D1213294

COSMOLOGY
PHILOSOPHICAL AND SCIENTIFIC

Christian Culture and Philosophy Series

GENERAL EDITOR
Donald A. Gallagher, Ph.D.
PROFESSOR OF PHILOSOPHY
BOSTON COLLEGE

The colophon for the Christian Culture and Philosophy Series consists of the Greek letters X and P, symbolizing Christianity, embraced by C, a variant of Σ, representing the Greek word *sophia.*

Cosmology

PHILOSOPHICAL AND SCIENTIFIC

By

LEO ALBERT FOLEY

PROFESSOR OF PHILOSOPHY
THE CATHOLIC UNIVERSITY OF AMERICA

THE BRUCE PUBLISHING COMPANY
MILWAUKEE

IMPRIMI POTEST:
CHARLES J. WILLIS, S.M.
Provincial

NIHIL OBSTAT:
JOHN A. SCHULIEN, S.T.D.
Censor librorum

IMPRIMATUR:
✠ WILLIAM E. COUSINS,
Archbishop of Milwaukee
April 13, 1962

TO
ST. ALBERT THE GREAT
THE ALBERTUS MAGNUS OF
BOTH PHILOSOPHY AND SCIENCE

Library of Congress Catalog Card Number: 62–16946

Made in the United States of America

FOREWORD

Intellectual developments proceed from a background either by way of building thereon or by way of reaction. This dichotomy is generally not so sharp as it might seem, since no movement can escape its background completely, and most movements can profit by it.

This is especially true of cosmology. Classical cosmology, in the tradition of Plato and Aristotle, is the oldest of man's intellectual endeavors. It is, moreover, the parent of metaphysics and the foundation of Western science. The cosmology of the Greeks was widely accepted until the seventeenth century. At that time, the great scientific advance which the Renaissance had inaugurated outstripped philosophical continuity, and the sciences made rapid progress almost completely on their own. Yet they were never completely divorced from their philosophical presuppositions. Francis Bacon, René Descartes, John Locke, Immanuel Kant, John Stuart Mill were all philosophers dealing with the problems originating in the scientific approach. On the other hand, Benjamin Franklin, Ernst Mach, Albert Einstein, Alfred North Whitehead, and Werner Heisenberg are scientists who have become philosophers either in fact or in intent.

That this is the case should not be surprising. Man has intellectual relations to the world in which he lives. He will attempt either to analyze the causes of his experiences or to correlate the events he perceives. In the former case he is philosophical; in the latter case, scientific. Both philosophy and the sciences are natural to man. Sometimes they seem close together. At other times they seem far apart.

We find both trends in the twentieth century. On the one hand, we find educators complaining that too much attention is being paid to classical thinkers. On the other hand, we find a Whitehead and a Heisenberg drawing near to the fundamental truths of Plato and Aristotle.

The fact is that truth is not the exclusive possession of any age or of any class of thinkers. There are truths that are eternal, and many of them are cosmological. On the other hand, there are new problems that both exemplify the perennial truths and open up new investigations. In brief, cosmology is philosophical and scientific. Each aspect is related to the other, and both are concerned with the ultimate answer to the universe.

There is a further fact that they have in common. Both are developments out of a background. Neither originated recently. Any study of either or both must take this into consideration. A problem can never be said to be examined completely unless it is seen against its background and in its various relationships. It can perhaps be better seen when viewed in its organic development.

That is the plan of this book. There are basic problems of reality that appeared early in Western thought among the Greeks of Athens, Asia Minor, Sicily, and southern Italy. These problems have served as the fundamental issues, cosmological and metaphysical, of Western philosophy up to the present day. It is with these that the first third of this work is concerned. The ramification of these questions into problems of quantity, extension, and quality — the immediate data of the senses whence we are led into both philosophical and scientific investigation — takes up the second section. In both parts, the treatment is historical, beginning with the simplest presentation of the problem and seeing it in its analytical and comprehensive development. The examples used are modern rather than classical. The third section is scientific cosmology. Again, it presents the problems historically and organically. Its purpose is to acquaint students of philosophy with the basic truths and directions of the sciences, just as the primary purpose of the entire work is to acquaint all readers with the unity of truth, both philosophical and scientific.

The author is indebted to many in the pursuit of this work: to the publishers for their constant and kindly interest; to colleagues of many faculties at the Catholic University of America from whom the author has sought information and assistance; to Miss Betty Goode for the final preparation of the text; to Dr. Donald A. Gallagher, general editor of The Chrstian Culture and Philosophy Series; to many friends for their constant interest and encouragement.

CONTENTS

PART ONE

Philosophical Principles of Material Reality

CHAPTER ONE

The NATURE of COSMOLOGY

"All men by nature desire to know . . ."
Aristotle, *Metaphysics*, Book I, Chapter I

THE NATURE OF PHILOSOPHY

Few, if any, widespread truths have been expressed in so few words as the above statement of Aristotle. The truth of this statement is seen in the existence and history of man. Rational knowledge is so exclusive a manifestation of man that he is defined, philosophically, as a "rational animal." *Homo sapiens*, or "wisdom-seeking-man," is one of his sociological and anthropological definitions. Lower animals show various degrees of knowledge and adaptation, characterized by instinct, the acquisition of habits, and a certain amount of improvisation. But man alone thinks, plans, schemes, develops his rudimentary awareness of things, enriches his mind with speculative knowledge, and expresses his love of the truth of reality in the sciences, in philosophy, and in theology, his love for reality in the arts.

Man's quest of knowledge is, moreover, a continual progress. Man, in general, has never limited his knowledge to any given content at any given time in his history. He has always continued to seek, to discover, to probe, to interpret, and to organize his discoveries and conclusions.

The fact that many men do not have the dispositions, the means, the time, and the occasion to seek knowledge does not deny the fact that they have the capacity for and the tendency to knowledge. The fact that all men *can* seek further answers to further questions, even that they can ask questions, shows man's natural tendency and desire to know.

Man not only tends to know. He tends to organize his knowledge.

He seeks to associate his discoveries with other known facts, products with sources, actions with doers, effects with causes. Sometimes he is mistaken as to the source and product, the cause and the effect. For example, two Canadian physicians, Drs. Banting and Best, spent many years seeking a cure for diabetes. They knew that insulin was the answer, but they thought that its source was the pancreas, since insulin, whenever it is produced, is produced in the pancreas. The simplicity of their conclusion was a mistake. They discovered subsequently that insulin is produced by two small glands, the "Isles of Langerhans," themselves within the larger gland, the pancreas. However, the cause-and-effect thinking that led them, at first, to the wrong conclusion was also the corrective that led them to the truth. Thus, not only does man seek ordered knowledge, he can also correct his own errors in the quest.

This tendency to know things in their associations and causes is known as the *virtue* or *habit of science*. In its ultimate, profound meaning, *science* is the possession of certain knowledge through causes. Yet, all things associated, various causes in relationship to effects, do not have the same importance. Some are more significant than others, and this naturally leads us to seek the one or ones which are the most significant. In other words, the tendency to know through causes leads man to attain knowledge through the most important, the ultimate causes and principles. Knowledge of this kind is called *wisdom*, and the scientific pursuit of ultimate causes is called philosophy, or the love of wisdom.

Philosophy is defined as *the understanding of all things, by the power of reason, in their ultimate causes and principles*. Although this definition may seem rather formidable and ambitious, it is only a formal statement that all men have the power to seek ultimate answers, to try to understand "what it is all about," and that some men have the opportunity to pursue such a quest.

Not all ultimate principles are the same. God, the Creator of the universe, is the absolutely ultimate principle. However, there are other principles, subordinate to God but supreme in their own order. For example, the ultimate principles of human behavior are different from those of the behavior of all other entities in the universe because man alone has a rational soul. Hence the principles that are the final expression of man are different from those that provide the fundamental explanation of other material beings. Since this is the case, for other beings as well as man, philosophy has a number of divisions. One of them, the field of philosophy that we are investigating, is cosmology, which is the pursuit of the ultimate principles of the material universe.

THE NATURE OF COSMOLOGY

1. *Verbal definition of cosmology*

The term *cosmology*, as its Greek etymology indicates, means: the science of the ordered universe. It comes from the Greek words κόσμος and λόγος. *Cosmos* is opposed to *chaos*, which means disorder. Hence, *cosmology* signifies the existence of order in the universe and the methodical pursuit of that order.

The term *cosmology* is comparatively recent. The Greeks, who originated western philosophy and western science, called the subject the study of natures (*φύσικα, naturalia*) or natural science. Medieval philosophers called it the philosophy of nature. The term *cosmology* was coined by Christian Wolff (1679–1754), a German philosopher and Protestant theologian. We should not attach too much significance, however, to the fact that this term appeared relatively late on the philosophical horizon, for the intellectual pursuit it designates stretches continuously from the Greeks to the twentieth century.

Even the word *cosmology* indicates for us the suppositions behind the science and its intentions. The basic supposition is that of order. It is a peculiar kind of order, i.e., order within change. It does not take much observation to notice that there is so much change going on in the universe that we can call the universe a process. Nevertheless, the change is not chaotic. It is ordered, definite, and measurable. For example, there is a regularity about the daily and seasonable changes of the weather, the trees, the position of the stars and planets night after night. Hence, there is order, but it is the order of a definite pattern of stability within change.

This pattern of stability is obvious enough to play an important part in all our thinking and activity. The farmer knows when it is time to plant and when it is time to reap, and that these times are generally the same year after year. The astronomer knows where to point his instruments night after night to take his observations, although the objects change nightly. When the physics teacher tells his students that they will continue the experiment in the next class, he and they are supposing that there is sufficient regularity about events and components of the universe that they can, at a future time, reproduce, with a high degree of accuracy, the same physical conditions that exist now.

Since we cannot reproduce the conditions with an exact sameness, there are, in these patterns, variations that we call chance, random activity, or some such similar name. Nevertheless, regularity and chance are so related that, through the use of statistics and the "calculus of probabilities," we can discover with a good degree of accuracy the regularity of the pattern of events that could easily be chaotic. As Alfred North Whitehead, a noted British-American philosopher and scientist, put it, our basic supposition in all learning is that there is an order in the universe.

2. *Real definition of cosmology*

This order can be described, recounted, explained in its details, and cosmology is the science that undertakes to be philosophical about it, i.e., to explain it in its ultimate principles. Hence, cosmology is defined as: *the perfect science of changeable or mobile being.* A few comments on the elements of this definition may be helpful.

Science. Science, as noted before, is, in its philosophical meaning, certain knowledge through causes. Thus cosmology is an attempt to determine with certitude the proper explanatory causes of changeable or mobile being. It is thus a disciplined investigation, involving evaluation and the proper subordination of the less significant to the more significant. In other words, cosmology seeks to order knowledge by discovering a hierarchy in things; it endeavors to grasp, with more and more precision, the ultimate, proper causes that will give us explanatory knowledge of mobile being and its properties. It proceeds from the proximate and hence better known causes of this object to its more remote but fundamental causes.

In order to attain this goal, cosmology demands not only that we seek facts, principles, and causes to explain what we already know, but also that we assimilate new facts with the old. In order to develop, to grow, cosmology demands a quest for discovery in the light of facts and principles already known. This means that cosmology proceeds both inductively and deductively. The quest for discovery is analysis or induction. That is, in seeking to discover *new* truths, we must mentally analyze the data to separate the pertinent from the non-pertinent, to discover the nature of the object known if enough evidence is available. In putting this knowledge to work, we deduce. That is, if our knowledge of any object is certain, we can apply it to every being that we recognize as belonging to the same class. Thus, by analysis or induction we learn that a dog is a mammal. Hence, we can infer immediately that it bears its young alive rather than in eggs, and that this is true for all dogs past, present, and future.

In learning we generally observe a sufficient number of cases to enable us to discover what is essential to the members of the class we are investigating. We learn the essence of the thing. In some instances we learn the proper or specific essence. In others we learn the generic or more common essence. In either event, we have enough knowledge for certitude. To come back to our example of dogs. It is doubtful that we know the essential difference between a dog and a cat. That is, we do not know precisely what makes a dog a dog and a cat a cat, distinguishing them from each other and from all other animals. However, we know that both are mammals and therefore have characteristic ways of living. We do not have to reinvestigate every dog or cat to verify this anew. We simply deduce that such is and will be the case because we have certitude about the more general or generic class, mammals.

Induction is a manner of learning, mental analysis. Deduction is the application of our knowledge to the members of a class. But deduction is more than that. It is also the recognition of the necessary relationship between the subject and predicate in the judgment that we may make about the member of the class. We not only say that dogs and cats are viviparous. We say they are viviparous because they are mammals.

Deduction is also used in cases in which we do not have certitude but only opinion. Here deduction is called dialectic. We shall investigate it at greater length later on, particularly in connection with the method proper to the empirical sciences. In brief, this consists in adopting an opinion, in making a choice between probable answers. We assume one of the opinions, consider it as a basis of deduction, as though it were established, and then extend it deductively to see to what we are committed on the assumption that it is true. We then seek further evidence to confirm or verify our fundamental assumption. Dialectical deduction, of great value in the physical sciences, is also used in cosmology.

Perfect science. It may seem a bit presumptuous to term any organized knowledge a perfect science. However, "perfect" as applied to cosmology simply means complete or self-contained (cf. Latin *perfectum*, "completely put together"). Cosmology is self-contained in the sense that it has the means of answering the questions that it raises without going outside of itself, because it can discover the explanatory principles of the changing universe. That does not mean that it is not helped by data from other sciences. However, it does not *depend* upon other sciences for its answers, nor is it founded on an extension of them.

In anticipation, we may illustrate with an example. At one time it was generally believed that all bodies consisted of proportioned combinations of four simple elements. Cosmology explained this philosophically by saying that these elements were ultimate in the line of substance. That is, these elements could either subsist of themselves or combine with one another into autonomous entities called substances. Today we know that there are ninety-two natural elements, and that these are most likely composed of atomic and subatomic particles. Nevertheless, we still use the same reasoning, namely, that these particles can be combined into elements in the free state and into autonomous combinations called substances. In other words, although the data are somewhat different and cosmology benefits from later discoveries, the answer remains the same because cosmology is not limiting its conclusions to the facts of any discovery or any time in the history of thought. This is so because cosmology goes behind the *fact* of combinations of elements or atoms to the *principles:* capacity for combination in relation to fulfillment of this capacity in reality, or, more briefly, *potency and act*, called *matter* and *form* in cosmology. In this way, cosmology remains a perfect or complete science simply because it contains within itself the capacity to answer its own questions in relation to problems it raises, independently of the limitations of the facts concerned.

A perfect science is not contrasted with an imperfect science, but with a particular science. Cosmology should not have to go outside of itself for the key to the answers to its questions. On the other hand, the particular sciences frequently must turn to other sciences for their answers. Many problems in biology require answers in chemistry, which in turn frequently depend on nuclear theory in physics.

The following example should illustrate the differences between a perfect science and a particular science. We may raise the question of mortality, that is, why living things die, or at least cease to exist as themselves. As a biological problem we are faced with the difficulty that we cannot say what death is since we do not really know what life is. Hence, we must describe death in terms of the disorganization of such vital operations as assimilation, digestion, nutrition, etc., and the consequent effect of this disorganization upon component tissues and cells. When we ask *why* this is so, we must consult organic chemistry to explain the nature and needs of cells. However, in explaining cell operations we must turn to their molecular structures, and this is a problem in chemistry, organic or inorganic. Nevertheless, since molecules consist of atoms and the latter of subatomic particles, we are then led from nuclear chemistry to nuclear physics, especially since the question of vital energy raises the question of any energy, and this is, again, a physical problem.

On the other hand, philosophically we need not become involved in all this interchange of scientific data. We base ourselves upon the obvious fact that each living body, like any other body, is composed of parts and can be resolved into those parts. The resolution into parts is what we call death. Hence, when we say that each living entity can be resolved into its parts we are saying that each living thing is mortal, since mortality is death, which is resolution into parts. This does not mean that each living entity *will* die. It simply means that each living being *can* die. However, while we normally expect the former, we are absolutely sure of the latter since each living body is composed of parts into which it can be resolved.

Changeable or mobile being. Since cosmology is philosophical in its quest for the ultimate principles of material being, it concentrates on those properties of material being which are most permanent and most indicative of its nature. These properties are two: extension and change.

Material being is extended. The physical bodies that constitute the material universe are spread out, even if only minutely. Bodies are not points, and even the energies that proceed from and activate bodies are extended. Philosophically, this means that they have parts. These parts need not be discrete, such as the hand of a man or the leaf of a tree. But they do mean that one end of a physical body is not the other, and that the top is not the bottom.

Whatever is extended, whatever has mass, is divisible. We can break bodies down into smaller and smaller parts, and there is always something left over. We cannot reduce bodies to points. The closest we can come to this is to reduce them to their energy states, and even here they have particle characteristics. No matter how small the remnants may be, they are not points and hence have some extension and *can be* divided further if we are able to produce the proper instruments to divide them.

The fact that material bodies are endlessly divisible means that in their very nature they can be broken down into their parts. In other words, *they are changeable in their very natures*. This is what we mean when we call them mobile — or changeable — beings. The outstanding property of material bodies is their capacity to undergo constantly a breaking down of parts, simply because they are bodies, not spirits, because they are extended and thereby have parts. They are intrinsically changeable because they are what they are and exist as they do.

The outstanding characteristics of bodies, material beings, is that they are composed of parts, spread out, and hence are intrinsically changeable. This is what distinguishes body from spirit and this is the proper object of cosmology, an investigation into the mobility or changeability of bodies.

PHILOSOPHICAL METHODS

Early in the seventeenth century, the noted English philosopher, political figure, and essayist, Francis Bacon, advanced the thesis that philosophy is exclusively deductive whereas the physical sciences are exclusively inductive. What Bacon might better have said is that philosophy is *demonstrative* whereas the sciences investigate an associative pattern of data. Philosophy, and hence cosmology, begins with *abstraction*, which does not mean an intellectual remoteness from reality. Abstraction is the mental process of analyzing the data of the senses, both external and internal, such as the imagination and memory, to attain to the essence of the object. The basic principle fundamental to abstraction is that things operate according to what they are. Hence, by analyzing the operations of physical things as experienced by our senses, we can be led to an understanding of the principle from which they proceed, the essence, in this respect called the nature. This is no more unusual than the fact that by an analysis of the marks on a tree stump we can tell whether it was chopped down by a man or gnawed down by a beaver. This is also the type of thinking behind much experiment. The whole point behind bombarding particles in an accelerator is to determine from their paths, their penetration in photo-emulsion, and the direction of their spins, whether or not they show wave characteristics, particle characteristics, or both together, or both at different times.

As mentioned several times, when we attain an understanding of the nature of the object under consideration, we can extend, with certitude, our knowledge to all members of that class. For example, were we to try to prove, by statistics, that all men are mortal, we could build up a good case and show a more than general trend. However, we would not eliminate the possibility that some men have such control over their body chemistry that they can evade death. Even if our statistics were complete, we would fail to overcome the possibility. Moreover, we could not be certain that some child with a type of body chemistry to allow him to live indefinitely might not have been born after we started our interviews. Nor could we really be certain that our statistics were complete. The only way we could really prove that all men are mortal, statistically, would be to kill all men and then commit suicide. Even then, we could not be sure that we had covered all men. There would be the haunting doubt of the adequacy of our coverage.

On the other hand, by demonstrating that all men possess parts, can be thus resolved into their parts, and hence can die, we have our conclusion without the haunting fear of doubt. The expression used here, the "haunting fear of doubt," may be an indication of certitude. Certitude is the mental assent to a proposition without the prudent fear of its opposite or alternative being true. Obviously, such mental commitment must be based on some solid foundation. Otherwise we have the stubborn acceptance of a dubious proposition because of illusion, delusion, or personal preference — all without sufficient evidence. There are many solid foundations, many sources of evidence for intellectual commitment, but they can be reduced to three which give three corresponding types of certitude. The three foundations are: being, natures, and uniformity of events. The corresponding types of certitude are: metaphysical, physical, and moral.

Metaphysical certitude is based upon the existence of an entity, an event, or a fact. To deny a proposition known with metaphysical certitude would lead one to absurd contradiction. Thus, for example, I am as certain as I can possibly be that the sun exists.

Physical certitude is based upon the natures of things. The example used above, the mortality of man, is a good example. Once I know the nature of man I am certain that he is mortal. Physical certitude is properly the field of demonstration, for demonstration is essentially the application of the truths of the class to the members of the class. Thus, once I know that a seal, by nature, is a mammal, I do not have to examine every seal to see whether he has lungs instead of gills.

Moral certitude is based upon our knowledge of human conduct, the usual responses men make to situations in which they find themselves. For example, mothers usually love their children. Nevertheless, it is not an absurdity or a contradiction for mothers not to love their children. Thus, in any particular instance, I can have moral certitude that this woman loves this child because she is its mother. Nevertheless I cannot have metaphysical or physical certitude of this truth.

Demonstrative reasoning, as noted above, is based upon a knowledge of the natures of things. Yet there are two difficulties involved in this. The first is that there is a limitation to what we can know about the natures of things. There may not be enough evidence for us to learn the nature of a thing, either specific or generic. In that case, the most we can do is to have an opinion concerning the object. Our reasoning about it must be, consequently, hypothetical. That is, we can take a point of view of the object, develop our opinion logically to see to what we are committed, and then seek out the evidence to verify our stand. This is the field of *dialectic,* which is the selection of an opinion for logical investigation. Notice that there is an *as if* or *as though* quality about such reasoning. We argue *as though* our choice were the only one. Such reasoning is called *hypothetical.*

COSMOLOGY AND THE PHYSICAL SCIENCES

The use of concepts rather than evidence plays a large part in scientific reasoning, and this because it is frequently difficult to obtain sufficient evidence to support an assumption.

Furthermore, whether there is or is not evidence, there is a limit to how far our knowledge of the natures of things extends. That is, there are valid fields of knowledge in which the natures of the objects concerned do not enter in. For example, knowledge of the speed of a body, its mass, inertia, rate of descent in a free fall, etc., does not depend upon the knowledge of its nature or essence. Since the intellect tends to know, and to know the answers to these problems, such fields are valid areas of intellectual investigation. However, since we cannot properly demonstrate in these fields, the best we can do is to associate our knowledge, attempting to synthesize our observations in such a way that we can discover a uniformity within the manifold of sense data which floods our observation.

Since the sciences concentrate on these and similar problems, they are not regularly concerned with the natures of things. They are concerned with the *uniformity of operations and events.* Uniformity must be established against time and space standards, which involve measurement. It also involves a theory of experiment. If I wish to rule out the possibility that such uniformity is the result of chance, *I must prove my point by attempting to observe all the conditions before an event,* note the consequences of these conditions to see whether the consequent follows invariably, generally, variably, or only occasionally. In any event, in order (1) to clarify the regularity of the consequences for the variable and occasional, and (2) to establish the sequence of antecedent-consequent, *I must try to control the ideal conditions. I must experiment.* Only then can I work around to a statistical average that out of N number of experiments involving N physical conditions I get N predictable results. Only then can I extrapolate into the general thesis that, for example, given rapidly rising warm air currents in the midst of descending cool air currents I will get sufficient ionization of the air molecules to set up a thunderhead and produce thunderstorms. Notice here that our reasoning is, again, hypothetical. That is, the basic theory is that, given certain conditions, I can expect determinate results. This is the basic form of hypothetical reasoning: ". . . if . . . then."

Basically, then, we can see that the *fundamental* difference between cosmology and the physical sciences lies in the type of thinking and in the area of investigation proper to each. Cosmology directs its investigation of reality toward an understanding of the *essences* of real bodies through a knowledge of their ultimate principles. In seeking this kind of knowledge, cosmology involves thinking that is both analytic and synthetic, that is, a type of thinking which abstracts the essence or nature of things and demonstrates the natural effects of such a nature.

The physical sciences, on the other hand, concentrate on an area that is quite different. Although they do involve abstraction, inasmuch as they are intellectual disciplines and must, consequently, leave out of consideration (abstract from) individual differences, they are not abstractive in the sense of eidetic abstraction or abstractive induction, which gives insight into the nature or essence of things. Moreover, they are dialectical, hypothetical, in their conclusions; they seek to determine the uniformity of events and to extend this uniformity into fields that seem to show the same physical conditions that give rise to probable conclusions. Such thinking is primarily conceptual, and the fundamental hypotheses are: (1) *if* my observations and experiments are correct, *then* I should meet such-and-such results; (2) if the association of *such type* is uniform, then I should be able to extend my conclusions to similar phenomena. For example, if the attraction of bodies in a gravitational field and the attraction of charged particles in an electromagnetic field have the same rate, then I should be able to use the same formulae in both cases. It works the other way also. If I can use the same formulae successfully, this indicates similarities between gravity and electromagnetic attraction.

This extension of concepts means that the physical sciences generally reason from concept to concept rather than from thing-to-concept-to-thing. The basis for such reasoning is the congruence of concepts. An example might be the applications of the concept of the conservation of energy. We represent it as *CE*. One of its applications is in the problem of work. In any mechanical system, work done equals the work put in minus friction and drag. We will call this the conservation of work, and symbolize it by *CW*. Since it is essentially the same idea as the conservation of energy, it is included in *CE* thus: CE CW . This also applies to the transfer of electricity and is called the conservation of charge (CC). Now we have CE CW CC . Furthermore, we can interpret many of the activities of atomic particles in terms of conservation. They seem also to be electromagnetic in character. Our symbol is now: CE CC CW IW .

On the other hand, concepts sometimes do not fit. For example, the concept of moving bodies (V/G) which applies to comparisons between bodies-at-rest, bodies-in-motion, body-at-rest to body-in-motion, and body-in-motion to body-in-motion, does not apply to bodies in a free fall, V. However, by enlarging our notion of comparison through a fundamental notion of general relativity, *Gik*, we can associate the concepts which hitherto eluded each other, thus: 

.

The basic difference between scientific theory and philosophical thinking, then, is that the norm for scientific thinking is the fittingness or adequacy of concept to concept, the *congruence of concepts*. In philosophy it is *the relationship of concept to reality*. Hence, whereas cosmology considers reality *as it is*, scientific theory generally considers nature *as it is thought about*.

As mentioned above, the uniformity sought in scientific observation and experiment must involve a theory of measurement against space and time. This leads us to a second difference between the sciences and cosmology.

The sciences consider matter as *measurable*, whereas cosmology considers its nature as *intrinsically changeable*, regarding measurability as a property flowing from its nature. The emphasis of science upon the measurability of matter derives only from the obvious need of measurement to discern uniformity. The mathematical approach of the physical sciences (foreshadowed even in Plato) goes back to the early seventeenth century when Johannes Kepler discovered that we could better understand the physical forces of the solar system if we substituted one mathematical figure for another: an elliptical orbit of the planets for a circular orbit for example. Galileo, in the same tradition, noted that we could correct many mistakes if we had the proper geometrical expression of many problems involving bodies moving in relation to one another. Hence, he concluded that if we had sufficient mathematical knowledge we could foresee any physical problem and anticipate many possible errors. The mathematical approach to physical reality reached its perfection with Newton. The latter was able to infer the rate of the attraction of bodies with such accuracy that we are able to apply his formulae to problems in electromagnetics and electrodynamics as well as to questions involving gravity.

Since many qualitative characteristics of bodies can be reduced to their quantitative states, many post-Newtonian philosophers inclined to let mathematics take over the role of philosophy.

Despite the rapid advances in discovery, the same philosophical problems remain. We still must consider the natures of the components of the universe. It is one thing to say that a given body of a given weight (m) is attracted to another body (M) at the rate of Mm/r^2, and it is something else to say that a man is falling off a building to the surface of the earth. There is room for different considerations of the same problem. The physical sciences look upon a problem from the point of view of *measurable matter*, whereas cosmology looks upon the same problem from the viewpoint of the *natures and changes of the entities involved.*

A third difference between cosmology and the physical sciences concerns the role of deduction in each. Francis Bacon, it may be recalled, had charged that philosophy is exclusively deductive and that the physical sciences are exclusively inductive. Bacon's thesis might have been true of the decadent philosophy at his time. Moreover, it is obvious that philosophy, as a science, uses deduction a great deal insofar as it uses logic a great deal. Deduction is a logical method.

Today the opposite to Bacon's thesis is more correct. Philosophy always is and always must be inductive because it must analyze its findings in order to learn the essences and ultimate principles of objects. On the other hand, scientific reasoning has become almost exclusively deductive. To give an example: if we could discover that another planet had the same general physical conditions of our earth, we could suppose that there could be forms of life on that other planet similar to our terrestrial forms of life. Also, if the latest theory of the formation of planets about our sun could be established, then we could suppose that any other main sequence star whose spectroscopic analysis seems to show a similar period of rotation on its axis as that of the sun would have planets to maintain its internal balance of forces according to the principles of angular momentum. The supposition in both cases, that of possible life on other planets and other possible planetary systems, is a form of deduction called hypothetical deduction or dialectic. It is based on the assumption ("hypothesis") of a position and the deductions therefrom to see to what we are committed in the search for verification. Thus, in the example cited, we can reason in the following way: *If* the principles of angular momentum are universal, and *if* they explain the stability of a star's internal forces through the restraining influence of a planetary system, *then* we can expect to find planets about any star similar in nature to our sun. We think that the principles are true, hence, we can expect to find other planetary systems. Its logical form is: If *A*, then *B*. *A* is true; then *B* must be true. This is deduction because it is an inference from a universal concept. The fact that it is an assumed universal does not make any difference in the logical form.

Because of the nature of scientific reasoning, the sciences have to assume more and more. Hence, they have to infer more and more from assumptions. Hence, they are also much more deductive than cosmology. In turn, this leads to a fourth difference between cosmology and the sciences. This is to be found in *the nature of truth.*

In general, truth is the agreement between the object known and its mental representation or idea. I know that my definition of man as a rational animal is true if it agrees with the operations and essence of men as composite beings possessing rational souls and organic bodies. However, much of what the sciences investigate escapes definition. Consequently, they do not give us knowledge of essences and cannot, therefore, reach the same degree of truth in their conclusions.

This means that the sciences must be satisfied with a congruence of concepts in investigating facts as well as in formulating theory. Scientific concepts are called *working concepts.* For example, is there an extremely minute particle of definite electromagnetic properties called an electron that corresponds with my concept of a *beta* particle? Or is my concept of a *beta* particle an idea postulated as a possible answer to a problem of electromagnetic stability? Since no one has ever seen an electron or is ever likely to, the easiest way to put my concept to the test is to see how well it agrees with other ideas about the same problem. If there is such general agreement of my concepts, if they do not contradict each other, they are said to be *congruent*, and congruence of concepts, as we have seen, is "truth," in a scientific framework.

However, I may have any number of congruent concepts that do not necessarily represent reality, and frequently reality shows that my concepts may agree among themselves without having the proper reference to physical entities outside the mind. For example, the old theory of the four elements to explain physical and chemical properties is congruent enough. It lasted until the seventeenth century. However, we now know that it does not agree with reality, and hence we say that it is no longer true even though it is still congruent. Thus we see that the congruence of concepts, although it may be an *indication* of truth and a good working notion of truth, can be extended too far. Ultimately an appeal to physical conditions outside the mind, that is, to reality, is required. Cosmology sometimes uses working concepts, but it has far greater direct relations with reality because it is seeking the natures of things and their changes and operations.

This, then, is a fourth difference between cosmology and the sciences. Cosmology follows the direct appeal to reality and makes primary use of *abstracted notions*. The sciences must depend heavily upon *working concepts*.

A fifth and final great difference between cosmology and the sciences has been seen earlier. It concerns the distinction between perfect (or universal) and particular sciences. Cosmology is a perfect science. That is, it is self-contained. It has the means within itself to answer the questions that it raises. The sciences, on the other hand, often have to go outside of their own fields for the fuller solution of the problems they raise.

The greatest difference between cosmology and the sciences, however, is that first mentioned, namely, the manner in which they get the information on which they erect their basic principles. Cosmology starts with the intuitive realization that things are, that they change, and that there is a pattern of stability within the constantly changing universe. Thus, the mobile being that cosmology undertakes to explain indicates in its *mobility* the change that is characteristic of the universe and in its *being* the stability of the components of the universe. This presents us, then, with the problem of being and becoming, the first truly philosophical problem undertaken by Greek and subsequent western philosophy. The sciences, on the other hand, start with some outstanding aspect or property of being and make great use of working concepts in the development of their principles. In order to see this point more clearly, we shall now comment on what are called the formal and material objects of cosmology.

MATERIAL AND FORMAL OBJECTS OF COSMOLOGY

The material object of a science is the thing which is considered. The formal object is that special note about the thing that gives rise to the special intellectual intention or direction of investigation. That is, the formal object is the intelligible mode in the light of which the material object is studied.

The *material object* of cosmology is the entire universe, the world of bodies, the world of material entities and energies. This is also the material object of the sciences.

The *formal object* of cosmology is the mobility or changeability of mobile being. We have seen that bodies are extended and are thus composed of parts. Because they are composed of parts they can be resolved into their parts and can have their parts rearranged. By that fact, they are changeable. Cosmology investigates the material universe and material beings precisely as changeable, movable. It is interested in determining the nature of mobile or changeable beings precisely as such. It wants to find out *why* they change and what causes are capable of explaining this primary and essential datum of the world of our experience. We see that the material universe not only *is* but is also *becoming*. The world of our immediate experience is a world of becoming, of change, but of a becoming or change that involves some element of stability. The principal concern of cosmology is to inquire into the causes for this becoming. Its formal object is, therefore, being as subject to change, to motion, to becoming.

COSMOLOGY AND THE DEGREES OF ABSTRACTION

Cosmology's first principles are intuitive, that is, they are immediately evident from experience and are not derived from something known prior to them. We cannot prove either that things are or that they change. These are obvious facts which we accept on the strength of their own evidence. The intuitive grasp of these principles is, as we have already seen, abstractive, as all speculative knowledge of the intellect must be. In coming to a close of this chapter on the nature of cosmology, however, it may be helpful to show in more precise detail why all speculative knowledge must be abstractive and to investigate the various degrees of abstraction. In that way, we shall see more clearly the nature of cosmology as a philosophic discipline and its relationship to the positive sciences, to mathematics, and to metaphysics.

Speculative knowledge, as a perfection of the intellect, an immaterial faculty, demands that the objects known be in some way immaterialized, disengaged from the limitations of matter and individuality. Moreover, as grasped in a scientific way, objects of speculative knowledge acquire a kind of necessity, that is, a degree of stability and fixity, immobility. Why? Because every necessary thing is, as such, immobile, whereas that which is unstable, unfixed cannot be anchored down with the certainty scientific knowledge demands. Consequently any object of a speculative intellectual knowledge is in some way liberated from both matter and motion or change, that is, abstracted from these two conditions of being. Consequently, the various speculative or theoretical sciences are distinguished from one another according to the degree in which their objects are abstracted from matter and motion.

The objects of some sciences are real things which depend on matter and motion for their existence, since they exist only in sensible changing matter. Such are the objects of this universe, the objects we have previously seen to be those investigated by cosmology. Furthermore, these objects depend upon matter not only for their existence but also for their intelligibility, inasmuch as they cannot be understood unless they are related in some way to sensible matter. For example, we cannot understand a man unless we in some way make reference to flesh and bones; without these, man simply does not exist. Yet, in order to be known intellectually, these objects must be freed from (abstracted from) the *here* and *now* which limits them to *this* individual at this given time and in this given place, e.g., the object of our speculative intellect is not this man, John Smith, but man as such. There is reference to flesh and bones in general, but not to *this* flesh and *these* bones. It is precisely with realities of this kind that cosmology and the physical sciences are concerned.

There are other realities, however, which do not depend upon matter in order for us to understand them, although they do depend upon matter in order to exist. Such, for example, are lines and circles, numbers and figures, the objects investigated by the science of mathematics. These objects exist only in sensible, changing things, yet in understanding them we do not make reference to sensible, moving things. In fact, we have to imagine them as free from the conditions of really existing material things in order to understand them. The line of the geometer, for example, has length but no breadth or depth. Lines of this kind exist only in the mind, for any really existing concrete line is something bodily, something having both breadth and depth in addition to length. Thus objects dependent upon matter for their real, physical existence, yet independent of matter for their intelligibility, form the subject matter investigated by the science of mathematics.

There are still other realities which are independent of matter and change both for their existence and their intelligibility. Such, of course, are God and angels, beings of a purely spiritual, immaterial nature. But other realities, found at times in sensible, material things, can also exist in immaterial things. As examples we can cite substance, act, perfection, intellect, will, which are found in sensible things such as men but also *can* exist in beings of a purely immaterial nature. In fact, being itself is such a reality, for being is indeed sometimes material yet it is not limited to the material. Realities of this kind are the objects of yet another intellectual science, the science of metaphysics or "first philosophy," the philosophy of being, which seeks the ultimate causes and principles of all things precisely as existent beings.

The degrees of abstraction pertinent to cosmology, mathematics, and metaphysics are called the first, second, and third degrees of abstraction respectively. We have noted that the objects investigated by the physical sciences, such as biology, physics, chemistry, etc., are, like those of cosmology, on the first degree or level of abstraction; that is, the objects investigated by these sciences are material beings which cannot exist nor be understood without some reference to matter. Yet, in the actual development of the physical sciences, there has been (as noted previously) a growing use of mathematics in ascertaining the properties and interrelationships of the realities under investigation. Thus the modern physical sciences seem to be "mixed" sciences; that is, they involve thinking that takes place on both the first and second degrees of abstraction. This is, perhaps, one of the chief ways of distinguishing these sciences from cosmology, although some hold, and with good reasons, that the modern physical sciences, since they are primarily directed toward a knowledge of physically existing realities, are fundamentally and properly objects lying on the first level of abstraction. They differ from the object of the science of cosmology, mobile being, in that they are more precise, determinate specifications of the mobile being which cosmology (called at times the "general science of nature") studies.

Cosmology is fundamentally in the first degree of abstraction. It deals with material entities as material and mobile and seeks their ultimate principles in the order of matter. However, cosmology as originated by Aristotle really dealt with a metaphysical problem because he treated of the mobility of mobile being. His problem was that of essences and whether essences exist in some existence apart, for example, in a world of ideas as postulated by some Greek thinkers. By the fact that Aristotle maintained that they exist in matter as natures, he did raise the question of an existential, that is to say, realistic,* philosophy and did introduce

* The term "existential" originated in recent years in France. It connoted an *empirical* approach to ethical and moral problems, and was used in opposition to the *theory* of morality which some postwar French thinkers considered inapplicable. With some degree of success, it claimed the authority of Søren Kierkegaard, Martin Heidegger, and Karl Jaspers. In terms of this trend, only the complete empiricist can be an existentialist.

The term "existentialism" became popular with Thomists. It has been taken to mean an investigation of essence in relation to existence rather than a purely logical consideration of essences alone.

As used in this work, "existential" means "realistic."

some fundamental metaphysical considerations into his philosophy of nature. To the extent, then, that he raised the question of existence, his treatment of mobile being as being does raise some problems that are both metaphysical and cosmological. Hence there is a tendency among some modern Thomistic cosmologists to consider cosmology in part in the third degree of abstraction as well as in the first degree.

There is a similar problem concerning the physical sciences. They deal with matter, forces, energies, all of them forms of matter. Hence, they are fundamentally in the first degree of abstraction as long as they remain experimental. However, since the time of Copernicus, Kepler, and Galileo, physical theory has become more and more mathematical. Much of it is almost pure mathematics, and hence must be considered in the second degree of abstraction. Furthermore, physical theory becomes so abstract that its very abstraction raises the question whether it is actually dealing with reality or not. Hence, it becomes a theory of concepts in relation to reality, of possibles in relation to existence, and hence has some aspects of the third degree of abstraction about it. In fact, in the hands of such theorists as P. A. M. Dirac, Albert Einstein, and Werner Heisenberg, physical theory undoubtedly becomes metaphysical.

Nevertheless, the only reason why we can speculate about the degrees of abstraction in relation to cosmology and the physical sciences is that we recognize the validity of the degrees of abstraction, which are only another expression of Aristotle's division of theoretical thinking into physical, mathematical, and metaphysical problems. Moreover, in recognizing these areas we realize the need for different patterns of thinking in dealing with objects lying within those areas and the necessity of rearranging these patterns before transferring from one area to the other.

The different patterns of thinking as laid down by the degrees of abstraction in association with the different areas of investigation are the focus of concentrated investigation by contemporary scholastic philosophers in the United States.

Some, chiefly Louvain-trained men working at Duquesne University in Pittsburgh, hold that cosmology is more closely related to metaphysics than an independent and autonomous science, since it is concerned with the being of mobile, changing objects.

The Dominican Fathers of River Forest, Illinois, and their colleagues elsewhere in the United States, are concentrating on the relationships between the physical sciences and cosmology. Their problem is whether the sciences are to be considered specifications of cosmology or of mathematical physics, or whether the principles of cosmology and the associated and assimilated data of the physical sciences are all to be part of a larger and more advanced philosophy of nature.

Vincent Edward Smith of St. John's University, Jamaica, New York, is working on the intelligibility of the sciences. Although the sciences give us models of how to think about the problems of reality, the scientist is, Smith argues, actually seeking essences, perhaps without being conscious of the object of his quest.

These and similar investigations by others throughout the United States are gradually bearing fruit. Whereas cosmology has of late been considered almost a synonym for astrophysics, philosophical and especially scholastic cosmology is once again making itself known.

SUMMARY

1. Philosophical thinking is natural to man because he has the tendency and ability to continue his questions about the nature of things. His knowledge has a tendency to become ordered and, hence, scientific. It also has a tendency to follow the order to the ultimate answers, and hence is sapiential.
2. Cosmology is the philosophical investigation into the ultimate principles of mobile being, or changeable being. Hence, it is the philosophy of the universe, of all material creation.
3. There are many aspects of material reality that demand a more specialized investigation than that undertaken by cosmology. The pursuit of these specialized problems is the work of the particular sciences.
4. Since this is the case, it is necessary to discover the proper objects of these intellectual disciplines bearing on the same material object. Hence, we define cosmology as the perfect science of mobile being. By perfect science we mean a self-contained, methodic investigation into the ultimate principles of the changes and being of the components of the material universe. The formal object, that which distinguishes cosmology from other sciences, is changeability or being as changeable or mobile. Because matter is composed of parts, can be resolved into its parts, can have its parts rearranged, it is changeable. It is material being as changeable that cosmology investigates. The particular sciences, on the other hand, investigate a different aspect of material things from a different point of view. They are not perfect sciences, but rather particular sciences insofar as their self-imposed limitations require them, sometimes, to turn to other particular sciences for a fuller pursuit of their problems.
5. Cosmology is fundamentally in the first degree of abstraction. However, some of its problems concerning the existence of the natures it investigates seem to lead it into the third degree of abstraction. The particular sciences are in the first degree of abstraction as long as they remain in the experimental order. Much of their theory is purely mathematical, and hence they have aspects of the second degree of abstraction about them.

Furthermore, insofar as many of their questions are highly hypothetical, they have many aspects of the third degree about them.

In brief, we might summarize the degrees of abstraction, especially as they are related to cosmology, in the following way:

a) There are problems wherein we must refer our concepts to the material existence of the object we think about;

b) There are problems wherein we deal with the conceptual existence of our objects of thought;

c) There are problems wherein we must refer our objects of thought, no matter what they are, to the basic question: Do they or do they not exist?

CHAPTER TWO

The HISTORICAL FORMULATION of the MAIN PRINCIPLES of COSMOLOGY

Not all of the fundamental principles of philosophical cosmology were discovered or formulated at once. There were two centuries of hard Greek reasoning before the first great philosophical attempt to account for the physical universe was undertaken by Plato. And even Plato, in his cosmological speculations, did not think that he could attain certitude, but only a "likely" or "probable" account (cf. *Timaeus*, 29).

The development of western thought and science began with the Greeks. It did not begin in Greece itself, but rather in Asia Minor. Athens and the city-states of Greece proper were at the center of an empire that was generally fomenting war with its neighbors. As is frequently the case in militarized cultures, more attention was paid to the practical than to the speculative. Thus philosophy was subordinated to Athens' military aspirations. Moreover, the official Greek religion — the mythology that is familiar to schoolboys — served the practically minded Athenians as a working explanation of the universe.

Thus philosophical development among the Greeks began in two sections of the Greek confederation of city-states that were somewhat removed from the activity attendant on Greek political movements. They were in Asia Minor at Miletus, not far from Ephesus, now in Turkey; and in southern Italy, at Croton, and Elia, now Velia. Since they were not at the center of Greek patriotic activity, the citizens of these Greek colonies could look upon Greek culture from the point of view of a disinterested spectator, and they did not seem to be impressed. The thinkers of these outlying Greek cities seem to have been discontented with the mythological explanation of reality offered by the poets, and they supplied the beginnings of what philosophy always needs: a sound, *rational* investigation of reality on its own terms.

THE BASIC PROBLEM

The basic problem facing these early Greeks was the same one that has fascinated all people. As far as anyone can tell, the universe is made out of the same material, yet there are in it many different types of entities. Being is one insofar as all things exist and seem to be made out of the same fundamental stuff or sources. Yet being is many insofar as there are many different types of entities made out of this same source or sources. This is the problem of *the one and the many*.

Furthermore, things do not remain the same nor do they always retain the same pattern. They *change* into other types of beings, undergoing what we call *substantial changes*. A tree, for instance, does not remain a tree permanently. It dies, becomes wood, and the wood, in turn, is usually reduced to its component elements which undergo further changes into further types of beings. Even beings which retain their substantial identities are constantly undergoing changes of some kind. The same tree sheds its leaves during the autumn, brings forth buds during the spring, and grows and changes in many ways while retaining the same identity. In brief, things may remain *substantially* the same yet undergo a variety of *accidental changes*.

So common is change that the entire universe, it soon becomes obvious, is a vast process of change. Yet there is a definite stability to this change. It is not disordered. It is definite, takes place in regular channels, according to a set sequence of events, in a determinate pattern of stability. This problem of the widespread existence of substantial identities, substantial changes, and accidental changes is the problem of *being and becoming*.

Fundamentally the answer to both of these problems, or rather this same problem with its two facets of the one and the many, of being and becoming, is the following. The material beings in the universe are limited by their own capacities. They are contingent, dependent; hence they are not absolute. They do not have within themselves the being that *must* exist as such. They can not-be. Consequently, they are changeable, at least as regards existence. They come into being and pass out of being. Furthermore, because they are limited, and thus changeable, they can be influenced by almost anything else. Whether they will be so or not does not depend upon their type of existence, since they are contingent, but rather upon whether they are stronger or more forceful than the entity that attempts to influence them. Even then, though they may resist change, they are still influenced somewhat, even if slightly.

The ultimate answer to this problem is the dependence of all contingent beings upon God. This then means that the problem is one of theology and religion as well as one of philosophy.

This basic problem is perennial. It has some aspects that are typically modern and contemporary, yet, as we shall see, some of the answers proposed by the Greeks seem amazingly modern. At least, we are able to see that they dealt with the same basic problem that faces us.

BASIC ANSWERS OF THE PRESOCRATIC PHILOSOPHERS

1. The Ionians. Three philosophers of Miletus in Ionia are regarded as the first physicists or philosophers of nature, i.e., cosmologists. These three are Thales (c. 640–562 B.C.), Anaximander (c. 610–546 B.C.), and Anaximenes (c. 588–524 B.C.). Although each differed in his response to the fundamental question of cosmology, all agreed in teaching that there is one original principle (ἀρχή, or *beginning*) whence everything in the universe of our experience is derived. That is, all three of these Ionian thinkers sought for the universal substrate of the many, changing beings of the sensible world. Viewed in the light of subsequent Greek thought they were looking for what Aristotle would call the material cause of change, that is, the perduring subject of change. They thus emphasized the need for any genuine cosmology to discover within the many, changing things of experience some common source to explain the similarity among different things and the perduring subject affected by change. In two of these thinkers, Anaximander and Anaximenes, we find evidence of a concern to explain why things change at all by seeking to discover within the underlying substrate some intrinsic principles of energy or dynamism. Moreover, each of these three Ionians regarded his ultimate principle as a vital, living force, as something divine, imperishable. Thus they were either hylozoists, affirming that life is fundamental to all sensible beings and that everything in some way partakes of the divine, or tended to this view.

Thales, the first of these Ionians, found the common source or principle of things in water. To us his principle seems absurdly naïve. Yet his effort to find a principle of this kind is profoundly important from the philosophical and scientific point of view. For material things are similar, and this similarity indeed may well be more significant and indicative of their nature than their differences.

Why did Thales choose water as the basic stuff, the ultimate principle of all things? We do not know precisely why, nor did Aristotle, who knew far more about these ancient thinkers than do we, who are dependent on scattered fragments, sometimes derived from secondary sources, for reconstructing their doctrines. Yet Aristotle did offer some conjectures of his own on the reasons leading Thales to his position, and the important thing to note is that Aristotle attaches significance to Thales because he believed that Thales reached his conclusion by rational, that is, philosophical thinking. According to Aristotle, Thales posited water as the first principle probably because of his observations that "the nutriment of things is moist . . . that heat itself is generated from the moist and kept alive by it . . . and from the fact that the seeds of all things have a moist nature, and that water is the origin of the nature of moist things" (*Metaphysics*, I, 3, 983b20–27). A further consideration that may have influenced Thales was the fact that water can exist as a solid, a liquid, and a gas or vapor, the three so-called states of material beings.

Thales' successor, Anaximander, differed from his predecessor in making the primitive stuff or first principle of material reality the "unlimited" or "boundless," rather than a definite substance like water. In the sole fragment of his teaching that survives, Anaximander declares: "the first principle of existing things is the unlimited . . . but into those from which the existing things have their coming to be do they also pass away, according to necessity; for they give justice and make amends to one another for their injustice, according to the ordering of time" (Fragment 1, found in Simplicius, *Phys.*, 24, 14–20). Anaximander seems to have been the first thinker to introduce "the unlimited" or "boundless" or "infinite" as a philosophical term, meaning by it the inexhaustible reservoir or source for the development of the physical world. Yet it is not the notion of the unlimited which is the characteristic feature of his teaching. After all, the "water" of Thales was likewise "unlimited" in the sense that it was the fundamental, inexhaustible source of cosmic becoming. The distinguishing feature of his first principle, as compared to the "water" of Thales, was its indeterminate nature. Why did he favor a first principle of this nature rather than one of some determinate kind, as water or air? According to Aristotle, Anaximander and others who posited a first principle of indefinite nature did so so that the determinate kinds of bodies existent in the physical world might not be destroyed by it. If the first principle were of a definite nature, e.g., water or the moist, then it would destroy utterly its opposite, the dry (cf. Aristotle, *Physics*, III, 5, 204b22–29).

More striking and more important in Anaximander's teaching, however, is his attempt — vague though it be — to explain *why* this primitive unlimited stuff evolved, giving rise to the determinate material bodies of the universe. He speaks metaphorically, attributing this process to necessity, to the judgments of time evening out the tensions produced in the plastic stuff of the opposites it contained. In other words, for Anaximander all the opposites — hot and cold, moist and dry, etc. — were already contained in the "boundless." They merely had to be "separated out" of it by the decrees of time. The "unlimited," therefore, was a mixture in which no one of the opposites predominated. It was Anaximander's successor, Anaximenes, who developed this aspect of his doctrine, introducing the terms "rarefaction" and "condensation" to explain in less poetic language the processes whereby the realities precontained in the original matrix separated out from it in such a way that the sensible bodies of the experienced world come into and pass out of being. Anaximenes, however, substituted "air" for the "indeterminate something," the "boundless" of Anaximander as the first principle or original matrix. Yet the positing of contrary forces to explain the generation and corruption of sensible existents is a notable advance. It is behind the thinking of Aristotle. It is the basis of the dualism characteristic of Western thought: potency and act, matter and form, coprinciples to explain being and becoming.

Anaximenes and the Ionian tradition were "succeeded" by Anaxagoras and the atomists. Before investigating these latter "physicists," however, the Pythagorean, Heraclitean, and Parmenidean movements must be examined, for all greatly influenced the later followers of the Ionians.

2. Pythagoras and the Pythagoreans. Pythagoras (fl. c. 53 B.C.), born on the island of Samos off the coast of Ionia, spent much of his life in Italy, at Croton, founding there a brotherhood primarily religious in character but stressing culture and learning. We do not know much about Pythagoras himself. We are fairly sure that he accepted the belief of metempsychosis, or transmigration of souls, most probably because of his enthusiasm for religious revival begun at Delos, the scene of the Orphic rites. We also know that he was fascinated by numbers. We do not know exactly how his interest in numbers arose, but we do know of his discovery of the vibrating string. Since lyre music was part of the Orphic rites, Pythagoras could be expected to have an interest in it. He discovered that the pitch of a note is in direct proportion to the number of vibrations. If the vibrations are doubled, the pitch is an octave higher. If the number of vibrations is halved, the pitch is an octave lower. The same is true for the column of air in a flute. The significance of this, of course, is that the material involved makes little difference. *The number is the determinant.*

This immediately introduces an outstanding landmark in the philosophy of nature: the consideration that any theory of nature must be developed by distinguishing between the determinable, the stuff, the source of change, and the principle of determination, the essence, the ideal, the form as the termination of the change. This is not the *immediate* result of Pythagoreanism, but in the course of time it most certainly was developed by the Pythagorean brotherhood. The immediate development was twofold.

First of all, the Pythagoreans stressed the significance of proportion. The elements, the sources, the changeable, have indeed an importance of themselves. If there were no sources, there would be no products and no natural processes. However, there are real differences in the products of the same elements. For example, not all the combinations of carbon are alive, and some of them cannot even be considered organic. Since the differences are not actually *in* the elements or sources, we must, the Pythagoreans held, turn to proportion to explain these differences; that is to say, the elements have many capacities that are actualized in and only in their proper combination with other elements.

Second, the Pythagoreans contributed to the theory of number itself, raising such questions as combinations of numbers, a possible infinite number, *odd* numbers as infinite numbers, *even* as finite numbers, an *infinite series* of numbers, etc. The Pythagoreans thereby introduced mathematical thinking into Western culture and began a movement that has still, perhaps, to reach its fruition.

We may, as Aristotle does, sum up the achievements of Ionian and Pythagorean cosmology in the following propositions.

1. There are in nature sources or elements to explain the similarity observed among the many beings that constitute the universe.

2. There must also be principles of contrariety to explain the equally remarkable differences among those beings and to explain their diversity of operation.

3. Proportion or order, represented by number, is necessary to explain the *proper* and determinate direction of natural processes. In other words, the ordered structure of the universe and the definite channels of development evidenced in nature demand some formal, determining principle as their adequate explanation.

The Ionians, in short, gave to subsequent Greek thinkers the notion that change or movement in the material universe required a basic substratum (the element of similarity and identity in things) which passed from one opposite state to another (the element of differentiation among things). The Pythagoreans had suggested that the opposite states into which the underlying substrate passes were like numbers, the principles of specification, of determination. We shall now see how sensible change was subjected to a metaphysical account, in terms of being and not-being, process and flux. For this account of sensible change we must look to Heraclitus of Ephesus and Parmenides of Elea.

3. Heraclitus of Ephesus. (floruit c. 500 B.C.). He is a fascinating character. Extensive study of the fragments we possess of his writings, oracular in style, has led scholars to see in him a man primarily interested in moral questions whose statements concerning the nature of the physical universe are largely incidental. His concern with morality is exemplified in his resignation from the hereditary office of the King of Ephesus in order to concentrate on the priestly duties associated with that office. Of the scroll containing his oracle, we possess only fragments, but from them we can gain an appreciation of his moral earnestness and outlook. The following points are indicative of his position.

1. Philosophers, especially Pythagoras, have put too much emphasis on explanations of the universe and have neglected the purpose of life.

2. Man's purpose in life is the pursuit of wisdom. Compared to this, all else is foolishness. There is no point in attaching oneself to any item in or any explanation of the universe, since compared to wisdom or *logos* all else is passing away. (This is the force of his statement that "all is change.")

3. Wisdom is the reconciliation of opposites: "Having listened, not to me, but to the *Logos* it is wise to agree that *all things are one*" (Fr. 150). The universe is full of all kinds of opposite and contrary forces and tendencies. The only stability is that of wisdom since it reconciles the opposites. Nothing has any meaning without wisdom.

4. Wisdom, symbolized by fire, enables man to see how the unremitting process of change, the ceaseless flux of reality, takes place eternally according to fixed measures.

A dominant person is often remembered by some minor statement or action that overshadows his true value. This was the fate of Heraclitus, who is remembered chiefly for his statement that all is change. He is thus written off as the philosopher who denied being and who explained it as an illusion, or as the cosmologist who tried to explain away matter and to reduce the universe to force.

Actually it was the followers of Heraclitus who advocated the doctrine of a Universal Flux. Some of them interpreted Heraclitus to the effect that, since all is change, permanence is an illusion. This philosophy is called *dynamic monism,* a doctrine subjected to devastating criticism by Aristotle and one which, in all its forms, is ultimately self-destructive. In order to learn, there must be some stability in things and in men: otherwise, by the time we think we understand anything, it is already something else. Moreover, we are something other than what we were. Furthermore, to say that being is an illusion is to raise the question, "Whence come our illusions?" We believe that we see a pattern of stability amid the change observable in things. Moreover, we believe that we who perceive this stability amidst change are ourselves perceiving subjects. If nothing abides, neither things nor ourselves, how can "we" be subject to illusions?

Yet the dynamism, the universal flux of the Heracliteans serves to remind us of the central feature of the material beings that make up the universe about us; that is, these beings are constantly changing; mobility, movement is natural to them.

Moreover Heraclitus, by attributing to a "divine" wisdom or *logos* the role of reconciling all opposites, of governing the ceaseless flux that constitutes the universe, calls attention to the need for cosmologists to face the problem of finality, of intelligent ordering of processes and movements. Despite the obscurity of his own teaching on the nature of the divine *Logos* directing all things, his remarks on the need for such a principle inaugurated a study of this problem.

4. Parmenides (fl. c. 485 B.C.). Perhaps the most influential of the Preplatonic philosophers was Parmenides. Parmenides lived in Elea, a Greek colony in southern Italy (Magna Graecia), yet he was thoroughly familiar with the physical views of the Ionians by reason of the ties between Elea and the Greek cities of Asia Minor. Although it has been customary, since the time of Plato, to oppose Parmenides to Heraclitus, we shall see that this device, dramatic and vivid though it be for illustrating diametrically opposed philosophical positions, does not do justice to either thinker.

Parmenides wrote his philosophy in poetic form. In the opening part of his poem he speaks as one who has been given an apocalyptic vision of truth by a goddess of light. In the first part of the poem proper, called the "Way of Truth," he presents what he believes to be the true vision of reality, one based on *logos* or wisdom. If we follow this path, Parmenides tells us, we shall see that being alone is and is thinkable, whereas not-being is not and is indeed unthinkable. Moreover, being, the object of wisdom, is ingenerate, imperishable, indivisible, continuous, motionless, perfectly self-identical. For how could it arise since beside it there is nothing? How could it perish, for what besides being could destroy it? How could it be divided into parts separate and distinguishable one from the other, since each part, in order to be, would have to be as much being as the whole? Or how could it move, since it lacks nothing, having no place either inside or outside itself in which it could move? Basic to all Parmenides' arguments on the nature of the one unique Being is his complete identification of *being* and *that which is*. In fact, the Greek text of his poem simply uses the verb "is" or "is not" without expressing any subject. Indeed, for Parmenides, there can be no subject that could receive or lose being. Such a subject would be, in Parmenides' eyes, other than being and hence wholly identified with not-being, and not-being, of course, cannot be at all. There is, for Parmenides, then, just being, in which no distinctions or gradings, no modes or characteristics of any kind whatsoever, can be found.

In the second part of the poem, known as the "Way of Opinion," Parmenides investigates the universe as it appears to men, the universe that Thales and the other Ionians had attempted to explain. In investigating this universe, he is trying to see *why* the world of sense appears as it does to men. It appears as though there are many beings within a common universe, that these beings are generated and corrupted, that they move from place to place, that they undergo changes of all kinds. The reason why the world so appears to men is that they have set up two forms for their thinking, whereas they should use only one. What are these forms? The first, symbolized by flame or fire, is that of truth and being. The second is that of "unknowing night," that of not-being and error. This second form should never have been set up by men on an equal footing with that of being, but once it is set up it furnishes a second basic principle and so allows an acceptable explanation of the world as it appears to mortals. Accordingly, Parmenides is then able to offer an account of the nature and genesis of the heavens, the sun, the moon, the stars, and of human activity.

Parmenides' interest throughout the poem is to explain the visible, sensible universe. Considered from the point of view of *logos*, of wisdom, it is one, changeless, perfect. Viewed under the aspect of opinion, it is many, changing, incomplete. Yet the being of Parmenides is sensible throughout. Thus Aristotle considers him along with the "physicists" or cosmologists, those who were concerned to explain the physical universe, the "being of sensible things." Aristotle indeed is very careful to state that Parmenides did not conceive of being as supersensible, *meta* or beyond the physical (cf. *Metaphysics*, IV, 5, 1010a2–3). Thus he was not, in Aristotle's eyes, a metaphysician. However, in spite of this limitation in his point of view, Parmenides saw vividly and expressed forcefully what it means for a thing to be. In his insight into the implications involved in saying of a thing that it *is*, Parmenides set before the eyes of subsequent Western thinkers the basic metaphysical problem, the problem of being. Against the background of Parmenides' notion of being, those who follow will have to strive manfully to allow some genuine being to multiplicity and change.

In concluding this section on Parmenides, it may be worth while to indicate why scholars believe that he and Heraclitus, despite their differences, are basically in agreement. Both philosophers, true enough from radically different points of view, agree in maintaining the basic unity of all things, in affirming that the sensible universe *appears* to be in a state of constant flux, in identifying wisdom and truth, and in seeing in fire the symbol for the inner constitution of reality.

5. Later Eleatics: Zeno and Melissus. Of the cosmologists between Parmenides and Plato, Zeno (fl. 465/455 B.C.) and Melissus (fl. 445–441 B.C.) are traditionally represented as the most important theorists who continued the monism of Parmenides, the position that being alone is and becoming is mere appearance. Neither of these men was as profound as their master Parmenides, their importance lying not so much in their contributions to physical theory as in their development of dialectical argumentation, the posing of alternatives to the Parmenidean position that becoming, movement, change is impossible and reducing these alternatives to absurdity. Thus Zeno's arguments against motion—the race course, Achilles and the tortoise, the flying arrow, the moving rows—have become classic. To take the Achilles-tortoise argument as an example, Zeno argued as follows: Achilles, proverbial in Greek literature as the fastest runner, can never overtake the tortoise, equally proverbial for its slowness. Why? Because Achilles must first reach the point whence the tortoise started. But in the meantime the tortoise has proceeded farther. Achilles, therefore, must cover new ground to catch up. While he is doing so, the tortoise has moved still farther. Thus Achilles must again catch up. The same kind of reasoning can be, Zeno argues, used an infinite number of times, with the result that Achilles can never catch the tortoise. The purpose of the argument was to make the opponents of Parmenidean changelessness look foolish; and Zeno's arguments are valid if his opponents adopted, as many did, the Pythagorean notion that motion is made up of an infinite number of mathematical points, themselves motionless. His reasoning did serve to show the futility of constructing motion of immobilities, of confusing mathematical discrete quantity with real continuous quantity.

Melissus is chiefly notable in that he made the being of Parmenides, which the latter had regarded as finite, infinite.

6. Empedocles. Empedocles of Acragas (c. 521–461 B.C.*) is best regarded as one who continued the Ionian tradition with an attempt to surmount the difficulties leveled against that tradition by the Parmenidean doctrine of being. Like the Ionians of old, Empedocles sought the ultimate source or principle of sensible things. He held that this principle was fourfold: "Hear, first, the four roots of things: bright Zeus /air/, life-bearing Hera /earth/, and Aidoneus /fire/, and Nestis /water/, who causes a mortal spring of moisture to flow with her tears" (Fr. 6). The use of the term "roots" to designate these fundamental principles suggests that for Empedocles the universe of sensible beings developed from them in the way that a tree springs from the soil. These "roots" are not produced by anything else. They are thus ultimate, first beginnings for all.

Empedocles' choice of four roots is itself not too original, since they seem to be concretizations of the traditional Ionian opposites of hot and cold, moist and dry. Aristotle notes that Empedocles, although positing four basic elements, uses them as if they were but two, fire on the one hand and earth, air, and water on the other. Empedocles has thus one fundamental set of contraries.

The Parmenidean influence is seen in the characteristics Empedocles ascribes to each of his four roots or elements. Each is, like the being of Parmenides, ungenerated, imperishable, unchanging. The very terms he uses to designate them bear striking similarity to those used by Parmenides to describe his being.

In explaining how the sensible things of experience arise from these four ultimate principles, Empedocles invokes the two opposite forces of love and hate, under whose influence take place the successive union and separation of the four basic roots. The four, mingled together in an original mass in which the characteristics of each are canceled out so that none predominate, are stirred up by the forces of love and hate, much as a mixture of pigments is stirred by a painter, in such a way that at determinate intervals of time the characteristics of one predominate. This process is cyclic and eternal, and the successive and continually changing world processes are "undeceptive" in contrast to the "deception" found in them by Parmenides.

Strictly speaking, Empedocles does not appear to be too original. He

* On the disputed question of Empedocles' chronology, see J. Owens, *A History of Ancient Western Philosophy* (New York: Appleton-Century-Crofts, 1960), pp. 103–104, 417–418.

seems rather to have been a successful popularizer of doctrines implied in the Ionians, but he stereotyped their basic opposites in such a way that the doctrine of the four roots is best known as the work of Empedocles. Of him Aristotle wrote that he was one of those "who, having nothing to say, yet pretend to say something" (*Rhetoric*, III, 5, 1407a33–34).

7. Leucippus (fl. c. 449 B.C.). He used the concept of atoms to reconcile the ancient Ionian theories with the Parmenidean concept of being. By "atom" Leucippus understood something that will not be cut or divided, being an indivisible extended unit. The atoms of Leucippus had the characteristics of Parmenidean being and were infinite in number. But Leucippus postulated the void or non-being in addition to the atoms, taking both as equal causes of the things that come into being. Because the atoms could move about in the void, they could join with one another to form the bodies observed by men in their everyday experience. The apparent differences in kind between the composites resulting from the motion of atoms in the world were explained by endowing the atoms with different shapes, and here we see the influence of the Pythagoreans on Leucippus. For example, fire, since it tends upward, has a pyramidal shape to its atoms. Since water is fluid, its atoms are tiny spheres. Earth has solid, cubical atoms.

This is the system generally called *atomism*. Its greatest champion is generally considered to be *Democritus* (c. 494–404 B.C.), a Greek philosopher from Asia Minor who had come to southern Italy. That Democritus has been known as the outstanding atomist is one of the ironies of history. Democritus was predominantly concerned with a unified moral theory of the universe, and most particularly with man's social role in the State. Leucippus' cycle of love and hate drew the attention of Democritus, and insofar as he accepted the philosophy of Leucippus in its entirety, he also thereby accepted atomism as an adequate scheme for the physical universe.

Atomism is mechanism. That is, it explains phenomena solely in terms of objects and forces. This may be twofold: physical and philosophical.

As a *physical* system, it still exists, although more as a conceptual system to tell us how to think about the universe in order to give us working concepts that help us use things rather than as a theory regarded as ultimate and explanatory of the inner nature of sensible reality, as was the atomism of Leucippus and Democritus.

As a *philosophical* system, atomism has two shortcomings. It attempts to explain the properties of bodies by the shapes of atoms and by their motion. Yet an explanation of this kind leaves unanswered the question,

"Why do atoms move at all and why do they combine to form definite bodies?" The ultimate answer is that if atoms constitute different essences by forming different proportions, they do so because they *can* do so, because they have the capacity, the potency to enter into proper proportions terminating in different essences. The ultimate answer, then, is not to be found in the *fact* of combinations — it is this fact that Leucippus, Democritus, and their modern successors acknowledge — but in the material *potency* for the combinations. This means, then, that atomism does not go far enough. It may be right as far as it goes, but to be philosophical it must go all the way.

Second, atomism does not explain the origin of the forces and energies assumed as necessary to cause the atoms to move. Atomism pictures atoms falling through a void, but that does not answer how energies can proceed *from* bodies. The answer to this is that somehow the energy must first *be* in the body before it can proceed from it. The answer to this difficulty was what Greek philosophy had been gradually developing into: an emergence from a factual account into an investigation of real principles. The problem of bodies reduces itself to a combination of activity and capacity to be acted on. This means that bodies must be composed intrinsically and essentially of a principle of activity and a principle of receptivity or passivity. The fullest development of this is called *hylomorphism*, a philosophical doctrine receiving its first adumbrations from Plato and its realistic development by Aristotle.

SUMMARY

1. The basic problems in cosmology as well as in metaphysics are how all the beings in the material universe resemble one another in their being yet differ from each other in their essences and existence. This is the problem of *the one and the many*. Furthermore, these beings remain what they are for a time and yet undergo changes. As far as anyone can tell, the pattern of stability amid change is as wide as the universe. This is the problem of *being and becoming*.
2. The *Ionians* tried to explain reality in terms of sources, such elements as air, water, etc., and such contrary forces as attraction and repulsion.
3. *Pythagoras* and the Pythagoreans began with a consideration of proportion of components. This became a theory explaining the essence of bodies as number. This began as a philosophy of immanence but became a philosophy of transcendence in the hands of some Pythagoreans who made the universe a material imitation of a world of numbers.
4. *Heraclitus* was violently opposed to mathematicism of any sort, and his philosophy is an interesting contrast between the transitory character of the material universe and the ultimate wisdom of the divine mind. His influence was felt in a subsequent emphasis on becoming by his followers.

5. *Parmenides* put ultimate emphasis on being at the expense of becoming. The subsequent development of Graeco-Italian philosophy is an attempt to follow Parmenides as far as possible, but making room for the reality of becoming. *Empedocles* sought to achieve this by an emphasis on elements and contrary forces, whereas *Leucippus* and *Democritus* sought to do so with their theory of atoms and of forces.

This is the background of the philosophical doctrine of hylomorphism.

CHAPTER THREE

The COSMOLOGY of PLATO

INTRODUCTION

The Presocratics had made the first attempts to reach a genuinely philosophical and scientific understanding of the physical universe, seeking the fundamental principles and causes of the changing beings that constitute that universe. Their efforts, especially those of Parmenides and the Eleatics, had raised the problem of reconciling the seemingly divergent reports of the senses and the intellect on the nature and structure of physical reality. They had brought into prominence the tension between being and becoming, sense appearances and intelligible, intrinsic natures.

The Presocratics, especially Heraclitus and Democritus, had likewise raised questions concerning moral conduct and the relationship between virtue and knowledge. Socrates, that inspiring figure in Western thought who exerted such profound influence on the young Plato and, through him, on all subsequent philosophers, was, in his youth, interested in cosmological pursuits. Disillusioned, however, by the sophistical dialectic of those who championed one particular theory or another, he soon decided to devote his life to questioning men on moral matters, those that deeply touch human life both individual and social, on the grounds that "an unexamined life is not worth living." His concern was to determine the principles that could serve men to guide their lives wisely, to choose the good and avoid the evil, to discover abiding, stable norms of conduct in the midst of change.

Plato was to draw together the various themes developed in preceding Greek thought — cosmological, moral, metaphysical, epistemological — probing each and contributing to them the riches of his own personal inquiry into the problems central to each. He was to explore, and to explore deeply, the philosophical implications involved in asserting that we know something, pursuing true knowledge to every area. We will be concerned primarily with Plato's teaching on the nature and structure of physical, mobile being, the sensible existents of the universe. But to understand his cosmology we must first view the larger philosophical framework against which his physical theory was elaborated.

THE THEORY OF IDEAS OR FORMS

Plato is best known as the advocate of the Ideas or Forms as true being. Yet his teaching is frequently misrepresented, at times quite seriously, and he is made to appear as a somewhat naïve simpleton who sought to flee the concrete world of sense, a world of flesh and blood human beings soiled by contact with earthy things, to a dreamworld of spiritual ideas where everything is perfectly ordered and in complete harmony. One common misrepresentation is to see in the term "idea" a mental construct elaborated by the mind, a "copy" of really existing things purified of their imperfections and "idealized" to the nth degree. Such is emphatically *not* what Plato meant by an Idea or Form. Perhaps a few observations on the terms Plato used and their meaning to the Greeks of his day will be helpful in dispelling any misconceptions on this score. The Greek word "idea" comes from the verb ἰδεῖν, meaning "to see." The word had the meaning of *something seen* by men rather than produced by them. It had been used by Greeks prior to Plato to signify both the outer form or shape and the inner nature of a thing. Plato took this word, along with its ordinary meaning for his Greek contemporaries, and used it as a philosophical notion of his own to signify what he regarded as the "really real" in things, as true, authentic being. One synonym Plato used for "idea" was εἶδος, meaning "form." This word also stems from the verb ἰδεῖν, "to see." In addition, Plato frequently uses the terms οὐσία, "being," γένος, "kind," ἕνας, "unit," or φύσις, "nature," to denote the same object as that pointed out by ἰδέα or εἶδος. Many times he adds the term "itself" to a word to get across the same point. Thus we see that Plato used a great variety of expressions to denote what he regarded as genuine reality, and in every case he is using terms that point to something objective, something independent of mind, discovered in things by man rather than constructed or fashioned by his intellect.

In the early dialogues — *Laches, Charmides, Euthyphro, Protagoras, Meno, Gorgias* — Plato's interest is chiefly in moral questions. He seeks, for example, to find out what courage, temperance, piety, virtue are in themselves. The point driven home in these dialogues is that actions are called courageous or pious or temperate or virtuous because they all possess some common character making them to be courageous, pious, temperate, etc. This common character, found in individual cases of virtuous activity, is what is being sought. Plato also links up virtue and knowledge in these early dialogues. For instance, if a man is to act bravely, temperately, piously, virtuously, he must know what bravery itself, temperance itself, etc., are. Indeed, he must know himself as well. Now to know what these virtues and what virtue in general are in themselves is to know that common feature running through particular instances of them. It is to know their Idea or Form, their inner nature or being, that which makes them to be what they are. And what is true of virtue and its parts is true likewise of the other objects of human intelligence. True knowledge, what Plato calls ἐπιστήμη (science), is knowledge of these Forms or Ideas which impart stability and self-identity to the varied, multiple individual instances. To ἐπιστήμη or scientific knowledge is opposed belief (πίστις) or opinion (δόξα), which is not based on a vision of the true being or inner structure of things but rather on a "probable" or apparently correct estimate of them on the basis of their sensible appearance.

The Ideas or Forms are as yet not "separated" from the things of this sensible universe. Thus far, the theory as set forth in the Platonic dialogues would seem to be common to both Socrates and Plato, at least if Aristotle's testimony is accurate. For Aristotle reported that Socrates, too, believed in the Ideas or Forms and that he linked genuine, certain knowledge to them. Yet he also tells us that Socrates did not "separate" the Ideas, that is, he did not maintain that they existed independently of sensible things. Yet this is a teaching central to the Platonic dialogues, beginning with the *Symposium*. Thus, when we find the "Socrates" of the Platonic dialogues teaching that the Forms or Ideas exist in a state of complete independence from material things, we must regard this "Socrates" not as the historical figure but as the dramatic spokesman for Plato himself.

Why, however, did Plato "separate" the ideas? Why was he led to conclude that they existed outside of as well as within physical things? As we have seen, Plato argued that there must be, within the many individuals of our experience, something common making all beautiful things, for example, beautiful or making all men men. Beauty itself, man himself, courage itself are embodied in individual cases of beautiful objects, of men, and of courageous actions, but as so embodied they are limited, scattered among many, in a way alienated from themselves.

Beautiful things are not beauty itself, courageous actions are not courage itself. They *have* beauty, courage, justice, etc., but *are not* these realities in an absolute sense. By examining these particular exemplifications of the "really real," however, and by letting love for truth take possession of his being, a man is gradually led to see a nature such as beauty itself, "which in the first place is everlasting, not growing or decaying, or waxing or waning; secondly, not fair in one point of view and foul in another, or at one time or in one relation or at one place fair, at another time or in another relation or at another place foul . . . but beauty absolute, separate, simple, and everlasting, which without diminution and without increase, or any change, is imparted to the ever-growing and perishing beauties of all other things" (*Symposium*, 210E–211B).

The unchanging nature, reached by this ascending process, is regarded as that which all concrete, material individuals, which we may call "beautiful" or "good" or "just" or "courageous," as the case may be, share in or partake of. The genuinely real, participated in by the individuals of our experience, is thus existentially independent of those individuals, anterior to them, the cause of the reality they possess and in final analysis the object and cause of our scientifically grounded and certain knowledge (ἐπιστήμη) of things. The ideas, in brief, are both immanent to sensible things and transcendent of them, constituting a "world of Ideas" (this expression never occurs in Plato himself, but is an accurate way for designating his thought).

Plato encountered many difficulties in his theory of participation, anticipating in his dialogue *Parmenides* the principal objections that would be leveled against this teaching by subsequent thinkers, in particular, by Aristotle. Such objections were based on problems such as these: Are there Ideas or Forms of such things as hair, mud, fingernails? If individual men are similar because they partake of the Form *man*, then must we not say that there is yet a "third man" in whom both individual men and the Form *man* participate in order that we might use the same term to denote each, and so on *ad infinitum?* Furthermore, how are the Forms or Ideas existing in this supersensible world related to one another? What gives unity to this universe of separated Forms? Why are there many Forms and not simply one? Plato well recognized the difficulties involved in positing a world of Ideas, yet he steadfastly adhered to his teaching, maintaining that, without these Ideas, not only would certain knowledge of things be impossible but also that there would be no stability or fixity in things themselves. Without these Ideas which transcended the sensible universe, yet were immanent to material things through participation, Plato held, all that would be left would be a universal flux, the ceaseless becoming advocated by the popularizers of Heraclitus' views. Moral conduct based on knowledge would be impossible, and without that there could be no *politeia*, no life of justice pursued by men with a common goal and common interests.

The upshot of Plato's discussion of the problem involved in the theory of participation in the *Parmenides* was that the fact of scientific knowledge is the unshakeable reason for admitting the reality of the Ideas. Such knowledge, as Plato seeks to show in the *Theaetetus*, is rooted in being and is attained by the intellect, not through any bodily sense. Since knowledge is grounded in being, however, the old Parmenidean problem of motion and plurality in the objects of knowledge is raised. This is discussed in the *Sophist*, where Plato undertakes to show that motion, despite its opposition to the Parmenidean concept of being, must exist in the realm of the Ideas and thus share being in some way. "Can we," Plato has the Eleatic Stranger ask, "ever be made to believe that motion and life and soul and mind are not present with perfect being? Can we imagine that being is devoid of life and mind, and exists in awful unmeaningness, in everlasting fixture? . . . Under being, then, we must include motion, and that which is moved" (*Sophist*, 248E–249B).

Motion as well as changeable things, consequently, has to be accepted as somehow sharing in being. This means that motion is one of the Forms or Ideas. Plato can, therefore, allow with Parmenides that being itself is unchanging, yet equally hold that change or motion is or *exists* in some way. The two, motion and being, mingle. Yet they are not the same. Being *is not* motion, it is *other* than motion; and conversely motion *is not* being, it is *other* than being. Motion is, thus, in a sense *non-being*, yet it is not absolutely non-being, for absolute non-being simply *is not*, whereas motion in some way *is*. Motion is in that it shares in being; it is not in that it is not identical with or the same as being. The purpose of the philosopher, accordingly, is to see what are the chief Forms of Ideas or Kinds, those that can mingle with one another. For Plato these are the Forms of being, rest, motion, sameness, and otherness (cf. *Sophist*, 254C–255E). Among these the Form of otherness is that of relative non-being. By its presence in all the Ideas (save that of the One or the Good, which is beyond Being) it renders the world of Ideas multiple and renders possible plurality in the sensible universe that exists only by participating in the supersensible Forms or Ideas. At the very summit of the world of Ideas and, consequently, at the summit of reality, stands the Idea of the Good or the One. Plato places this Form above being itself (cf. *Republic*, 476A–D), but he does not elaborate on this doctrine in any subsequent writings. The reason seems to be, however, that the Good or the One is not only the final cause of all sensible things, bringing them into being, but is likewise the ultimate condition or principle underlying the Ideas themselves. Eternal, the Ideas do not come into being. Many, they yet constitute a single *uni*verse, a coherent and harmonious realm. Whence derives the bond that unites them, that holds them in being? For Plato, the ultimate source welding them together, making them a cosmos and not a chaos, is the Idea of the Good or the One. To discuss this matter further would involve us too deeply in Plato's metaphysics than is necessary here. We shall now see how Plato related his Ideas to the sensible universe, how he explained the origin, structure, and nature of the physical world. In other words, we shall turn our attention to the Platonic cosmology as contained in the dialogue *Timaeus.*

PLATO'S COSMOLOGY

The chief interlocutor of this dialogue, Timaeus of Locri, commences by distinguishing between "that which always is and has no becoming; and that which is always becoming and never truly is" (*Timaeus,* 27D). The first is the "really real," the genuine reality, the being, that is, which we have just seen to be proper to the Platonic Ideas or Forms. The latter, which is apprehended not by the intellect itself but by "opinion with the help of sensation," is the world of sensible experience, the physical universe examined by the Ionians. Because it is not the genuine object of intelligence, Timaeus does not pretend to give a "scientific" or certainly true account of its origin and nature. All that he can hope for is a "likely account," one of whose truth we can never be certain but must be content to know only with a high degree of probability (cf. *Timaeus,* 29C).

From the fact that the sensible universe is in a state of constant becoming Timaeus argues to some cause, a divine craftsman or Demiurge. Throughout the dialogue the Demiurge is referred to as the "father and maker of this universe," the "god" or artisan of the world of our experience. For this reason, some have seen in the Platonic Demiurge a being strikingly analogous to the Christian God. Yet this is definitely not Plato's position. For the Demiurge, indeed, seems to be a symbolical figure. He is certainly not to be identified with the Idea of the Good (which, as we have seen, is the highest principle, the absolutely first in the Platonic hierarchy of reality). He is introduced, moreover, in a dialogue expressly devoted to giving but a "likely account" and not a necessarily certain report on the origin of things. In all likelihood, he is a symbol, standing for the divine element at work in the physical universe. The Demiurge is pictured as fashioning this world after an eternal and uncreated pattern, i.e., after the pattern of the world of Ideas. Note that the world of Ideas is represented as independent of the Demiurge; never is he said to be the cause of the Ideas. The world of Ideas definitely does not exist in the mind of the Demiurge, as do the eternal ideas of St. Augustine, for example, exist in the mind of the Creator God. The Demiurge is led to fashion the physical universe after the pattern of this ideal world because of his goodness; yet the Demiurge is not free in his work. He must, by an intrinsic necessity, bring the sensible world into being. In addition, the goodness that the Demiurge could impart to the world is represented as subject to the limitation of the material at his disposal. He does not make this universe out of nothing. Rather he takes over preexisting matter which, prior to his action, lay in a state of chaos and disorderly motion and upon which he confers order and beauty.

Because the physical world is ordered and because order implies intelligence and soul, the Demiurge first fashioned a world-soul that makes of the body of the entire universe a "living thing with soul and reason." We see here how the ancient Ionian notion of universal animism is adopted into the Platonic cosmology. The body of the world, being visible and tangible, requires fire and earth among its constituents. Yet these must be united, and the "fairest" bond between these is that of mathematical proportion. Since a solid, unlike a surface, has a double and not just a single mean, two intermediary constituents, air and water, are necessary as the link joining together fire and earth. In this way the four Empedoclean "roots" are justified mathematically as the four primitive constituents of the sensible world.

What shape should the universe take? That of sphere is Timaeus' answer, because it is the most perfect figure and is moreover most suitable for the world-soul. The striking feature of this aspect of Plato's "likely account" is the fact that the shape he confers on the universe is precisely that which Parmenides had given to his unique being. The result is a universe that is one and solitary, being, in fact, a "blessed god" (*Timaeus*, 34B).

That this living god might more completely be like the ideal and eternal, the Demiurge next makes a "moving image of eternity," making this image "eternal but moving according to number, whereas eternity itself rests in unity; and this image we call time" (*Timaeus*, 37D). Time was made along with the universe. This quite evidently means that for Plato, time, the ordering of motion according to mathematical succession, had a beginning. Time was not present in the "disorderly" motions of the preexistent material prior to the action of the Demiurge. Such indeed is the explicit testimony of Aristotle (cf. *Physics*, VI, 1, 251b17–19), who implies that on this point Plato differed from all other Greek thinkers. Yet Plato expressly declares, and Aristotle is again a witness, that motion itself is eternal (cf. *Timaeus*, 30A, and *Metaphysics*, XII, 6, 1071b32–33); apparently, then, while Plato regarded motion as eternal, he did not so regard time. Time is a type of duration that began only when the Demiurge constituted an ordered universe out of the materials that he found already there and set in *ordered* motion.

The Demiurge then made the other living things required for the completion of the universe, modeling them after the Idea or Form of living things: the heavenly gods, the birds, creatures of the sea, and those which live on land. The first, the so-called gods, are the stars. Yet Plato implies that other divinities were also constructed, to whom was given the responsibility for making the bodies of men and lower living things. The final production of the Demiurge himself is the souls of men.

Up to this point the dialogue has been concerned with describing the cosmos from the viewpoint of its intelligent causes, those endowed with mind. Yet there is necessary also a study of those causes which lack intelligence and which produce chance events. For the universe is a mixed effect, embracing both necessity and mind. Necessity, called the variable or errant cause, signifies the purposeless or unintelligent agent at work in the universe. It is identified with the "receptacle" or "nurse" of all generation. Plato's description of this necessary cause, this receptacle of sensible beings, is very halting. It cannot be identified with any definite thing, such as fire or earth. These are rather elements that appear within this "matter." This receptacle, "while receiving all things, never departs at all from her own nature, and never in any way, or at any time, assumes a form like that of any of the things which enter into her. . . . But the forms which enter into and go out of her are the likenesses of real existences modelled after their patterns in a wonderful and inexplicable manner" (*Timaeus*, 50BC). Hardly real, this receptacle is apprehended by a kind of "bastard reason" (*Timaeus*, 52B). The receptacle always remains the same. It thus partakes, though in a mysterious way, of the intelligible, being eternal and indestructible. It is finally identified by Plato with "space" (*Timaeus*, 51A), providing a "home for all created things."

As one commentator has noted: "Interpreted in later language, this would be the doctrine of a prime matter that is a matter *in which*, but not *from which*. . . . It is by no means identical with the Peripatetic [Aristotelian] matter, which receives forms and is perfected by them" (Ignatius Brady, *A History of Ancient Philosophy*, p. 96).

Nonetheless, and this will help us see how Plato leads to the Aristotelian doctrine of hylomorphism, the doctrine presented in the *Timaeus* regards the sensible things of our experience as composites involving in their essence both material and formal elements. The formal element, making them to be what they are, comes to them from their participation in the ideas. The material element, limiting them to the here and now, is located by Plato in the work effected by "space," a principle independent of the ideas and co-eternal with them and not identical with the individual composites either, being prior to them and *unchanged* within them.

SUMMARY

1. The cosmological views of Plato cannot be understood unless they are seen against the background of his entire metaphysics. Basically, Plato's philosophy can be understood as an effort to determine the causal principles that account for the intelligibility and structure of the individual existents of our experience. Plato located the supreme causes of this intelligibility and structure in the Ideas or Forms. The latter, because they are characterized by self-identity, stability, eternity, and immutability, are purely spiritual or immaterial in character. They are the product of no mind, but are truly existent. They are, in fact, more truly existent than are the material things of our immediate experience, inasmuch as they are free from any spatial or temporal limitations. There is, moreover, a hierarchy of Ideas or Forms, at the summit of which is the Idea of the Good or the One, which is the source of all the reality and intelligibility both in all other Ideas and in the sensible things that in some way partake of or share in them.
2. Although the Forms or Ideas transcend the material universe by reason of their supersensible being, they must in some way be immanent in the things of this universe; otherwise the intelligibility we do discover in things would be inexplicable. Although Plato himself maintains that it is impossible to determine precisely how these Forms are "participated in" by sensible things, he offers a "probable account" to explain their immanence in material beings. Accepting matter as a given datum, a receptacle in which individual sensible things appear, Plato indicates that the order and intelligible structure these things manifest is caused by a "Demiurge" or divine artificer who "overcomes" the chaotic condition of materiality by endowing sensible existents with a likeness or resemblance of the Forms or Ideas.

CHAPTER FOUR

ARISTOTLE'S HYLOMORPHISM

INTRODUCTION

Greek cosmology, from Thales and the early "physicists" on, was a search for principles that would explain the nature and structure of the physical world. This quest for principles was continued by Aristotle, who takes pains to show us why a philosophical inquiry into nature must be concerned first and foremost with determining principles. "When the objects of an inquiry," he tells us, "in any department, have principles, conditions, or elements, it is through acquaintance with these that knowledge, that is to say, scientific knowledge, is attained. For we do not think that we know a thing until we are acquainted with its primary conditions or first principles, and have carried our analysis as far as its simplest elements. Plainly, therefore, in the science of Nature, as in other branches of study, our first task will be to try to determine what relates to its principles" (*Physics*, I, 1, 184a9–16).

In determining the principles of physical reality, Aristotle proceeds in a dialectical fashion by subjecting to analysis the theories of his predecessors. Underlying this approach is his belief that the labor of those who went before him has not been pointless. Despite the conflicting, at times contradictory, accounts of the Ionians, the Eleatics and the Heracliteans, the Pythagoreans and the Platonists, Aristotle is convinced that each has seen something of genuine significance, that they have been compelled, as it were, by the truth itself, to discern something within physical beings that gives some clue as to their ultimate principles. Thus we shall begin by recapitulating Aristotle's review of his predecessors.

ARISTOTLE'S REVIEW OF HIS PREDECESSORS

Considering the principles of nature dialectically, that is, from the point of view of the alternatives open with respect to their number and nature once one grants their necessity, Aristotle observes: "The principles in question must be either (a) one or (b) more than one. If (a) one, it must be either (i) motionless, as Parmenides and Melissus assert, or (ii) in motion, as the physicists [that is, the Ionians and the Heracliteans] hold. . . . If (b) more than one, then either (i) finite or (ii) an infinite plurality. If (i) finite (but more than one), then either two or three or four or some other number. If (ii) infinite, then either as Democritus believed one in kind but differing in shape or form; or different in kind and even contrary" (*Physics*, I, 2, 184b15–22). The next thing to do is to examine each of these alternatives, to see whether some can be discarded as involving absurdities or contradictions and to see which seems most promising for subsequent inquiry and verification.

The Eleatics, that is, Parmenides and Melissus, maintain that there is only one principle and that it is motionless. For them, in other words, everything is one; plurality is mere appearance whereas in truth being alone is and is changeless. Aristotle, in addition to noting that this position runs directly contrary to the obvious fact of change and multiplicity in nature, goes on to show that it is based on a failure to distinguish the meanings of "is" and "one," for both terms are used in many senses (cf. *Physics*, I, 2, 185a20–21). Fundamentally, Aristotle tells us, the Eleatics had not distinguished between the subject and the attribute which is predicated of it, between, for example, "what has whiteness" and "whiteness" itself. Put in a more general form, they had not made the distinction between "what has being" and "being." To put this criticism in more concrete form, consider the following three propositions: The man is, the dog is, the stone is. If there is no distinction between the subjects (*man, dog, stone* respectively) and the predicate (*is*), then the three subjects are totally one. This would seem to be what Parmenides would say. Yet it is obvious that all three are different. All are "one" in the sense that all exist; each one *is*, but each one's manner of existence differs according to what it is, according to its essence. This is what Aristotle affirms in saying that there are many ways in which we say of a thing that "it is." Put briefly, his argument against the Eleatic monists is based on his realization that to use the same predicate "is" of many different things does not mean that these things are identically one.

The Heracliteans (and here, we should recall, Aristotle's arguments bear chiefly on the popularizers of the Ephesian thinker, who was himself principally interested in moral questions) can be criticized on the same score as the Eleatics, in that they admit of only one principle in nature, namely, in affirming that all things are one. They differ from Parmenides and his followers, however, in making their "one" dynamic in character rather than static. For them change, ceaseless flux, is characteristic of the one ultimate principle of all things, whereas the one of Parmenides was absolutely changeless. Because of this feature of their doctrine, Aristotle could charge them with making knowledge impossible. Why? Because, for knowledge to be possible, there must be some element of stability in reality. If reality is a flux, an endless succession of change, we can never gain knowledge of it. For in the very moment that we believe we apprehend it in a knowing act it is already becoming something different (cf. *Metaphysics*, I, 6, 987a25 ff.).

In discussing the views of the Ionian thinkers (Thales, Anaximander, Anaximenes) and subsequent "physicists" such as Anaxagoras, Empedocles, and the atomists, Aristotle observes that they can roughly be divided into two groups. Of these, the first posits one fundamental principle at the basis of the physical universe (e.g., water for Thales, air for Anaximenes) from which they generate the various objects that go to make up the universe by invoking forces such as condensation and rarefaction, considered as contrary properties of the basic underlying stuff. The second group, and this includes Anaximander and Empedocles, "assert that the contraries are contained in the one and emerge from it by segregation" (*Physics*, I, 4, 187a12–16, 20–23). Aristotle's basic objection to the account of the various "physicists" — including those of both groups and including as well those who make their "one" from which everything else emerges a plurality of units of the same basic kind — is this: none of them sufficiently explain the nature of the "forces" at work to bring into being from the basic underlying principle the individual sensible existents of our immediate experience. In other words, these thinkers did not have an adequate notion of efficient causality, and the "forces" they invoke are closer to the "mythological" explanations of the poets than to the philosophical principles demanded of a scientific cosmology. The same criticism, Aristotle believes, can be directed against the Pythagoreans, who derived all things from numbers, and against the Platonists who sought to account for all things on the basis of their Forms or Ideas. Neither Pythagoreans nor Platonists, Aristotle argues, tell us precisely how their numbers or ideas can be the efficient causes of things.

Nevertheless, Aristotle goes on to point to something of profound significance in the thought of the early Greek "physicists." This lies in their acceptance of the belief that "nothing comes into being from non-being." Because of their acceptance of that opinion, they reasoned that the individual sensible beings of our immediate experience must have arisen in some way from some primitive, underlying principle. In other words, these early Greeks had reasoned along the following lines:

> Since everything that comes into being must arise either from what is or from what is not, and it is impossible for it to arise from what is not (on this point all the physicists agree), they thought that the truth of the alternative necessarily followed, namely, that things come into being out of existent things, i.e., out of things already present but imperceptible to our senses because of the smallness of their bulk. So they assert that everything has been mixed in everything, because they saw everything arising out of everything. But things, as they say, appear differently from one another and receive different names according to the nature of the particles which are numerically predominant among the innumerable constituents of the mixture (*Physics*, I, 4, 187a33–187b3).

As we shall see, Aristotle himself accepted this common opinion, but with significant distinctions which enabled him to avoid the difficulties to which previous explanations were subject.

Finally, in summarizing the trend of Greek cosmology up to his time, Aristotle returns to a theme running through all preceding accounts, the theme, namely, that the principles of physical things are in some way contrary to each other granted that one accepts the obvious datum of experience that there is a genuine plurality of sensible existents and that motion or change is a property of these existents (cf. *Physics*, I, 1, 185a13). Some reference to contrary principles is found even in those who, like Parmenides, maintained that everything is basically one being, for even he invoked the "hot and the cold" and principles under the names of "fire and earth." In brief, practically all those who in any way sought to give some kind of rational account of the universe "identify their elements, and what they call their principles, with the contraries, giving no reason indeed for the theory, but constrained as it were by the truth itself" (*Physics*, I, 5, 188b27–30).

Aristotle's chief concern, in his own positive teaching on nature, will be to discover *why* the primary principles of sensible existents must be contrary, the number of such principles, and the way to admit the validity of the principle "nothing comes into being from non-being" while allowing for real changes within things and a plurality of existents that will not be swallowed up and lose their identity by some underlying stuff which alone can be called genuine being.

ARISTOTLE'S POSITIVE ACCOUNT

1. Two contraries and their subject. The first question Aristotle considers in his own theory is this: Why must the principles of natural things be contrary? The *fact* that these principles are contrary had more or less forced itself upon his predecessors, but no one among them had seen why this must be so. Aristotle gives us the reason behind this fact in the following acute analysis:

> First principles must not be derived from one another nor from anything else, while everything has to be derived from them. But these conditions are fulfilled by the primary contraries, which are not derived from anything else because they are primary, nor from each other because they are contraries (*Physics*, I, 5, 188a27–29).

The abstract reasoning behind this analysis will become clearer if we consider what it means for a thing to "come-to-be." Moreover, by examining what it means to say that *something comes to be*, we shall be in a better position to see just how many principles are required. For purposes of illustration, let us take the following example. *An uneducated man becomes educated.* If we consider what actually takes place in the process described in this proposition, we shall see that several elements are involved. First of all, something comes into being, namely, an "educated man." Second, something becomes an educated man, namely an "uneducated man." Closer inspection discloses that the "uneducated man" can be further analyzed into "uneducated" and "man," and that the former of these ("uneducated") is present prior to the process and absent at its completion, whereas the latter ("man") perdures throughout the entire process, being present both at its inception and at its end. Thus, as Aristotle tells us:

> Whatever comes to be is always complex. There is, on the one hand, (a) something which comes into existence [the "educated man" of our example], and again (b) something which becomes that — the latter (b) in two senses, either the subject ["man" in our example] or the opposite ["uneducated" in our example] (*Physics*, I, 7, 190b10–12).

The "contraries" disclosed by this example are "educated" and "uneducated." Of these the former comes to be as a result of the process, whereas the latter, present at the inception of the change, is no longer present at its end. Furthermore, the one contrary "uneducated" has the nature of an imperfection, a lack of being. It is what Aristotle calls a *privation* affecting the subject undergoing the process of change. The other contrary, "educated," on the other hand, has the nature of a perfection, a fullness of being, which the subject acquires as a result of the change. This other contrary is what Aristotle calls "form" or "act," that is, a perfection or actualization in some way determining or modifying the subject which undergoes the change.

Note that Aristotle, in his analysis, introduces a third element essential to change or "coming-to-be" in his discussion. This is the subject ("man" of our example) which perdures throughout the change. Two contraries are in themselves insufficient to explain change. They cannot act on each other but demand some third principle upon which both exercise their influence. In other words, there are three principles involved in any process of change or "coming-to-be," namely the two primary contraries and an underlying subject or substratum (cf. *Physics*, I, 7, 190b28–191a1). This underlying subject or substratum is what Aristotle later calls "matter," that is, the potential principle of change which is perfected, determined, actualized by the form or act resulting from the change and affected by a contrary privation prior to the process.

2. The various types of change. The illustration we have given of change or "coming-to-be" is relatively simple, yet the truth of which it is an example is of profound significance for understanding the nature of physical reality. Change, motion, process — all this is going on constantly within the things we see and touch and hear and smell. Motion or change is such an outstanding feature of the sensible, physical world that some of Aristotle's predecessors, such as the Heracliteans, had been led to see in process or becoming the only genuine reality. Nothing abides, everything is changing, was the conclusion they thought inescapably forced upon them. And they are not without their modern counterparts, especially among those of our own day who have been so profoundly influenced by the data that give such persuasiveness to the theory of evolution. Aristotle himself recognized that the physical universe is characterized by change, by motion, by becoming, yet he also recognized that "there is no such thing as motion over and above the things" that move and change. In other words, motion or change presupposes a subject that perdures throughout the entire process. Change is of various kinds, but "it is always with respect to substance or to quantity or to quality or to place that what changes changes" (*Physics*, III, 1, 200b32–33).

Put in another way, change, the universal characteristic of the world of sensible objects, is of various kinds, but in all its types it presupposes some underlying subject or substrate that passes from one state of being to another. The various kinds of change noted by Aristotle are the following: (1) *Substantial change* — change "with respect to substance"

— the generation and corruption of individually existing things, such as the generation of oxygen and hydrogen from the "corruption" or passing out of being of water. (2) *Quantitative change*, or increase and diminution, such as the change evident in a human being as he passes from childhood into adulthood. (3) *Qualitative change*, or alteration, such as that undergone by a body when it passes from the state of being hot to that of being cold. (4) *Change in place or local movement*, surely one of the most obvious types of changes, when a body moves from one position to another. In subsequent chapters we shall take up in more detail these various types of change, in particular, local motion and the conditions required for it, but for the remainder of this chapter we shall be concerned primarily with what Aristotle called change in substance or substantial change, the generation — "coming-into-being" of individual existents — and the corruption — the "passing-out-of-being" of those same existents, for it was with respect to his explanation of this type of change that he developed his hylomorphism. That is, it was in explaining substantial change that he showed that the intrinsic structure of the individual sensible existents of the physical universe requires two complimentary principles, matter (*ὕλη*) and form (*μόρφη*).

3. Substantial change and hylomorphism. In their attempts to explain how something could come-to-be, that is, be generated, one of the chief difficulties facing Aristotle's predecessors was to show how the emergence into being of something genuinely new and real was possible, chiefly because they believed that "nothing comes to be from non-being," but only from being. Thus, as indicated before and as Aristotle well recognized, they either ended up in a monism like that of Parmenides or the Heracliteans, denying anything really distinctive about the individual beings we perceive, or else concluded that what appears to come to be actually derives from "things already present but imperceptible to our senses because of the smallness of their bulk." In other words, the things which seem to come into being actually existed prior to their apparent emergence into being. Aristotle's genius lay in showing how the fundamental principle behind their thinking, namely, that "nothing comes to be from non-being" could be accepted without denying the obvious fact that *new* things, which actually did not exist before, really do come into existence.

Take the example adduced previously, that of our educated man. Prior to the process whereby he became educated, whereby the "educated man" came into being, the man was "non-educated." The process of education changed him from a state of being non-educated to a state of being educated. Yet the end product, the educated man, did not come into being from nothing. There was, antecedent to the process, the "non-educated man" and one of the elements of this antecedently existing being perdured throughout the entire process, namely, the man who became educated, whereas one of the elements of this antecedently existing being passed out of being during the process, namely the status of the man as being "non-educated." This, obviously, is not an instance of substantial change or change in substance. It is rather what Aristotle would call an accidental change in the category of qualitative change. Nevertheless the process is fundamentally the same in an instance of unqualified or substantial coming-to-be. Take, for example, the coming-into-being of flesh in a human being who eats and digests an apple. Something entirely new, which did not actually exist prior to the digestive process, results from it, namely human flesh. Nevertheless it does not come into being from non-being pure and simple, for antecedent to the change the "non-flesh" matter of the apple existed. Its character of being "non-flesh matter" disappeared as a result of its being eaten and digested by the human being, but something perdured, that is, remained of the original matter throughout the entire change. This perduring subject, actually existing under the form of apple prior to the change, was potentially human flesh; and the work of the process was to change it from being informed or actualized by the form "apple" to being informed or actualized by the form "flesh." It is this perduring subject which Aristotle calls prime matter, or the potential element within things allowing them to change from one state of being to another. The perfection or act making this matter to be the matter of an apple at the beginning of the process and to be the matter of human flesh at its end is what he called the substantial form.

In his own analysis of processes of this kind, Aristotle effectively uses his notions of "privation" and "matter" to get around the difficulties facing his predecessors. As will be remembered, the privation affecting the subject of a change prior to the change itself is one of the two "contraries" demanded as principles in explaining this phenomenon. In the examples we have used, the privative contraries are "non-educated" and "non-flesh" respectively. The "matter" or perduring subjects of change are "man" in the case given of an accidental change and the "primary matter" in the case of the substantial change from the apple to human flesh. Now Aristotle admits the validity of the principle "nothing comes into being from non-being," if "non-being" is taken in an absolute sense, that is, as signifying *nothing*. Nevertheless, if "non-being" is taken in a qualified sense, there is a way in which something comes from "non-being." For, Aristotle writes, "a thing comes to be from the privation," that is, the contrary affecting the subject prior to the change, "which in its own nature is not-being — this not surviving as a constituent of the result." In addition, Aristotle can say that the resulting new being emerging from the process of change does not come from being in the sense that it does not come from a being which actually existed prior to the change; that is, the human flesh resulting from the process of digestion does not come from human flesh which actually existed prior to that process. Nevertheless, it does come from being, in the sense that it comes from a being which *potentially* was the product that results from the change; that is, the human flesh comes to be from a "matter" which, prior to the change, was potentially human flesh although not actually so (cf. *Physics,* I, 8, 191b12–18).

4. Matter and privation. The central role assigned to matter in explaining the nature of physical things and the possibility of change within them is brought out very clearly by Aristotle in his discussion of the relationship between matter and privation and the distinction between these two principles. Privation, the privative contrary present at the beginning of change but absent at its terminus, is a lack of the being, of the perfection, of the form actuating the perduring subject of change at the terminus of the process. In other words, privation is, in its own nature, "not-being," the *absence* of a given kind of perfection within the subject that changes. Matter, on the other hand, is "not-being" not in its own nature but solely by reason of an attribute that it has, that attribute being precisely the privation (cf. *Physics,* I, 9, 192a2–5). As Aristotle puts it:

> The matter comes to be and ceases to be in one sense, while in another it does not. As that which contains the privation, it ceases to be in its own nature, for what ceases to be, the privation, is contained within it. But as potentiality it does not cease to be in its own nature, but is essentially outside the sphere of becoming and ceasing to be. For if it came to be, something must have existed as a primary substratum from which it should come and which should persist in it; but this is its own special nature, so that it will be before coming to be. For my definition of matter is just this — the primary substratum of each thing, from which it comes to be without qualification, and which persists in the result (*Physics,* I, 9, 192a25–32).

In other words, primary matter is for Aristotle something *given,* ultimate in its own order, and absolutely necessary as an intrinsic constituent of things if real changes are to be explained in any satisfactory way. It is the perduring subject of change, affected at the beginning of any process of becoming by one of the contraries, namely the privation, and at the end of the process by the other contrary, namely, the form or act which brings to completion and fulfillment the potentialities contained in matter or rather the potentiality that matter itself is. Here we must point out that no Greek ever seems to have attained the notion of creation. That is, for the Greeks the potential element within things, the constituent of really existing beings which borders on the unintelligible because it is of itself undetermined (recall Plato's remark that the receptacle of becoming, matter, can be known only by a spurious or bastard reasoning), was something *there*, something eternal and given in things. The essential role of the "Divine Mind" or artificer of the universe was, not to account for the being or existence of the material universe, but to account for its intelligibility, its structure as something ordered, its nature as a cosmos (harmonious interrelationship between the many). For Aristotle the determinate natures or essences that make the individual existents of the physical universe be what they are are *potentially* within the underlying subject of change, that is, matter. Since the intrinsic element within things making them to be of a determinate nature or essence is called by Aristotle *form*, this means that form is contained potentially within matter. Matter, indeterminate in itself, thirsts for determination or perfection; that is, it is essentially an *appetite* for a given type of form (cf. *Physics*, I, 9, 192a10–20). Nevertheless, because the matter cannot actualize itself, another principle, this time extrinsic and not intrinsic to the changing being itself, is required. This principle is the *efficient cause*, which is responsible for the emergence of the form from the potentialities of matter (cf. *Metaphysics*, VII, 8, 1033a24, 1034a4–5). Because the efficient cause, in its acting, operates for an end, a fourth and final principle is required, the *final cause*. We shall have more to say about these Aristotelian efficient and final causes in later chapters of this text, where we take up his teaching on the need for a first unmoved mover to account for the movements we observe about us. The point remaining for our examination of form and matter as intrinsic principles or constituents of physical things is to see more closely Aristotle's teaching on them within the context of the problem of substance.

5. Hylomorphism, substance, and being in Aristotle. The word Aristotle used to signify what we call substance or entity is *ousia*. This in itself is quite significant, for, as will be remembered, this is one of the terms Plato used to signify what he regarded as the "really real," the authentic being of things, namely, the Forms or Ideas. Thus, in determining what Aristotle had to say about *ousia*, or substance, we shall discover what for him was the "really real."

Aristotle notes that the term "substance" is predicated of at least four main objects: (1) the "whatness" or defining element of things, e.g., "humanity" in a man; (2) the universal or the common element in things allowing us to predicate the same term of many different individual existents, e.g., "man" as said of John and Peter; (3) the genus, which is really the more remote and determinable element of the definition, e.g., "animal" in the definition "rational animal"; and (4) the substratum or underlying subject (cf. *Metaphysics*, VII, 3). At first it might seem that the fourth of these, namely the underlying substrate or subject, is the one to which the term "substance" primarily refers. For, if we strip an individual existent of everything else that can be predicated of it — affections, products, length, breadth, depth, qualities, etc., etc. — something must yet remain as long as there is to be anything at all. What remains is the purely indeterminable and potential element in things, their matter. In fact, Aristotle himself declares that "matter is nearly, in a sense *is*, substance" (*Physics*, I, 9, 192a2–5). Nevertheless, Aristotle cannot bring himself to conclude that matter or pure potency is the authentic being of things, the "really real." Basically, his reasons for rejecting matter as substance in its primary significance is this: matter, of itself, does not even exist; it is not a "this," a concretely existent thing exercising its own proper activity and affecting others. As such matter is pure indeterminacy, unintelligibility, potency. Likewise neither the universal nor the genus can serve as genuine, authentic being. Both exist as such only in the mind, not in the actual physical universe (cf. *Metaphysics*, VII, 3 and 13).

It seems then that "whatness" or essence is the genuine being or substance of things. Essence is the determining feature of things, the element explanatory of their intelligibility and perfections. But what precisely is the essence of things? Whence does it derive? It cannot come from the matter, the underlying substratum, for this, as we have seen again and again, is purely potential, indeterminate. It must, therefore, derive from the active principle within things, namely, the form. The form is what gives determination to things, making them "what" they are. Form, thus, is the primary instance of substance or *ousia* in things. It is the "really real," authentic being (cf. *Metaphysics*, VII, chs. 4–8, 17). In brief, "substance or entity is the indwelling form, from which and the matter the so-called concrete substance is derived" (*Metaphysics*, VII, 11, 1037a30).

Strikingly enough, the word Aristotle uses to signify "form," which he has just identified with the "really real" within things, is εἶδος. As will be recalled, this is precisely the same term most frequently used by Plato to designate his Ideas.

Now, if it is the form in virtue of which a thing is and is called a "this," some definite thing, then the form must be that something in the highest degree; thus it is the primary instance of "thisness" as well as of substance or authentic being within things (cf. *Metaphysics*, II, 1, 993b24–26). Yet, if this is so, it raises certain difficulties for Aristotle. For one thing, he admits that only individual things exist in the sensible universe. Nevertheless, the object of scientific knowledge must be other or higher than the individual objects of sense knowledge: "for all things that we come to know, we come to know in so far as they have some unity and identity and in so far as some attribute belongs to them universally" (*Metaphysics*, III, 4, 999a28–33). It seems as though we are faced with a dilemma. Either form is a universal, and can, as a consequence, be known scientifically, but then it cannot make matter a "this." On the other hand, if form is purely and simply singular, it is intellectually valueless (cf. *Metaphysics*, III, 6, 1003a8–17).

Aristotle's way out of this problem seems to lie in making the form of itself neither singular nor universal. It is not singular, but it is indivisible: "Callias and Socrates are different in virtue of their matter, for that is different, but the same in form, for their form is indivisible" (*Metaphysics*, VII, 8, 1034a6–7). Because it is not, of itself, singular, it is knowable, definable, and the principle of intelligibility within individuals; yet, because it is not of itself universal it can in some way *be the being of singular things*. To know the form is for Aristotle both to know the singular and to know the universal (cf. *Metaphysics*, XII, 5, 1071a28–29).

Although a full-fledged investigation into and evaluation of Aristotle's teaching on form as the substance or genuine being within things would carry us too deeply into his metaphysics, we believe that an indication of the direction of his thought on this point is of value. It is of value first of all because it shows us that Aristotle did not depart so much from Plato as many popularizations have tended to stress. Like Plato, so Aristotle saw in form or εἶδος the ultimately real, the authentic being in things. He agreed with Plato in seeing that *ousia* or substance is the clue to the intelligibility and identity of things, but in addition saw in it the key to the further problem of how and where it exists.

SOME CHRISTIAN CONSEQUENCES OF HYLOMORPHISM

Plato, as will be recalled, accepted matter as a primary given. It was just *there*, in a state of disordered chaos, and the work of the Demiurge or divine artificer was simply to bring it into order, to confer intelligibility upon it. For Aristotle, as we have just seen, the situation is almost the same. Although matter never is without a determinate form whence derives the intelligibility and structure of the things of our experience, matter is, for Aristotle, a presupposition. It is, he notes, free from either generation or corruption, from coming-into-being or passing-away. In other words, neither Plato nor Aristotle arrived at the notion of creation, of the need for inferring a cause to account for the existence of matter. When the early Christian Fathers turned to the philosophy of the Greeks, they sought to find a basis in Plato and Aristotle for the biblical notion of creation. Some Christian thinkers, more deeply influenced by Plato than by Aristotle, have toyed with the notion that God created prime matter and then informed it, that is, gave formal, as well as potential, existence. However, this offers difficulties, the first being that *primary matter cannot exist as such.* It is potency, capacity. However, potency is always the potency *of* something. It supposes the existence of the subject of which it is the capacity. Furthermore, even the vaguest sort of stuff we can imagine as existing and operating has some formal determination, a certain "thisness" about it, at least insofar as it is something. It is to that extent informed. In other words, in the material order, anything that exists, simple or complex, either is or inheres in a composition of form and matter. And again, this means that when God created, He created beings. These beings then go through their further changes according to their essences: according to what they are, their forms, and according to their potencies, their matter. In other words, God "concreated" matter rather than created it. For what He created was material beings, composites of matter and form.

These material beings that God created are substances. They are substances having the potentialities for substantial and accidental changes. God, the first and principal cause, is responsible for their being. Yet He endowed them with innate principles that serve as causes for their changes and subsequent development.

This consideration opens up the possibility of a philosophy of evolution. Once we conclude that God created substances composed of matter and form, once, in other words, we admit the creation of actual beings in potency, we can think in terms of the emergence of the higher from the lower *according to the potencies of the lower*. This was first advanced by St. Gregory of Nyssa, one of the eminent Cappadocian Fathers of the Church, in his works the *Hexaemeron* and *De Hominis Opificio* (*The Work of the Six Days of Creation* and *On the Creation of Man*, respectively). It reached its highest development by St. Augustine in his doctrine of the *rationes seminales*, or fundamental types, in his work *De Genesi ad Litteram* (*On an Interpretation of the Text of "Genesis"*). St. Augustine teaches that God created a few fundamental types which were actuated into more precise and higher types according to their natural tendencies, from their forms, their potencies, their matter, and brought about by the energies in the universe. Augustine's fundamental insight was accepted by St. Thomas Aquinas, though with profound modifications because of the different metaphysics underlying his thought.

SUMMARY

1. In reviewing the thought of his predecessors, Aristotle brought to light a common theme running through their speculations. All who sought to give some kind of rational account of changeable being, even those who advocated but one principle, were compelled in one way or another to make their principles contraries or to allow for some kind of contrariety in their principle if they advocated but one. Thus, Aristotle concluded, the philosophy of nature or cosmology is first and foremost a search for first principles which are contrary or opposed to one another.
2. Aristotle himself located these contraries in the privation affecting sensible things prior to change and in the form or determination perfecting them after the change. Thus there are at least two first principles necessary to explain change or motion, namely form and a privation contrary to it.
3. Since, however, these contraries cannot act directly on each other inasmuch as the presence of one necessarily entails the absence of the other, Aristotle saw the need for inferring the existence of a third principle of changeable being. This he called matter, a term he used to designate the potential, determinable element within things. Prior to any given change, this matter is deprived of the determination or actuation it is to receive as a result of change; that is, it is the subject of a privation. After the change, this same matter possesses a new determination or actuation. In other words, it is now the subject of a new form.
4. Change is itself a generic term. Specifying its kinds, Aristotle distinguishes the following types of change: (1) generation and/or corruption, that is, change in the substantial identity of the subject; (2) qualitative change, called alteration; (3) quantitative change, or change by increase or diminution in size; and (4) change of place or local motion.
5. Matter and form are intrinsic principles of change; that is, they exist within the being that changes. Yet they alone are not sufficient to explain why change occurs. For an adequate explanation of change Aristotle saw the need for two extrinsic factors or causes, namely, the agent or efficient cause, operating on the changing being by reducing it from its status prior to change to the act of change itself; and the final cause, which is the reason why the efficient cause acts at all.
6. Aristotle, most likely because of his Platonic heritage, ultimately found in the form or *eidos* within things the source of their reality or being.

Nor did he ever attain the notion of creation, accepting matter as a primary given. Nevertheless, the principles explanatory of change within things which Aristotle brought to light were taken over by Christian philosophers who were able to extend them in such a way that they could be incorporated into a metaphysics of being influenced by the biblical notion of creation.

CHAPTER FIVE

NATURE and the NATURAL

A presupposition of philosophy, the sciences, calendars and almanacs, and plans for the future is order in the universe, or, as we call it, the "order of nature." It is true that certain scientists concerned with theoretical physics and philosophers influenced by German idealism find it convenient to look upon the universe as a determinable and inchoate mass upon which the mind imposes determination and order. In other words, these thinkers find the "order of nature" in the mind rather than in things. Nevertheless even they admit that a "natural order" is the basis of our thinking, the basic assumption or fundamental intuition upon which all subsequent thinking regarding the physical world is based.

Our knowledge begins with the senses, whose objects are the singular existents of the physical world. Although these objects are subject to constant change, there must be some element of stability or order within them to account for the regularity and patterned structure of the events we perceive.

Although this order is not absolutely rigid, and although there are chance variations and spontaneous deviations and improvisations with it, nevertheless the pattern is such that we are confident of: (1) the orderly operations of the universe as a whole; (2) the orderly operations of the components of the universe; and (3) the orderly interplay of these components according to their essences in themselves and their actions and reactions with one another. This confidence is not merely an intellectual conviction. When we speak of the general order of the world of nature or of the particular order of one of its elements such as "the nature of a dog or of a man" we are reflecting a way of life, a way in which we live. We are stating our expectation that the universe will be generally the same tomorrow as it was yesterday, that it will be, both in its stability and changes, generally the same for the next five thousand years that it has been for the past five thousand. We live in this expectation even though we discover more and more about nature day by day.

INDIVIDUAL NATURE

1. Verbal definition. The word "nature" is etymologically derived from the word for "living things." The Greek word *φύσις*, which we find reflected in *physics* and *physical*, has reference to the life of plants. Its Latin equivalent stems from *nasci*, "to be born." This has several forms: *na(c)tivitas*, "birth," and *na(c)tura*, "vitality," "vital operation," etc. This would imply that nature is conceived of as an intrinsic principle; that is, it refers to those basic operations which spring from the essence of an object, being developed in, from, and by the object rather than imposed on it from the outside. In other words, "nature" has always been considered as an existing principle of development from within. In short, "nature" is an intrinsic principle of operation within things.

2. Real definition. The first accurate definition of nature is given us, again, by Aristotle. He defines nature as "the source or cause of being moved and of being at rest in that to which it belongs primarily and in virtue of itself and not in virtue of a concomitant attribute" (*Physics*, II, 1, 192b22). At first sight this seems rather formidable, yet there is a reason for all of the words Aristotle used. They deserve further investigation.

Source or cause. Our concept of nature originates with properties and proper operations. From these externally observable acts we learn the natures or essences of things. In other words, we learn the natures or essences of things by seeking to determine what it is within them which is explanatory of their operations. This learning process is illustrated in the sciences when the astronomer seeks the origin of solar flames or of cosmic rays and in philosophy when we attempt to learn the ultimate nature of an object by examining its properties. In either case we affirm that there is a source or cause of the operations and properties we investigate. This source is ultimately the essence of the thing, and in the order of existence and operations essence means nature. Thus, since solar flares seem to be magnetic storms that radiate all types of particles, we state that the sun, by nature, is a thermonuclear process that is generally stable in the visible end of the spectrum but somewhat unstable in the ultraviolet end of the spectrum. Similarly, since the beaver cuts down trees by gnawing, having a characteristic jaw and tooth formation for this purpose, we say that he is a rodent by nature.

We should note here, however, that in only very rare instances do we attain the proper essences of things. Their activities and operations give us a clue as to their specific natures, yet often we must be content with the more generic, that is, with the nature common to a wide variety of things, e.g., do we really know why a dog is different from a cat? But knowledge of the proper essence remains as an ideal.

Motion and rest. Nature is a source or principle or cause of motion. This means that the nature of a thing is related to the motions which flow from it as a cause is related to its effects. The running of a deer, the galloping of a horse, the growth of a tree — all these are movements springing from a source within, and this source is their nature. Nature is also a source or principle of rest. A child is born, grows, reaches maturity. Although the child-become-a-man is still a changing, moving being, at a certain period in his life he attains his full stature, remaining at rest in it. Why? The ultimate source explanatory of his rest in a determinate size is his nature.

We shall return to examine motion and what it means for a material being to move or change in a later chapter. For the present it is sufficient to note that the movements or changes that take place in the universe spring from the natures of the beings that exist within it.

In that to which it belongs. Nature is *in the thing* to which it belongs, and in this way nature differs from art. We speak, for example, of the "movement" of a poem or play. Yet the source for this movement is not a principle intrinsic to the poem or play itself; it is rather within the person who wrote the poem or play, the artist responsible for their being. But the movements of natural as opposed to artificial things flow from their own being, and the wellspring or source within them responsible for their movements is what we call their *nature.*

Primarily in virtue of itself, not in virtue of a concomitant attribute. By putting these words into his definition of nature, Aristotle intended to signify that nature is within the *whole* of the being in question, not by reason of any part. For example, man is rational by nature; that is, his whole being is to be a rational animal. Man is also a material substance, having weight and mass. Both weight and mass are essential to man, but neither is primary or proper to him. Why? Because he shares these qualities with all other extended material beings. They are not, therefore, primarily or properly *human* qualities and do not belong to man by reason of his nature as man. Thus, nature signifies the proper essence of a being. In addition, by stipulating that nature is what belongs to a being primarily and in virtue of itself, Aristotle distinguishes it from what might belong to a being incidentally or accidentally, that is, what belongs to a being by chance. For example, it is natural for men to have eyes. Yet at times men are born sightless or even without the physical organ called an eye. Such incidents are "chance" events, freaks of nature, in some way counter to nature. They raise the problem of chance, a problem which we shall discuss in detail later in this chapter.

3. Further notes on the definition of nature. A material substance is an integrity, a substantial union of matter and form. This means that essentially it is what it is and that it is changeable. It further means that it is autonomous in its existence (granting, of course, its dependence on God), and expresses itself outwardly through its acts or modifications; that is, it is a substance operating through its accidents. Since nature is in the order of existence and operation, it gives rise to a threefold classification according to its integrity, its material characteristics, and its formal characteristics.

Integral operations. A material substance operates as a whole. This means that it not only exists as it does and operates according to what it is, but also according to what its components are. Some bodies operate slowly. Others are almost inert. Still others are extremely active. Some are stable, whereas others are unstable. This depends not only on what they are but also upon their intrinsic energy. The latter, in turn, depends on their elementary composition, the structure of their molecules and atoms. Hence, in order to explain essence as nature, we must look to the structure of the body to see the general type of its operation. Since this is so, we must examine the components of a body to identify its nature. This is not the primary notion of nature. The primary notion is always essence. Nevertheless, essence demands structure both for its existence and operations. Thus, the concept of nature in its extensions must include the structure of the body, elementary and atomic.

Material characteristics. By these we do not mean primarily mass characteristics of a body, although those are proper to the structure, to the integrity of the body. Here we are first of all concerned with matter as the potential element within things. Since material beings are passive as well as active, their intrinsic natures must be capable of explaining why they are affected as they are by the beings with which they come in contact. The ultimate intrinsic source within their natures explaining their passivity is primary matter.

Formal characteristics. These refer primarily to form itself. An essence operates as a nature because of what it is. It is what it is because of the form, which is the determination of the potencies of matter. Hence, nature always refers primarily to form. If there were only one meaning to nature, if we had to eliminate all meanings save the most appropriate, it would have to be form. Nature signifies not only that a body is and operates, but far more properly that it exists as *this kind* of a body rather than *that*, that it operates *this way* rather than *that way*. Hence, nature means primarily form itself. It is form that identifies and specifies all else that is included in the concept of nature.

However, we also speak of secondary matter in this connection. The reason why a body can be acted upon is that it is not a point. It must be spread out, extended, to be affected. Hence, extension and quantity are considered properties more closely allied to matter than to form. Form has to do with specification. It explains why bodies are what they are; that is, it shows us why bodies can be classified according to types or kinds. But all bodies, precisely because they are material beings, are extended. Hence, insofar as becoming and reception demand extension, and insofar as extension is more closely allied to matter than to form, matter is the fundamental principle of mass properties. It is the principle allowing for a given structure which then draws its further properties from the form.

THE GENERAL ORDER OF NATURE

We began our consideration of nature on the level of the individual natures of things. In reaching knowledge about individual natures, however, we begin with the general order of nature, nature as a whole.

It is here that we find a significant difference between the philosophical and scientific methods. In philosophy we look to the *essences* to explain operations. In the sciences we look to the *pattern of the whole* to classify the uniformity of the repetition of some events and the variations of other events. We develop this uniformity in a pattern of mathematical constants and variables. This development gives us a set of adequate and comprehensive concepts under which we are able to classify physical constructs. The emphasis in the sciences of nature, then, is on adequacy and elegance of a *conceptual scheme*. In the philosophy of nature, it is on *analysis* of individual operations to discover the essence. Then by *synthesis* we see the operations of the individual in relation to the whole.

As we pursue this analysis and synthesis further, we see that it consists in gaining a knowledge of the operations of the four causes. This leads us to consider: (1) the four causes in respect to nature; (2) matter and form in respect to the four causes and in respect to nature; and (3) the laws of nature.

1. The four causes in respect to nature. Bodies are what they are and operate as they do because they have the potential to be acted upon and to act, need energy to do so, and tend to fulfill their natural tendencies both in acting and being acted upon. Looking once again to the four causes we discover that they are:

The material cause. This is a body as the source of a new entity or of the changes it undergoes while persisting as a substance. In short, the material cause is a body as the subject of substantial and accidental changes. In the order of concrete existence, the source or principle for receptivity is *secondary matter.* In the order of essence or nature, and as a principle of secondary matter, this is *primary matter* or the *essential, potential, determinable principle allowing for the determination and becoming of a new material entity and for the modifications in the persisting subject.*

The formal cause. This is the determination of the body, the *determined fulfillment of the potencies of matter into a definite essence with its subsequent determined existence and determined operations.*

The efficient cause. Neither matter nor form is capable of explaining the act of existence. Form is act, but act as determining or perfecting matter. The essence or nature composed of both form and matter is itself a potency for existence. As a potency, it does not actualize itself. As a potency, it cannot be operative in the order to which it tends. Hence, it must be fulfilled or actualized by something else. This is the efficient cause. The efficient cause is that being which by its activity positively influences the becoming of something else. It may be the worm that spoils the apple or it may be the unidentified energy in the universe that is responsible for hitherto unexplained phenomena.

We must note that although the identification of the cause is an intrinsic part of the scientific method in trying to ascertain the invariance of a given sequence, it is not necessary for causality philosophically understood. Philosophically we know that an efficient cause is required whenever a given being is not able to serve as a total explanatory principle of itself or of its properties. We may not be able to identify precisely the efficient cause required as an explanation, but we at least know that a cause is necessary. The popular statement that whatever changes is changed by another must be understood in this light, that nothing reduces itself from potency to act. Something else must do so whether or not we understand or are able to identify what that something else may be.

The final cause. There must be a reason why a being acts and why it acts one way rather than another way. This is the classical statement of finality. Action implies an operation to achieve some sort of a balance, some sort of stability. It may be in the thermodynamical and electrodynamical tendencies of physical matter, the chemical affinities of elements, the trophisms of plants, or in the tendencies of the senses to their proper objects. One way or another it originates in the *appetites* or tendencies or privations both of the action of the efficient cause and the reactions of the effect. This tendency must exist before it begins to be realized in activity. But for it to exist, there is required the final cause, the satisfaction of the tendency, *the good attracting action toward its attainment or fulfillment.* Since no actions ever take place without the influence of this cause, it has frequently been called the cause of causes.

The general finality of the components of the universe is called *teleology*. It implies that since the individuals in the universe obey their natural tendencies, the universe as a whole is ordered. Teleology is opposed to *mechanism,* which maintains that all that is necessary to explain the order and operations of the universe is the coincidence of forces and masses. We might exemplify this by saying that the mechanist maintains that given force *F*, proceeding from energy *E* and meeting mass *M;* then: displacement *D* involving velocity V over resistance *R*, and covering distances d_1, d_2, d_3, d_n, . . . , in directions dv_1, dv_2, . . . will occur. The occurrence is called an *event* and is plotted on a quadrant describing the space *S* covered and the time *T* involved. The quadrant is an application of the familiar Cartesian coordinates involving an *S* axis and a *T* axis instead of the familiar *x* and *y* axes. Sometimes the time axis is represented by the imaginary number $\sqrt{-1}$, represented by *i* (for imaginary number) in some problems involving relativity.

We should be able to see readily enough that the above mechanistic statement is really a geometrical description of a physical event. Geometry fulfills its purpose with formal description. Consequently there is no finality in the representation or the statement thereof. Hence, mechanism, insofar as it is a *geometrical* expression, pays no heed to finality in its formulations.

Finality enters into the realistic account of an event, however. It enters into it whether the force is that of cosmic rays and light pressure on a small satellite depressing its orbit somewhat or whether it is the force of the wind pressing the keel of the sailboat against the resistance of the water. Hence, it investigates what cosmic rays or wind or water may be, in order the better to understand their tendencies in the expectation of learning *why* they operate and why they operate as they do. A mechanical description, on the other hand, is trying to find what is common to all force apart from its origin and tendencies, no matter whether it is the force of light or wind. Its purpose is to seek what is common in order to make comparisons. The teleological or finalistic purpose is to investigate being in the order of existence, as it is, rather than as it is represented. Hence, it must take reality on its own terms.

Both positions are valid, but they proceed from different degrees of abstraction. In the case of mechanism, the object of consideration is represented as a *point event*, a meeting on the time-space (*TS*) coordinate. In finality, the object is a *real or actual event* involving the tendencies of real beings in the order of existence. Actually, teleology and mechanism complement one another and should never have spent the centuries they have in such complete separation. Philosophically, teleology is the focal point of all the operations of nature, and it is periodically reaffirmed and rediscovered as such through the centuries. After several centuries of mechanism, Socrates, Plato, and Aristotle advanced it. Then after several centuries of the necessary mechanical explanations following the philosophical lead of Descartes and the mathematical lead of Newton, it has been reaffirmed and rediscovered in our own day not only by such moral philosophers as Kierkegaard but more especially by the scientific philosopher Whitehead.

2. Matter and form in respect to the four causes. This is a rather brief statement of the obvious, but it is at the heart of cosmology and metaphysics. In one of his shorter works, *On the Principles of Nature*, St. Thomas links up the four causes with matter and form in this way:

Matter is fundamental to the existences and changes in the universe of matter because these depend on potency, and matter is potency.

Form is necessary not only for the existence and determination of the components of the universe but also for their operations and tendencies. Form is thus required:

a) *For efficiency*. A body acts and reacts according to its essence, and this is determined by form. Hence, form gives the order whereby an activity is definite and determined.

b) *For finality*. A body acts and reacts according to its tendencies. These are the familiar privations, the extension of the form guiding operation.

Hence, the whole universe of matter is explained in terms of matter and form, in terms of potency and act. Through these notions we gain an insight into the nature of things. We derive, from a knowledge of their forms, an understanding of why they tend as they do, act as they do, and react according to their formal essences. We may summarize our findings thus:

Matter — the potential principle

Form — the determination, further specified as:

Substantial form — the determination *into which* the product is specified;

Efficient cause — the determination *by which* the product is produced;

Final cause — the determination *for which* the cause and effect act and react as they do;

Exemplary cause — the determined pattern *according to which* the action proceeds.

Mention of the exemplary cause in relation to matter, form, efficiency, finality, and the general order of nature, reintroduces the problem raised by Plato, questioned by Aristotle, and reaffirmed by St. Augustine and St. Thomas, that God planned, created, and governs the universe immediately.

3. God and the universe of nature. Without God the universe has no ultimate meaning. It consists of a system of limited entities each of which depends for its existence on something else. The explanation of a limited entity may be partially explained by another limited entity, but only partially so. Insofar as this other is limited, it too must be explained. An infinite series, or infinite distribution of matter, or an eternal process, all these only postpone the difficulty that much the more. We are led to the explanation of limited being, or being-by-participation, only by entitatively infinite being, God Himself. As this applies to the order of nature, it means that God and God alone must be the author of nature.

4. The laws of nature. We all know what a law is. We know that it is a statement of an ordered way of doing or avoiding something. We know, furthermore, that it must proceed from proper authority. Not just anyone can legislate and get away with it. A lawmaker must have a proper legislative office to do so, otherwise no one pays any attention to him. Lastly, we know that the law must be promulgated. It must be expressed in such way that its subjects can know that it exists and what its prescriptions are. Hence, we define a law as: *an ordinance of reason, prescribed by competent authority, and sufficiently promulgated.*

The laws of nature as we understand them today do not fit under this definition. Hence, there must be some adjustment of concepts when we speak of laws. A law of nature, as it is used in the sciences, is a generalization of an observed regularity. This fits in with the aim of the physical sciences, which is to systematize our knowledge of the observed world. Since system implies order, we try to pursue and classify the order in such way as to see physical events as instances under a few far-reaching and more inclusive generalizations that we call laws.

Since there are observed phenomena, we see them against a background of space and at a definite time. Hence, both spatial and temporal measurement become important in the statement of any generalization or law. Any generalization is conceptual, and hence the laws of nature are fundamentally concepts. Furthermore, since they are measurement-generalizations, they are mathematical in essence. Their expression is statistical. The laws of nature are not really principles of nature. They are conceptual expressions of facts which occur with regularity.

The laws of nature are in the mind, just as any concept is in the mind. When we see this, we discover that Immanuel Kant's *a priori* categories are not the shocking innovations that at first sight they seem to be. They are simply a further application of the theory of the laws of nature. Furthermore, when modern physical theorists such as Lindsay and Margenau maintain that they are not concerned with extramental reality in its nature or causes, they again are affirming that they are interested in the regularity of phenomena as observed, not as caused, or as necessary or contingent, or anything like that. They are being theoretical, but they are not being philosophical. Their approach can be summarized in this way: we do not know what gravity is. Yet our observations of the regular attraction between bodies provide us with statistics allowing for the formulation of a generalized statement. Thus, when Isaac Newton noticed that the deviation of the moon from a straight, tangential path toward the earth is sixteen feet a second, the same as that of the fall of an apple from a tree, he was able to express a mathematical generalization of the attraction of bodies against which the attraction, or fall, or influence of any body throughout the universe might be measured.

This understanding of the laws of nature also indicates how a law can be "overthrown," or seriously questioned, without any corresponding change in the natures of things outside the mind. This is normal. It begins to become a bit serious when epistemologists maintain that these mathematical concepts impose an order in nature. They do nothing of the sort, of course, and such epistemologists frequently run into difficulties when their theory forces them into the position that the change of a law, for example, the overthrow of the "law of parity" in early 1957, should change reality. And, of course, reality remains pretty much the same. Our generalization of its observed phenomena has to become a bit more accurate.

The laws of nature are not the principles of nature. The principles of nature are the four causes as explained earlier in this chapter. St. Thomas, dealing with law in respect to nature, simply calls it the participation in the wisdom of God. That is, God conceives of possibles, of which some are actualized. Since God designs them to act according to their natures even though most of them are unintelligent, in their actions they reflect the creative design of God in operation. Hence, they are said to participate in the wisdom of God. This is the position of St. Augustine in his doctrine of the *rationes seminales*, the evolving types.

APPARENT EXCEPTIONS TO NATURE — VIOLENCE, CHANCE, AND ART

1. Violence. Although violence is generally considered as force contrary to the natural order, it is not thereby unnatural, and this for two reasons: (1) violence proceeds from existing entities which must have a certain degree of orderliness in order to exist; and (2) violence is always relative to whatever it affects. We must examine these points in detail.

Violence is in the order of force. Hence, it proceeds from something existing. But in order to exist, a thing must have some sort of an essence, even if only for a short time. Even in the most violent processes we know, the thermonuclear processes in the stars or in humanly devised processes, the sequence is orderly, predictable, recognizable in its operation and effects and remnants. Its violence is not in disorder but in its intensity. Intensity, however, is relative to something, and this leads us to the second point about violence.

Violence is always relative to that which it affects. For example, when the wolf kills the sheep, it is violent for the sheep but quite natural to the wolf, which, as a carnivorous animal, lives on flesh that it must kill for itself. Or again, on our own planet, what would be a violent change in temperature for people on one part of the earth would be quite normal for people on another part. This implies three conclusions.

The first conclusion is that violence cannot be universal. Violence is variation or intensification in and of order, and hence presupposes order. Even if violence existed of itself in some way, it would be ordered, to a certain extent, in its existence because some essence or essences would be involved. In other words, the violence would be the order.

Second, violence could be a good deal more general than it is. In the world that is familiar to us, we know of many, many natural processes that could be intensified into what, at present, we call violence. For example, a slight tilting of the earth's poles farther away from the ecliptic could bring about violent changes in the weather, involving stronger winds, more moisture in the air blocking off sunlight and, with the shifting of ice caps consequent to the earth's new position, terminating in another ice age. A shifting of the Gulf Stream closer to North America could bring results almost as disastrous. The rising warm air closer to the land mass would attract cold air from the north arctic zone. The meeting of the cold air and warm air would result in both violent storms and heavy fog periods, consequent blocking off of sunlight, and the beginnings of a new ice age. The same could result from the addition of a slightly greater amount of carbon particles, "smog," to our already polluted atmosphere. On the other hand, the slightest thinning out of our ionosphere would allow more harshly penetrating primary cosmic rays, ultraviolet rays, and x rays through the atmosphere with their consequent violent effects on man.

Third, any act of violence involves subsequent natural readjustment. This is generally disastrous when the action is the result of man's tampering with the order of nature. For example, a farmer may decide to do away with all the hawks in the neighborhood to protect his poultry. If he is successful, he discovers that this poultry is now destroyed by rodents, which up to now had been kept under control by the hawks. Should he manage the extremely difficult task of controlling the rodents, he discovers that the insects multiply destructively. This applies in the field of ecology, but a moment of reflection shows its application to any other system. The reason for all of this is that there is no such thing as an isolated entity in the universe. All things are related, many of them so closely that to affect one is to affect many others that are closely interlinked. If one is affected violently, the rest react equally violently.

In summary, then, *violence is force against a restricted order but is itself a part of the greater order of nature*. With sufficient information it is predictable save in one case: the abuse of free will by man. Only man can select the forces he wishes to abuse, and only man can be deliberately destructive.

2. Chance. Chance has many phases and it goes under many names. We speak not only of chance, but also of luck, the fortuitous, and fate. Furthermore, chance is a concept proper to many developments in theoretical physics and in theories of evolution. Actually, there are two understandings of chance, the classical notion and the modern physical notion.

The classical notion of chance. This is what we generally consider as luck, and it does exist. Luck can be good or bad. There are people who are lucky and people who are accident prone. Many outstanding events in history, such as the defeat of the Spanish Armada and the discovery of x rays, have been influenced by chance.

The classical view considered chance as an element in any consideration of nature, and hence Greek philosophers investigated it as such. Christian theology was interested in the problem of fate and superstition. As these are presented, they are tied up with natural phenomena, the movements of stars and planets, some of the aspects of numbers. People such as Joseph Balsamo, the self-styled "Count Cagliostro," have taken advantage of human interest in these and have turned this interest to their own advantage.

We see an excellent example of chance in the discovery of x rays. Wilhelm Roentgen, of Munich, was working on the conductivity of gases in vacuum tubes, Crookes tubes. Since he wished better visibility for his experiment, he worked in a darkened room. Someone working on another experiment involving photographic plates took advantage of the dark room and left some plates there. Roentgen, following his own pursuits, put his apparatus to work and noticed that the plates, in another part of the room, became fogged. This unforeseen event suggested to Roentgen that radiation was leaking from the tube. This set him on the experimentation that discovered the photoelectric effect and was behind the magnificent work on the electron performed by Sir J. J. Thomson. Although such a discovery was bound to occur some time or other, as it did occur, it was an accident, a chance product.

Upon analysis of this event, we notice that only the event was unplanned. Everything else involved in it was the result of intelligent direction. The event was the crossing of two orders, as follows:

a) *First order.* Roentgen was working on the problem of how well or how poorly gases conduct electricity. Since he was using direct current, the electron flow was from the cathode to the anode. A phenomenon involved in this is what is called the Crookes dark space, the result of the pressure of electrons moving away from the cathode at extremely high velocities. This causes a greenish glow difficult to see except in the dark. Hence, Roentgen deliberately darkened the room.

If the photographic plates had not been placed in the dark room, Roentgen would have then further pursued the dark space, and perhaps with a slit objective would have discovered that the sharpness of shadows seemed to indicate the emission of particles instead of, as Roentgen thought at the time, the pressure of waves. Thus, he might have been the discoverer of the mass of the electron rather than Thomson. At any event, he could easily have been the great pioneer of the interaction of waves and particles in a planned direction. For his work there was no need of the presence of photographic plates.

b) *The second order.* As a matter of fact, someone was interested in photographic plates, better emulsions, etc. However, photographic plates must be kept in the dark to prevent their being "lightstruck," or fogged by light. Here was a dark room temporarily at hand. Hence, it fitted in perfectly with the experimenter to store his plates in this room for the time being.

If Roentgen had not carried out his experiment, the photographer would undoubtedly have continued his experiments and might have come up with better, faster, and more sensitive plates years in advance of later discoveries in this field. This activity, too, was planned.

c) *Resolution.* All that we can say is that the consequence was unforeseen, although the components of the event were planned. It was unforeseen simply because the contingencies of events in nature are so wide in possibility that no one can possibly foresee every eventuality.

We are led to the conclusion, then, that chance is the *unforeseen eventuality of several necessary and natural sequences of cause and effect.* In the cases cited above, deliberation has entered, although this is not necessary. There can be the inability to foresee the outcome of a natural sequence of events. For example, many people have suffered extreme bad luck simply because they did not see that they had erected a building in a spot subject to earthquakes.

All of the above is within the order of nature, and, to a certain extent, within the operations of the four causes. However, there are these differences:

There are *material causes* of the event. It has proceeded from several sources in virtue of their primary matter. Since matter has no intrinsic determination or direction apart from existence through form, primary matter is actualized no matter what occurs.

Since chance is in the order of an event and an occurrence, material and formal causes do not enter into the consideration. They are causes of the essence of the entities concerned. However, these have their essences, chance or no chance.

However, since chance is in the order of events, efficiency and finality must be considered. Since, moreover, the problem is that of the unforeseen, finality plays a big part.

There is no final cause of the chance event as chance. There is the finality of the orders involved, and with the accidental meeting, there is the realization of new appetites and tendencies with the event. Hence, the event is the initiation of a new order of finality.

Since the event is accidental, the efficient causality is in the order of the incidental rather than that of proper causality. However, there is efficiency, or else the event would not occur.

Nevertheless, chance is part of the order of nature finding its objective basis in the contingency of the operations of dependent beings. Coupled with this is the inability to foresee the outcome. If man were omniscient, he would be able to foresee the outcome, and there would be no chance. For the same reason, since God is omniscient, and since His knowledge is the cause of reality, there is no chance to God. Chance is in the order of secondary causality.

The *scientific concept of chance* enters into our considerations later. It is essentially the same as the philosophical notion. However, it deals with problems concerning the random distribution of matter, the unpredictability of events, and to what extent statistical averages of these need be taken into account, will suffice, or can be overlooked in the development of scientific theory.

The following consideration illustrates what we mean by random. In the corridor of a school pupils rush from one classroom to the other. They are going to different rooms, not all to the same room, and, consequently, there is a certain irregularity to the tide of all of the students. Furthermore, some are walking rapidly, some slowly, some by themselves, and some in friendly groups. The distribution of students is about as random as can be, even more than if there were a panic when all would be rushing toward the same few exits. Nevertheless, despite the random character of the individual actions, there gradually appear signs of a general average. For example, the floor wears down where there is the average of the heaviest traffic. Along the wall, about elbow high, there begins to appear a continuous streak from the contact of many different elbows over a period of time. The random actions of the individuals average out orderly if not geometrically.

Needless to say, in the above considerations, the concepts of the chances of random distribution and of chance events do not militate against our philosophy of nature and of the four causes. In random distribution and random motion, things still act as they do because they are what they are. The problem is not one of nature but of our knowledge of nature. Hence, chance, random distribution, random motions, etc., are problems not so much in cosmology as in epistemology. They are not problems of nature so much as problems of the interpretation of nature.

3. Art. Art is natural to man, a part of the natural order of human beings, but not nature. Nature is the process of the fulfillment of the potencies of matter, formally, finally, and efficiently. Art is the imposition of an ideal on matter or on other ideas. Nature proceeds from matter and terminates in matter. Art proceeds from an idea and may terminate in other ideas or in material representatives of the idea. No matter whether nature proceeds efficiently or inefficiently, orderly or somewhat disorderly, smoothly or violently, it still proceeds naturally. It is still nature. Art, on the other hand, corresponds well or poorly to an idea. Hence, whereas there is not good or bad nature — save from the point of physical integrity, a whole product or an incomplete product, sometimes called physical good and physical evil — art is by its very nature either good or bad art. Briefly, art and nature proceed in diametric opposition.

There are different truths in the understanding of nature and art. Nature is what it is, and our knowledge of it corresponds to what nature is in itself. Hence, truth in relation to nature is scientific truth, that is, the agreement of our idea to extramental reality. We must *learn* what nature is and we must adjust our concepts to what it is. On the other hand, we *make* art to be what it is. An art product is truly what it is when the product agrees with the idea. The truth of nature is the agreement of the idea to the thing. The truth of art is the agreement of the thing to the idea.

There is causality both in nature and art. The causality of nature is that of the four causes. The causality of art is that of exemplars and efficiency. Art really has no material cause, since it proceeds from an idea. There is the use of material, but in either case, material causality is only analogous. The formal cause of an art product is identical with the exemplar. So is the final cause, save with the following extensions: the exemplar can express something useful, something didactic, or something pleasurable. In these cases, the arts will be, respectively: crafts, liberal and rhetorical, and fine.

We might say a few brief words about the extensions of the arts to fill out this summary consideration. Art is a human devising. It has been defined as: *the right reason of making*. Now, we can "make" with ideas or with material beings. If we make with ideas, the purpose may be to develop the truth. In this case, the art will be what we call a *liberal art*. The purpose may be that of delight at the *beautiful*. In this case, the art will be a *fine art*, characterized by the aesthetic contemplation of the beautiful expression of ideas. It will be characteristically *poetic*, which notion includes the novel and the play. If we make with things, again, if the purpose is aesthetic, the art is a fine art such as painting, sculpture, etc. If the purpose is useful, the art is a *craft*.

Both the liberal arts and the fine arts are higher, ontologically, than the crafts. That is because both arts terminate a tendency, in this case, the satisfaction of the intellect. Although the liberal arts are not truth, they are logical erections of true concepts for the purpose of the better unfolding the truth. Truth is a transcendental property of being, and hence the liberal arts are fulfillments of the intellect's transcendental relation to being. The same is true for the fine arts. The objects are not contemplated for any useful purpose. They are contemplated for their beauty, which is either identical with being or such a close aspect of being as to be almost identical with it. Hence, since both the fine arts and liberal arts tend to being as the good of the intellect, they are in a unique position metaphysically. The crafts, on the other hand, deal with means to an end, and hence are ontologically lower. In descending order we might consider the hierarchy of the arts as follows:

Type of Art	Terminative Purpose
Liberal	Truth as the good of the intellect
Fine	Beauty as the good of the intellect
Craft	The useful good, and hence incomplete in itself

The older division of the arts into liberal and practical was based on the work done by a free man (liberal) and the work done by a slave (practical). In the scholastic period, liberal became the free development of ideas for their truth or aesthetic content whereas practical became the work done on material objects for their aesthetic or practical purposes. This latter consideration is that of the schoolmen, most particularly that of St. Thomas. The Renaissance division into liberal, fine, and practical arts is implicit in St. Thomas' consideration.

The threefold division while not identical with nature is still natural to man. Man naturally thinks and develops his ideas of truth. Man naturally loves beauty and naturally produces it artistically. He also naturally manufactures useful objects as means to his own good and work.

Nevertheless, since the directions of art and nature are diametrically opposite, art is not identifiable with nature, and aesthetic theory should avoid too naturalistic an interpretation of art.

SUMMARY

1. Nature is defined in terms of the individual nature as the first and intrinsic principle of motion and of rest in that in which it is primarily and not in virtue of a concomitant attribute.
2. Although accidents, structure, and properties apply to the individual nature, nature means primarily matter and form. In this sense it is defined by St. Thomas as the essence as the source of operations.

3. Scientifically, the world of nature is described mathematically in terms of the uniformity of the whole. In philosophy, the whole is interpreted in terms of the actions and reactions of the individuals.
4. The principles of nature are the four causes. The laws of nature are statistical expressions of the concepts of constants and variables drawn from the pattern of nature.
5. Violence is a more intense expression of natural forces insofar as they interfere with individual natures.

   Chance is the unforeseen in the face of the contingent. In science it is the statistical expression of the immeasurable or the unpredictable.

   Art is the application of an exemplar to ideas or matter for a didactic, aesthetic, or utilitarian purpose. The respective areas are the liberal arts, the fine arts, and the crafts.

CHAPTER SIX

ATOMS, ELEMENTS, and HYLOMORPHISM

We have already seen how some of the Presocratics, especially Leucippus, Empedocles, and Democritus, sought to explain the generation and corruption of bodies, their physical changes and their qualities, through minimal parts or *atoms*. By investing each of these atoms with the attributes of the being described by Parmenides, and by making the changes we observe in physical things consist simply in the external arrangement of the atoms, they sought to avoid the difficulties against change and multiplicity raised by Parmenides and at the same time to give a natural foundation for the apparent movements that take place in the sensible world. This Presocratic atomism was completely materialistic in the sense that it saw no need for going outside of matter or for discovering within matter any principle of an order higher than matter.

THE ATOMISM OF PLATO'S "TIMAEUS"

The Presocratic atomists held that an explanation of physical reality by means of elements or atoms was a complete one. Plato, in his dialogue *Timaeus*, incorporated much of the atomism of his predecessors in his "likely account" of the origin and development of the universe. Although the precise status in the order of being belonging to "atoms" and "elements" in Plato's theory remains an open question because of the "probable" nature of his physical views, one point does stand out. No matter what the degree of reality to be assigned to them, atoms and elements are not, for Plato, the total explanation of physical things. He saw that atomism could be turned to good account as affording a conceptual framework or scheme for dealing with physical things in a rational manner, but insisted that the ultimate explanation for the structure and order observable in the visible universe must be located in causes which transcend that universe, namely, in the Ideas and the Demiurge.

Plato drew heavily upon the Pythagorean mathematics of nature in describing the "atoms" or "elements" of traditional Greek thought, that is, the four "roots" or primary bodies: fire, earth, air, and water. Thus the Platonic theory of atoms and elements is more geometrical than physical; that is, Plato looked upon the universe from a mathematical point of view; and, in explaining the proper places of bodies, for example, he was more interested in the geometrical concept of place than in the physical properties which bring a body to, and maintain it within, a place. This is just another indication that, in the *Timaeus,* Plato was more interested in providing a conceptual frame of reference for ordering our knowledge about visible things than in offering a properly physical, that is, cosmological explanation.

In brief, Plato saw the visible universe as a unified whole whose individual constituents were hierarchically arranged. Physical bodies are as such visible and tangible. To explain their visibility, fire is necessary; and to explain their tangibility, earth is necessary. Thus fire and earth are the primary basic elements. But, Plato urges, "two things cannot be rightly put together without a third." Hence a bond is needed to join fire to earth in the individual physical bodies we see and touch. Since fire and earth are both solids, that is, extended in three directions, a single bond is not sufficient to unite them. Two means or proportions are required, and these are the "elements" of air and water (cf. *Timaeus,* 31–32). In giving more precise account of the four basic elements, Plato observes that we cannot properly refer to them as substantial entities, as they "slip away and do not wait to be described as 'that' or 'this' or by any phrase that exhibits them as having permanent being" (*Timaeus,* 49e). They can perhaps best be regarded as qualities that make their appearance in the receptacle or nurse of becoming, that is, in space. As extended qualities, the four primary elements possess a geometrical shape conferred upon them by the Demiurge. Plato takes things as far back as triangles, choosing the right-angled isosceles (half-square) and the right-angled scalene or half-equilateral, from which are to be built up the square and equilateral sides of the solids (cf. *Timaeus,* 53c). If anyone should ask that the description be carried beyond triangles, Plato would reply, "the principles yet more remote, God alone knows and such men as are dear to him" (*Timaeus,* 53d). Solids are then constructed of these triangles. To earth Plato assigns the form of a cube as being the most immobile or hard to move; to fire, he assigns the pyramid, as being the most "mobile" and "having the sharpest cutting edges and sharpest points in every direction"; to air, the octahedron; and to water, the icosahedron (cf. *Timaeus*, 55d).

The elementary solids may be and are transformed into one another, since water, for example, may be broken down into its constituent triangles under the action of fire, and these triangles may recombine into the same figure or into others. Earth, however, is an exception. It may be broken up, but the constituent triangles from which it was fashioned (isosceles or half-square) are proper exclusively to it (cf. *Timaeus*, 56).

Thus, by utilizing some of the mathematical concepts advanced by the Pythagoreans, Plato saw that the doctrine of the four elements or roots, traditional in Greek thought, could be given some kind of rational basis as a partial explanation of the structure of material beings.

Nevertheless, it is important to remember that Platonic atomism should not be interpreted too literally. He insists that his account of the visible world is only likely or probable. The Platonic doctrine on the elements is intended to facilitate thinking about physical things; it is not intended as the final word on the intrinsic nature of those physical things. Strikingly enough, Plato's views are quite similar to those of modern physicists regarding the atoms, elements, and molecules. The modern physicist will maintain that structurally matter consists of minimal parts, yet the properties he ascribes to these in molecular, atomic, and nuclear theory are largely conceptual. In other words, modern atoms are reality *as considered by man rather than as it is in itself*. They are metaphors rather than realities. This is basically the same position as Plato's.

ARISTOTELIAN ATOMISM

Aristotle makes several sharp distinctions in his consideration of atoms and elements. Like Plato, he maintains that matter, structurally, consists of elements and that elements consist of atoms that have the properties of the element. Furthermore, he agrees that fire is the element of lightness and activity, earth the element of heaviness and inactivity, and the other elements in between and relative to fire and earth. However, there are these notable differences:

1. Atoms and elements are in the real order of bodies rather than in the conceptual order.

2. They are in the order of bodily properties and not in the order of essence. Hence, they are accidental and not essential to bodies.

3. They are in the order of bodily structure. Hence, they help explain

a different problem than that explained by hylomorphism. This means that in the Aristotelian system, *hylomorphism remains valid no matter what subsequent discoveries may be made or conjectured in or about elements, molecules, and atoms.*

The foundation of the Aristotelian consideration is the distinction between a body's essence and its properties. A body can remain constant in its essence even if it undergoes changes in its properties. For example, gold is gold even though it may be the slightest flake of gold or a huge ingot. There will be different physical properties. The flake will be more ductile and malleable, whereas the ingot will be soft but practically inert. Similarly, hydrogen is hydrogen, whether it is in a gaseous or liquid form. Again, both its chemical and physical properties will be somewhat different in either case, but it still remains hydrogen. Likewise, a dog is a dog, whether he is old and fat or young and active, whether he has good health or poor health. There must be a reason, then, why the entity can retain its essence yet differ in its properties. This reason is to be found in its structure.

Since Aristotle was able to give a good mechanical explanation of the universe and its operations in terms of the physical properties of bodies, he saw no need to go any further than this mechanical explanation when applied to the bodies that compose the universe. Like Plato, he had a tendency to associate physical with chemical properties, that is, he associated lightness with activeness and heaviness with inactivity. Taking one thing with another, he was not too far wrong. With the exception of helium, the actinide series, and some of the heavy radioactive elements, most light elements are chemically active and most heavy elements are chemically inert.

Thus, Aristotle arranged the elements as follows:

Element	**Chemical Properties**	**Physical Properties**
Fire	Absolutely active	Absolutely light
Air	Relatively active	Relatively light
Water	Relatively inactive	Relatively heavy
Earth	Absolutely heavy	Practically inert

Aristotle, like most of his contemporaries, realized that no body is absolutely inert. His reasoning was simple: even earthy bodies are somewhat active. This activity must come from the body itself. Hence, the body in its elementary structure must be somewhat active.

This system was easy to visualize. Everyone saw and experienced that fiery objects are light and have a tendency to rise. They are also active.

Earthy objects are heavy and practically inactive. This fitted in with Aristotle's mechanics of the universe, which hinged about the tendencies of bodies to seek their proper places, light objects upward and heavy objects downward. The highest, that is, the farthest away from the earth, are the stars, while the most downward, that is to say, the most central object in the universe toward which all heavy objects tend, is the earth.

Since these atoms and elements are so important for the composition of bodies, how do they exist in themselves? Aristotle rejected the atomic theories of his day, those of Leucippus, Democritus, and others, because he saw them as no more than attempts to patch up the philosophy of Parmenides.* Furthermore, he thought that in this patching up the atomists accepted too much, the monism of Parmenides, and they supposed too much. His position was that they might have done better in starting from a different position than that of Parmenides. They were hampered in accepting the unchangeability of being. Hence, they had to work hard to explain the obviousness of change by considering it the changeability of the parts of the unchangeable One. They then supposed too much. In order to explain obvious generation and corruption, obvious spatial change in the motionless and full universe of Parmenides, they postulated the universal void both outside of and within the universe in order to guarantee room for the changes they accepted.

Furthermore, the atomists failed to explain difference and differentiation. If they took the position that the atoms were all the same, then they failed to explain how the products were different. If we represent the atoms by the letter X, then no amount of X's or combinations of X's are going to give us Y and Z. All we get are variations of X. If the atomists took the position that the atoms were already different, then they went against the basic postulate of their leaders, Parmenides and Melissus, who maintained that all are the same and unchanging. They also failed to explain the differences that they postulated. The answer, as we know, comes from Plato and Aristotle, that there are determinations known as Forms (Plato), which Forms are the fulfillments of the potencies of matter in really existing bodies (Aristotle).

Although Aristotle was opposed to the atomism of his day, he was not opposed to atoms. He looked on atoms as "relatively small parts" of elements (cf. *On Generation and Corruption*, I, 2, 317a16), and he put the emphasis on the whole rather than on the parts. In fact, he uses "atom" and "element" almost interchangeably.

Elements are simple bodies (cf. *Metaphysics*, V, 7, 1017b10). Bodies

---

* For Aristotle's criticism of his predecessors see: *Physics*, VI, 1, 231a21 ff; *On the Heavens*, III, 1,299a2 ff.; *On Generation and Corruption*, I, 2, 315a26 ff.

are divisible, composed of parts. Their relatively small parts are atoms. Although in theory bodies are infinitely divisible, there are practical difficulties about dividing infinitely. Hence, there are minimal parts. And these minimal parts are what the Eleatics had called the "indivisibles," or "atoms."

Since the atoms are parts of the elements, they have all the properties of their elements, and are of the same essence as their elements. The parts partake of the essence and the properties of the whole in simple bodies; and, for Aristotle, the elements are simple bodies. Among the properties of the elements, of any other bodies for that matter, is intrinsic activity. Hence, the atoms are intrinsically active. Thus Aristotle has the germ of a kinetic-atomic theory.

Elements have identities, and according to the Aristotelian tradition, they have forms (cf. *Metaphysics*, V, 7, 1017b10). What happens to their forms in combination? Do they retain their identities? Do they submerge their identities? Do they lose their identities completely? If they retain their identities, their forms, what are their relations to the substantial form? Aristotle's answer is that the substantial form is the identity of the whole, and that a substantial change is a change ". . . from *this* to *that* as a whole" (*On Generation and Corruption*, I, 2, 317a22). Hence, the problem of accidents, parts, qualities, and properties is proper to elements and atoms, and accidental changes are in this order. On the contrary, substantial changes are on the part of the whole involving rearrangement of the component elements and atoms.

The works of further resolution of these questions was left to St. Albert, and his position was followed by his disciple, St. Thomas.

ELEMENTS IN A COMPOUND

The problem as undertaken by St. Albert is this: if the elements remain in a compound, are there several substantial forms?* This question gives rise to several considerations:

1. If the elements remain in a compound, then it is not one substance but an aggregation of several substances. However, against this simple answer is the fact that there are different types of unity. There are aggregations, of course, but they are easily recognizable as such. On the other hand, there are substantial unions, discernible from the unity of their operations toward a fulfillment beyond the individual fulfillments of the elements themselves.

* See *Commentary on De Caelo*, L. III, Tract. II, C. I; *Commentary on De Generatione et Corruptione*, L. II, Tract. 1.

2. If the elements enter into a compound to the extent that they completely submerge their identities so as to lose them, then the product is a simple substance. This, however, cannot be held because the properties of the elements are discernible in the compound and because the elements emerge from the compound when it breaks down.

We are led to the conclusion, then, that the elements remain *somehow* in the compound. The question is, in what manner? In a true substantial union, the substance is not merely the sum of its elements and their atoms. The substance as such has some domination over its component elements in the retention of its own identity. Hence, there is some subordination of the elements to the substance.

The subordination is the key to the answer. The elements exist as parts in relation to the whole and are subordinated to the essence of the whole.

Since the Arabian philosophers were all physicists, the scientists of the day, they had faced this question. Among them there were two outstanding points of view, that of Avicenna and that of Averroës. *Avicenna* had maintained that the elements remain only potentially. However, their properties are actually operative, and it would be difficult to see how only potential elements could be the source of actual properties. *Averroës* had maintained that the elements remain in a "confused" state. Again, however, there are precise manifestations of the presence of the elements in properties, which would lead to the conclusion that the elements are present as such in the compound.

St. Albert's answer is in the distinction between essence and substance. In brief, it is that the elements retain their essences in the compound but sacrifice their independent existence. Since the substantial form is a principle of existence, the elements as parts draw their existence in the whole from the substantial form of the whole. This means that in the free state they are substances. Upon their entering into a compound, they sacrifice their substantiality and change into parts, drawing the essence and existence of the whole from the form of the whole. Thus, although they retain their identities in the order of essence, their identity is no longer substantial but componential. They are thus informed by the substantial form of the whole and are subordinated to it.

Technically, St. Albert distinguishes between the *first being* of the element, its essence. This is *what* the essence is, what the element is. However, to say *what* it is is not to say *that* it is. The form is the principle of substance, and St. Albert calls substance the *second being* of the element. This, incidentally, is what is meant by the dictum uttered repeatedly by St. Albert, St. Thomas, and Duns Scotus, that "form gives existence to matter." It means that matter is in potency to existence through form. In the case of an element, the primary matter of the element is in potency to existence in the free state as a substance through its own substantial form. It is also in potency to existence as a subordinate part of a compound substance through the form of the compound which is, simultaneously, the principle of the existence of the compound through the proportion of the elements. In this way, in the substantial order, the form of the compound is the equivalent of the forms of the elements. It does the work, so to speak, of the elementary forms.

St. Thomas follows St. Albert on this. He adds the term "virtually," and says that the form of the compound is "virtually," that is, equivalently, doing the work of, the forms of the elements in the order of the substantial existence of the compound.

All of the above development is in St. Albert's commentary on Aristotle's *On the Heavens,* Book III. It is also repeated in his commentary on Aristotle's *On Generation and Corruption,* Book II.

As long as the elements are in the compound, they lend their properties to the compound through their elementary or atomic properties. Upon the breakdown of the substance, they can: (1) resume their own identities as substances or (2) be rearranged into other compound substances as subordinate parts.

At any event, this theory of elements and atoms as real components of real bodies does not militate against hylomorphism. Any and all particles and elements enter into combinations because they *can* do so. This potency to be actuated in existence through proportionate combinations is their primary matter. The fulfillment of the proportion, the fulfillment of this potency, is their form, and it is through this form that they are capable of existence.

THE ORGANIC FORM

The importance of organization in the existence of material entities in the explanation of the Aristotelians is similar to the problem of life. That is why many modern scholars look upon the Aristotelian explanation as "organic." This gave rise to a new problem, the possible plurality of truly substantial forms.

To recast for a moment, we have seen how even though the elements remain in a compound, there is only one true substantial form since there is one existence to the proper compound, the proper substantial unit. The problem of the *organic form,* or the *forma corporeitatis* as it was called in Latin, arose from the problem of life, and arose from the convictions of Aristotle about the nature of life.

Aristotle maintained that life is merely the higher organization of the same elements out of which the rest of bodies are made. This is a modern point of view, and is the occasion of a dispute between mechanism and vitalism among contemporary biological theorists. However, Aristotle made a distinction between rational and irrational life. Even though he apparently never settled to his own satisfaction whether or not the human soul is immaterial, he did maintain that the rational principle in man is the form of man and is the principle of life in a rational entity.

Christianity introduced a new interpretation of this based upon the Christian belief in the spirituality of the human soul. It is possible on purely rational grounds to argue from the nature of contemplative operations to the immateriality of the soul. Since the soul is immaterial, it is not limited to the restrictions of matter. It is incorruptible, and hence has a natural immortality. Plato maintained the survival of the soul for the purposes of the pursuit of wisdom, although his argumentation does not establish the nature of immortality. It rather shows the fittingness of survival for the attainment of wisdom beyond matter.

Although the tendency among early Christian thinkers was more toward Plato than toward Aristotle, many accepted the Aristotelian principles of potency and act, essence and existence, and matter and form, almost completely. This was certainly the case for St. Augustine. Hence, the consideration of the human soul as the form of the body was the perfect answer for the Christian understanding of man. It guaranteed the potency for the spiritual life without any underestimating of the goodness of man's body and material possessions, a heretical notion that plagued the Manichaeans, Gnostics, Docetists, and, later on, the Albigensians.

However, the consideration of the spiritual soul as the form of the body also posed problems. Chief among these was the consideration that the soul, as spirit, is indifferent concerning the principles of matter. That being the case, the body must satisfy its own needs. Among its needs is that of organization. Since the soul is above this sort of thing, the body must have its own principle of organization, a principle of bodiliness, or an *organic form.* Hence, in man, there are two forms: the organic form as the principle of bodily organization and the fulfillment of the potencies of matter; and the spiritual soul which is not the form of man's primary matter but of man's body.

The finest exposition of this organic form is by John Duns Scotus.* His reasoning is that since the form is the fulfillment of the potencies of matter, and since spirit can in no way be such a fulfillment, the human soul cannot be the form of man's primary matter. Hence, there must be such a material fulfillment, the organic form. Once again, this organic form is the form of man's prime matter, while the soul is the form of man's body and the principle of man's existence as man.

Scotus had based himself on the Aristotelian principle that the higher is the fulfillment of the lower. St. Albert and St. Thomas had also maintained that the higher is the fulfillment of the potencies of the lower. However, they also maintained that in cases where the higher cannot be the *fulfillment* of the lower, the lower can still be the *preparation* for the higher. They looked upon the soul in relation to a prepared body.

The close interplay of soul and body is seen in the process of learning and thinking. We learn from individual material objects, and yet our knowledge is trans-material, or meta-material, just as it is meta-temporal or trans-temporal, that is to say, immaterial, beyond the limitations of time and place. Similarly, in our abstract, conceptual knowledge, we still make use of the resources of the body in visualizing our ideas in fantasies and memory images. Today psychologists see in detail what St. Thomas saw in general, the use of the central nervous system in knowledge.

Although both St. Albert and St. Thomas lived before Scotus, they anticipated his difficulties in their answers to the older theories of the organic form. Their position was that learning and knowledge show such a close union of soul and body that we cannot consider the soul merely as the resident of the body. Similarly, man's actions proceed from such a unique principle that it demands one and only one form, not the cooperation of two forms, no matter how close this cooperation might be.

Their answer was that the soul is the unique form of the body, and although it is not the fulfillment of matter, it is the equivalent of such a fulfillment because the body is especially prepared for the soul. The soul is, thus, *virtually* the fulfillment of the potencies of matter.

Concerning the manner of this, they differed. St. Albert maintained that the spiritual soul was created in the diploid cell immediately upon conception. St. Thomas maintained that there was a succession of forms (cf. *ST*, I, 76, 3, ad 3). There was a vegetative form as the principle

* In the *Opus Oxoniense*, L. II, dists. 11 and 16.

of organic development, a sense form as the principle of sense development, and finally, when the foetus has become *viable*, the creation in this of the spiritual soul. Each form is virtually the former one, and upon the accession of each latter one, the former recedes to the potencies of matter.

In this way, despite theories of atoms, elements, despite theological problems, they were able to maintain the unicity of man's substantial form in his rational soul. It is a perfect interdevelopment of faith with Aristotelian philosophy.

There are further problems in connection with modern atomic theory that have come back in a philosophy called *hylosystemism*. However, modern atomic and nuclear theory are far more conceptual than the realistic atomism and element theory of Aristotle and the earlier of the modern scientists. This demands a special investigation to be seen later in this work.

SUMMARY

1. Greek thinkers never really unified their theories of atoms and elements; that is, atom theory was postulated with a view to one set of problems. Element theory was postulated according to the needs of another theory.
2. The first significant unification of atom and element theory was by Plato. He did this predominantly in the conceptual order, and his atoms have geometrical properties.
3. Aristotle united atom and element theory in the physical order. His atoms have the physical and chemical properties of the elements of which they are the minimal parts.
4. Since substance is autonomy and identity, it does not, of itself, explain variations of accidents and properties in a body. The structure and its elements are called on to explain these.
5. The forms of the elements persist in the compound substance, but in the compound they draw their existence as parts from the substantial form of the whole.
6. Because the spiritual soul in man was considered to have little to do with bodily organization, and actually is not the fulfillment of the potencies of matter, early Christian thinkers postulated a material organic form called the *forma corporeitatis*.

   St. Thomas maintained that there is a succession of forms, vegetative succeeded by animal, in the foetus to prepare it for the spiritual soul. The soul then performs the formal operations of the lower forms. It is thus the *equivalent* or, *virtually*, the lower forms.

PART TWO

General Properties of Bodies

CHAPTER SEVEN

MOTION and CHANGE

The reality of change and its understanding have been matters of primary concern to all philosophers. Plato tolerated change as an inferior state, impossible to grasp intelligibly and characterizing the shadowy sensible things which in some way or another "imitate" the unchanging Forms or Ideas. Aristotle regarded it highly and considered the universe as a process striving to imitate in temporal fashion the life proper to the Self-Thinking Thought. St. Thomas gave a Christian interpretation to the Aristotelian doctrine, looking upon change as a state in a being's quest for the perfection of its existence, in striving to imitate God's being. Mechanistic science and philosophy made it a mere conceptual entity as background for other conceptual entities. Relativity physics and the new mechanics make it the stuff of the universe. Two outstanding modern philosophers, Bergson and Whitehead, identify reality with the duration of change.

These positions have a great deal in common if we understand change in terms of its basic components, potency and act. Its perfection is that it is. Yet, it is fundamentally imperfect since it is an unfulfilled being, an actuality tending to the fulfillment of its unsatisfied tendencies and to that extent deprived of the fulfillment of its potencies. The reality of change as a mode of being and the imperfection of its being are expressed in the Twelfth Book of Aristotle's *Metaphysics*. Here Aristotle points out the essential imperfection of the universe as changing, and hence imperfect, being, in contrast to the entitative perfection of the Prime Mover or Self-Thinking Thought as pure act.

In general, we consider change as the transition from one state to another. Every type of change fits under this description. For example, the transition from motion to rest or from rest to motion is a transition from one state to another. The motion from place to place is the transition from the state of being in this place to the state of being in that place. The change of a quality is the transition from this type of modification to that type of modification. A substantial change is the transition from this type of being to that type of being.

It is obvious that change must be explained in terms of potency and act. Since the transition is from something to something, we are once again faced with a result proceeding from a source. This means that the result must be explained in terms of the potencies of the source. The result came from the source only because the source had the potency to be actualized in the result. Hence, any consideration of change must be explained in terms of potency. And potency, in material beings, is ultimately rooted in primary matter.

Immediately, then, we can eliminate substantial changes in spiritual entities. Change is fundamentally based upon the parts of a body. A body is changeable because it is composed of parts and can be resolved into its parts. Spiritual beings do not have parts, and hence, any change as regards them is accidental to them. Their changes are those of relationships, not of intrinsic potency in relation to act. Their potency is their essence in relation to act. Any changes in angels, for example, are not *in* them and *from* them but *between* them and other entities.

Furthermore, purely metaphysical changes are not properly changes at all, because there is no development from one contrary (*terminus a quo*, or "former state") to another contrary (*terminus ad quem*, or "later state") according to the potencies of the subject. Such purely metaphysical states are creation, annihilation, and transubstantiation.

Creation is the production of the entire being from nothing. In other words, creation does not presuppose any material cause. Any true change is from a material cause, that is, from the subject deprived of a perfection at the inception of change and actualized or perfected by it at the terminus of the process. In creation, there is the making of the entire being, essence and existence, and in the case of bodies, matter-form-essence and existence. Creation is not *from* nothing. It is simply the instantaneous appearance of being by the creative power of God where before there was nothing.

Annihilation is the reduction of being to nothing. In every natural change there is always some residue, that is, some being at the end of the process. Annihilation, then, would take the direct action of God who alone has the power to reduce to nothing the beings He has called into existence. It would, however, seem to be contrary to the divine wisdom to destroy utterly what is naturally indestructible. Hence, we must interpret the scriptural accounts of the end of the world not as the destruction of the universe but rather the end of the human race, perhaps by some natural cataclysm or perhaps by divine intervention. A natural cataclysm might be, for example, some deviation of the earth's orbit that would bring it closer to the sun, brought about by some foreign interplanetary body coming close to the earth or moon. Perhaps, although it is a remote possibility, the sun might collapse and become the kind of exploding star that we call a *nova.* On the other hand, this period of destruction might be the result of ultimate war. At any event, although God could annihilate the universe, it would seem that such an act would run counter to His wisdom, governance, and providence. Any such destruction would better be considered as the rearrangement of conditions in the universe, fatal to man but not involving the utter annihilation of matter.

Transubstantiation is the total conversion of one complete being into another complete being. It is not the annihilation of one and the substitution of a newly created being. It is a change that goes beyond ordinary material change. In the latter, there is the reorganization of matter according to its components into another material being. However, something of the old passes over into the new in that the potency of the secondary matter that is reorganized is always awaiting fulfillment in the newly organized product. It is an exchange of determinations or forms, and is sometimes called a formal change. In transubstantiation, every particle of the old becomes the new. It goes beyond an exchange of forms or a process of reorganization. The whole being, matter and form, becomes the new being with its matter and form.

The only example of transubstantiation that we know of is in the sacrament of the Blessed Eucharist. In this case, the bread becomes the Body and Blood of our Lord, and the wine becomes the Blood and Body of our Lord. We know of no cases of transubstantiation in any other order. It is possible, otherwise the Blessed Eucharist would be impossible, but it seems beyond the powers of created agents to bring it about.

TRUE CHANGE

In this chapter we will be concerned with changes or motions in the strict sense, the ones with which we are familiar from our experience. These are those transitions, modifications, and incessant movements characterizing the universe of sensible existents; and they can all be explained, as will become evident, in terms of potency and act within things, set in operation by the ordinary forces and causes in the universe.

Before giving a proper definition of change, it is essential to note carefully the characteristic features of change or movement and the being that is the subject of change. First and foremost, we should note, with Aristotle, that "there is no such thing as motion over and above the things. It is always with respect to substance or to quantity or to quality or to place that what changes changes" (*Physics*, III, 1, 200b32–33). Change, in other words, does not exist in itself and by itself. It is always the change of *something* which is in transition. When contemporary physicists declare that mass is fundamentally energy, it might seem as though they are denying this rather obvious fact. Nevertheless, in explaining what they mean by saying that mass is energy, they show that they recognize this truth. They are not stating that only change, energy, exists. Rather they are saying that energy and mass are two ways of viewing sensible existents, what Aristotle would call secondary matter. They are saying that things possess an inner identity that abides as the center or subject of various levels of energy, that there is a relationship between this subject and its energy levels, and that these energy levels can be predicted and charted mathematically in virtue of the abiding identity of sensible things regarded as so many units of mass. Whatever activities sensible things exhibit, whatever modifications they may undergo, all in some way or another proceed *from* them as their source. In other words, any individual sensible thing contains within itself the capacity or potency for the various energy levels it may attain.

Seen in the light of potency and act, change or motion may be defined, as in Aristotle, as "*the fulfillment of what exists potentially* in so far as it exists potentially" (*Physics*, III, 1, 201a10–11). After some words of comment on this definition, we shall proceed to examine the various types of change characterizing the world of mobile or sensible things, that is, the physical universe of our experience.

Our definition contains three elements, which must be exemplified and explained: (1) motion or change is fulfillment or act; (2) it is the fulfillment of the potential; (3) it is the fulfillment of the potential precisely as potential.

1. Motion is fulfillment or act. A changing, moving thing was, prior to its movement, not in motion. Yet it was in potency for motion; that is, it *could* move. Were it incapable of moving or changing, it is obvious that it would never move or change. When, then, it *is* moving or changing, it is obviously no longer in a state of potency for motion but in a state of act. An example will help. A green leaf turning yellow in the fall is no longer *merely* in potency to be yellow. It is, however, not yet actually yellow, but turning or becoming yellow. Thus we are led to say that what was previously in a potential state had a potency to two acts. The first is a perfect act; in the present case, this is the leaf already yellow. The second is an imperfect act, the act illustrated by the leaf turning or becoming yellow. This is the act of motion or change. It is act, because it is fulfilling a potential state of the green leaf. Yet, it is imperfect act, because it does not completely fulfill the potency of the green leaf to *be* actually yellow.

Corresponding to the distinction between perfect act and imperfect act is a twofold potency within the being that changes or moves: a potency to become and a potency to be. The leaf that is green has both a potency to become yellow and a potency to be yellow. The act of the first kind of potency is the act or fulfillment that we call motion or change; the act of the second kind of potency is the term or end or result of motion.

2. Motion is of the potential. Motion or change is the fulfillment or act of the potential. Only a being in potency can be affected by change or movement. Once a potency is fulfilled the movement or change corresponding to it is completed. Thus, for example, a cooked goose cannot any longer undergo the change from being uncooked to being cooked. It can indeed undergo other changes, but precisely as a potency for being a cooked goose it is completely fulfilled, actualized. It is for this reason, as we have seen, that immaterial beings, such as God and angels, cannot undergo change or motion in the proper and strict sense.

3. Motion is of the potential precisely as potential. The explanation of this element of our definition of motion is more difficult than that of the first two elements. Yet it is the most important element in the definition, for it signifies that the act which motion is is an act that is *continuing, changing, ever proceeding on.* The thing to see is this: why not define motion or change as the "act of fulfillment of the potential"? Why must we add the words "precisely as potential"? The reason can be seen in this way. Were we to identify motion with the act of the potential we would be speaking of motion as *already complete.* We would be referring to the term or result or completion of the movement or change, not to the movement itself. Take our green leaf that becomes a yellow leaf. If we defined motion simply as the act of the potential, then we would be referring to act making the leaf *actually yellow,* we would be referring to the state of the leaf once it had already become yellow. But the motion or change that the green leaf undergoes in passing from the state of being green to the state of being yellow is not the act whereby the leaf is ultimately yellow. The latter is the perfect act to which we referred before. Motion or change is rather the imperfect act stretching from the prior state of being green to the final state of being yellow. It is for this reason that the words "precisely as potential" are essential in our definition of motion or change.

TYPES OF PHYSICAL CHANGE

You will recall, perhaps, our previous citation from Aristotle, in which he was emphasizing that motion or change is not something over and above the things that change or move. As he so shrewdly noted, change or motion "is always with respect to substance or to quantity or to quality or to place" (*Physics*, III, 1, 200b32–33). If we analyze this statement of the Stagirite, we shall see that motion or change is fundamentally of two distinct kinds: substantial and accidental, and the latter of these may be subdivided into three distinct groups. A change is substantial or accidental depending on whether the termination achieved, the result of the act of motion, is a new identity or a new modification of a persisting identity. Accidental changes are subdivisible into: (1) purely spatial change, local motion (Aristotle's change of place); (2) qualitative change, the most proper form of change in modifications, alteration; and (3) vital change, the modifications involved in organic processes, corresponding to the change in quantity noted by Aristotle.

Substantial change is in the order of autonomous identity, autonomous existence. It is the actuation of a new and different type of autonomous form on the part of the primary matter of an old autonomous entity. It must be noted that the change is by way of the actuation of potencies on the part of an already existing substance. The new comes from the old.

The process of the actuation of the new is called *generation*. Its simplest definition has been advanced by St. Thomas Aquinas: *change toward the acquisition of a form* (*motus ad formam*). Since it is the fulfillment of potencies of something already existing as a definite actualized essence, it involves the breakdown of the old. This breakdown is called *corruption*, and is defined as: *change from a form* (*motus a forma*).

The generation of one thing is the corruption of another. This is a precise way of saying that change is never by creation and annihilation. In this, the determination of what is generation or what is corruption depends upon two points: (1) whether the terminant of the process is higher or lower ontologically than the source; and (2) whether it is considered more or less desirable.

Generation and corruption as the directions of change, the terminations and sources respectively, are examples of conservation as necessary to any sound philosophical theory. The new comes from the old by rearrangement of the old according to the natural tendencies of the old and of the energies acting upon it. Since change is never creation and annihilation, it always involves rearrangement. This fits most closely with the fundamental principles of bodies. The possibility or potentiality of change is in the source, the *material cause*, according to its intrinsic potentiality, or primary matter, which is involved in its composition of parts. The change terminates in something new with a new essence as the fulfillment of the potentialities of the source. This new formal termination, necessary for the full actuation of primary matter into existence, is the *formal cause*. Energy and activity are necessary to actualize the potentialities involved, and hence we must have an *efficient cause*. Finally, appetites, or tendencies, or privations guide the direction both of the change and of the efficient cause. In other words, *final causality* is involved.

Accidental change more or less fulfills the fundamental conditions and requirements of change. It does not do so perfectly because the fundamentals are presumed in substantial changes. An accidental change is the *acquisition or exchange of modifications* in a substance that retains its identity. Among these modifications are location, quality, and vital processes.

Local motion or change in place is not the acquisition of a form. It is, however, the fulfillment of a potency within material things for a new location. In this way it fulfills both the general description of change as a transition and the proper definition as the actuality of a being in potency insofar as it is in potency. Although there is no absolute place and everything is in motion in relation to everything else, bodies are at relative rest with their immediate local surroundings. In this way, then, there can be motion from place to place. Any such motion is the fulfillment of potency to a new location.

In connection with local motion or movement from place to place, it is necessary to take up the question of inertia. The law of inertia was formulated by Isaac Newton in the seventeenth century A.D. Nevertheless, Aristotle, writing in the fourth century before Christ, touched upon the principles involved in his discussion of the void advocated by the atomists. Aristotle maintained that there is no need to postulate a void in nature to explain the motion of bodies, and one of his arguments (one attempting to reduce his adversaries to absurdity) ran as follows:

> Further [on the supposition of a void], no one could say why a thing once set in motion should stop anywhere; for why should it stop *here* rather than *here*? So that a thing will either be at rest or must be moved

> *ad infinitum*, unless something more powerful get in its way (*Physics*, IV, 8, 214b20–215a22).

Moreover, Aristotle also held that all bodies would fall at the same rate of speed in a void, if a void existed or was possible (cf. *Physics*, 216a17–21).

Although Aristotle himself argued against the existence of a void or vacuum, it is highly interesting to note that he came to the same conclusions regarding the motion of bodies in a void as did Newton. Newton, of course, idealized the situation by making the void or vacuum and the laws that would regulate the motion of bodies in a void the *desideratum* for handling movement in a highly efficient mathematical way. Yet modern physicists realize that a perfect void is impossible. In fact, the modern "vacuum" tubes and the notion of a vacuum in contemporary physics is far from the "void" of Aristotle. For the latter, the void was non-being as such, pure nothingness. For modern physics, the vacuum is pervaded by forces of various kinds. It is no way equivalent to non-being, to nothingness.

Nevertheless, it will be useful to examine more closely the reasoning leading Aristotle to his conclusions both that there is no void in nature and that, were a void possible, all bodies would fall within it at the same rate of speed and would continue moving infinitely in the same direction if unimpeded.

First let us put Aristotle's statement in its context. It is really a dialectical or hypothetical argument, which can be formulated in this way: if there is a void, then a body once set in motion will not stop anywhere. Aristotle denies the consequent of this hypothetical syllogism, for he believed that experience clearly showed us that moving bodies do actually stop somewhere. Consequently, he effectively denied the antecedent of this syllogism to establish his point that there is no void in nature. Arguing more positively, Aristotle put forth two basic defenses to his proposition that a void does not exist in nature. The first is that a void is not necessary to explain movement, as those who postulated it thought. Replacement, the fact that one body is moved out of the way to allow room or passage for another, suffices to handle the difficulties they had encountered.

His second argument is based on the experience common to all of us, and to the chariot drivers of Aristotle's day, that once a body is set in motion it tends to keep in motion. We notice this when, in driving, we apply the brakes. The car tends to keep moving so much so that deceleration is often a marked strain and a car cannot stop in time. This is not necessarily because the brakes were applied too late. It is because the car tends to keep on moving.

As explained by Aristotle, motion is twofold: (1) natural, free motion; and (2) motion by constraint, motion constantly subject to forces. In neither case does motion, considered in itself, explain its own stopping. (1) If the motion is free, there is nothing to stop it. (2) If it is by constraint, the constraint is from the outside. As he points out: ". . . the medium causes a difference because it impedes the moving thing . . . especially a medium that is not easily divided, i.e., a medium that is somewhat dense . . ." (*Physics*, IV, 9, 215a29 and 30).

This is the same argument as that developed by Galileo and Newton, except that Galileo added that the medium evens out the mass velocity — speed — of the moving object, while Newton pointed out that further forces are needed to change the directional velocity of the moving body. It is interesting to notice about Newton that, in treating of this (cf. *Principia*, Axioms I, II, and III), he regards it as a physical fact about which he then constructs the proper geometry and calculus.

Actually, Aristotle's statement about the movement of bodies in a void is a restatement of potency and act in relation to a quality, the quality of local motion. Motion, imperfect as it may be compared to being or to the state of a movable thing once the terminus of the motion has been reached, is nevertheless an act in the category of quality. Thus a body actualized by motion as its act tends to continue not only in physical existence but also in the mode of that existence. The modern problem of the perfection of motion in itself as opposed to the Aristotelian treatment of body-in-motion is a point of mathematical-physical theory, exemplified in lines and curves on a graph, rather than of cosmology.

Alteration, or qualitative change, is "the transition to and through the full realization of a quality." A quality is an accidental modification. Qualitative changes are somewhat different than substantial changes not only insofar as they are accidental but also in the matter of their further changes. The first acquisition of a quality by a subject may be called generation. However, there can be *gradual* changes within the full range of the quality. A substance is or is not, and there is no middle term between these extremes. There can be degrees of a quality. A flower either is or is not a rose. Once that is determined, however, there can be degrees of the redness of the rose. That is why we define qualitative changes as the transition not only to but also *through* the full realization of a quality. Thus, although the first possession of a quality is instantaneous, the further development is gradual and temporal. Fundamentally, this is explained by greater participation in the quality on the part of the potency of the subject.

Organic development is the perfecting of an organism in its growth. This is its fundamental growth by intussusception, by the manufacture of its own cells and organs. This is primarily quantitative, but is also qualitative insofar as it affects figure, density, etc. This is accidental as long as the subject remains the same, and in its details is more properly a biological study.

IMPORTANT CONSEQUENCES OF CHANGE

There are two important facts to be considered about change. The first of these is that change itself is not subsistent. This is true whether it be local motion or substantial change. Qualitative change does not enter here since, properly, it demands a subject and pushes the problem back into substantial change.

Philosophers have disagreed about this point. Even though Heraclitus seems to have been a moral philosopher, some of his followers attempted to maintain that reality *is* change. This would be substantial change. At a later time, under the influence of John Locke, whose doctrine reduced substance to the sum of the qualities of a body, there have been those who maintain that there is no substance, no qualities, only change.

Their arguments are based upon the fact that there is no such thing as static being. Yet they misunderstand the nature of substance, which is persistent and autonomous identity, no matter how much activity there may be in its structure and activity. The consideration of substance as autonomous identity is the key to the understanding of this problem. A being cannot be pure change. If that were so, it would never retain any of its identity from instant to instant, from moment to moment. Since it would always be changing, it would always be something else. Nevertheless, it retains its identity, no matter how active, even how explosively active it may be. Hence, we must conclude that the existence of change points to the deeper and more fundamental existence of being. We must further conclude that material being is extremely active in its material components.

If, at any stage in the process of any change, no matter what, we could interrupt it and reduce it to a purely static state, we would always find a being or beings. They would be beings in potency for the completion of the change, but they would be beings. Earlier in this work we saw that the approach to the consideration of potency and act, matter and form, began through change. We saw that in every change there is something of the old in the new, something of the source in the product. This was called the *substratum*. Generally, this substratum is simply called primary matter. More properly, it is material being in potency. The actual substratum, it must be repeated, is material being in potency. However, the change itself must be traced back to the fundamental principle, primary matter. Beings do not change unless they can change. This changeability, then, is the fundamental principle of actual change, and this principle is primary matter. It is in this way that we speak of primary matter as the substratum involved in change.

A second consequence of our consideration of change is the formulation of the principle of efficient causality. The first formulation of this was by Aristotle, and is worded as: "ἅπαν τὸ κινούμενον ὑπὸ τινος ἀνάγκη κινεῖισθαι." This is translated into Latin as: *Quidquid movetur ab alio movetur*, which, in turn, is translated into English as follows: "Whatever is moved is moved by another." This statement has little meaning in English, and its rather poor, tautological expression is the result of poor translations. In Greek, there is a middle voice, besides the active and passive voices. The middle voice governs intransitive actions. In English, when we say: "I ride," the verb "to ride" has no direct object. In Greek, the middle voice, λύομαι, is used. In form, the middle voice is exactly the same in much of its conjugations as the passive voice, and unless a translator is alert, he is liable to translate the middle voice, which is active but not transitive in meaning, into a passive meaning. This is what happened in Aristotle's statement about causality.

The original meaning of Aristotle's statement of causality is: whatever changes or moves is changed or moved by another. As pointed out by St. Thomas, the full meaning of this is that no potency reduces itself to act. We have seen this illustrated in our consideration of change. A capacity does not fulfill itself. A potency does not actualize itself. The reason for this is that in relation to its proper act, the potency is a deprivation, a non-being that should be. However, non-being is inoperative, and the fulfillment must be by something else. This something else, whatever it may be, is the efficient cause. This efficient cause may be the energies in the universe or it may be a clearly recognized agent. However, some actuality must be the extrinsic principle of reduction to actuality.

In contemporary philosophy as well as in physical theory the principle of causality is not widely recognized. Causality is recognized. After all, every thinker is trying to recognize the responsible principle explicative of phenomena. However, since Francis Bacon's time, causality has been associated with the attempt to identify the responsible cause. Frequently we are unable to do so. In fact, statistically, it is morally impossible to recognize many causes. If the principle of causality depended upon the identification of the cause in every instance, then we could not maintain it. However, as we have seen, the principle of causality in scholastic philosophy is approached not through the attempt to recognize or identify the cause in every instance but through the realization of the insufficiency of the effect to explain its own becoming. Hence, the principle of causality really means that what is unable to explain its own coming-to-be demands an explanation in something else. This something else is the cause.

COROLLARY

There is one other problem we must face here. One of the points involved in the special relativity theory of Albert Einstein is the transformation of mass into energy. This is expressed in the formula: $E = mc^2$. Many have interpreted this to mean that a substance can be transformed into a quality. Actually, that is not the case at all, nor is such an interpretation proper to this point of relativity physics. Actually in this case both *mass* and *energy* are concepts descriptive of the fact that bodily being is intrinsically energetic. The Einsteinian equation is expressive of the rate of energy within the structure of any body. It has a long history.

The problem developed from quantum theory. The latter, advanced as an explanation of radiation by Max Planck at the turn of the twentieth century, sought to reconcile two theories of the nature of light. Sir Isaac Newton, while working with prisms, noticed that as light enters a denser medium it bends in a fashion characteristic of the mechanics of bodies. He concluded that light consists of extremely small particles. On the other hand, Newton's contemporary, Christian Huyghens, noticed that light has some wave characteristics. In transmission, it has many of the characteristics of the waves that we find in the ripples of water or any other liquid. Hence, he concluded that light consists of waves, and his point of view prevailed for many years.

Toward the end of the nineteenth century, Roentgen's discovery of x rays and the discovery of radioactivity by Becquerel and the Curies again focused scientific attention on the possibility that radiation consists of particles. This was verified by Sir J. J. Thomson in the Crookes tube experiments wherein he discovered the mass of the electron. The radiation of electrical energy gave off all the properties of the emission of particles.

Max Planck assumed that both the wave and particle characteristic of radiation could be maintained if we could hold that emission consists of bundles — *quanta* — of particles. the individual *photons* (as he called the particles) would give the particle effects whereas their grouping in bundles would give the wave properties. We can visualize this is we think of the puffs of smoke in a steam locomotive. The actual smoke consists of individual particles of carbon and sulphur compounds. Yet the groupings give off wave properties.

A wave is a traveling influence not necessarily requiring a medium. If there is a medium, as, for example, water, there is a certain amount of material displacement. Medium or not, however, a wave is always energy. Since the experiments of Michelson and Morley, in Cleveland, Ohio, in 1887 showed that there is no evidence of any universal medium (called the *ether*), people began to look upon waves as pure energy having mass effects. Einstein, knowing nothing of the Michelson-Morley experiments and not being particularly interested in ether, looked to the quantum theory from another point of view. Scientists such as Sir James Jeans had been interested in the wave-particle properties of light, and in order to discover more about it, had been carrying on intricate experiments. Among these was the transmission of light through slit screens of gold. The supposition was that if light consists of particles, these particles would accumulate on the target area in the form of a glow. If, on the other hand, light consists of waves, the alternate crests and troughs would set up a pattern of diffraction rings. This is exactly what happened, as in the diagram below.

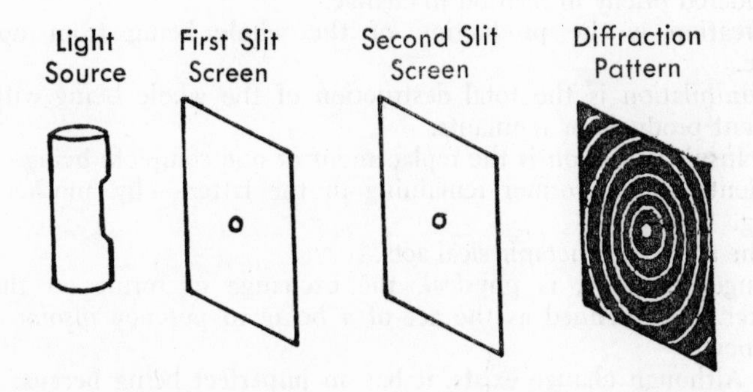

This posed a further problem. Experiments with prisms indicate that light consists of particles. So does electron radiation. On the other hand, the interruption of light in transmission seems to argue that radiation is waves. Einstein developed the quantum theory by assuming that it is both. In emission and reception, radiation is particles with mass properties. In transmission, it is waves. Particles can be handled under the concept of *mass*, whereas waves are treated under the concept of *energy*. Hence, radiation has both mass and energy properties. The formula: $E = mc^2$ simply tells us how much energy these particles have, or, conversely, the fact that in given states energy has mass.

Furthermore, radio theory and the conclusions of nuclear and atomic physics show that anything can radiate electrons. Simply by heating any solid sufficiently, it emits electrons. This is called thermionic radiation. These electrons are considered particles. In their transmission they are considered waves. The waves proceed from the mass of the body, and hence mass is considered to be transformed into energy, once again at the rate of mc^2.

This does not mean that substance is transformed into a quality. Substance is the sufficient reason for a thing's identity and autonomy. Mass is a quality of matter. So is energy. Hence, $E = mc^2$ simply indicates the transformation of one quality into another, and in a sense is no more unusual than the transformation of the same substance, water, into a solid, a liquid, and a gas.

SUMMARY

1. Change, in general, is the transition from one state of being to another state of being.
2. Although creation and annihilation are not properly change, they are considered briefly in relation to change.

   Creation is the production of the whole being from no material cause.

   Annihilation is the total destruction of the whole being with no consequent products or remnants.

   Transubstantiation is the replacement of one complete being — only the accidents of the former remaining in the latter — by another complete being.

   The above are *metaphysical* acts.
3. Change, properly, is *physical*, the exchange of forms on the part of matter. It is defined as the *act of a being in potency insofar as it is in potency*.

   Although change exists, it has an imperfect being because its nature it is on the way to fulfillment.
4. Changes are: *substantial* — change to another identity; *quantitative* — change in size; *qualitative* (alteration) — change to and through a quality; and *local* — movement from place to place.
5. Change does not subsist in itself. It is always the change of some subject.

CHAPTER EIGHT

QUANTITY and EXTENSION

One of the most obvious characteristics of bodies is that they are spread out, that they have some extension. Any body, however minute, has some extension simply because a body cannot consist of points. As we have seen, the divisibility of bodies is an indication of their fundamental changeability. There are few, if any, properties of any created substance as close to their subject as extension is to bodily substances.

The question then arises of the relationship between bodies and quantity, between bodily substance and extension. All bodies are necessarily extended, and whatever is extended is a body. Does this mean that extension and body are identical, that extension is the essence of bodily substance?

A number of philosophers and scientists have identified bodily substance with extension. Some of the more important proponents of this thesis are the materialists and René Descartes. Gottfried Wilhelm von Leibniz may also be regarded as upholding the identity of bodily matter with extension, although we must note that for him any genuine substance — which he calls a monad — is spiritual in nature, matter being in reality a subordinate grouping of monads which provide functional aids to the clarification of the perceptions of the dominant monad or entelechy which confers upon the being in question its unity and substantiality. We shall briefly consider these representatives of the thesis that bodily substance is extension and then offer some of the more important reasons for affirming that extension is really distinct from the substance of bodily things.

It is not too surprising that materialists should maintain the identity of bodily substance and quantity. After all, they maintain that all being is matter, thereby shutting off any consideration of being as non-material. Since he is committed to the basic supposition that the only being is that which can be perceived by the senses, the materialist naturally concludes that only bodies are genuinely beings, genuinely substances. Moreover, since bodies are perceived by the senses solely because of their character as extended masses, it is again only natural that the materialist should identify bodily substance with extension or quantity.

Descartes, the founder of modern rationalism, approached the problem of the relationship of bodily substance to quantity from the point of view of the mathematician. This was in large measure the result of his own training in mathematics and of his conviction that the right method in philosophical reasoning should be modeled after the clarity and distinctness characteristic of mathematics. Using the proposition "I think, therefore I am" as the bedrock of philosophical certainty, the proposition whose truth can in no way be denied, or even doubted, Descartes continued by examining minutely what further truths could be deduced from this fundamental proposition, coming to the conclusion both that the nature of man was to be a substance "the whole essence or nature of which is to think . . . so that the 'me', that is to say, the soul by which I am what I am, is entirely distinct from body" and that "I might assume as a general rule that the things which we conceive very clearly and distinctly are all true" (*Discourse on Method,* Part IV). One immediate corollary to the thesis that man is essentially spirit or mind is that the body is not a part of man's essence or substance as man. It is rather another kind of substance in some way or another joined to mind or soul. When he turned to an examination of the essence of body, Descartes concluded that material substance or body is nothing else than an extended thing, having figure and motion. Thus, in Descartes, a radical distinction is made between mind or thinking thing, what he called *res cogitans,* and body or extended thing, what he called *res extensa.* He viewed each as a complete thing or finite substance, derived from the infinite substance, God. Mind or thinking thing is known through its proper attribute, which is thought, and body or extended thing is known through its proper attribute, which is extension (cf. *Principles of Philosophy,* I, 53). Since the proper attribute of any being is the one "which constitutes its nature and essence," then extension is the nature or essence of bodily substances.

In evaluating the position of Descartes, it may be helpful to throw into relief the difference between mathematics and a science of real beings, such as cosmology. Certainly, in analytic geometry it is true that $L(x_2,x_4y_2)^2 = L(x_2,x_4)^2 + L(x_4,y_2)^2$. This is the Pythagorean theorem represented as:

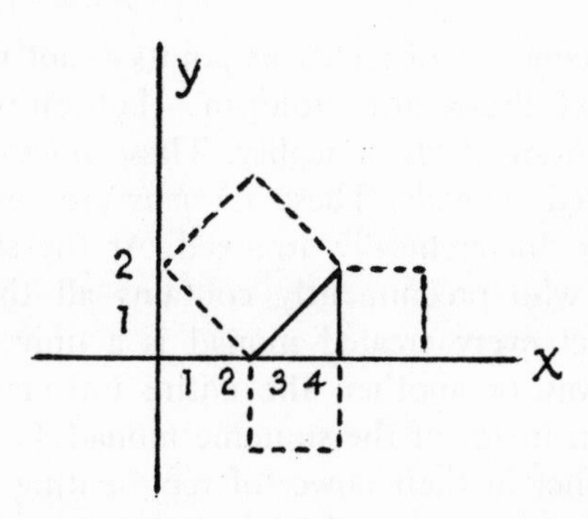

But is this certain physically? First of all, any mechanical means or human means of drawing that figure has shortcomings. As a result, I can be sure that the square of the physical hypotenuse I draw is *not* exactly the sum of the squares of the opposite sides. In my mind that is certain, but outside of my mind the lines, the physical lines objectifying that theorem, are more or less perfect since they are drawn more or less to scale, which scale is more or less accurate, etc. Furthermore, although in asking the question: "What is that figure?" I can answer that it is a triangle, in answering the same question I can also say that it is ink on paper. Ink is mostly carbon and water. Paper is cellulose, an extremely complicated carbon compound. In other words, mathematical bodies are not physical bodies. The obviousness is in the mathematical, or conceptual, or ideal, or mental bodies, not in real bodies. Hence, although the essence of mathematical bodies may be extension, the same is not true of physical bodies. They are of wood *shaped like* a triangle, metal *shaped like* a circle, polyethylene *shaped like* a sphere. However, in their essences, they are not a triangle, a circle, and a sphere. They are wood, metal, and polyethylene respectively.

Leibniz resurrected Greek atomism. The inventor of the infinitesimal calculus, he looked upon the Cartesian coordinates as approaching a point. Not only did he see geometrical figures as points on coordinates, he also visualized historical events as capable of being represented on coordinates by using the symbols *S* for space and *T* for time. Thus, let S equal England. Then, if S_1T_1 = Hastings, 1066, and S_4T_5 = Bosworth Field, 1497, the points S_2T_2, S_3T_3, and S_4T_5 could represent events in the War of the Roses. The entire series (S_1T_1–S_4T_5) could represent the Plantaganet dynasty in England.

All of this history is represented by points. It is here that atomism enters in. We can conceive of reality as points — not merely small masses after the manner of Presocratic atomism — but units filled with all of the forces and qualities of all of reality. These *microcosms*, or tiny universes, Leibniz called *monads*. These *monads* are spiritual in character. They are, moreover, hierarchically arranged. At the summit is God, the *monas monadum*, who preeminently contains all the reality found in created monads. Yet every created monad is a universe to itself, representing, in some way or another, the entire universe of being because it is in some way an image of the supreme monad, God. Created monads differ from each other in their power of representing the universe. Some are fully self-conscious, purely spiritual. Others are not fully conscious and need the assistance of other, auxiliary monads which they gather around themselves to facilitate their representations. The monad of any composite being that confers unity and substantiality upon it is called by Leibniz the entelechy of the being in question. The subordinate monads grouped around this entelechy monad to facilitate its powers of representation "extend" it, as it were, and form its "body." Extension, thus, is the same as body. But note that for Leibniz the term "body" does not indicate a genuine substance. Rather it stands for an aggregate of substances, of monads, each of which is spiritual in nature insofar as it is genuinely real.

It must be obvious by now that attempts to identify bodily substance with quantity and extension are fundamentally attempts to identify ideas with matter. In every case we have seen that although the conclusions of the philosophers who try to identify bodily substance with extension may achieve logical rigidity and cohesion in the intellectual order, their conclusions fail when applied to the very matter which is the object of their theories. This breakdown in the face of matter is the basis of our arguments to show the distinction between body and extension.

There are two arguments to show the real distinction between bodily substance and quantity or extension. The first has to do with an analysis of the nature of any body in itself. The second is based on how we learn of bodies and of quantity.

First argument. All bodies are extended. All bodies have some sort of identity and some sort of autonomy. Hence, they are either individual substances or aggregations of individual substances. At any event, their autonomy and their existence is due to their substantiality and their identity.

With this as background, we argue thus:

1. If extension and quantity are identical with substance, any change

in quantity will be a change in substance. A quantitative change would mean a change in identity.

2. However, such is not the case. There are many changes, quantitative and qualitative, in a substance persisting in its identity. For example, we can fuse gold into one dense lump. We can also hammer it out into a widespread, extremely thin sheet. Yet it still remains gold. Again, the fact of growth is a quantitative change. Hence, if quantity were the same as substance, when a small tree or a young dog matured, each would be constantly undergoing substantial changes. Obviously this is not the case.

3. Hence, since changes in quantity do not necessarily involve changes in identity in such way that the body becomes another existence, we cannot say that quantity and bodily substance are identical. Somehow, they are different, really different.

Second argument. There is a real distinction between that which demands a sufficient reason for its existence and the sufficient reason itself.

1. We perceive quantity intuitively. All of our sense perceptions, which are intuitive, depend upon the extension of matter. We see because light comes from a source across a distance and reflects off a surface. We hear because sound waves travel through an extended medium. We feel because there is sufficient extension in the object of our senses to offer them resistance. In other words, quantity is the intuitive object of sense knowledge.

2. On the other hand, we soon perceive that quantity or extension is not self-existent, self-sufficient. It is always the extension of *something*. It must be explained in terms of something self-sufficient, something autonomous, some independent subject, as its sufficient reason. We call this sufficient reason *substance*.

3. Since there is a real distinction between that which needs the sufficient reason and the sufficient reason itself, there is a real distinction between substance and quantity.

If quantity and substance are not identical, and yet never naturally separated from each other, what is the type of distinction between them? We say that it is a *minor real distinction*. By this we mean that, although quantity *is not* substance, still, they are not separable. In brief, there are two kinds of distinction: *logical*, the distinction between different ideas of the same thing, and *real*, the distinction between different things.

Real distinctions depend upon concepts, of course, but concepts which indicate that their objects are not identical. This non-identity may be obvious from the separability of the two objects. We are told that the

American Indians first thought that a man on a horse was one object until they saw a Spaniard fall from a horse. The separation showed the obvious difference between the horse and the man. The difference between objects apparent to the senses because of separability is called a *major* real distinction.

There are cases where one thing *is not* the other, but there is no separation between them. For example, when a body moves, it moves at a rate of speed in relation to something relatively at rest. Hence a body moves swiftly or slowly, and its motion can accelerate or slow down. Hence, there is such a thing as a rate of speed. The rate of speed is not identical with the motion of the body. Movement implies a rate of speed, and there is no movement without a rate of speed and there is no rate of speed without movement. Yet the one is not the other. They are really distinct but not separable. Such is a *minor real distinction.*

Since, as we have seen, there is no body without quantity and extension and no extension without body, we conclude that *the distinction between bodily substance and quantity is a minor real distinction.*

THE NATURE OF QUANTITY

What, then, is quantity? To determine this, we must return to our original problem. As we say, quantity is the universal property of all bodies. There is no body without extension and no extension without a body. Substance is identity, autonomous essence. Extension is the physical state of "spread-outness." Since substance is not identical with extension, there must be some principle *whereby a substance has extension.* This is quantity, and is defined as: the *absolute accident whereby a material substance has parts outside of parts.*

1. Quantity is an *absolute* accident. This simply means that quantity is an accident modifying the substance in itself, without considering any relationship that might exist between that substance and other substances. If there were only one body in the universe, it would have extension in virtue of quantity. Its extension would not depend upon any other body. Hence, quantity, the principle of extension, is absolute, not relative.

2. *Parts outside of parts* simply means that the body is not a point. One side is not the other. The top is not the bottom. One end is not the other end. This property of parts outside of parts is, most properly, extension. The term "extension" is simply the Latin term for "stretched out."

Briefly, then, a substance is extended through quantity. The parts are the parts of the substance. They are extended by quantity.

PRIMARY AND SECONDARY EFFECTS OF QUANTITY

The consequences of quantity are called the *formal effects*. Formal effects are not necessarily the effects of action, since in this case quantity does not "do" anything efficiently. Formal effects are consequences of a given determination or disposition. The formal effects of quantity are the consequences of the presence of quantity as a principle. They are twofold: primary and secondary.

Extension, or the possession of integral parts, is the primary effect of quantity. Once again, a material substance has parts because of quantity. Hence, the first consequence of quantity is that the body has parts, i.e., is spread out. This is, again, extension. Extension is therefore the first formal effect of quantity.

The parts have a twofold formality. Insofar as they are the parts of *the substance*, they have a substantial formality. Yet *as parts* they have an accidental formality. Thus a man's hand is not identical with the man. It inheres in the man and is an accident. Yet it is a man's hand, and as long as it is a part *of the man*, it has a substantial aspect or formality. Here we must remember that the nature of quantity is not, of itself, to introduce plurality. Plurality follows on quantity. Its nature is simply to be a principle of the distribution of the parts of the substance. Hence, quantity is only incidentally a principle of division and plurality.

Since no body is infinite, it has edges, and consequently its *parts are distributed in a definite manner*. This manner or mode of distribution is the first secondary effect of quantity following upon the first effect which is the distribution of parts.

The manner whereby parts are distributed is called *figure*. Hence, figure is the first secondary effect of quantity. Primarily, figure refers to the body itself, to the relationship of parts to the whole and to each other. This is another example of what we mean when we call quantity an absolute accident. Were there only one body in the universe, there would still be extension and figure.

Figure in relationship to surroundings is called *position*. When we say that a body is erect, vertical, horizontal, supine, etc., we say that it is vertical or horizontal *in relation to* something else. An isolated body simply is extended and figured, but not erect or supine, as the principles of space science are beginning to make clear. In Latin, this is called *situs,* and is the next secondary effect of quantity.

The general relationship of a body to its surroundings and to other bodies is called *place.* The area background of a body is called *space.*

Hence, the first formal effect of quantity is the distribution of parts, or extension. The secondary formal effects are the manner of distribution, or figure, and figure's relationships with surroundings: position, place, and space.

PLACE AND SPACE

There is no such thing as an isolated body in the universe. That is, there is a plurality of bodies. Hence, bodies have an immediate background, an immediate set of surroundings. This is called *place.* They also have a general background, a general set of surroundings in the distribution of matter in the universe. This is general place; and, as measurable, it is called *space.* Both place and space have physical and mathematical aspects. They have physical aspects because there are physical forces at work holding bodies in their places and relating them to other bodies. There are mathematical aspects because we can measure the location of a body in the geometrical distribution of matter.

Place was first defined by Aristotle as: *the innermost boundary of what contains a mobile body* (cf. *Physics,* IV, 4, 212a20). Aristotle's definition was given in the course of his discussion of the problem as to whether place was a body. As Aristotle pointed out, if place were a body, then two bodies would be simultaneously located in the same area, namely the body located and its place. Furthermore, we could then ask about the "place" of the place. After giving some examples of how a place can be a container such as a vase, and how this can be filled successively with liquids or air, which are in the container, Aristotle concluded that these surroundings are considered as a container and are called place. Thus, physically, place would be the innermost surface or surfaces of what comes into immediate contact with the body in question. Hence, the place of the tree in the plain would be the air making contact with the trunk, branches, and leaves, and the earth making contact with the roots.

Place can be both proper and general. Proper place is the place of the definition above. General place would be the surrounding neighborhood. Thus, the proper place of the second volume of an encyclopedia would be the front cover of the first volume, the back cover of the third volume, the shelf immediately under it, and the air immediately above it. Its general place would be a bookcase in a given room of a given building.

The investigation into the meaning of general place has arisen out of the problem of bodies constantly moving through a medium or of a body at rest in a moving medium. For example, if a fish under a bridge is swimming upstream at the rate of one mile an hour while the river is flowing downstream at the rate of one mile an hour, the fish remains under the bridge. Yet his proper place, the immediate surface of water enveloping him, is constantly changing. Thus, to locate or "place" the fish, we look more to general conditions than to his immediate surroundings. We then locate the fish through his relations to the bridge and to the riverbank rather than to the immediate surface of water touching him. Similarly, since the earth is constantly moving in its orbit, it does not have a proper place in terms of immediate surroundings. Hence, we call its orbit its proper place and refer it to the sun as the focus of the ellipse.

Aristotle generally associates the term "mobile body" with the definition to show that presence in a place is incidental to a body, not essential. A body can change places, and its presence in this place rather than in that place is the result of motion. A body has either moved to a place or has been put in a place. Since this is the case, a body can also change places if there are sufficient physical forces to bring this about. As a matter of fact, Aristotle looked upon the universe as a process in which bodies are generally on the go. Hence, a place is temporary and changeable. It is not a being. It is a relationship between beings. This relationship consists of the physical forces that hold a body in this place now. They might easily move it to another place some other time.

Place, then, as the immediate surroundings, consists of the relationship of a body to its physical environment as the result of physical forces. This is its proper place, because properly as a molar being it is subject to physical forces, and if these forces reach a balance bearing on the body, the body remains here rather than there. This can apply to orbits as well as to bodies. The same balance of forces applies in this case.

Since place is a relationship and not a substance, all places are relative. There is no absolute place. Place is usually judged in terms of the relationship of the smaller body to the larger body, the body on top to the body below, etc. For purposes of measurement, this is insufficient. Hence, we *select* a place, consider it absolute, and use it as a basis for measurements by considering it point zero in a coordinate system. This is *mathematical* place, and is a selected point of demarcation. For example, when we say that Baltimore is thirty-three miles northeast of Washington, we start from a Coastal Geodetic Survey marker on the lawn of the White House, and consider that point zero. There is a similar marker in Baltimore, in Mount Vernon Place on North Charles Street, which is simultaneously point thirty-three for measurements from Washington and point zero for measurements from Baltimore.

In conclusion, then, place is essentially relative. Physically, or *materially*, place is the termination of a balance of forces setting up a body in an immediate physical environment and considered as a background or container. Mathematically, or *formally*, it is an arbitrary point of demarcation as the basis for scaler (two-dimensional) and topical (three-dimensional) measurements between bodies. Any "absolute place" is a universally recognized — and hence arbitrarily selected — marker for international, interplanetary, interstellar, and intergalactic measurements. Such, for example, is Greenwich, England, which is internationally agreed upon as point zero for longitudinal measurements of the earth's surface. Interplanetary and interstellar measurements would be from the center of the sun. Intergalactic measurements would be from a point at the middle of our galaxy to a point in the middle of another galaxy such as that of Andromeda, Perseus, etc.

Sir Isaac Newton tried to ascertain an absolute place in the universe. Realizing that we do not know the size of the universe, he looked upon the "fixed stars" as quasi-absolute places. If a true absolute were required, we would have to fall back upon the omnipresence of God. This is an inversion of the true concept of omnipresence. Omnipresence means that God, who is spirit, upholds matter creatively and providentially by His power wherever matter may be.

Albert Einstein maintained that since there is no absolute place, and since all bodies are constantly changing places in relation to each other, it would be more convenient to abandon any given point, straight line, or mass as our basis, rooting the latter rather in the three-dimensional concept of the distribution of matter in relation to the times of bodily motions. Thus, relativity is a logical development of the classically philosophical concept of place both physically and mathematically.

Space, too, is both physical and mathematical. This concept is also founded on the plurality of bodies. Bodies are more or less close to each other, more or less apart from each other. Because of this, there are measureable relations between them since there is matter within them and matter between them. This matter can be measured. Even if there were no matter between bodies, the fact that they are at a distance would allow us to consider this absolute vacuum as measurable. This measurement is called space, and is defined as: *the distance within and between bodies*. The distance within bodies is called *internal space*. *External space* is the distance between bodies.

Space is a more mathematical concept than place. Place is primarily a physical relationship giving rise to measurement. Space is a measurement of the distribution of matter, regardless of the physical relationships of the individual bodies save that they are near to or far from a given point. For example, the objective basis of measurement is the distribution of matter, regardless of whether this distribution is thick or thin, solid, liquid, or gaseous, binding or tenuous. These are problems proper to place, not space. They enter into the physical process of measuring, but the measurement as such abstracts from these physical conditions. On the other hand, physical conditions must be considered when we deal with place, as will be seen when we consider relativity.

Space, as a geometrical-physical concept, has its own properties. These depend upon both geometry and physics. Geometry has its own theoretical development and its own logic wherein the norm is the validity of the deduction of concepts from other concepts. A measurement, on the other hand, is the application of a norm to a physical state. Thus, as a geometrical concept, space is immaterial, subject only to the validity of geometry. As a measurement, however, it must be applicable to things and is modified by the physical conditions to which it is applied. This has given rise to some errors in the interpretation of astronomical findings.

Theoretically, space as a geometrical concept can be developed according to the constructions of any valid geometry. In general, there are three such geometries: the rectilinear geometry of Euclid and Descartes; the positive curvature geometry of Riemann; and the negative curvature geometry of Lobarchevsky. In all three of these geometries, space is an area set up by lines. It can be two-dimensional or three-dimensional or multidimensional according to the direction of the lines. Furthermore, the direction of the lines constructs finite or infinite space.

Before proceeding any further with spatial theory, we had better make several references to reality, most particularly what we mean by "dimension" and by "infinite space." We say that any real body is three-dimensional. We also say that mathematical theory can involve many more dimensions than three. There is no contradiction between these statements if we remember that in the former case we are dealing with applied mathematics while in the latter we are dealing with theoretical mathematics.

A body has edges, and as described mathematically these edges or boundaries are called dimensions. A dimension is a linear measurement in a given direction. Direction is part of the definition of a dimension, and if there is a change in direction, there is a new dimension. Consequently, in the *theory* of measurement there are as many dimensions as there are changes in direction. Thus, in problems of projective geometry, there can be many more than three dimensions. In the *practice* of measurement we limit changes in direction to the general character of bodies. The mass of a body is extended in every direction from its central point, although more in one or two directions than in all unless the body in question is a perfect sphere. In a mathematical linear measurement of this mass, that is, in a dimension, if we start in one direction, we have a measurement of the body's length. We change direction to measure its width. That makes two dimensions. We make another change and, hence, have another dimension, to measure its depth. That is all we need: an initial direction and two other changes to describe the mass properties of bodies. This is what we mean when we say a body is three-dimensional. We need no more than three directions. Yet, since there are many problems of moving bodies involving frequent and regular changes in directions, three-dimensional bodies moving in a three-dimensional distribution of background matter may require a multidimensional theory.

Concerning the concept of the infinite, we have already seen that metaphysically the infinite is that being which has no limitations whatsoever. This, in reality, is God and God alone. The mathematical infinite varies according to the context in which it figures. In other words, there is a lack of limitation within the definition of the mathematical entity, whether it is a number series or space constructed from lines.

Any number sequence, line, area, or volume that does not close back on or limit itself is a mathematical infinite. For example, we can have an infinite series of *prime numbers*. Prime numbers are those which are divisible by one and by themselves. They are 1, 2, 3, 5, 7, 11, 13, 17, 19, 23, 29, 31. . . . We cannot prove that there is any prime number that is the end of the series, and so we say that it is an *infinite series*. This, of course, means that it is infinite from a given point of view and in a given context. No individual number is infinite, since it is divisible if it is an even number and will become divisible by the addition or subtraction of one, if it is an odd number. Since the series consists of components, it is not *really* infinite. It is infinite by *theoretical definition*.

We speak in a similar fashion of lines and areas. A circle, sphere, or cylinder closes back on itself. Geometrically it is finite. On the other hand, the axes x and y of the Cartesian coordinates continue to extend thus:

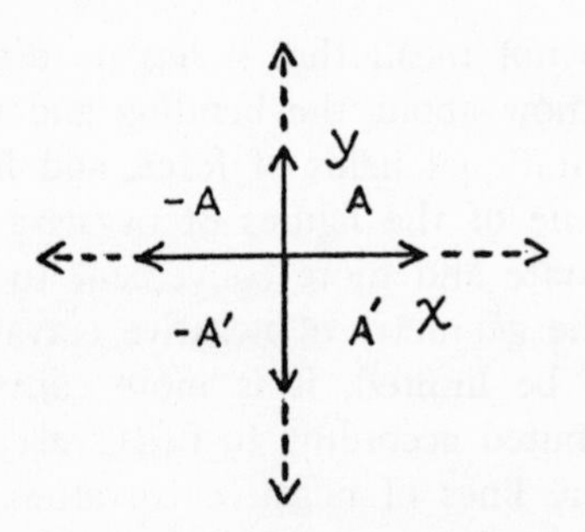

The areas A, –A, A′, and –A′ are called infinite. There is no reason for these areas to close back upon themselves. They are not self-limiting.

The same is true for curves and curved areas. Curved lines and curved areas which close back upon themselves are called positive, and are finite. Curved areas and curved lines which do not close back upon themselves are called negative and are infinite.

We cannot say whether the curve C is infinite or not, but we can say that the curve C′ is non-closing and, thus, infinite. Also, the curved area A_c is finite, whereas A_c' is infinite. So is the negative sphere, that is, a theoretically inverted, or inside-out, sphere shaped somewhat like the cover of a baseball or the shape of a saddle, since from points P and P′, the curved area diverges in every direction, because the figure is constructed out of non-converging parabolae.

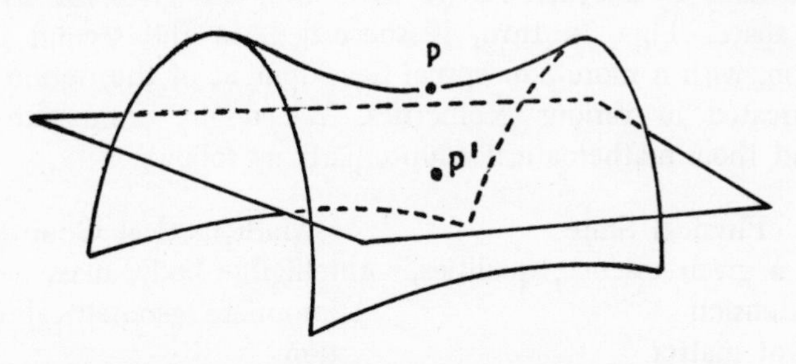

Notice that these figures, as physical entities, are neither physically nor metaphysically infinite. They are measurable lines on paper. Hence, they are physically limited. So much the less can they be metaphysically infinite.

When astronomers and physical cosmologists discuss the infinity of the universe, they do not mean that it has no dimensions. They mean that from what we know about the bending and direction of light, we can say that the gravitational fields of force, and hence the distribution of matter, resemble one of the figures of negative curvature. Since this is so, it is more accurate and more convenient to measure it according to the theorems of the geometry of negative curvature of Lobarchevsky. Even though it may be limited, it is more convenient to consider it either infinitely distributed according to negative curvature or expanding in the direction of the lines of negative curvature.

Some of the above points are taken from the theory of projective geometry. Some are an application of that geometry in a theory of measurement. As seen earlier, measurement is the meeting of mathematical theory with physical conditions. Mathematical theory begins with two real physical conditions: the continuity of the matter of one or several bodies, called the *continuum;* and the *plurality* of bodies. The former gives rise to geometries. The latter gives rise to arithmetics and calculations.

Here we are interested in the continuum. This is *an even distribution of matter within one set of boundaries*. This is more theoretical than actual, however, since matter seems to be made up of particles having fields of force between them. If the continuum is interrupted, it is called an *imperfect continuum*. This seems to be the general order in nature. However, it can still be *considered* as even, and it is said to *flow* from one boundary to the other.

Whether the continuum is perfect or imperfect, it ends in boundaries. Furthermore, between bodies the distribution of matter is said to flow from one body to another. As we have seen, this gives rise to the concept of space. This, in turn, is succeeded, in the second degree of abstraction, with a more conceptual development of the notion of space, and is treated in various geometries. We might summarize the real states and their mathematical counterparts as follows:

Physical State	**Mathematical Counterpart**
Body of a given essence, qualities, and extension	Intelligible body, mass
Amount of matter	Appropriate geometrical consideration
Boundaries	Dimensions
Apartness	Space
Distribution of matter	Conceptual space
Three-dimensional	As many dimensions are required by the problem.

Physics takes a neutral stand in this question. It simply considers the size and density of bodies and calls this *mass*. It considers a substance as a *portion of mass* rather than as an autonomous essence in the order of existence. Frequently it overlooks the matter between bodies and speaks of "empty space." The force relations between the bodies are expressed by considering the bodies as enormous points and the force between them as a straight line (classical mechanics) or a three-dimensional force with given permeability or impermeability (relativity mechanics). In the former case, the "point-mass relationship," the emphasis is on the body as *setting up* physical conditions. In the latter case the body is considered as *influenced by*, or even *constituted by*, physical conditions. The proper geometry used here, that of place and space, is called *topography*, or *analysis situs*.

INFINITE DIVISIBILITY OF BODIES

Since points have no extension, they are not bodies. Thus bodies which do have extension cannot consist of points. That means that bodies cannot be reduced to points in their division. Every remainder will have some extension and can never be reduced to points, simply because points have no extension. Hence, bodies are always further subdivisible. This is the theory, and of course it is based on the fact that points connot be the constituents of bodies. We cannot get mass, which bodies have, from no mass. There are also practical difficulties about the continued division of secondary matter. In order to see these difficulties, we must first examine the theory at greater length and then examine the practice.

In *mathematical theory* there are no difficulties, because mathematical bodies are conceptual constructs. Hence, as long as we stay within the logical framework of the concept, we can do just about anything that fits within that framework. For example, in a number series we can develop many types of infinite series of numbers. Similarly, we can develop many types of geometries in this latter field. We can also pass from one to the other.

A famous instance of this is illustrated by Jacob Cantor and his transfinite numbers. One application of his theory concerns the number of points in a line. If we define a point as the intersection of two lines and define a line as length without breadth, then there are the intersections of two entities having no breadth and thus constituting a point, which has no dimensions. We can do so by having sectors S_1, S_2, S_3, S_n,

. . . from point Q intersecting line L, as below. If the distance between points P_1, P_2, P_3, . . . is always one half the preceding distance, the process of constituting points by division can go on endlessly.

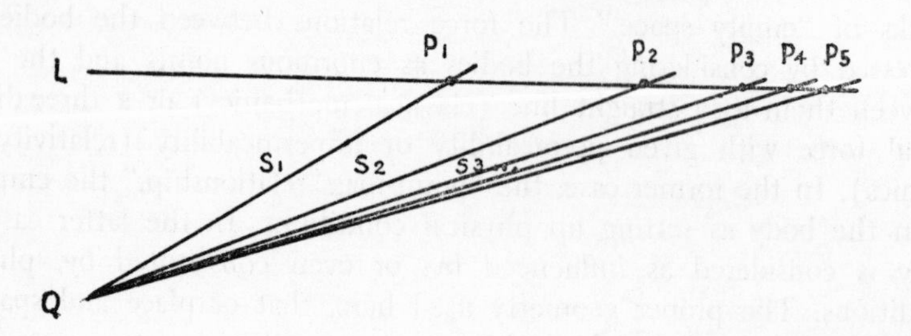

Jacob Kantor developed this into all types of geometry under the ℵ *aleph* () series, which consists of: (1) the number of points on a line, on a plane, and in a series; (2) the number of lines on a plane and in a solid; (3) the number of planes in a solid. In each case, the answer is an infinite number.

Here we can note difficulties in projection that make proper projection difficult, if not impossible. Projection is the extension of one figure upon another. But it is difficult to project from a plane to a sphere simply because the surface of the latter changes any point-to-point relationship. The Mercator Projection, the attempt to represent the spherical earth on a flat map illustrates this.

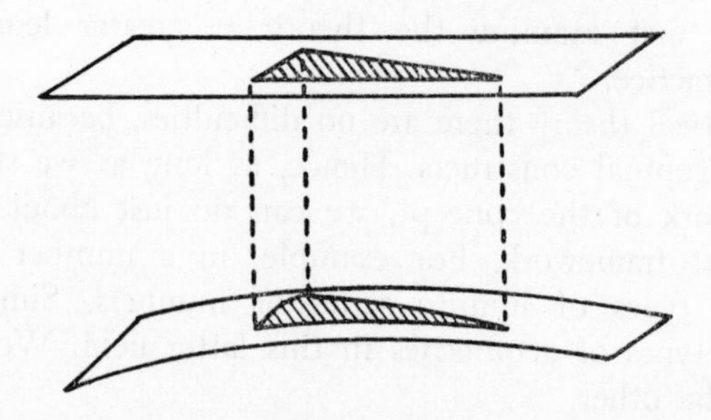

However, even a projection from plane to plane constitutes difficulties. Since points have no extension there cannot be a proper point-to-point relationship at all. Some geometricians conclude from this fact that if we cannot reproduce points from body to body, we cannot reproduce events properly, since the physical conditions which are inevitably reduced to the bodies concerned cannot be repeated accurately. This gives a new twist to the supposition that history does or does not repeat itself.

Fundamentally, however, these problems in projection are based on the infinite divisibility of matter, all theoretically correct. Although the conclusions in mathematical theory can be applied to reality with proper adjustment of concepts, they are fundamentally conceptual entities. By adhering too closely to these theoretical and conceptual entities, Descartes and Leibniz encountered difficulties in working around to a properly realistic philosophy. They did not take the extension of bodies as it exists but rather as it is conceived in the mind. Hence, their philosophies are more properly conceptual systems than realistic analyses of matter on its own terms.

Theoretically, in the physical order, matter is infinitely divisible. This is so, briefly but essentially, because bodies have parts, parts have extension, and neither can be reduced to points.

There are *practical difficulties*. These difficulties are basically two in number.

1. Sooner or later, in any physical division, the dividing instrument becomes larger than the thing to be divided. We then devise a new instrument, a smaller knife, a more accurate microscope. For example, in a microscope, sooner or later the object viewed becomes smaller than the wavelengths of ordinary light, at least at its edges. Hence, we devise an electron microscope with shorter wavelengths. However, we again run into difficulties because the dividing instrument itself meets the same threshold or barrier of practicality. Here we meet the second difficulty.

2. When we get into the extremely small, the submicroscopic, we are dealing with the imperceptible. We cannot sense what we are dealing with. We must reconstruct. This we do by bombarding the imperceptible with energy. In theory, we attempt to tell from the results what the mass and position of the remainder were before the bombardment. Here the difficulties multiply. We can never tell what the position was because we never knew it in the first place. Even though we have an idea what the mass was, and what the remainder should be according to the forces and direction of the bombarding energy, the resultant entities seem to be energies having wave and particle characteristics rather than pure particles. Furthermore, there is no appreciable change in mass of the resultant particles. Actually, we are getting down to fundamental energies, to the binding force of the particles, which is harder and harder to break and which seems to be energy with wave and mass characteristics. This makes it harder and harder to reconstruct exactly what we have been working with.

It is right at this point, incidentally, that physical theorists have different interpretations. Dirac maintains that the difficulties are so insurmountable that we can never go from the macroscopic — or observable — level to the microscopic level. This level is properly conceptual, since what we cannot observe we must interpret. Einstein, on the other hand, maintained that by the use of better and better instruments we would obtain more data, enough to resolve difficulties. Heisenberg maintains that the uncertainty makes no difference. Even if we admit that we are uncertain of the masses, positions, velocities, and properties of entities below a certain level, we still have enough data to guarantee our basic interpretation of nature.

Our difficulties in dividing matter below certain levels should be foreseen. After all, bodies do have extension. They consist of parts, and these parts must have an extremely energetic binding force when we take into account the energy content of any body. Hence, there must be increasing resistance to division as we get into the lower orders.

A further characteristic of such division is that things are more vague and less certain as we get lower. This results, in part, because organization is breaking down from the more complex to the more simple. It is also due to the fact that we are dealing with the more imperceptible. We are not getting clear evidence, and hence we are less able to form judgments. We are not exactly getting down to primary matter, but we are getting close. And it must be remembered that primary matter is in itself unknowable, since form is the principle of order and intelligibility.

SUMMARY

1. All bodies have extension, and whatever has extension is a body.
2. Extension is not, however, identical with substance. If it were, any change in extension would be a substantial change, that is, a change in identity. Such is not the case. Furthermore, extension is intuitively perceived by the senses whereas substance is inferred as the sufficient reason of extension and other accidents.
3. Extension is the distribution of parts in the whole. Since this is not identical with substance, it must be in virtue of some accidental principle. This is *quantity*, which is defined as an absolute accident disposing the distribution of the parts in the whole.
4. The formal effects of quantity are: extension — the first formal effect; and figure, position, and location, the second formal effects.
5. Physically, place is the first innermost surroundings of a mobile body. Mathematically, it is a point of demarcation in reference to other bodies against a spatial background.

6. Space is the distribution of matter. Geometrically it is a construction set up by the direction of lines. These linear directions are called dimensions, and they allow for a correspondence to the edges of bodies, to changes of direction in moving bodies against a spatial background.
7. Theoretically, matter is infinitely divisible. In practice, difficulties arise from the energies holding the minimal parts together.

CHAPTER NINE

The PRINCIPLE of INDIVIDUATION

Individuation, that is to say, the division of an individual nature or essence or species into many individuals to whom that nature or essence or species belongs is a problem peculiar to material or bodily substances. This is so because bodies and only bodies are composed of parts and are divisible into their parts. Spirits are not divisible and hence are not further individualized. Spiritual substances are individual, but their individuality is the product of direct creation, not of generation from a source, and the unity of their individual existence is their being, transcendental unity.

Furthermore, bodies are individualized in several ways. In every change, substantial or accidental, there is some rearrangement of matter. From substantial changes there are two possible results. Either (1) other types of substances are generated in the corruption of a substance; for example, in the electrolysis of water, hydrogen and oxygen are generated. Or (2) a new individual of the same substantial essence comes into being. For example, some worms, when cut in two, become two other worms. Starfish, when cut to pieces, become other starfish as long as there is a complete arm and part of the central disk. A tree divides off part of itself into specialized tissue known as a seed, which, after breaking away from the parent tree, becomes a new tree after fertilization.

It is this second type of substantial change that we are dealing with here. Our problem is how it is that there are many numerical individuals having the same essence or nature.

This is not a new problem. It was introduced, perhaps, by Pythagoras and is at the essence of Platonic philosophy. Aristotle considers it realistically, and St. Thomas treats of it at length. In anticipation, we may say that the answer is primary matter having some relation to quantity in the order to existence.

The problem is metaphysical and physical. The above consideration illustrates the physical aspects of it: division of a body because it has parts. It may seem strange that this problem has a metaphysical aspect until we realize that division is limitation. It is a limitation upon every human being, for instance, to say that he *is not* mankind, that is, that he is not the completion of the essence of man, but that he *shares* mankind. It is a limitation that one man is less healthy, less talented, than another man.

What, then, is the principle that limits individuals within the same species? This question must be considered metaphysically and physically.

Metaphysically. At first sight, it would seem that the differences between beings of a given essential class can be explained in terms of their *accidents*. One man, after all, is greater than another because he has more talents, a better brain, a more sensitive central nervous system. However, a moment's reflection will show us that this is only a partial answer demanding a deeper principle for its explanation.

A being has accidents only because it is already a limited being. Furthermore, its accidents depend upon its capacity or potency to be perfected by accidents. So much the more, then, does its degree of accidents depend upon potency. After all, it cannot have more-or-less in accidents unless it has the capacity to have accidents in the first place. Hence, potency, rather than accidents, is the principle of limitation.

Another attempt to solve the difficulty, again a rather simple answer, puts this limitation in the *efficient cause*. An entity is an individual because it has been made so or created so. Again, a moment of reflection will show the incompleteness of this answer. A knife can cut a loaf of bread into slices, but only if the bread is cuttable. The same knife cannot cut marble. Hence, the knife, or efficient cause, is limited according to the potency of the object it is working on. We may say that another tool can cut the marble. True enough, but the fact that we must shift the tool with a view to the material proves that the potencies of the object figure in in the ultimate consideration.

This metaphysical examination shows, then, that since individuation is limitation the answer must be found in potency. In bodies, this individuation is matter, primary matter.

In the physical order we see this when we consider the relations of matter and form to efficient cause.

Form is the fulfillment of matter, educed from the potencies of matter subject to privations by an efficient cause for the perfecting of both the cause and the effect. Form, as the fulfillment of matter, is act in relationship to potency. As act, form is in itself unlimited. Yet the forms perfecting and fulfilling all bodily substances are, in fact, limited by some principle intrinsic to those substances. This other principle is matter. Hence, form is limited by matter.

This argument presupposes that an actuality or perfection is not of itself limited or self-limiting. To show why this is true, we can set up the following dialectic argument. Act is either self-limiting, rejective of limitation, or indifferent as regards limitation and therefore limited by something else.

Act *is self-limiting*. If this is true, then any actuality that exists is by its very essence limited. However, God is an actuality. Hence, on the basis of the proposition that act is *self-limiting*, we could argue that God is self-limited by His very existence. This is obviously absurd, since, if it were true, God would not be the Pure Actuality, the Absolute Being that He must be to be God. God would then be a limited being. But being by limitation needs unlimited being to explain its existence and essence. Hence, God must be unlimited, and we immediately see the weakness in assuming that act can be self-limiting.

Act *positively rejects limitation*. This, of course, is absurd. Anything which exists is an actuality. Yet all things except God are limited. Hence, the only conclusion that we can come to is that *act is indifferent as regards limitation*. Thus, if an act is limited, it must be limited by something else. This "something else" cannot be, as we have seen, either an accident or an efficient cause. The only principle left is potency, which in bodies is primary matter.

However, the limitation that belongs to bodies is not merely the metaphysical limitation of an act by a potency, the participation of many in the same act. Limitation is always appropriate to the manner of the existence of the type of being. In the case of bodies, consequently, limitation involves division into parts, arrangement of parts. This implies the existence of quantified secondary matter.

Yet the principle of individuation in bodies cannot be secondary matter as such. Secondary matter *is* the individual, presuming limitation as already achieved. Nor can it be quantity as such. Quantity is an accident presuming the existence of the individual. Yet, since individuation is a peculiar sort of limitation in relationship to quantity, quantity must somehow enter into the principle of individuation.

We must turn, once again, to the nature of primary matter. It is a potential for existence through form as a substance composed of integral parts. It must be remembered that primary matter, although it is one of the principles of bodily essence, is as such a potential for existence.

The manner of existence in question is that of quantified existence, simply because a body's existence is that of a substance composed of integral parts, and it has these parts through quantity. Hence primary matter, as a potential for existence through form, also has a relationship to quantity as the principle of parts outside of parts.

This relationship, this potency of matter for quantity as a condition for existence, has been termed, in Latin, *materia quantitate signata.* Its translation, "matter signed by quantity," has little if any meaning in English. What is meant is the relationship of primary matter to quantity as a condition for its bodily existence as an individual material substance.

St. Thomas Aquinas uses the expression *materia quantitate signata.* However, there are different opinions as to what he meant exactly by the expression. These opinions are those of Sylvester Ferrara and Thomas de Vio Gaetana, or Cajetan.

Ferrara's point of view is simply that a body exists as a body and as such is divisible. Hence, he looks to the previous body, the source, in its divisibility for the relationship of matter to quantity. In order to explain the origin of this process of division and divisibility, he must fall back on creation as the creation of beings, among them bodies, which are then further divisible because of their primary matter.

Cajetan's point of view is based upon the nature of potency as fulfilled in act. For Cajetan, *materia quantitate signata* means the transcendental relationship of primary matter to quantity. A transcendental relationship is one wherein at least one of the terms of the relationship has no meaning without the other. Its whole meaning is in terms of the other. It may seem strange that matter should be so considered when it is necessary to maintain that its entire signification is to its correlative act, form. However, we must also remember that its full signification is in existence, and since the existence of a body requires quantity, Cajetan maintains that primary matter is also transcendentally related to quantity.

Actually, it would seem that both points of view, that of Ferrara and that of Cajetan, are fundamentally the same. Primary matter exists in a body. Hence, the body is required for the product. Yet the body is divisible only because of its primary matter, its potency, its capacity for change. That this requires quantity should be obvious from the nature of a body. The differences between Ferrara and Cajetan seem to be that Ferrara puts his emphasis on the process of change while Cajetan puts his emphasis on the principles and conditions of change.

SUMMARY

1. Individuation is the multiplication of an individual nature or essence or species into individual substances. It is peculiar to bodies since only bodies are divisible.
2. Since individuation is limitation it is in the order of potency. The individuating activities of the efficient cause and of accidents presuppose the potentialities of bodies.
3. Since form is actuality, it is indifferent to individuation. Hence, individuation is in the order of primary matter. It is also in the order of quantity, since it is numerical.
4. Hence, individuation is rooted in the transcendental relationship of matter to quantified existence. The proper expression for this is *materia quantitate signata*.

CHAPTER TEN

The NATURE of TIME

Any theory of the universe, whether philosophical or scientific, must consider the problem of time. We find the question of time beginning to assume its proper importance in Plato, who regarded time, "the moving image of eternity," as a continuum created to be subdivided into numbers and as essential to sensible things. In addition, we find time to be of great importance in classical mechanics as well as in relativity. Theories of organic evolution and newer theories of the evolution of the universe have raised the question of time to such significance that Bergson would consider the essence of his metaphysics to hinge about the problem of time and duration.

The key to the nature of time is our experience of it. Time as an experience involves personal observation and personal duration in relation to change. At least that is the general point of view whereby we speak of past and future. Time is also a measurement. The astronomer measures through time, and the commuter considers the distance between his home and his work in terms of a railroad timetable rather than in terms of miles.

Time, as we experience it, involves a contrast between the permanent and the changing, the problem faced by Plato. Time, as experienced, includes the notes both of change and of duration. We contrast changing things with more permanent entities. This contrast is the basis of the two traditions of the consideration of time, Platonic and Aristotelian. The Platonic tradition looks to time as a metaphysical and physical principle. This is reflected in the emphasis on time as a principle in the post-Renaissance physics which was in many ways inspired by a resurgence of Platonism. The Aristotelian tradition is to look to time as a measurement of motion, the type of thinking whereby we measure velocity in terms of the time taken to cross a given distance. This assumes newer importance in relativity physics.

Plato, as we have seen, was fascinated with the contrast between the changing and the permanent. This led him to infer that the principles accounting for the stability we find in things exist apart, autonomously, in a world of eternal and immutable Forms. Somehow these eternal Forms must be "participated in" by the objects of our senses, the beings of the material world.

Sensible things, therefore, somehow share in the Forms; and their duration, while not eternal and abiding, is in some way an "image" of the duration of the Forms. Plato calls their duration "time," which he understands as a continuum which can be divided into numbers. These numbers are in some way related to the essences of the changing imitations of the eternal realities.*

There is a great metaphysical truth contained herein. Plato properly contrasts the temporal with the eternal, arguing that since the eternal is immutable, it is timeless, beyond time, trans-temporal. Most properly, time is intrinsic to the changeable, the mutable, and is the principle of their changing duration. This is the beginning of the great note of participation-as-imitation in philosophy: that those things which are limited and changeable have no meaning without the eternal and immutable.

This is the background of Aristotle's consideration of the contrast between the mutable and the immutable. However, whereas Plato looked upon time as a principle, Aristotle considers it a measurement based on our observation of change through the concepts of before and after.** As a matter of fact, that is exactly how Aristotle defines time: "*the number of motion in respect of 'before' and 'after'*" (*Physics*, IV, 11, 219b1).

THE NATURE OF DURATION

Once again, this is an expression of duration, except that it is the measurement of the duration of the changeable as opposed to the duration of the eternal. This gives rise to the three considerations of duration based upon this Platonic-Aristotelian philosophy of time. These are:

1. The duration of an existentially immutable being. This being is God, and we call His duration *eternity*. Eternity, thus understood, is identical with God's existence which is identical with His essence. Thus,

*On this see *Timaeus*, 37d.

** Cf. *Physics*, Bk. IV, chs. 10–11.

eternity is but an aspect of the nature of God. It is not endless time. It is altogether beyond time. Any temporal references to God are on our part. We live in time and we think in temporal terms and images when we consider the duration of anything. Hence, we have a tendency to look upon eternity as "endless time." Actually, it is but one aspect of the nature of God.

2. The duration of an essentially or substantially immutable being. This is the duration of a created spiritual entity. A spirit has no parts, and hence is to that extent immutable. Nevertheless, it is a creature, and does not have the *existential* immutability of God. Its existence depends upon God. Even though it is incorruptible once created, its duration is that of participated existence, and is not, properly, eternity. We call this *aeviternity*. Strictly speaking, the human soul has this type of duration. The human soul is a spirit. On the other hand, it is also the form of the body and is so intimately united with the body that it habitually operates in sequence. We naturally think in time, and aeviternity seems rather far from the soul, although strictly speaking it is the proper existence of the soul as spirit if not as form.

3. The duration of a mutable being. This is, most properly, continued existence whose measurement is time.

THE NATURE OF TIME

We have been speaking of time both as a measurement and as motion. This was the problem that faced Aristotle. Against his Platonic background he realized full well that time represented a contrast between the stable and the changeable. He was familiar with the Platonic consideration of time as a metaphysical and physical principle. On the other hand, he knew full well that we use time as a measure of change. It always involves an observer in relation to change. Hence, it has both subjective and objective aspects. Is time completely subjective? completely objective? Or is it partly both?

Aristotle first considers the assumption that time is completely extramental, a purely physical thing. However, if that is the case, it offers certain difficulties.

The first difficulty is that if time is extra-mental, it is bodily. If it is bodily, it must have parts. If it exists, its parts exist. Obversely, if its parts do not exist, then time does not exist. Now the parts of time are past and future, which are divided by the present. The past, as such, does not exist, nor does the future. At best, the past exists in the duration of *things* which have come to be in times past and which continue to exist. The future is the expectation that things will continue to exist, that the universe will not cease to exist, at least for a while. And insofar as *now* is the divisor, it has no parts and cannot exist as such.

Moreover, even granting that time could exist as such, what is it? It seems to be continuous, and since it passes, it would seem to be some sort of motion. Now it is either the motion of the universe or the motions of the components of the universe. If it is the former, then there is one universal time, and everyone has the same past and the same future. Yet we know that past and future are set up by the *now*, or the simultaneous, and this varies with the observers. The only case in which coincidence in time means simultaneity of experience occurs when the observers are equally distant from the event.

If time, on the other hand, is the movement of the objects of the universe, then there are as many times as there are movers. Furthermore, movements are relative and variable. Some are faster, some slower. Nevertheless, the time-motion relationship is fundamental to general relativity.

In the former case we would have only one time. In the latter case, we would have innumerable times. Yet we break down the former into many times by subjective agreement, and we correlate the latter into one time scheme by equally subjective agreement.

Consequently, we must take more than motion into consideration when we consider time. It is not completely objective. It has subjective aspects about it. Otherwise we would not be able to agree about hours, days, months, and years — or even, for that matter, about the "now." In other words, we consider variations in time and motion only if we consider time a constant and not a variable. This implies a subjective selection of a norm for the constant.

On the other hand, subjective as time may be, we cannot consider it completely subjective. After a period of unconsciousness we have a tendency to connect the first period of resumed consciousness with the last moment of remembered consciousness, and we become aware of the passage of time by discovering that changes have occurred during our unconsciousness. The example used by Aristotle is that of the fabled sleepers of Sardinia who slept through twenty or so years without realizing that so great a time had elapsed. Washington Irving's Rip van Winkle illustrates the point just as easily.

Again, if time were only subjective, there would be as many times as there are observers. Further, the psychological factor whereby a given period of time seems to drag for one and to speed for another shows the need of correction in terms of objective motion in order that both agree as to the duration of the time involved.

Clearly, then, time is both objective and subjective. Its objective basis is change, motion. Its subjective interpretation is past and future as subdivided by the immediate perception of surroundings, the present, the "now." Thus it is that Aristotle defines time as the "number of motion according to 'before' and 'after.'"

THE "NOW"

From our experience, we know that we define the past and future in their relationships to the "now." We see the past in the realities that have existed "up to now," and we think of the future as an extension of the present in terms of "from now on." Furthermore, in our measured times, we agree on a "now," with which we set our watches or stop-watches.

The "now" or present that we can be sure of is the immediate, because by the time we advert to it, it has already passed. This immediate is outside the faculties of observation because it involves some sort of realization beyond the observation. This makes it the immediate observation of something. However, it is the person, not merely the sense, that observes. Hence all of his observing faculties are involved in the observation of the "now." This means the competent senses required. The observation of an event means not only sight but also hearing and any other sense that may be involved, as, for example, the sense of smell when we realize that there is a fire taking place now. The fact of personal, rather than merely sensile, apprehension in the "now" is a point in special relativity. The same event can frequently be seen before it is heard. However, with little if any conscious effort, the person adjusts this apprehension of the event in such way that he intuits it as one event even though it comes through two sense channels at slightly different times. This means that the principles of sense adjustment, the internal senses of memory, the combining sense, and the particular reason, enter into the apprehension of the "now." This is further verified, as we have already seen, in that memory is implied in our observation of "up to now," and in our expectation of "from now on."

TIME, THE MEASURED AND THE MEASURER

The basis of time as a measurement, thus, is the "now." However, as noted above, the now is based upon either a consciousness of one's surroundings, or upon some change, even in the individual, that can be noted as occurring. Hence, although *motion*, and to that extent the foundation of time, continues despite the observer, *measured motion*, or time, depends upon the observer. It depends upon the notation of some event considered as "now" and used as the beginning of a continuous sequence of *observed time*. This is the numerical measurement of any sequence of changes considered as one motion. Hence, the "now" takes on the character of an indivisible instant at the beginning of a continuum. The continuum is motion, which may be any number of independent motions considered as one process.

The comparison of "now" as an instant in relationship to a continuous time line to the point as an indivisible in relationship to a spatial line is an interesting illustration. Just as there is no thing such as a point, yet we consider one, so also there is no such thing as a "now" save in the senses and in our intellectual advertence to it. So also, just as a line is not a point, or a series of points, yet is also considered a moving point allowing for an infinity of points on it, so also time is not a succession of "nows" and yet can be considered a "now" moving into the future and changing it into the past.

As a matter of fact, there is an intrinsic relationship between time and space insofar as both magnitude and motion involve a continuity that is measured by an assigned number representative of an indivisible. In the case of magnitude it is the point. In the case of time it is the "now." This gives us a basis for intermeasurement, the measurement of space by time and time by space and velocity. In fact, the notion of time as the measurer is a commonplace one. We measure distance by time just as we can infer time by distance and velocity. This receives its most elegant presentation in special relativity, as we shall see in the next chapter. However, it has a philosophical basis, namely the fact that both time and space are rooted in the same physical reality. This foundation or reality is motion.

Motion is from place to place, from this place to that place. In the moving, area is crossed, so that by the very fact that there is the relation of a movable body to its surroundings, a common continuity is set up: the geometrical continuum of space and flowing continuum of motion. The continuum is a point-area-point relationship for space and a now-motion-now relationship for time, since it takes time to cross space. This sets up a *before and after* relationship since the moving object is *now, at this former place, before* it arrives *now, at this latter place, afterward*. Consequently, a twofold continuum is set up. As Aristotle puts it:

> But what is moved is moved from something to something, and all magnitude is continuous. Therefore the movement goes with the magnitude. Because the magnitude is continuous, the movement too must be con-

> tinuous, and if the movement, then the time; for the time that has passed is always thought to be in proportion to the movement.
>
> The distinction of "before" and "after" holds primarily then in place; and there in virtue of relative position. Since then "before" and "after" hold in magnitude, they must hold also in movement, these corresponding to those. But also in time the distinction of "before" and "after" must hold, for time and movement always correspond with each other. The "before" and "after" in motion identical in substratum with motion yet differs from it in definition, and is not identical in motion (*Physics*, IV, 11, 219a10–21a20).

This amounts to a two-dimensional continuum: space and time. However, since the space spoken of by Aristotle is the real distribution of real matter, and since real space is three-dimensional, this amounts to being a four-dimensional continuum.

As we shall see shortly, the word "dimension" is not proper to time, although it is used in relationship to it. The immediate question to be faced is an application of time as the measurer and time as the measured.

As we have seen, time is not purely subjective, although individual psychological states make the duration of an action seem of different times to different persons concerned. Hence, in order to get away from this confusion of individual viewpoints, we look to a constant motion as the norm and then set our hours and calendars by it. In this way, time is the measured. On the other hand, no motion is so constant as to be absolutely invariant. Hence, we use the measurement to contrast one motion against another for the constancy of the measurement itself. For example, for daily measurements into twenty-four hours, we use the rotation of the earth on its axis. However, the earth's rotation is not absolute. The earth is gradually slowing down in its rotation. It also has a 28,690-year wobble that we call the precession.

Furthermore, we use the earth's orbit as the basis of our year. Here again, though, the extremely precise movement of the earth about the sun is modified by all kinds of physical conditions: the positions of other planets, the appearance of comets close to the sun and hence close to the earth, the position of the moon in relation to the earth, etc. We correct this by observations of the earth's position in relation to the stars. By this, we also correct the mathematical — as opposed to physical — length of the day. In this case, and in similar cases, time is the measurer.

The use of physical movements as the basis of measurement is sometimes called *natural time*. In brief, it consists of the observation of a physical motion as the basis for measurement. The motion is observed as continuous and is broken down into measured segments. For a time, the position of the moon was used for an annual measurement of a year of thirteen months. However, the orbit of the earth became the accepted motion for the year and the rotation of the earth for the day. These motions are at the basis of *solar time* which is used for our twelve-month year and twenty-four-hour day. Its correction by the earth's position in relation to the stars on both a daily and annual basis is called *sidereal time* and is the measurement used by astronomers.

For the sake of convenience we use instruments, watches, clocks, sundials, etc. The use of these is called *artificial time* because it is measured by a human device. Its basis is some natural motion, the swing of a pendulum, the unwinding of a spring, the dropping of sand, etc. However, it has been devised for man's convenience, and is considered artificial. The latest and most accurate method of measuring time is by a device that measures the periodic motions of atomic particles. This is far more accurate than any movements of such big bodies as planets and far more accurate than any human device for measuring time.

However, it must be noted that, whether natural or arbitrary, time as the measurer is fundamentally *arbitrary*. We *select* a motion for the foundation of our time measurements. We select other motions for the more correct approximation of the first.

When we consider what is measured by time, the answer must always be motion or something under the aspect of motion, something changeable. What we have been speaking about immediately above has been the proper notion of time, time as the measure of motion. However, we also measure the duration of movable things, and speak of a building as so many years old, or of a structure built to last so many years. In either case, we are considering it as changeable and we are speaking of it in terms of its becoming and its duration, its change from its sources to its present existence. Similarly, we speak also of the change involved in the ending of something when we speak of it coming to an end after so many years. Even though we are measuring the duration of a being, we are measuring the duration of a changeable being and we begin and end the measurement of its duration with the notation of a change, its beginning and its ending, all of which involve motion in their changes.

TIME AS A DIMENSION

As noted above, time is often called a dimension. The use of the expression "fourth dimension" became popular when Leopold Infeld based himself upon Einstein's emphasis of the constancy of the velocity of light in a vacuum. He considered that in relationship to light one second is the equivalent of 300,000 kilometers. This was nothing new. For centuries light had been used to measure the universe since the universe is too vast to be measured conveniently in miles or kilometers.

If by dimension is meant a measurement, then time is a dimension, for time measures as well as is measured. If by dimension is meant the boundary of a body, then time is not a dimension. However, since a dimension is a linear measurement in a given direction, then we can call time a dimension since there is a time line, a succession of events in an overall motion. In this way, time is an intrinsic part of a coordinate system, not only because events take place in space and time, not only because it takes time to cross space, but also because the validity of observation frequently depends on: (1) the time of observing them, and (2) their age when they are observed. For example, a key to the physical understanding of the universe is not only the distribution of types of stars, but also the age of these stars as they are distributed in space and interpreted according to the time it takes their light to reach us. The Hartzsprung-Russell diagram of main sequence spectral types of stars is essentially a union of the ages and physical properties of stars, and is a key to the age of the universe.

It must be kept in mind, however, that although we speak of time as a dimension, it is a one-way dimension. Fundamentally, this has nothing to do with the calculus of probabilities about whether the universe is running down, although that may be involved. It simply means that we cannot undo what has been done. We cannot undo our own age, our biological age, nor can we repeat the same action so that both are the identical unit. We can reduplicate an action, more or less approximately according to the physical conditions, or we may repair it. Once it has been done, however, it has been done.

SUMMARY

1. Plato considered time as a physical principle that limited eternal essences to changeable and material imitations.
2. Aristotle considered time a measurement, and defined it as "*the number of motion according to 'before' and 'after.'*"
3. The parts of time are past and future. These are enumerated by the "now," which is the personal intuition of the extra-mental.
4. Time as a measurer is considered *natural* if its computative basis is a natural movement; *artificial* if its basis is some sort of artificial device.
5. Time is called a fourth dimension insofar as space and time are intrinsically related and space is frequently measured by time. It does not correspond to the configuration of bodies. In that sense it is not a dimension. However, it is a linear measurement and in that sense may be called a dimension.

CHAPTER ELEVEN

RELATIVITY

As we have seen in the previous chapter, space and time are intrinsically associated. In fact, St. Thomas flatly states that they have the same formal note: *prius ac posterius* (*In Phys.*, IV, l. 17, n. 572 ff.). The basic reason for this is the fact that bodies are extended and that motion is a continuum across bodies. This is why it takes time to cross space. After almost three centuries of classical physics, Albert Einstein introduced this consideration as a basic postulate for the more accurate understanding of the basic principles of classical physics (cf. *Relativity, the Special and General Theories*). The reintroduction was hailed as an outstanding achievement because it introduced an economy of measurement in problems that proved more and more difficult to explain. The problem then arises: When did the doctrine of time get separated from that of space, and why did Einstein have to reintroduce their relative character?

THEORETICAL BACKGROUND

In practice, time and space have always been associated simply because we can measure space in terms of time and time in terms of space. The emphasis, then, was largely one of technique. The emphasis on time can be traced back to Galileo. The emphasis on space, or, rather, the doctrine of space, can be traced to Descartes.

Galileo was fascinated with gravitation and with the acceleration of falling bodies. He was fascinated with the problem of the pendulum, wherein the time remains constant, although the swing of the pendulum decreases in its arc. He thought of this in terms of a downward pull of gravity. In his attempts to discover the constant rate of falling bodies, and to discover why bodies tend to fall at the same rate of speed, he concluded with Stevinus that a falling body should constantly accelerate and that only the resistance of the air prevents this. This led him into the problem of the increase of velocity, and he thought of this increase in terms of distance covered. However, here he met a circle in argumentation. A body cannot cross any distance unless it has attained velocity, and it cannot attain any velocity unless it has crossed some distance. Hence, Galileo looked to *time* as the means of explaining acceleration.

Descartes, on the other hand, began with geometry and its emphasis on conceptual space, and reduced the essences of bodies to their outstanding characteristic, extension. This reduced their components to points, and hence began the point-mass relationship. This meant that any relationship between entities was to be considered a straight line joining two points. Descartes also had a tendency to look upon time the same way. Whereas time is based on motion, Cartesian doctrine made it spatial and, hence, formal and almost motionless.

Newton realized the necessity of the interrelation of spatial and temporal measurements. His constant for the attraction of masses was based upon temporal statistics carefully and painstakingly drawn up by Gunter and Halley, the statistics of the successive positions of the moon at the same time of night over many successive observations. However, he too had a tendency to look upon time as one direction of measurement and space as another.

This, however, poses a difficulty. There is no absolute space and no absolute time. There is no absolute point whence we can begin our spatial and temporal measurements. Newton tried to save the phenomenon by falling upon the omnipresence of God for space and the eternity of God for time. This, however, is no answer since God is a spirit. The nearest in the physical order that Newton could attain was the apparent fixedness of the "fixed" stars.

Actually, in the mechanics of Newton, which, we must remember, are always valid in the macroscopic (that is, observable) order, there is no need for any absolute time or absolute space. All that is needed is international agreement on distances and times.

The real difficulty came to the fore in the application of the laws of mechanics to atomic and subatomic particles. Nuclear and atomic theory would have little meaning without the laws of mechanics. No one has ever seen an atom, nor, for that matter, do we suppose anyone ever will see one. We must reconstruct the atom in terms of problems wherein atomic theory gives the best coverage of both salient and divergent facts. The reconstruction must be in terms of what we know, and our supposition is that the universe should obey the same laws throughout since it seems to be made up of the same basic materials. Hence, what holds for the observable order can safely be projected downward into the unobservable order.

A word must be said about "obeying the laws of nature." As seen earlier in this book, the laws of nature are really a statistical expression of mathematical concepts. This results from the scientist's preoccupation with the uniformity of phenomena. Phenomena are in the order of sense observations, and the science of uniformity is something in number, something geometrical, rather than philosophical. Hence, the scientist's approach to reality is that of measurement, and the laws of nature are really the constants of measurement.

The scientist's position, then, is that we can apply measurement to the extremely minute with equal validity as to the extremely huge. Nevertheless, he must check on his measurements, and in the atomic and nuclear order, he cannot do so directly. He must devise a theory of measurement to interpret the results of the observable disturbances which serve as substitutes for direct measurement.

The basis whereby he justifies his disturbing matter is that matter consists of particles. However, the same particles, in motion, give every evidence of being waves. Consequently, he assumes that matter at rest consists of particles, whereas matter in transmission, radiant matter, consists of waves. In order to see how this can be, he must suppose that he can measure matter at rest and matter in transmission. There are two difficulties here. The laws of mechanics as applied to matter at rest maintain that matter can never be at rest. Radiant matter travels at nearly the velocity of light, and the only way to measure this is to interrupt it. However, the interruption gives evidence of wave properties. On the other hand, we can never measure matter at rest simply because matter never is completely at rest according to the theory behind mechanics. There is always some molecular motion presupposing more fundamental atomic and nuclear orbits and spins.

This has led to three interpretations in physical theory. P. A. M. Dirac maintains that we must face the fact that we are always stopped at the barrier of the extremely small, and we must doubt the validity of our suppositions when they are applied to the extremely minute. Werner Heisenberg maintains that we need never worry about the times and places of individual particles since a statistical expression is sufficient for a firm basis for the application of theory. Albert Einstein maintained that human ingenuity would come up with an answer to the problem with more complete and congruent concepts, if not with better measuring devices.

Einstein had entered this problem in anticipation of many of the problems mentioned above. His problem began with quantum physics, a theory which maintained that the old dichotomy of light-as-waves or light-as-particles could be resolved by supposing light to be the emission of bunches of particles at different frequencies of emissions. The bunches or "quanta" of energy emitted would be in the red end of the spectrum at a low frequency, which would give the impression of long wavelengths, and in the violet and ultra-violet spectrum at a high frequency, which would give the impression of extremely short waves. Since all the particles, called "photons," travel at the same speed, the difference would be only in the emission, and the result would be a wave effect. The difference in frequency would also explain how the prism could break up the components into the rainbow effect.

However, putting this to the test would again raise the problem of the impossibility of measuring position and velocity simultaneously. Or, more simply, putting it to the test would simply show that matter is both waves and particles. It would simply verify the old difficulties. On the other hand, however, it was a conceptual scheme that accounted for the difficulties. Moreover, it solved the old dilemma raised by the fact that electromagnetic wave transmission should ionize all in the wave front whereas it does not. Quantum mechanics maintains that there is no wave front, only the effect of one, and that the reason why everything is not ionized along the "wave front" is simply that statistically only a few radiating particles strike a few impeding particles.

Einstein had earlier maintained that the impossibility of measuring velocity and position simultaneously can never be resolved. Whereas we can agree that a physical marker of sorts is point zero, we can never agree what is the "now" of the beginning of a time measurement. The "now" is in the senses, not in objective reality, and two observers cannot agree as to the exact "now" of the seeing or hearing of the same phenomenon. For example, observation will depend upon the position of the observers, and if a time sequence is to be started with the observation of the same event, the time sequence will depend on the position of the observers. If the beginning of a naval maneuver is to coincide with the sound of a gun, any ship in the fleet over eleven hundred feet from the sounding gun will hear the signal at least one second later. Now, if the responsible officials were to set their watches at the sound of the gun, we would find several local times in the same coordinated effort.

One would think that all could coordinate their watches with a chronometer. However, the same difficulty remains. The chronometer had to be set at some time, and that would depend on further temporal standards which would, in turn, depend ultimately upon the positions of observers. In other words, we cannot set two clocks or watches at a perfect simultaneity. Not only that, we may say that two events are *coincident*, regardless of observers, but we cannot say that they are *simultaneous* unless the two observers are equally distant from the events and from each other. And even to say that they are simultaneous requires a system of clocks, and we are once again in the old difficulty.

After a few moments' thought, this seems to be obvious. However, like many obvious points, this difficulty arose only within the context of the classical position of space and time as absolutes and the classical space and time transformations. As a matter of fact, Einstein's relativity of observation and the inability to achieve perfect temporal adjustments became the focal point of a lot of tag ends of physics that had been more or less loosely associated.

The points were: (1) extensions of the consideration of an absolute space and absolute time, and (2) the possible existence of an all-pervading medium called "ether" for the transmission of the transverse waves of light and other forms of radiation.

The classical coordination of space and time, as noted above, began with Descartes but received its sanction from Newton. In his *Principia*, Newton had the following to say:

> All things are placed in time as to their order of succession, and in space as to their order of situation. . . . It is from their essence or nature that they are in places . . . (Introduction).

As things developed, Newton's position was reduced to the following simple propositions:

1. Each thing has from its nature mass and motion.
2. Mass immediately puts it into spatial relations, whereas motion immediately puts it into temporal relations.
3. There must be a coordinate system of space and time for proper measurement of motion in relationship to place against which we can measure the motions of bodies from place to place both spatially and temporally.
4. We can measure from moving body to moving body only if their motion is uniform to each other. The key to this statement is "uniform." This does not mean that the bodies must be in perfectly parallel motion or anything like that. It means that, in respect to one another, one body could be considered at rest and the other in motion or vice versa. This is the principle that grants validity to our measurements from one moving automobile to another, from the earth to any other planet, or from the sun to any other star.

5. Nevertheless, to determine the uniformity of motion, there must be a point of reference whereby we look on conceptual space as absolute and geometrical time as absolute. For this purpose, the Cartesian coordinates are excellent. Physically, however, the zero point must be some molar body, a fixed body.

In the development of these principles, nature is *conceived* of as a system of masses and forces operating in absolute space and time. The points of reference for these are the fixed stars. Changes in direction are vectors brought about by forces. Time is conceived as an endless and unidimensional series of instants. These temporal instants must be simultaneous and assigned to the same instant by all other observers who measure correctly.

SPECIAL RELATIVITY

The essential doctrine of relativity is the intermeasurements of space and time. This was obvious to the Greeks and scholastics because they considered a spot on the stable earth as point zero for measuring time by space and space by time. After Copernicus, Galileo, and Kepler, the sun became point zero. With Newton, point zero became the fixed stars. In the twentieth century, serious doubts, since verified, arose concerning the local stability of stars and galaxies. Hence, since we still measure space by time and vice versa, Einstein made the observer the basic point for all spatial and temporal measurements.

Einstein substituted a new constant. Instead of the hypothetical absolute point and the unattainable absolute instant or now, he substituted the velocity of light in a vacuum. In this way, then, one second of time could be the equivalent of 300,000 kilometers of space and all measurements could take on a more accurate spatio-temporal determination. Thus, the proper geometrical approach would not be through a space *and* time conceptual system, but through a space-time continuum.

Actually, Einstein's conclusion made little difference in classical physics in the macroscopic order. Very little in classical physics at the time depended upon precise observation where a difference of microseconds would interfere seriously with theory. Furthermore, the field where differences might be noticed, particle physics, was just at the beginning of its development, and here relativity was more a handy tool of measurement than a theoretical change.

Nevertheless special relativity caused consternation in mechanistic philosophy. We must remember again that the object of the physical sciences is an understanding of the uniformity of phenomena observed in the physical universe. Although Kantian philosophy maintained that the observation of phenomena was not even a gateway to a record of the extra-mental, the average physical theorist generally took the stand that there was something corresponding to and somewhat responsible for the observations. Physical scientists usually reasoned that whatever came first temporally in any series of events in which there was an invariant association of *A* and *B* was the cause of whatever followed. The event first observed was generally considered the cause of the event observed afterward. This is not the philosophy of causality. It is rather mathematical thinking in the sense that the point at the beginning of the line is the cause of the line drawn as its continuation. When Einstein pointed out that what was observed first, *A* or *B*, depended upon the position of observers, consternation gradually began to spread as people realized that they could then speak of effects occurring before their causes; in their own eyes they were committed to a topsy-turvy world in which up and down, right and left, before and after had no meaning save from the point of view of the observer.

These problems mean little to scholastic philosophy as philosophy. They have no reference to such fundamental principles as those of identity, contradiction, and sufficient reason. These, not positions or times, are the bases of causality. Relativity does not come even close to essence and existence, substance and accidents, matter and form. However, for the mechanistic philosopher, whose predecessors had dismissed these metaphysical and physical principles, relativity posed a serious problem unless he realized that his epistemology of phenomenon and formula required a more basic foundation than that of geometry. What Einstein actually did in philosophy was to suggest that since we could substitute one conceptual scheme for another without thereby changing the universe in the least, we could doubt the real relationship of any conceptual system to reality unless there were a more direct dependence of concepts upon reality itself. In other words, the fact that we could change the theoretical picture without changing the universe suggested that the mathematical picture might not be the exclusively proper one at all. This is what Sir Arthur Eddington maintains when he states that the world of green grass and blue skies is as true as the world of photosynthesis and wave propagation in the atmosphere (*The Nature of the Physical World*, p. 321 ff.).

Special relativity brought focus on another problem that had vexed theorists for several years. This problem was the transmission of radiation and the need of a medium if such radiation were a wave.

For centuries thinkers had speculated whether light traveled instantaneously or with extremely fast velocities. Gradually the conviction arose that it took time to travel but that it would be difficult to measure the exact time. The characteristic properties of light gave rise to differing theories. These properties are: propagation in a straight line in the form of beams and rays and the bending of light on entering different media. For example, we have all had the experience of seeing a long object such as an oar seem to bend in water. Actually it is the light that bends. Light also has an angle of incidence in its reflection whereby the angle at which it lands on a mirror is also the same angle at which it reflects.

Sir Isaac Newton concluded that light is the emission of extremely small corpuscles, whereas Christian Huygens maintained that light consists of transverse waves.

There are two types of waves, transverse waves and longitudinal or compression waves. When a boat travels through still water, waves are set up and they move from the scene of the disturbance in ever wider divergence from the source and with a velocity independent of the source. There is some motion of the water, but the water does not travel with the wave. It is disturbed by it. If the water traveled with the wave, there would be a separation of water at the source and a piling up of water along the wave front. However, we can see this if we float an object in the water before the wave front. As the wave comes, the object rises with the wave, goes forward a bit, and then settles back close to its original position. These waves are called *transverse* waves because the motion of the medium is at a right angle to the direction of the wave.

On the other hand, we have probably noticed that when a locomotive nudges into the first of a long string of freight cars, a shock travels along the entire length of the train with almost instantaneous speed. In this case, no one of the individual cars moves more than a few inches. The shock is transmitted through and from car to car. The transmission of such shocks by a pressure on the components of the medium is called a *compression* or *longitudinal* wave. Sound waves are of such a nature. The vibrations of the source are impressed upon the molecules of the medium, each of which is pressed upon the one in front of it in such a way that the shock travels through and from the molecules in the medium.

Experiments with polarization begun by Descartes seem to show that light, if it is a wave, is a *transverse* wave. The consideration that light might be a wave was based on the fact that if light travels at different speeds through different media it would seem to be more a wave than an emission. As a matter of fact this is the case, and hence light is generally considered to be a transverse wave. The fact that light travels in rays and beams rather than spreads spherically is explained by the extreme velocity with which it moves and by the extremely short wavelengths proper to it.

However, a wave is the propagation of energy through a medium. When physicists tried to determine this medium, they had to postulate the *luminiferous ether*. It is easy to suggest that we could not perceive this, since as a matter of fact we would not see *it*. We would see *by* it. However, the nagging question persisted that there should be some means of perceiving it directly or indirectly. This is especially true when we consider the properties demanded by the work done by the ether. It would have to be universal, yet imperceptible. However, insofar as it would have to be something, the passage of the planets and the earth through it should be indicated by some sort of drag and slowing down of the planets in their orbits over a reasonable period of years. Yet such has never been perceived. The passage of celestial bodies through it should build up a compression wave in front of the body. This, too, has never been observed. We could perhaps suppose that each planet is surrounded by its own ether moving with the planet through the all-pervading ether. But this has never been observed, especially where the moons of Jupiter should show the slight deviations of light in the passing from the proper ether of Jupiter to the all-pervading ether between the planets.

An extremely sensitive experiment was carried out in Cleveland, Ohio, in 1887, by two physicists, Michelson and Morley, who had done significant work in the passage of light into denser media. By use of an interferometer and the passage of light between a system of reflectors, they should have been able to perceive some influence of ether on light. As frequently as they performed the experiment, they simply verified the conclusion reached by Fizeau, DeSitter, and Foucault, that light arrives at the earth at exactly the same velocity whether or not the object emitting it is approaching or receding from the earth. This was observed from the moons of Jupiter and from binary stars. As one binary comes toward the earth, the other recedes from the earth. Yet the light from each, when they are equidistant from the earth, one receding and one approaching, comes to us at exactly the same time.

More important, however, is that the Michelson-Morley experiment not only verified the above conclusions about the velocity of light, it also showed that we seem to have no way of proving the existence of the ether. We can only infer its existence. The Michelson-Morley experiment has been repeated frequently in modern times, especially during the International Geophysical Year, with the use of extremely sensitive ammonia gases instead of reflectors, and there has been no variation in the velocity of light by the supposed disturbance of ether occasioned by the earth's passage through it.

Actually, Einstein knew nothing of the Michelson-Morley experiment. His approach was that of x-ray radiation and photoelectric phenomena, the problems of radiation that occasioned the quantum theory. When Einstein advanced the consideration that light might be a better constant, he also entertained the notion that a wave might simply be pure energy which in transmission might take the form of a wave because of the emission of photons. Light is never at rest, and hence we speak of a photon having "zero mass at rest," and the same might be true of other forms of electromagnetic radiations. If we looked upon radiation as a wave with particle characteristics, then we need not worry about a medium. We merely maintain that waves and particles are two forms of the same fundamental stuff, in one state energy, in another state mass. The rate of interconversion from one state to the other is $E = mc^2$.

The consideration of light as the ultimate constant of energy is simply the realization that electromagnetic radiation approaches the velocity of light but never exceeds it. Hence, as far as anyone knows, light is the ultimate in velocity.

In trying to explain the immeasurability of ether, two physicists, Lorenz and Fitzgerald, had maintained that a body at high velocities contracts in the direction in which it is going. They estimated that the rate of contraction is that of $\frac{m}{\sqrt{1-\frac{v^2}{c^2}}}$ where c is equal to the velocity of light and v is the velocity of the moving object. As the object approaches the velocity of light, as v^2 approaches c^2, then the formula approaches m/0, which is mathematical infinity. If the object were large enough to have clocks on it, then the clocks would slow down approaching zero because their mechanism, according to the principles of angular momentum, would retard with the expansion of their parts. This has given us the formula $M \rightarrow \infty :: T \rightarrow 0$. This, in turn, has given us the picture of the space ship wherein the approach to the velocity of light means the contraction of time so that the members would age, biologically, much slower than their fellows on earth. On their return they would be that much younger.

Einstein was not particularly interested in space ships. He was interested in seeing if the formula had any foundation in fact. He developed a number of predictions of the acceleration of electrons and their increase in mass. Later on, after accelerators were perfected, his statistics were fulfilled. The interpretation is, however, that the electron picks up energy in its acceleration and that this energy is converted into mass.

All of the above is an application of the formula $E = mc^2$. This, we must remember, is a statement that in radiation matter is fundamentally energy that sometimes has mass properties and sometimes has wave properties. This was the first successful reconciliation of wave and particle theory, and any successive reconciliation, even in the face of new difficulties, has been a development of this fundamental statement.

Actually, this does not change the basic consideration of matter in philosophy. It is rather a development of the Aristotelian-scholastic position that matter is intrinsically energetic. Concerning the problem of space and time, Aristotle and St. Thomas both maintained the relativity of space and time. Einstein shifted the emphasis from body-at-rest to body-in-energy and postulated a new constant, the velocity of light in a vacuum. It is as fundamental as the consideration that since nothing is absolutely at rest, since everything is in motion, then a constant motion is a better norm than a hypothetical state of rest.

There has been a great deal of philosophical objection to the fact that Einstein has shifted stability from matter to motion, whereas traditionally matter has been considered absolute and motion relative. But this tradition is different in Cartesian and scholastic philosophy.

From the *Cartesian* point of view, this is a valid objection. Matter is supreme in Cartesianism and motion is simply a hypothetical line between masses. However, we must remember that Cartesianism is fundamentally geometry with philosophical overtones.

In *scholastic* philosophy, we must remember that matter, in the sense of extended particles of masses, can be to a certain extent necessary since bodies are *de facto* extended. However, since all bodies are *mobile beings*, they are intrinsically changeable and are always changing accidentally. On the other hand, motion *is*, but it is always relative since it is from something, on the part of something, and terminating in something. Hence, there is really no absolute, except God, and scholastic philosophy has no quarrel with relativity.

Actually, special relativity is a theory of measurement, a conceptual scheme, that comes somewhat closer to reality than its preceding conceptual systems in mechanism. In so doing, it cleared up a number of loose ends in former theories of measurement. Einstein *never* maintained that truth is relative. As a matter of fact, toward the end of his life he took the stand that reality is always the measure of theory, even though his concept of reality was more that of Ernst Mach than that of St. Thomas. Nevertheless, toward the end of his life he looked upon his life's work as a constant attempt to correct preceding theory in view of reality rather than in view of ideas.

GENERAL RELATIVITY

Special relativity had theorized on two levels: that of the atomic constitution and that of measurement. On the atomic level it had introduced new concepts to quantum theory and helped to reconcile the problems of waves and particles through the concept of energy. In the area of measurement, it introduced the consideration that absolute space and absolute time are but concepts, and hence maintain their validity only in their conceptual usefulness. Where other concepts are more applicable, they should be adopted. Among these was the more steady constant of the velocity of light in a vacuum. However, since light takes time to travel, relativity introduced a time element to measurement and substituted the concept of *interval* for that of *distance*.

This raises a basic question. If our familiar foundations of measurement have only a limited value on a scale as small as our solar system and local galaxy of stars, what foundations are we to have for measurements as wide as the universe supposing we could measure the size of the universe? This is the subject of *general relativity*.

General relativity is a mathematical expression of many of the principles of Ernst Mach, a physicist turned philosopher. "Mach's Principle" is a statement of the fact that although Newtonian physics fell back upon the fixed stars as points of reference for the utility of the concepts of absolute time and absolute space, we should not lean too heavily upon the fixed stars since we have no evidence that they are fixed. Mach's reasoning was in advance of the spectroscopic evidence that the stars seem to be moving away from a common point of origin. His reasoning was that if the earth and other planets undergo a great deal of motion we have no reason to suppose that the stars are at rest. Their apparent rest may be explained by the fact that the distances between them are so vast that their motions are imperceptible.

Early in the nineteenth century, an astronomer named Olbers advanced the view that the diameter of the universe was 2000 million parsecs, or 4×10^{22} miles. This may sound naïve to us today when we are accustomed to envisioning the universe as one huge expansion of galaxies and stars over immeasurable distances. Olbers' reasoning was that the sky should be much brighter at night than it is, on the basis of the number of visible stars. The only loss of intensity of starlight that he could see was that of spread from a distance. Light from a simple point source loses intensity according to the inverse square of the distance, the same ratio as gravity. Hence, Olbers saw a similarity of measurement between gravity and light. What we can conclude about light we can apply to gravity, and vice versa. Basing himself upon a quantitative analysis of all the light that strikes the earth and of all the gravitational forces that influence the earth, and supposing a uniform distribution of matter throughout the universe, he arrived at his conclusions about the size of the universe.

Mach and Einstein went along with the concept of a limited universe, although they did not restrict themselves to the size advanced by Olbers. Einstein maintained that the universe could not be infinite. Taking the supposition that gravity influences every body in the universe, he argued that gravity would be infinite if the universe were infinite. However, were this the case, its force would be so great that matter would be radiant energy according to the formula $E = mc^2$, and the universe would be an infinite blaze rather than the system of bodies that it is.

The supposition in all reasoning from Galileo, Newton, up to Mach and Einstein was that of *uniform distribution* of matter throughout the universe. Astronomical evidence gradually showed that this supposition can be questioned. Now, a word must be said about uniform distribution. The contrary of *uniform* is not disordered. It is *random*. Uniform would mean a geometrically systematic distribution, for example, one molecule per cubic yard of interstellar space. *Random* distribution would mean a distribution of matter according to physical influences. It would mean, for example, an average distribution of dust on a floor which changes position according to drafts, passersby, etc., always remaining average but not uniform.

Since the geometry of Euclid is that of uniform distribution, the consideration of random distribution would raise the question of the applicability of Euclidean geometry to reality in a theory of measurement. Euclidean geometry works hand-in-hand with the physics of Newton for the following reasons:

1. Euclidean geometry is based upon an ideal distribution of matter following the construction of a line as a moving point, the construction of a plane on three points or one line and one point and crossed by straight lines, and the construction of volumes by a simple change of direction perpendicular to the plane.

2. Conversely, points can be considered the crossing of two straight lines or as the end of any line.

3. The shortest distance between two points is a straight line simply

because it is the most economical distance between them. It may be considered as *natural path* or *natural avenue* between them.

4. The above is the basis of trigonometry in the practical order and topography in the theoretical order. For example, we consider any mountain as pyramidal or conical in shape and simplify our measurements accordingly.

In Newtonian physics, we put those points to work in the following manner:

1. Newton noted that moving bodies, in a measurable distance, have a tendency to travel in and persist in a straight line. This, for him, is then the most economical type of motion, and any curved motion, such as that of planetary orbits, can be explained as vectors, that is, a most economical balance to two rectilinear motions.

2. Hence, a straight line is a *natural path* or *natural avenue* of the motions of bodies.

3. Since moving bodies move according to the forces that influence them, these forces have a straight line as their natural avenue.

4. The universal force of gravity can then be represented as a straight line between enormous points.

However, the introduction of the consideration of *random* rather than *uniform* distribution of matter in the universe raises questions not only of the applicability of Euclidean geometry but also of Newton's interpretation of gravity. Gravity takes two forms: resistance to being raised, called "weight" or *mass gravitation*, and resistance to being moved or stopped, called *inertia*. Actually, these are the same. If we take all the work required to raise an object, it is the same as all the work required to move it over any distance if we consider the distance a factor in the work. This was thought to be a coincidence. Newtonian physics could not explain it because it considered gravity a product of *mass and distance*. Aristotle would not have been surprised because he considered gravity a product of *mass and position*. Einstein, too, considers gravity a product of position. In this he followed Mach.

If the distribution of matter in the universe is *random*, that means that there are denser and rarer areas between stars and galaxies. This would mean, according to the classical concept of gravity, that gravity would vary over huge areas according to the density and closeness of bodies and matter in those areas. This would mean *local* rather than *universal* gravitation. In turn, this would mean that the actions of molecules and atoms would be slowed down in denser material conditions, as, for example, in the center of a star. This should be shown up in a spectroscopic analysis of the radiation of their elements from a star, for example, the sun. This has been verified by observation of hydrogen and helium in the sun. Their characteristic spectroscopic lines lean a bit toward the red. In recent times, this has been verified not only from the components of the sun but also from other stars in our galaxies as well as from starlight from other galaxies.

With the confirmation, it would then seem that curvature geometry would better describe the distribution of matter than Euclidean geometry. Just as a straight line is considered a natural path in Euclidean geometry and corresponds to rectilinear motion of moving bodies, so also, in curvature geometry, a curved line is the natural path. However, does there correspond any natural curved motion in the universe and on a scale much vaster than that envisioned by Newton? As a matter of fact, there is a lot of curved motion in the universe, but this can be explained in Newtonian fashion. The test of "curved space," that is, such a distribution of matter that curvature geometry applies to it better than Euclidean geometry, could be verified in the direction of something moving with extreme rapidity.

This could be light. If this supposition is true, light, following the naturally curved path, should be detected in some sort of curvature. The *assumption* of the bending of light was able to clear up one difficulty almost immediately. Despite more and more careful observations in astronomy that had led to the discovery of the velocity of light and more accurate descriptions of the orbits of planets, there was still the uncomfortable realization that our measurements were inaccurate by forty-two seconds of an arc every hundred years in the orbit of the planet Mercury. Even though Mercury's closeness to the sun makes it difficult to observe, such a discrepancy is a major problem in astronomy. The assumption that light bends could account for the discrepancy. The only major object nearby to account for this bending would be the gravitational pull of the sun. Assuming this, then, it would give us the rate of the bending and give us a key to putting the tentative conclusion to the test of further observation.

In 1919, Sir James Jeans put this to the test with the assumption that the curvature of light could be detected by the apparent displacement of stars behind the sun and apparently close to the sun's disk. The only way to detect this would be during a total eclipse of the sun, and in the 1919 total eclipse he was able to see an apparent displacement of a star close to the sun's disk. The explanation is that the light is curved in coming to us, and although we know where the star *is*, the light coming from it is curved and we apparently see it elsewhere. This experiment was repeated in 1924, and can be repeated any time now with the coronascope.

Now, if universal gravitation were true, there would be so much gravitational force influencing the light that it would follow the line of least resistance and proceed in a straight line. The fact that it sometimes curves is an indication that there are local gravitational forces. G. F. Fitzgerald, in 1894, had maintained that gravity is probably due to a change in the structure of the ether produced by the presence of matter. Einstein, taking over from Fitzgerald, urged that gravity is produced by the bodies, not by a change in the ether. So conceived, gravity is a product of bodies in a certain place, whereas older physicists had held that bodies are in a certain place because of gravity. *Gravity is, as it were, not an independent force but rather an environmental extension of the body itself.* And this is remarkable, for it is a restatement that gravity is a secondary effect of quantity, which, in turn, is a principle of bodies. This is almost a reiteration of the Aristotelian-Thomistic position.

Once we understand gravity as a natural position, then we have seen the reason why weight, or mass gravitation, is identical with inertial gravitation. Both are effects on a body of its position in relation to another body or other bodies. Hence, the body, whether at rest or in motion, is, as the scholastics say, *in situ naturali,* in its proper place, and it naturally tends to maintain that place since it tends to maintain its accidental being. This place may be a position, or in motion it may be the line of least resistance, its natural path. Once again, these are fundamental tenets of Aristotelian mechanics.

This brings about a further development in one of the principles of special relativity, which states that under different physical conditions we might not know the difference of the effects of the physical conditions on ourselves and our environment, or if we did know, we might not be able to measure them. The same force of gravitation that slows down the molecules would have the same effect upon our bodily states, our weights and measures, our notions of distance, and our measurements of time.

For example: the gravity of the planet Mars, if we take the earth as a standard, is 00.38. This means that a hundred-pound weight would weigh only thirty-eight pounds on Mars. This also means that on Mars we would weigh a little over one third of our earth weight. Our system of weights, measures, and distances, then, would be different from that of the earth in a rather confusing way. Weights and measures are based upon the convenience of our muscular system, namely, what the healthy man can lift conveniently. Our system of distances is based upon what a man can conveniently walk in a day. It is then subdivided into about twenty units. Hence, we could, if we wished, state that a mile is one twentieth of a day's march, or state that a day's march is twenty miles.

A human being would, at first, find life on Mars, granted that it would have a livable surface (which it most likely does not), easy for a time. He would find it easy to run, to carry objects about, to throw objects. He could cover vast distances with a great amount of ease, all because his muscular system would find Martian gravity almost inconsiderable compared to physical conditions on earth. He would find it harder to stop once he had started. On the other hand, a Martian would find life on earth almost unbearable. Compared to his muscular system, earth standards would be almost impossible for him. Everything, including himself, would weigh two thirds more than what he was adapted to, and a walk of several miles would almost be out of the question for him. Hence, in any interplanetary travel, we would have to have four standards: (1) earth men on earth; (2) earth men on Mars; (3) Martians on Mars; and (4) Martians on earth.

There would be further differences. Mars is a smaller planet than earth. Hence, its horizon would be closer. Our planetary notion of distance would be that much smaller on Mars than on earth. The earth man would think it easy to cover vast differences, since we usually judge "vast" by a horizon scale. The Martian, on the other hand, would think the earth abnormally vast.

Our systems of time would be different. Mars rotates on its axis at about the same rate as the earth. Hence our notion of a day would be about the same. On the other hand, the Martian year is almost twice that of ours. There would be different notions of the seasons.

Our notions of color would be different. Mars is almost twice as far from the sun as we are, and the sun's light is almost four times weaker and dimmer than on earth. Hence, colors on Mars would be more subdued and warmer than on earth. The temperatures would be that much colder, depending not only on the distance from the sun but also on the rarity of the atmosphere.

In certain ways there could be mutual compensation. In other ways there would not. The lightness of gravity would also affect our watches and clocks. For example, when a clock is wound up, a spring or a weight exerts pressure on the machinery of the clock. This pressure is regulated by the pendulum, which, in turn, is measured by the standards of earth gravity. On Mars, since this gravity is weaker, the clock would speed up, and we would not really know what time it might be. We would have to devise new machinery with a view to the different gravity.

Nevertheless, in such close proximity between earth and Mars, we would have some basis of comparison. Suppose, on the other hand, that we could be transported to a totally unknown planet of a distant star. The only thing we could trust would be our muscular system since all of our weights and measures and their instruments and our clocks would be affected, even an atomic clock.

In other words, universal gravitation would have no meaning. In every case, the determinant would be local gravitation, and we would have no way, apart from our muscular system, to determine what this is or whether there could be universal gravitation.

The consideration of the manner of this local influence, this local extension of bodies that we call gravity, led Einstein, in 1949, into his *universal field* theory.

UNIVERSAL FIELD THEORY

In 1784, Coulomb discovered that magnetism has an influence over intervening space. He also discovered that the force of this influence is the inverse square of the distance. This consideration was developed practically by Faraday who discovered that the disturbance of a magnetic influence can induce a charge. Thus Faraday invented the dynamo, which induces either direct or alternating current by the disturbance of a magnetic influence with another magnet. Henry, Maxwell, Ohm, Poisson, Gauss, and Green did much theoretical work on the properties of these magnetic influences. They also discovered that a similar influence is set up about a conductor, except that whereas the magnetic influence radiates in a three-dimensional field from the north pole outwardly and bends back to the south pole of a magnet and similarly from the south pole, a conductor, or "boreal" field, spirals about the conductor in such way that its direction is perpendicular to the direction of the conductor. Thus the disturbance of a magnetic field creates an induced charge, which, in turn, sets up a boreal field.

The strength of either field is the inverse square of the distance from the source. As noted above, Fitzgerald had suggested that gravity is probably due to a change in the structure of the ether. The same could be said for the magnetic field and the boreal field. The common note running throughout these observations and conclusions is the ratio of the inverse square of the distance. Maxwell had drawn these together and had thus applied the laws of dynamics to electronics. He thus became the father of electrodynamics.

Einstein added a new interpretation to this. Just as the magnetic field and boreal field are constituted by their source, Einstein had concluded that gravity is constituted by a body as its source, and hence is a function of a body at a certain position. He gradually came to the conclusion that the similarities between a gravitational influence, or gravitational field, and magnetic and induced fields are overwhelming. Although a magnetic field is much stronger than a gravitational field (1×10^{12} stronger), nevertheless there is the same ratio, the inverse square of the distance. Hence, the field seems to be the constant in the universe. Furthermore, the field is constituted by objects, and not the inverse. Hence, we must reinterpret space not as the constituent factor of the position of bodies but rather the effect of the positions of bodies. Hence, the bodies are the sources, not the effects.

EINSTEIN'S UNIVERSE

The geometry followed by Einstein in his theories was that of Riemann. Riemann's curvature geometry is that of positive curvature. The fundamental postulates and the theorems developed therefrom curve back upon themselves. Hence, any consideration of the distribution of the matter in the universe according to Riemannian geometry would picture the universe as a closed universe; that is, if the geometry of positive curvature best describes the universe, it does so because the distribution of matter closes back upon itself. Actually, we did not know enough about the matter in the universe at the time to get more than a suggestion of the proper geometry. This had to await the hundred-inch telescope of Mt. Wilson and the two hundred-inch telescope at Palomar Mountain. Early in the 1920's, Friedmann, a Russian mathematician at Kiev, discovered an error in Einstein's calculations. The correction of the error required taking Einstein's fundamentally sound postulates and putting them in the framework of the negative curvature of Lobarchevski. This meant that matter, instead of folding in on itself, was rather curving away from a common center. This seems to have been verified by both telescopes mentioned above as well as by some of the findings in radio astronomy, and is a significant point in the expanding universe theories.

Before closing this chapter, we must ask what exactly Einstein did. Before making him too metaphysical, we must remember that Einstein corrected conceptual systems of measurements by adding more accurate norms of measurement. Hence, he dealt primarily in the order of concepts. However, a theory of measurement is not purely a conceptual system. It is fundamentally a system of ideas having a reference to reality. It is because relativity is a theory of measurement that it can be applied readily to reality in such problems as the velocity of light and the bending of light, the interpretation of gravitational fields, etc.

Yet Einstein seems to have gone a step farther. In one of his last written statements, in a short autobiography included in an anthology about him,* he went so far as to maintain that fundamentally all science must attempt to discover the extramental conditions of bodies and interpret them theoretically rather than to try to force conclusions into a conceptual system. In this, again, he was greatly influenced by Ernst Mach, who as physicist had maintained that the mathematical principles of Newton were being pushed too far, and who, as a philosopher, became interested in sensation as caused by extra-mental objects. Einstein states his indebtedness to Mach, and although he does not come close to what we would call realistic philosophy, he does maintain that the emphasis should be from the object to the mind.

There is nothing about relativity that is alien to scholastic philosophy. The fundamental relationship of time and space, which is at the heart of the special relativity theory, had been maintained explicitly by Aristotle and the scholastics long before Galileo discovered it was easier to explain certain phenomena about velocity and acceleration by time than by distance. The development from general relativity into field theory, the fact that gravity is a product of mass and position rather than mass and distance had been maintained by Aristotle and scholastic philosophers under the consideration of the secondary formal effects of quantity. Einstein never maintained that truth is purely relative. Although his theodicy is that of Spinoza and his epistemology that of Mach, nevertheless his entire lifetime is the record of a man trying to seek the true relationship of theory to reality.

SUMMARY

1. *Special relativity* is a theory to correct the difficulties of measuring the positions and velocities of objects.
2. Einstein proposed that since measurement depends on the position of the observer and thus makes the correlation of time and space difficult, a new constant, the velocity of light in a vacuum be used.
3. *Special relativity* is applied successfully to the resolution of wave and particle properties of fast-moving particles. The rate of the conversion of mass properties to wave, or energy, properties is $E = mc^2$.

---

* *Albert Einstein: Philosopher-Scientist*, Paul Arthur Schillp, ed.

4. *General relativity* was occasioned by the manner of the distribution of matter in the universe.

   Just as Newtonian physics looked upon a straight line as a natural path for moving bodies, general relativity looks upon a curved line as a natural path for moving bodies.
5. There is no universal gravity. Gravity is a property set up by the masses of bodies and their positions, not vice versa.
6. Similarities between magnetic fields, boreal fields, and gravity — although varying in strength — are the basis of Einstein's *universal field theory.*

CHAPTER TWELVE

QUALITIES and QUALITATIVE CHANGES

It may seem strange to consider qualities after this long treatment of quantity, extension, their secondary effects, and the interrelation of time and space. However, much of what we have considered recently has been qualitative. Apart from quantity and relationship, all accidents are either qualities or have many qualitative aspects about them. Furthermore, such secondary effects of quantity as figure, position, etc., are qualities, and every material quality is based on the fact that a body is extended. Points do not exist in physical reality. Hence, even for a body to have qualities, it must first of all be extended in virtue of its quantity. This relationship between quantity and qualities is so close that St. Thomas maintains that the rooting of material qualities in quantity is so close as to have misled philosophers into identifying quantity with material substance (cf. *Summa Theologiae*, I, q. 52, art. 1; III, q. 77, art. 2).

In any consideration of the accidents of a body, the most obvious are quantity and extension. Nevertheless, we soon discover that there are types of modifications over and above the amounts of matter there are in a body. For example, there is a typical but variable shape of a body. There is a typical but variable density or rarity about it. It will be typically active or inactive. These types of modifications, expressive of a certain *kind* of accident rather than a certain *amount*, are called *qualities*. The Latin term "quality" means "of a certain sort," just as the term "quantity" means "of a certain amount." We define "quality," thus, as a *formal modification of a substance*.

Since any accident apart from quantity and relationship is either a quality or rooted in a quality, it would be hopeless to attempt to classify all qualities. The best we can do is to classify general types of qualities. These are classified according to their proximity to the type of existence of a substance, starting off with the manner of their existence and then proceeding to their operations and changes. These general classifications are called *orders* of qualities, and are as follows:

1. *The first order* of quality is the manner in which a substance exists, and is called *habit*. The term "habit" comes from the Latin *modus se habendi*, which simply means "manner of existence." Habit, thus, as understood philosophically is much wider than the common acceptance of the term. Since it supposes self-existence, it is not substantial. However, it describes the general manner of something's existence over and above its substantial or accidental particularities.

The full treatment of habit is in connection with the categories in logic or ontology. In general, though, we may say that habits are *entitative* or *acquired*. Entitative habits are simply the manner of existence. Acquired habits are manners of operation gradually acquired through a repetition of acts. These may be non-conscious, as, for example, in the manners picked up by plants in growing, by animals in the search for food, etc., or they may be consciously acquired. Consciously acquired habits are what we ordinarily call habits, and like all other acquired habits they are gained through a repetition of actions. They become so much a part of the possessor that they have been termed, by Aristotle, second nature.

2. *The second order* of quality is the ability for operation, *power and potency*. This is the expression that all bodies are intrinsically active and that they have powers of operation called *active potencies*. These have to do with their properties of activity, and deal, for example, with the activity of hydrogen, the valency of carbon, the inertness of helium, etc. On a more highly organized scale, they treat of the activity of one person and the general slowness of another. These may be traced back to their body chemistry, but they are definitely qualities of the substance.

3. *The third order* of quality is *action and reaction*. These are the first actual expressions of the existence of a being in operation. Both the actions and the reactions express the existence of a substance. Insofar as any being is intrinsically active, it is either active or, when affected by something else, reactive.

There is a special importance to activity and reactivity insofar as we learn of the nature of something through an analysis of its operations. From quantity we learn *that* something is. Through an analysis of its activities and reactions we learn *what* it is. Hence, we can scarcely underestimate the importance of this order of quality.

4. *The fourth* order of quality is *figure and alteration*. As seen in the

chapter on quantity, a body not only has a distribution of parts. It also has a manner of this distribution. This is figure. Also, by the fact that it is active as a body, it has qualitative changes as well as quantitative changes. This is *alteration,* and is of special importance in cosmology.

Insofar as qualities are determinations, they proceed from form. This, again, accounts for their importance in learning the nature and essence of their subject.

ALTERATION OR QUALITATIVE CHANGE

The term "alteration" signifies a change to "otherness." Qualitative changes in bodies have a characteristic all their own. They can be both instantaneous and yet gradual. Because they are based on form, and are in themselves accidental forms, their first possession is in an instant. However, since they are the qualities of bodies, their changes are subject to material conditions, and these, as a general rule, are gradual. For example, there is an instant when the illuminated wall first becomes lit. Then it gradually becomes brighter. There is an instant when an active body begins to change its shape. However, the successive changes involved in the overall transition take time.

The above is the fact, and hence we define "alteration" as *a change toward the acquisition and full possession of a quality*. We can illustrate this by going back to the examples above. When a surface becomes bright, this is the result of photons of light striking it and reflecting from it. The first photon to strike the wall does so in an instant. It is likely that many photons simultaneously strike the wall. However, the first one or the first number of photons strikes in an instant. After that, the gradual brightening results from successive photons striking the already brightened surface. Similarly, when an active body changes shape, there is an instant when the first molecule changes its physical position or chemical condition. Gradually the other molecules in the body move after the first.

After the first possession of the quality, there is a gradual, successive change tending to the fullness of the possession of the quality. For example, after the first cell in the rose undergoes the chemical change of pigmentation whereby it reflects red wavelengths and appears red, there is the successive change in all the cells in this chemical change of pigmentation. Furthermore, as all the cells change, they change gradually from greenish white to pinkish white to the fullness of red before corruption sets in, cell by cell, and they turn an ugly brown.

The gradual character of qualitative changes, the fact that after the first instant the change is a gradual one toward fullness, has occasioned several explanations in philosophical rather than physical or chemical terms. In general, they consist of explanations in terms of the addition of more of the quality to the subject. For example, the rose becomes redder because more red is added to it. It is true that we can quote Aristotle along these lines. He often speaks of a non-white becoming white, and he speaks of the medical man becoming musical. This is Platonic language, and it is interesting to note that the sections of the *Physics* and *Metaphysics* where Aristotle speaks in this manner are the sections that textual scholars have identified as Platonic periods in Aristotle's thinking.

The explanation through addition can be considered in some qualitative changes. Obviously, a state of density or rarity can be achieved by the addition or diminution of the possessed in the possessor. Similarly, it can be achieved by the constriction or extension of the possessor.

On the other hand, changes involving figure or color must be explained not by the addition or subtraction of anything but by physical or chemical changes. A body does not become round because "roundness" is added to it. Nor does it become green because "greenness" is added to it. There are no such things as "roundness" or "greenness." These are concepts abstracted from physical qualities. A body becomes round by the redistribution of its parts. A body becomes green because of the qualities of the surface whereby it absorbs all wavelengths except green and reflects the wavelength of green. Hence, we cannot think here of the addition or subtraction of abstractions to a physical body. We must explain qualitative changes in some other fashion.

There is one common principle running throughout every qualitative change, and that is *potency*. In its simplest form, a qualitative change takes place because the subject is changeable in that regard. However, in order to be changeable regarding the quality in question, or regarding anything else, for that matter, it must be intrinsically changeable. In the case of density and rarity, the qualitative condition depends upon the capacity of the subject as regards the quality possessed. As we saw, density can be constituted either by adding to a fixed capacity, like forcing more air into a container, or by constricting the container of a fixed amount of matter. In either case, the container is the potency as regards the possessed, and the answer is in terms of the container as a potency. The same is true for rarity, except that either some of the possessed material is removed from a fixed container, or the container of a fixed amount is enlarged. Once again, the container is the variable or fixed potency in respect to the fixed or variable actual material contained.

Other qualitative changes are variations on potency. For example, an increase in heat can be achieved by raising the energy state of the contained, for example, air in a room. However, this depends upon the potency of the air to be so agitated that its raised energy state gives off the quality we call heat. On the other hand, the constriction of the container can force the molecules so close together that their more frequent collisions raise the energy state of the contained. In this latter case, we have a twofold potency, that of the air molecules and that of the container. The changes in figure and color are explained in terms of the potency for the redistribution of parts on the part of the subject, or its potency for changes in the physical and chemical states of its surface so that it either transmits, reflects, or allows to pass through certain frequencies or wavelengths which we see as color.

In every event, the fundamental explanation of alteration is to be found in the potencies of the subject to change qualitatively. It is in this way that St. Thomas considers substance and accidents a further example of the complete explanation of created being in terms of potency and act. The first is the limitation of existence by essence. The second is the limitation of form as the fulfillment of material potencies by matter as potentially existing form. The third is the limitation of qualities and other accidents on the part of substance as a potency for further perfection by accidents.

We see, then, that qualities are not abstract ideals of "greenness," "redness," "roundness," etc. They are physical states of the body itself, actualizations of the subject's potencies for further perfections.

A word must be said about spiritual qualities. Spiritual qualities are the proper accidents of a spiritual substance, which, of course, does not allow for quantitative accidents. Hence, they are such accidents as justice, benevolence, etc. In the case of man, his soul, as a spirit, has the obediential potency to participate in supernatural qualities such as sanctifying and actual grace and the infused virtues. Thus, the soul, as the form of the body, participates as such in grace. The intellect participates in faith. The will participates in hope and charity.

As seen above, qualities are too diverse to be classified save in the four orders considered. However, we may point out that there are such common qualities of bodies as shape and figure, activity or inertness, etc. On the other hand, there are proper qualities, such as the proper shape of arsenic crystals or the proper activity of hydrogen. These qualities are what we call physical or chemical *properties*.

LOCATION OF SOME QUALITIES

There is one problem peculiar to certain types of qualities, and that is whether the quality is properly in the object or properly in the perceiver. This is especially true of color.

For centuries it was generally considered that color was in the object only. The eye faithfully recorded the color of the object. It was admitted that there could be deficiencies in the eye whereby it failed completely, as in the case of blindness, or partially, as in the case of color blindness. When asked what color might be, it was considered a quality natural to types of entities such as plants, stones, animals, etc., that could be applied artificially to objects through pigments in paints.

Sir Isaac Newton's experiments with prisms introduced the consideration that colors might be wavelengths and that light might be a proper proportion of all visible wavelengths. Furthermore, experimentation in neurology, the discovery, for example, that dogs and cats do not see color but rather view reality in terms of black, gray, and white, raised the question that the objectivity of the color could be no more than proper wavelengths and frequencies and that color is in the eye of the perceiver.

This latter caused concern in scholastic circles since it seemed to undermine the character of the objectivity of reality, especially since we learn the essence of an object from its properties, and color is often among the properties of an object. Meanwhile, further investigation into the central nervous system, especially in brain functions, seemed to verify the position of the color in the perceiver. Actually, the nerves seem to operate like wet cell batteries. This led to the further conclusion that light in activating the eye caused a slight electric charge which was registered in the brain as a color. Experiments in brain prodding with electric needles evoked certain colors, pure colors apart from representation of colored objects. Furthermore, colors are often manufactured with a view to electronics rather than to human perception. For example, in the selecting of the colors green, yellow, and red for traffic lights, the selecting and testing is done not with a view to human perception, since that is taken for granted, but with a view to penetration of radiation through fog. In other words, it is not as though a board of color testers would agree as to which hue is recognizably green or red. Rather, it is the selection of tinted glass allowing for the most penetrating radiation of certain wavelengths or frequencies which can penetrate through fog and haze in such way that it will be recognized as green or red by the average viewer, and a shade of gray differing from two other shades of gray by the color-blind viewer.

Is there, then, objective color, or is it purely subjective? The only answer is that it is both. The objectivity of the color is that there is something about the surface of an object whereby it absorbs all frequencies or wavelengths except one and reflects that predominantly. We say predominantly, since there is a slight reflection of all the wavelengths, although one predominates sharply. This, then, is perceived and stored in the brain, and we call its effect on us a definite color such as blue or red. If the surface absorbs all partially and reflects them all partially, we call the result some shade of gray.

In conclusion, then, a color is partially objective, in the character of the emitting or reflecting object, and partially subjective as recorded in the brain. Since there is a commonness about the frequencies or wavelengths and about the human brain, we can agree as the color concerned. It is thus not purely subjective. On the other hand, there are certainly subjective aspects to it. One person will see red as rather dull, another will see it as bright. Yet both will agree that it is red since their brains are similar and the wavelengths are common. Hence, we might call a color a sense being with a foundation in reality.

SUMMARY

1. A quality is a *formal perfection of a substance.*
2. Since there are so many qualities, we cannot classify them all. We classify the general types, or orders, of them as follows:
   First order — habit;
   Second order — power and potency;
   Third order — action and reaction;
   Fourth order — figure and alteration.
3. *Alteration,* or qualitative change, is the *change toward the acquisition and full possession of a quality.*
   The first acquisition is in an instant. The fulfillment of full or partial possession is gradual.
4. The ultimate principle of the possession and change of qualities is the potency of the possessing subject.
5. There are objective qualities. However, their perception, especially in the case of color, undergoes frequent subjective modification.

CHAPTER THIRTEEN

ARISTOTELIAN SCIENCE

One of the problems facing the physical sciences today is that they have come to exist almost in isolation. This is the result of many factors: discoveries, historical events, theoretical developments, and vast cultural changes, particularly in the success of technological advances. Of late, however, many theoretical scientists have been seriously considering the need for philosophy both as a starting point for and a fulfillment of scientific investigation, both theoretical and practical.

Aristotelian philosophy is an excellent introduction to the sciences because Aristotle saw and explained several persistent points in his philosophy of nature which continue to be significant problems in the sciences. One of the basic problems in contemporary philosophy is called indeterminacy or uncertainty. The problem is this: although there is a uniformity in reality and symmetry in theory, it is not the same on all levels. In the lower levels we must face the fact of a wider range of possibles and alternate developments. This variability is a manifestation of potency, and is explained in Aristotle's teaching on primary matter. The regularity of the universe is explained in form and in the four causes. The tendencies of the beings in operation are explained through privations. Hence, in his significant cosmological points, those that are peculiarly Aristotelian, Aristotle has the key not only to the understanding of nature but also to the fundamental points of the science of nature in its epistemological developments and difficulties.

ARISTOTELIAN SCIENTIFIC CONTENT

Among the problems that continue to occupy the attention of scientists and philosophers are: the structure of the universe, its size or its possible infinity, the movements of its components, the energies of its components, the fundamental structure of matter. These problems today are developments of Renaissance science, which in turn was inherited from the Platonic-Aristotelian tradition against a background of Greek classical thought.

The first truly scientific development of these problems was by Aristotle. The treatment is in his works: *Physics, Metaphysics, On Generation and Corruption,* and *On the Heavens and the Earth.* In these works Aristotle maintained:

1. That the universe is finite in being and in mass;
2. That it is spherical in shape, with the stars in regular orbits, the planets in epicyclical orbits, and with bodies gravitating (literally) to their proper places in a balance of forces;
3. That the earth is at the center of the universe;
4. That bodies are composed of intrinsically energetic elements that can be broken down into particles;
5. That the universe is an eternal, evolutionary process of beings tending to the fulfillment of their potencies before corrupting into new beings similarly tending to a fulfillment of their potencies, etc.

The problem of the infinity of the universe as Aristotle met it was inherited from Eleatic philosophy. The Greeks found it hard to consider the universe as limited because that raised the question of what would be outside it. They postulated the void to answer that question.

Parmenides had maintained that being is the same, identical, timeless, ingenerable, and incorruptible. He should have maintained an infinite universe because the being he postulated had no limitations. The metaphysical infinite is that which has no limitations whatsoever. Instead, Parmenides visualized equality, and maintained this to mean equidistance. Hence, he portrayed the universe as a sphere. This gave rise, in the Platonic dialogue *The Sophist,* to the concept of distance and divisibility, the division of the one into the many. What is divisible is not absolutely unlimited. It is metaphysically finite since division supposes intrinsic divisibility. We recognize herein another argument for Aristotelian primary matter rather than the development within Platonism of extrinsic matter, or space, as the principle localizing forms.

Parmenides' disciple, Melissus, rightly maintained that the being of Parmenides is matter, and he flatly maintained that since we say that being is and that there is no way we can say that being is not, we cannot say that being or matter ever ceases to be either in time or in space. Hence, it simply is, infinitely and eternally.

Aristotle's answer to this is metaphysical, mathematical, and physical. His *metaphysical* answer is brief.

Parmenides based himself on the idea of being. However, we may have the *same idea*, but this does *not* mean that *being is the same*. We may say that a man is a being, a dog is a being, a plant is a being, and a stone is a being. However, in reality, we do not thereby maintain that the man, the dog, the plant, and the stone are identical, even though we use the same term "being" in relation to them. As Aristotle realized, not only are the individual beings of our experience not identical, but the concept of being itself shifts its meaning according to its application. The concept is analogical. This is the basis of the metaphysical treatise on the analogy of being. Hence, we cannot argue on Parmenidean grounds either for or against the infinity of the universe. No matter what Parmenidean logic may say, reality forces us to shift our concept of being in its real application to things ". . . for *is* is used in many senses" (*Physics*, I, 2, 185a20).

Thus, if we use the term "infinite" to designate the universe, we use it in a modified sense rather than in the properly metaphysical sense. Why? Because being, if "infinite," is unique and can properly be referred only to the Being who is by His own nature, God, and who is the cause of being of all else.

Since Melissus had maintained that the universe is an infinite distribution of matter, we can reject his position on metaphysical grounds. Matter consists of substances which, in turn, are modified by accidents. By the very fact that composition enters into this, any use of the term "infinite" is only by appropriation. The universe is not one infinite substance since it consists of many components. There cannot be an infinity of accidents since this would suppose an infinite substance or an infinite number of substances. However, this is a manner of speaking, not proper metaphysical infinity. Hence we must investigate this manner of speaking. The term "infinite" is properly used in mathematics, and is used only in an accommodated sense in physics or philosophy of nature (cf. *Physics*, III, 6, 206a15 ff.; cf. *Metaphysics*, XI, 10, 1066b 22 ff.).

Mathematical infinity, by definition, includes the concept of not self-limiting. This is threefold. In the *numerical order* it simply means a series of numbers which does not close back upon itself. In the *linear order* it means a line which does not curve back upon itself. In the *geometrical order*, it is the space, curved or straight, set up by infinite linear boundaries. These, however, are mathematical abstractions — the perfect line or perfect curve never found in nature but which natural objects might resemble. Thus, when astronomers speak of the infinite universe, they mean that its distribution of matter resembles one or another of the geometrical infinite patterns. Any of these figures and certain of these numbers are *infinitely divisible* simply by dividing by a segment or multiplying by a fraction respectively.

Aristotle maintained that the outermost objects of the universe, the stars, were separated by measurable distances and that the estimation of these set up finite areas. Consequently, he argued, the universe must be finite and can be measured as finite, although he also maintained that it is a good deal bigger than his contemporaries thought it to be.

Physical infinity of the universe would mean that there are no boundaries to it and that matter continues to be distributed without end. Aristotle's position is that if we are dealing with one universe, we are dealing with one collection of bodies that influence one another and are somehow held in various relations with each other by one force.

If the universe is infinite, the force holding it together would have to be infinite because it would have to be at least as strong as the whole in order to maintain the components of the whole in their physical operations. These operations are moving and being held at rest. We would thus have an infinite force, with an infinite effect, infinitely keeping bodies in motion or at rest. This would mean that moving bodies would never stop and that bodies at rest could never get started. We know that this is not the case (cf. *On the Heavens*, I, 5 ff., 271b1 ff.; 7, 275b12 ff.; *Metaphysics*, XI, 10, 1066a35, 1067a8 ff., 1067a14).

If we suppose that the force holding the universe together is less than infinite, it follows that the force, being weaker than the universe, would be unable to hold it together and it would fall apart of its own weight. It would no longer be one infinite universe but a number of finite universes. This, incidentally, is exactly the reasoning used by the champions of the modern expanding universe theory.

It might be interesting to go back to the first argument for a moment. One of the consequences of the special relativity theory of Albert Einstein is the conclusion that the energy of a body is equal to its mass times the velocity of light squared ($E = mc^2$). This is finite. However, if the universe were one and infinite, gravity would be stronger than any known force and would be sufficient to reduce all bodies to energy. Hence, the universe would not be an infinite distribution of matter but rather an infinite distribution of radiant energy, an infinite glow.

Aristotle's position was, then, that the universe is finite. If that is the case, what can we learn of its structure?

The structure of the finite universe

Aristotle bases his analysis of the structure of the universe on two principles: the nature of the mass properties of bodies and the nature of motion. Starting from the fact that bodies have different relative weights, that some bodies weigh more than others according to their component elements, and that a body at rest tends to remain at rest while a body in motion tends to remain in motion, he then analyzes the types of motion (cf. *Physics*, IV, 8, 215a19).

Motion is *natural* when its source or origin is a principle within the body. Natural motion is, for Aristotle, of two basic kinds. The first is circular motion, which is the line of least resistance between the radial and the tangential, as illustrated below.

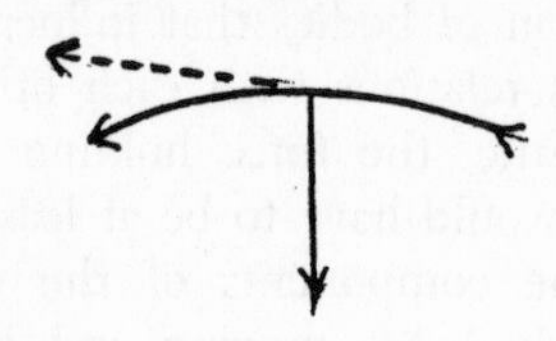

This type of natural motion is realized in the stars. It is not only the line of least resistance, but it also involves no coming-to-rest and no starting again. It simply continues. In its perfection it is realized in the stars or in any orbital motion. Thus, as we now know, the orbits of the planets would be perfect circles if the centers of gravity were in the exact center of the sun and the planets, and this would be a fulfillment of Aristotle's concept of natural, rotational motion as a perfect circle. The reason why the orbits of the planets are ellipses, not circles, is that their centers of gravity do not correspond to their geometrical centers. Because of the law of the mutual attraction of bodies, the centers of gravity are eccentric, thus setting up foci and a consequent elliptical orbit.

The second type of natural motion is the rectilinear motion of light objects tending upward and of heavy bodies tending downward. This is illustrated by the free fall of heavy bodies and by the pushing up of lighter elements because of the heavier mass of the atmosphere (cf. *On the Heavens*, I, 2, 268b12 ff.; II, 13, 294b31 ff.).

Any other motion is *constrained motion*, that is, motion subject to the constraint of some restraining force, for example, gravity, air resistance, etc. This can be rectilinear, rotational, or a combination of the two. The motion in a straight line of an object thrown directly upward would be an instance of constrained rectilinear motion. Its motion upward is overcome by the force of gravity, it stops, and it falls back. The motion of a boomerang illustrates constrained rotational motion. It goes in a circle, but it comes to rest because of gravity. Its rotational motion balances the force moving it in the direction in which it is thrown and the force of the air resistance it meets because of its shape. Nevertheless, there is the restraint of gravity that brings it to rest. A combination of both rectilinear and rotational constrained motion is illustrated by the parabola of an artillery projectile. It starts off in a straight line, but gravity curves it downward.

An inference from the above is a reaffirmation that the only natural rotational motion is that of the stars (according to Aristotle). There is nothing to stop them. Their motion is perfect. Hence, they move eternally.

Proper place is the termination of natural motion (cf. *Physics*, VIII, 3 and 4, 253b33 ff.). Bodies do not stop haphazardly. They stop here rather than there because the spot where they stop is the termination of a balance of forces. Aristotelian scholars puzzle over the precise meaning Aristotle had in mind when he spoke of a moving body being constantly subject to force. This gives us the impression that he maintained that the impulse still had some sort of contact with the moving body, or that there was some sort of "pinch effect" of the medium through which it traveled whereby it was kept moving forward. Aristotle had stated explicitly that a body set in motion tends to remain in motion, because motion is an actuality and any actuality tends to remain in act. Hence, he seems to have been close to our notion of inertia. Nevertheless, in constrained motion, there is some force or other which wears down the force of the propulsion in such way that the body is brought to rest. However, both the propulsion and the resistance vary the direction of the moving body in such way that it lands either where it is aimed or where the balance of forces brings it. Even in the aiming, types of resistance have to be taken into consideration and compensated for, as any artilleryman or target shooter will explain. The formula for this implies the propulsion (Mv) and the resistance (R), and in its simplest form is Mv/R.

"Proper place," then, is for Aristotle the place where a body stops after its propulsion has been overcome by resistance. It is important to understand Aristotle's notion of proper place. It is the place to which a body properly tends because of the forces influencing it. Hence it is a result rather than a purpose. The place does not exist for the body eventually to be put there. The body properly lands in the place because of the forces influencing it in its movements. The area of Meteor Crater in Arizona did not exist for a meteor to land there. It landed there as the result of atmospheric friction and terrestrial gravitation, and Meteor Crater is the result.

Briefly, then, proper place is: (1) the termination of the downward motion of heavy bodies and the upward motion of light bodies; (2) the orbits of the stars; and (3) the spot where a body stops as the result of the balance of forces achieved in its movements.

The fullness or emptiness of the universe (cf. *Physics*, IV, 6–8, 213a12 ff.)

Today we know that the expression "empty space" is a convenient mathematical term rather than a description of physical conditions between stars. In mechanics it simply means that we look to the stars as enormous points and the distances between them as straight lines without any reference to the areas included. When we take these into consideration in such way that we must represent the areas as curved and the measurements as curved lines, the notions of general relativity and field physics come into play.

We know that there is relatively a lot of matter between the stars: clouds of hydrogen gas, dust, etc. The physical problem of the nature of the space between heavenly bodies was that which the Greeks undertook to explain.

Once again we begin with the Eleatics. Parmenides and Melissus had argued that the universe is full since it is being. For a body to move, it would simultaneously occupy the place occupied by another. This would involve compenetration, which Parmenides and Melissus considered impossible. Subsequent Greek thinkers, in particular the atomists Leucippus and Democritus, refused to accept the Eleatic denial of local motion. They accepted, however, the Eleatic concept of being as the full. Hence, in order to account for the evident fact of motion, they postulated the "full" and the "void." The full consisted of individual units of atoms, each endowed with the attributes of Parmenidean being, and the "void" or "non-being" was the empty space through which the atoms moved.

Aristotle saw that the postulate of the void by the atomists was unnecessary. He maintained that local motion need not involve compenetration or the simultaneous occupation of the same place by two different bodies. Rather it could be explained as a replacement (cf. *Physics*, IV, 7, 214a28). A body can move to another place by taking the place of whatever was there previously. It can follow another body into a vacated place or it can force the former out of the place, just as the air follows the water into the vacated vase or just as, vice versa, the water can force the air out of the vase. We experience this when we move about. We feel a breeze where there is none simply because we feel ourselves moving the air out of the way. We experience directly that no void is required to explain movement. Consequently, the void is unnecessary.

What is more interesting and to the point is whether or not there is a void *within* the universe, whether or not there is emptiness within the universe (cf. *Physics*, IV, 8, 214b13 ff.).

The void within the universe would be either total or partial; that is, there would either be nothing between the larger components of the universe, or there would be areas of emptiness surrounded by areas of relative fullness.

Aristotle maintains that there is no total void within the universe. He reasons that since a body set in motion tends to remain in motion, a moving body would never come to rest unless something would bring it to rest. However, bodies do come to rest, and hence something besides themselves, some restraining force, has brought them to rest. This restraining force is the omnipresent *ether* (or *aether*). Here we must notice an extremely significant point introduced by Aristotle. The void was a conceptual entity; that is, it was an idea postulated by the Greeks to explain something as well as the lack of something. The *ether* was postulated by Aristotle as a physical force, a physical presence exercising its restraining influence on those things which would not otherwise stop. The ether made its reappearance in the seventeenth century as a conceptual entity, an idea postulated to explain the wave characteristics of radiation. It was later supplanted by the idea of the field to reconcile quantum theory with wave characteristics of light. However, in Aristotle's plan, it was a real entity between the heavenly bodies and beyond the earth's atmosphere of which it seems to have been an extension.

Just as there is no total void within the universe, so, also, is there no partial void (cf. *Physics*, IV, 8, 215a ff.). There are no vacuoles in the universe. Today we would say that even if there were such between the stars, the surrounding matter would drift into them filling them up. Aristotle's reasoning is again based on the properties of moving bodies.

A moving body is constantly being influenced by the resistance of other forces, among them the medium through which it passes, and in definite proportion (cf. *Physics*, IV, 8, 215a ff.). Consequently, its movement is a slowing down after the initial acceleration according to the formula Mv/R. If there were a partial void within the universe, there would be areas of non-resistance which would show up in the movements of bodies; that is, the moving body would be slowing down. On entering the void, it would continue at a non-slowing-down rate. On leaving the void, it would resume its slowing down. This should be perceptible as a change in the body. The process would be like the following:

Before the Void	In the Void	Outside of the Void
Mv/R	Mv/0	Mv/R

This would be perceived as an apparent acceleration of the body when it was in the void. The body would not speed up. It would cease to slow down for a time, but the impression of speeding up would be apparent, much as when the same runner, running with the same amount of energy, runs through water, on dry land, and again through water, successively. For the time that he is actually out of the water, away from the resistance of the water, he actually speeds up. A better example might be that of a car running in gear. In this case there is the constant drag of the engine block. When the clutch is disengaged, the drag ceases for a time and the car seems to accelerate. Upon re-engaging the gears, the motor slows down noticeably.

By similar reasoning, Aristotle argues that there is neither a partial void nor a total void within the universe. It is interesting to notice that this reasoning is confirmed day after day by the orbits of artificial satellites circling the earth.

The geocentric universe

Aristotle's scientific acumen is frequently questioned because he maintained that the earth is the center of the universe. Perhaps he accepted this originally because Platonism has the earth as the center of the universe. However, he later fortified his position with arguments from mechanics in the face of the positions of the Pythagoreans and Archelaus.

In Aristotle's time there were two hypotheses about the possible orbiting of the earth around some central body. The first, that of the Pythagoreans, was a somewhat fanciful development of the number "ten." They classified the heavenly bodies known at the time as the following: Earth, Moon, Sun, Mercury, Venus, Mars, Jupiter, Saturn, and the stars. This gives us nine heavenly bodies, counting the stars as one unit. This seemed unacceptable to the Pythagoreans because of their conviction of the harmonic qualities of the number "ten." Hence, they postulated a "counter earth" for the tenth body, and then proclaimed that the entire solar system revolved about a "divine fire." Aristotle had little patience with this theory since he considered it a rather unwarranted extension of mathematical aesthetics. He considered it rather a theory of art than a scientific theory (cf. *On the Heavens*, II, 13, 293a25).

The position of Archelaus, on the other hand, had much more to it. He maintained that the universe is a whirlpool of steamy water. In the center of this the empty sun floats, and since it is an empty sphere, it is not drawn into the whirlpool. The planets are in the whirl of the water, and they thus float around the sun. In a serious consideration of this, Aristotle argues that if the earth and planets changed position in this manner, the different positions of the earth would be shown up by observations of the stars which would appear to be changing their positions in relation to the earth. As a matter of fact, the parallax, the triangulation of stars over a six-month period when the earth is at opposite sides of the sun, does show such displacement. However, Aristotle had no means for such precise measurements, especially when the subtending is less than one second of one degree for the nearest star. Aristotle's argument was good. If the earth moves, its movement should be apparent against a background of stars. He saw no such displacement, and hence he concluded that the earth did not move (cf. *On the Heavens*, II, 14, 296b1 ff.).

Proceeding from this basis, Aristotle advanced his own reasons in favor of the geocentric universe.

There have been various representations of the earth in early thought. The most common representation, borrowed apparently from the Babylonians, pictured the earth as a flat disk surrounded by water and resting on a mountain, or an elephant, or a turtle, or something either physical or mythological. Yet there were always a few who maintained that the earth is a sphere. Among these was Aristotle. His argument was simply that the shadow cast by the earth on the moon could have no other explanation than the earth as a sphere (cf. *On the Heavens*, II, 14, 297b21).

Like Plato, Aristotle maintained that the earth is at the center of the universe. However, Plato had the earth revolving on its axis, thus giving the appearance of motion to the stars (cf. *On the Heavens*, II, 13, 293b 32). This, however, failed to take into account the epicycles of the planets. Moreover, the general opinion, with which Aristotle seems to have gone along, was that if the earth revolved, rivers and seas would overflow their banks much the same as a contained liquid slops over the edge of the container when it is moved. Aristotle maintained that the earth is at rest and that the stars move about it in spheres, the planets in epicycles.

Apart from the reasons given above, Aristotle adds an argument from mechanics. Once again, it is based on the natural movements of bodies, in this case, falling bodies. Briefly, it is this: all bodies, including such heavenly bodies as meteorites, fall toward the center of gravity. All such bodies fall toward the earth. Therefore, the earth is at the center of universal gravity (cf. *On the Heavens*, II, 13, 295b20 ff.). It is the absolute "down" from all sides of the universe. Furthermore, bodies coming from directly overhead on any point on the earth's surface fall toward the center of the earth, not to one side, or in parallel paths through the earth to a further center of gravity, as in the example below:

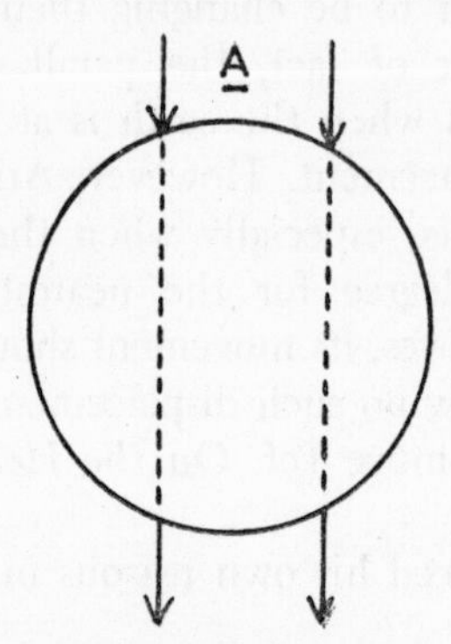

As bodies would fall if the earth were not the center of the universe.

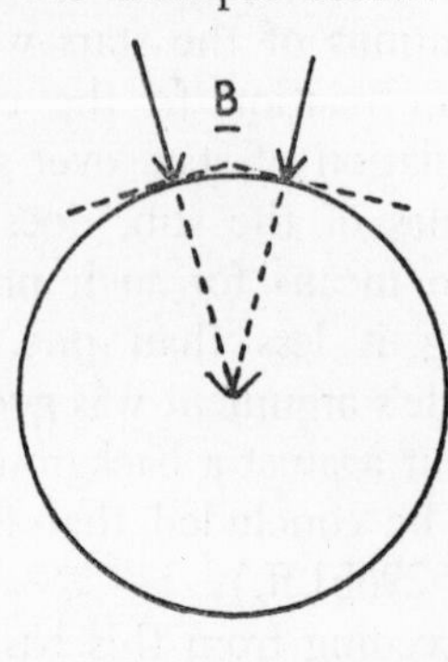

As bodies do fall. Hence the earth is the center of the universe.

Thus, because of the nature of falling bodies, the center of the earth must be the center of gravity, and the earth must be at the center of the universe.

The interesting point about such a position is not that it is based on the dignity of man or anything of that sort. The earth is not the center of the universe because man lives on it. It is the center of the universe because it is at the center of gravity. Man's presence on the earth is incidental to this. The reasoning involved is scientific, based on principles that are fundamental to mechanics. Exactly the same type of reasoning is the basis of the gravitometer whereby scientists have shown that the earth's gravity varies over the earth's surface and that the earth's center of gravity is not exactly at the center of the universe because of variations in its shape and its mass distribution. This, in turn, gives us a lead to an investigation of the forces acting on the earth in the period of its formation that would give it such a shape. The reasoning is good. Aristotle's difficulty was the failure of precise instruments. Even a telescope would have shown the many, many stars invisible to the naked eye yet distributed on such a large scale that the earth could not possibly be the central focus of such a great distribution of matter. It must be remembered that Copernicus argued to the heliocentric system against a background of Nicholas of Cusa and Novara who maintained that the planets go around the sun and that the sun is just another star. Copernicus' calculations were a revision of the geometry of Claudius Ptolomaeus. Galileo did not argue that the earth was not the center of the universe. He followed Copernicus' lead and, through a telescope, saw the many more stars, the moons of Jupiter, and the rings of Saturn.

The eternity of the universe

Contemporary scientific cosmology has expended much investigation in the problem of the age or eternity of the universe. There are two general positions about this problem: the *expanding universe theory* and the *steady state theory*. The former maintains that the universe began in some definite time in the past in some sort of cosmic explosion, and that by known methods and available data it is possible to achieve a time value to the process and to determine that time with a certain degree of accuracy. The latter theory, also called the "continued creation" theory maintains that there is no need to fall back upon a temporal creation. On the contrary, the evidence seems to be that the universe is an eternal process of the sudden appearance of matter in such way that the recession of distant galaxies is simply the making room for new matter. Neither of these theories deal with creation, properly speaking. The expanding universe theory maintains that some preexistent matter — hydrogen and some fundamental particles and molecules — are the source of the explosion. The steady state theory does not even raise the question of creation.

These theories are a modern and ornate expression of a problem known to Aristotle and his predecessors. The Greeks, too, were concerned with the age or eternity of the universe. For example, Aristotle maintained that the universe is eternal. Anaximander maintained that the universe was surrounded by a source that kept pouring elements into the universe which were differentiated by love and hate as principles of attraction and repulsion, generation and corruption. Parmenides' philosophy of being-and-no-change precluded creation since his concept of being was that of an eternal one. The Eleatics restored limited change only by basing themselves on the eternity of the sphere. Although Plato is sometimes considered to have advocated temporal creation, this would be difficult to establish. There is nothing in any of his writings that would lead us to the conclusion that he maintained any temporal character to this process. At least, Platonic doctrine can be just as easily interpreted in favor of eternal creation as it can for temporal creation.

As a matter of fact, the Greeks seemed to have found it difficult to visualize a time when there was no created being. Their mythology is full of explaining the beginning in terms of something emerging from a preexistent source. In fact, their acceptance of the eternity of things is clearly seen in their cultural concept of the cycle of the Iron Age, the Bronze Age, the Silver Age, and the Golden Age.

In the mythological development, it was the Greek tendency to visualize a time before time just as some of their concepts of the void were a visualization of a space outside of space. In the scientific expression, according to the science of the day, it was an attempt to explain the constant replenishment of the matter and the energy of the universe. Such realists as Anaximander and Anaxagoras fell back upon a source outside the spherical universe. For Anaximander it was infinite in extent. For Anaxagoras it was finite. In both cases, however, it was eternal, an eternal source of matter and energy. It should be noted here that the Greek word ἀρχή means "principle," as well as "beginning."

Plato, as we saw in Chapter Three, explains the duration of the universe in terms of the eternity and being of the Forms. So does Aristotle, but in a different manner (cf. *Physics*, VIII, 1 ff.; *Metaphysics*, XII, 7 ff.).

Aristotle never gave expression to the principle of the conservation of energy, but he uses the concept of conservation all through his physical and metaphysical works. Conservation, as understood in mechanics, means a property beyond our theory and our experimentation. Thus, the principle of the conservation of charge means that beyond our theory and experimentation, matter seems to be electromagnetic in character and that there is nothing that we can do about it. Similarly, the principle of the conservation of energy, first realized in its fullness by Leibniz and first expressed in mechanics by Joule, means that there are limitations to what we can do with matter. We can rearrange it, but we can neither create it nor destroy it. Hence, fundamental to any physical theory is the basic assumption that all change is a rearrangement of matter, and that the appearance of new forms of matter, for example, the "creation" of an electron, or of a new type of being, for example, a higher form of life in evolution, is but a rearrangement of matter. This is fundamental to Aristotle, for it is another expression of his philosophy of change, of generation and corruption, of the explanation of the changes and development in the universe according to the four causes.

Aristotle extended conservation into the order of being. There is nothing that we can do about being as such. It is. Material being changes, but as long as it exists, it is a being and tends to remain what it is in existence. Its change comes from corruption. However, this corruption may remain only in the order of potency as corruptibility. The process of corruption depends on some activity proceeding either from an extrinsic energy, intrinsic instability, or both. As long as it remains only a potential, the being tends to persist in existence. Even in the process of change, something is. Something is, and we can neither create nor destroy being. Hence, although in universal process individuals may change, being always is, and there is no reason for being as being not to be. This, then, suggests an eternal process, an eternal universe in which the components change but the being always exists.

As specified in the physical processes of the universe, Aristotle bases himself upon this conservation notion. What is incorruptible will remain eternally. What is corruptible proceeds from a source and itself is a source for further products. In each case, the source is a temporal antecedent. Hence, every change involves a before and after, and the measurement of that is time. In no case is any matter destroyed in change. It is rearranged so that its basic potency, primary matter, is fulfilled in existence and its formal appetites are fulfilled in a new being. This is developed in several principles: (1) matter is eternally rearrangeable and (2) the eternal and incorruptible stars are the sources of energy that continue the work of rearranging limited being in the eternal process that is the universe. Hence, the universe *exists* eternally because it is being and being is indestructible. The universe exists as an *eternal process* because the energy proceeding from the eternal stars keeps up the eternal rearrangement of the eternally changeable.

What, now, is the direction of its change? Is it a cycle after the fashion of the Iron Age, the Bronze Age, the Silver Age, and the Golden Age? Or is it an evolution? Aristotle takes the stand that it is spiral rather than cyclical and that its exemplar and final cause is the Prime Mover or Self-Thinking Thought (cf. *Metaphysics*, XII, 7, 1072b1 ff.). If Aristotle did not introduce God as the exemplar of the universe in the order of being, if he retained his concept of the first immovable mover in the *Physics* as either a world soul or some physical agent, he would have been led into a theory of thermodynamics. The constant exchanges of energy in the generation and corruption required for the constant actualization of things would have led him to the consideration that the universe was tending to a maximum of entropy. This does not mean that energy would be lost. Rather it would be so occupied in retaining the existence of higher entities that there would be less and less available for work to be done. Incidentally, this type of thinking is at the heart of the philosophy of Spencer and of the dialectic of the philosophy of Engels and Marx. This is why Communists who understand the Hegelian and Marxist philosophy of nature are led to the constancy of the dialectic on the one hand, but on the other to the supposition of the ideal state of affairs. This ideal state of affairs is the maximum of entropy that the dialectic seems to lead to.

However, with the introduction of a Mind as the final cause and exemplar of the universe, Aristotle has a universe that is a restless process always tending to what it cannot attain and always moving forward, never ending in a stagnancy of the complete fulfillment of anything.

In the *Physics*, Aristotle had dealt with a mechanically self-sufficient universe. Yet, in this process-universe, there is always the supposition of earlier sources and available energy. What is not explained is the existence of all this. Process is toward a goal, the individual good and perfection of the individual entity. The individual goal of each entity is the perfect fulfillment of its potentialities. The universe as a whole has a goal. This is the perfect operation of each existing entity within it, for the perfect existence of anything is not merely the fact that it is, but that it is constantly striving toward self-perfection in the ultimate fulfillment of all of its potentialities. Insofar as the Prime Mover, Aristotle's God, is the exemplar of all of this, he is the principle of a completely teleological universe wherein each entity is striving for existence in the substantial changes that replace worn-out beings with new beings and new opportunities, and the accidental changes which are the expression of the components of an organic-like universe of each being striving for the fullest expression of its capacities.

Aristotle's philosophy of nature is, thus, a theocentric consideration of the significance of all being only in terms of the pure actuality of the Prime Mover. His consideration of nature is a hierarchy from the Prime Mover as the exemplar and beings as imitation not of Platonic forms but of the Prime Mover, pure being, pure actuality. Thus, potency tends toward actuality. Appetites tend toward fulfillment in formal essences. These are the limitations of the existence of beings, for what a thing is by nature limits the manner of its existence. Hence, all creation is the process of the production of types of being of which the Prime Mover is the exemplar. This imitation of an exemplar is what, metaphysically, we call "analogical participation." Hence, in Aristotle we find analogical participation in being in his theory of the eternity of the universe.

St. Thomas maintains that philosophy cannot prove demonstratively that creation took place in time (*De Aeternitate Mundi; Summa Theologiae*, I, q. 46, arts. 1 and 2). Philosophy can, of course, demonstrate the need for creation, insofar as limited actualities are caused, and created causes require an absolutely First Cause. Creation, thus, for St. Thomas, is the metaphysical question of causality and dependence of limited actuality on Pure Act. The time element introduces the question of becoming, which for material things is the process of generation from material causes by efficient causes. The time element enters in insofar as each material cause is also a temporally antecedent source.

St. Thomas' argumentation is already of a different nature than that of Aristotle. Aristotle did not consider his Prime Mover as the efficient cause of the universe. Hence, he had to fall back upon the science of mechanics. St. Thomas maintained that arguments from this are only relatively demonstrative; that is, taking the state of the question, no one can disprove Aristotle's arguments, any more than today anyone can disprove the arguments of the expanding universe or steady state theories.

For St. Thomas, we must consider either the non-eternity or eternity of the universe through the eternal and creative will of God. However, since that is the case, we cannot, on grounds of reason, rule out the possible eternity of the world. God always existed, and since He is not limited by time, nor limited by His creatures, and since His action is identical with His nature, His causality is not limited by time. It is instantaneous and not in any way temporal. Furthermore, even though the processes of the universe are all temporal, they will last as long as matter lasts, and there is no reason why God could not always have had matter in existence. Furthermore, the very arguments advanced for the existence of God, based as they are on the contingency of creatures, argue to an eternal and omnipotent God, and thus our theodicy almost inevitably leads to the fact that God could always have had the universe in existence.

St. Thomas' argumentation reduces itself to two points: (1) that God is not limited to any given time when it comes to creation, (2) that the question of creation is not that of becoming but that of being. We cannot rule out the possibility of eternal creation. Hence, we cannot demonstrate that the universe began in time, for true demonstration must take possibilities as well as actualities into account. His conclusion is that the fact of creation in time is an article of faith.

SUMMARY

1. The Aristotelian system had a science content, based on the principles of mechanics, as well as a philosophy. When the sciences are seeking the further philosophical development of their implications, they might well look to Aristotelian realism.
2. Aristotle maintained that the universe is finite, because:
   a) It is not one limitless being, and hence is not *metaphysically* infinite.

b) It seems to be a sphere, its contents are at measurable distances from each other, and it cannot be said to be *mathematically* infinite.

c) Since the forces that hold the universe together are finite, the universe cannot be *physically* infinite.

3. Within itself, the universe is not empty since the movements of bodies within the universe indicate that they are meeting resistance from the *ether*.
4. The earth is at the center of the universe because bodies in an unimpeded fall tend toward the center of the earth as the center of gravity.
5. The universe, according to Aristotle, is eternal, although no individual process in the universe is eternal. Matter can be renewed eternally and is constantly renewed by the eternal motions of the stars.

The ultimate reason of the existence and processes of the universe is the Prime Mover, Pure Act. The universe is an eternal process of self-improvement after the unattainable perfection of God.

St. Thomas agrees with the eternal renewability of matter, but he adds that the universe *could* be eternal because the activity of God cannot be limited to temporal limitations. It is only by faith that we know that the universe was created with time.

PART THREE

Main Problems in Scientific Cosmology

CHAPTER FOURTEEN

BACKGROUND of MODERN ATOMIC THEORY

Modern atomic theory is sometimes considered to have begun with John Dalton, sometimes with Wilhelm Roentgen. No matter with whom it began, modern atomic theory is no sharp break with the past. It is rather a continuation of fundamental physical and chemical developments, and these, in turn, depend upon the more elaborate and earlier development of basic principles in mechanics which have always been treated by human thinkers. The eminent historian and philosopher, John Burnet, is as correct as can be when he states that the unique beginnings of Western science can be traced to the Greeks.

GENERAL BACKGROUND

The Greeks were the founders of Western science because of their emphasis on a rational and not mythological answer for the problems of the one and the many, being and becoming. Since so many of them were materialists, their notion of being was that of matter. Hence, their speculations necessarily required investigations into physical and chemical changes. They thus became acquainted with some of the basic problems of mechanics: motion, force, energy, inertia, heat, and magnetism. Even though such giants as Pythagoras, Plato, and Aristotle transcended materialistic limitations, they did not lose their interest in the basic problems of physics and chemistry.

Greek science was developed, in Christian times, by the true scientists of the Middle Ages, the Arabians. Their discoveries, observations, and experiments were assimilated into European thought and were the background of Renaissance science, just as Renaissance science was the background of modern science.

At the beginning of this development prime attention was given to the analysis of motion and the description of movements in geometry. This was carried out both for falling bodies and for the motions of heavenly bodies. From the inception of Greek thought thinkers devoted much to these problems of static and dynamic mechanics.

Among the Greek *atomists*, the following points were maintained either explicitly or implicitly:

1. The conservation of matter, and hence of energy proceeding from matter;
2. The explanation of displacement, pressures, bodily states, volume changes, and qualities through the energetic state of atoms.

The *Ionians* contributed the following:

1. An emphasis on elements for physical and chemical properties;
2. An explanation of physical and chemical states in terms of attraction and repulsion according to contrary properties.

Pythagoras and Plato developed the conceptual scheme of mathematical proportion as the significant reason for the physical and chemical states.

Aristotle gave a more realistic interpretation of the Platonic conceptual scheme, and explicitly maintained the following:

1. The fundamental explanation of the *structure* of matter — as opposed to the *hylomorphic* essence — in terms of both elements and atoms.
2. A conservation theory of matter and energy applicable to every manifestation of secondary matter, even evolution. In this way, he anticipated Leibniz and Joule in envisioning the conservation of energy.
3. The fact that we call inertia, that a body at rest tends to remain at rest while a body in motion tends to remain in motion.
4. The explanation of what today we call gravity in terms of the body and its position, rather than its mass and distance.
5. The interplay of time and space for true measurement.
6. The principle that rotational motion is more economical and more perfect than rectilinear motion on a sufficiently large scale.

Constant developments were made on these principles, especially by the Arabians. With the assimilation of these principles by such medieval and early Renaissance scholars as Albertus Magnus, Stevinus, Novara, and Nicholas of Cusa, the background was complete for Renaissance science.

THE BACKGROUND FROM MECHANICS

General principles of mechanics

Mechanics is the treatment of the motions of masses and of the effects of forces in causing or modifying these motions. One of its natural subdivisions is the consideration of the forces involved in the motions. This is *kinematics,* which treats of the characteristics of different kinds of motions and reactions (*strain,* if the body is notably affected in its structure; and *rigidity,* if the body is only slightly so affected).

Another subdivision of mechanics is *dynamics,* which is concerned with the effect of motions on bodies. Dynamics is subdivided into *statics,* which deals with bodies in equilibrium as a result of their inertia or as a result of the balance of forces. The second division of dynamics is *kinetics,* which treats of the effects of forces in changing the motions of bodies. Thus, statics deals with the effect of force on bodies. Kinetics deals with the effects of force on motions. We must notice that all of the points mentioned above were treated explicitly by Aristotle. Since his emphasis was on the relations of force and body rather than force and motion, his consideration of mechanics is more statics than dynamics.

1. Some of the fundamental concepts of *kinematics* are displacement, vectors, velocity, and acceleration.

Displacement is the area crossed by a body in a given time. This may be rectilinear or rotational.

Vector quantities are displacements involving not only magnitude but also direction.

Velocity is the *rate* at which a body passes over a given area in time. The fundamental formula of velocity is: $v = s/t$, where v is velocity; s, space; and t, time.

Acceleration is the change either in the magnitude (speed) or direction of the motion of a body. Notice that a change in direction is also acceleration. Thus, two bodies can be going at the same speed, but if one changes direction, it is thereby accelerated.

Since direction plays an important part in displacement, vectors, and acceleration, measurement is not only a question of magnitude but also of the angles involved in changes in direction. Hence, geometry as well as arithmetic plays an important part in physical measurement.

2. The fundamental concepts of *dynamics* are inertia and force.

Inertia is the property whereby matter resists change, either from rest to motion or motion to rest, without the application of some force. We know that we must use force to start a body in motion. We must also use force to stop the body or to change its direction. Furthermore, in the free motion of a body, when it stops or changes direction "by itself," we know that this is the result of friction.

Force is the application of energy. Force can be known and measured by: (*a*) the weight that it can support; (*b*) its ability to strain an elastic body; and (*c*) its ability to give motion to a mass.

Theoretically, any force, when properly applied, can move any mass if applied long enough. Hence, such things as rapid accelerations or slow but steady applications, directions of application, etc., constitute important problems in physics and in engineering. For example, a weight can be placed on a paper. A slow but steady pull on the paper will move the weight. A sudden jerk will pull the paper out from under the weight. In engineering, for example in automobile design, the car must be designed to handle the sudden spurts of certain types of drivers. The measurement of many of these applications of force is time.

Newton's first law of motion, that *every body continues in its state of rest, or in its state of moving with constant velocity in a straight line, unless acted upon by some external force,* is the classical expression of the fact of inertia. For that reason, it is often called "the law of inertia."

His second law, that *change of motion is proportional to the moving force impressed, and takes place in the direction of the straight line in which such force is impressed,* is an example of magnitude and vector characteristics of force as well as of motion.

His third law, that *to every action there is an equal and opposite reaction,* is a statement that force proceeds from a body. Therefore, a body is intrinsically forceful and can be expected to react according to the amount of energy impressed on it.

3. The fundamental concepts of *statics* are equilibrium, work, energy, and power.

Equilibrium is the state of a body when the forces acting on it are so related that the body is not accelerated. One illustration of equilibrium is found in a body at rest. In this instance the attraction of gravity is matched by the resistance of the object on which the body rests. Another example is provided by a body suspended between several forces, as, for example, an iron object suspended between two magnetic fields. Again, it may be seen in a body on a slope wherein the downward pull of gravity is balanced by the resistance of the surface.

Two further concepts are involved in the concept of equilibrium: center of gravity and moment of force. *Center of gravity* is associated with weight, which is the force with which the mass of a body is drawn toward the center of the earth. Since the earth is much bigger than the object it affects, it attracts every portion of the body's mass. On the terrestrial scale, as opposed to the astronomical scale where gravity seems to be three-dimensional, the attraction of gravity is rectilinear. It can be represented in terms of parallel lines, and when an object is raised at one point on its surface, it will rearrange itself according to these parallel lines. Thus, when object A is raised at point of suspension *P*, it rearranges itself to hang in the following manner:

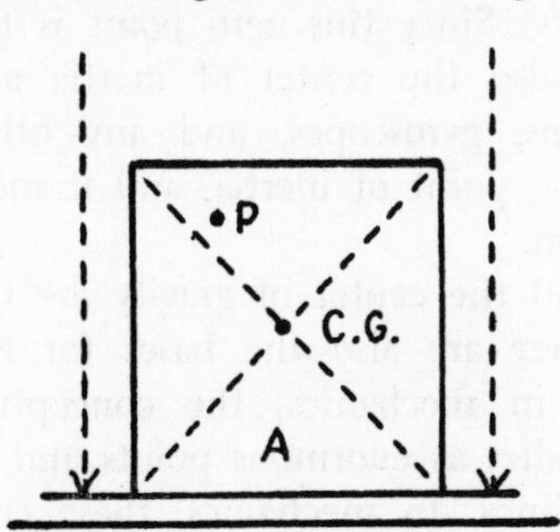

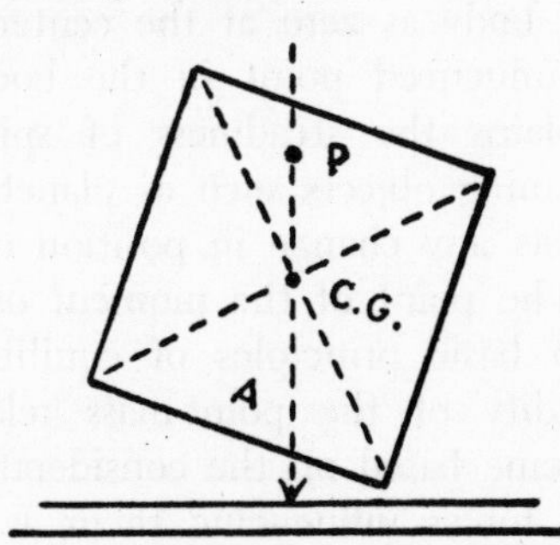

This means that although gravity affects the entire body, for purposes of consideration in mechanics it is enough to consider the mass and inertia of a body as concentrated at a point CG which is the crossing of a line perpendicular to the earth (the line of suspension) and at right angles to its center.

Unless the forces acting on a body are perfectly parallel, they have a tendency to rotate a body because of the body's inertia. This tendency toward rotation is called the *moment of force*, or *torque*. The effect of the moment of force will be the product of the magnitude of the force and the distance from the point of rotation or axis. At the axis, it will be zero. Farther away from the axis, it will be proportionately greater. However, it is always zero at the point of rotation, just as there is the least motion of a swinging door at the point where the door joins the hinge and just as, theoretically, there is no motion at the fulcrum.

The moment of force is called the *lever action*, and since the result, or the work done, is the product of both the magnitude of the force and the distance from the fulcrum, the longer the lever arm, the greater the work done. The lever action is the most fundamental concept in the doing of work, and is behind the ratio of gears as well as the length of levers. The reason is that the work done is the product of the length from the fulcrum and the magnitude of the force. If gears are distributed in such way as to represent longer distances from a fulcrum, more work can be done but at a slower rate. Consequently, in steam locomotives the wheels of freight engines are always smaller than those of passenger locomotives. This results in a greater distribution of the work load, although the train will run more slowly.

Note that the arrangement about the center of gravity is similar to that about the point of the moment of force. Hence, the body seems to rotate about that force, and we can consider the gravitational torques on the body as zero at the center of gravity. Since this zero point is the uninfluenced point in the body, it is also the center of inertia and explains the steadiness of spinning tops, gyroscopes, and any other spinning objects such as planets. It is the point of inertia, and it most resists any change in position or direction.

The point of the moment of force and the center of gravity are the two basic principles of equilibrium. They are also the bases for the validity of the point-mass relationship in mechanics, the conceptual scheme based on the consideration of bodies as enormous points and of the forces influencing them as parallel lines. In mechanics, these considerations work and work well. It is only in some of the problems of general relativity that they are insufficient.

The destruction of equilibrium is sometimes called work. Strictly speaking, however, work is *the product of force by the distance through which the force acts along the line of action*. Briefly, it is expressed as: $W = Fs$. Since distance is crossed or since there is some displacement involved, motion is necessary to work. Hence, a workman upholding the end of a beam would not be said, properly, to work, even though he is exercising muscle power.

Again, since work is the product of force by distance, any variation of either the force or the distance will vary the work done. For example, a greater magnitude of force will influence the work. Two men will find it easier to lift a barrel onto a truck than one. On the other hand, an inclined plane will make it easier for one man to do the same work, because the distance is greater and thus requires less force to accomplish the same amount of work.

Variations on the distance are the simplest contributions to machines. For example, a pulley makes work easier since it adds distance. The same is true for a gear ratio. The perfect machine, then, would be the optimum by way of most efficient force or fuel coupled with a perfect distance or gear ratio over a frictionless surface. A machine is simply a device to increase the output of work. The great opponents of work are friction and inertia. For example, the greatest work done by a machine is in starting, in overcoming inertia, in accelerating, and in increasing the magnitude or direction of force. Friction is the resistance of any surface to motion across it.

Energy is *the capacity to do work*, and the doing of work is an expression of the principle of the conservation of energy, namely, that *energy can neither be created nor destroyed*. It can only be distributed. The conservation of energy has two more specific considerations: the conservation of mass and the conservation of charge.

4. *Kinetics* is the science of motion and forces on motion. Although it is highly ornate, it deals with two fundamental concepts: momentum and direction. Its ornate development does not lie in the introduction of many new physical concepts but rather in devising better and better means of measuring the action of motion and the influence of force on motion. For example, one of its experimental discoveries is that the effect of a force in changing the motion of a mass is not in any way affected by the state of rest or motion of the mass which is acted upon. This was and has been of invaluable assistance in the logistics of projectiles. Kinetics has also shown how it is possible to discover the mass of planets from the gravitational effects they have on their satellites. The principle involved can be applied to the action of double stars on one another in order to discover the masses of the stars concerned. With masses and colors and brightness as known factors, we are able to couple color, brightness, and mass of a star and calculate its distance against the same properties of stars already triangulated. When this distance is associated with a spectroscopic analysis of their chemical components and when the interference of intervening interstellar and intergalactic dust is subtracted, we have a fairly good idea of the distances of all stars and galaxies.

Momentum of a body is the product of the amount of its mass by the amount of its velocity, and is a directed or vector quantity. What we have seen about direction and vector quantities previously can be applied to momentum. We have, thus, not only rectilinear and rotational and angular directions. We also have rectilinear, rotational, and angular momentum. Moreover, we are able to transform the basic formulas of each to the other. For example, we can use the same formulas for each with the adoption of Latin characters for rectlinear values and Greek characters for angular values. Thus, for the magnitude s covered in time t in rectilinear motion, we have the angular magnitude θ through which a body turns in time *t*. Similarly, the formula for displacement $s = \left(\frac{v_2 + v_1}{2}\right)t$, or $s = v_2t + \frac{at^2}{2}$ becomes $\theta = \left(\frac{\omega_1 + \omega_2}{2}\right)t$ or $\theta = \omega_2 t + \frac{at^2}{2}$.

Involved with the concept of momentum is the concept of potential and kinetic energy. *Potential* energy is energy of position or physical state. *Kinetic* energy is energy in motion. Strictly speaking, *potential energy is the capacity to do work which a body or system of bodies has in virtue of position or configuration.* By configuration we mean the distribution of parts as in a coiled spring, but also the association of energy sources. Thus, the association of certain hydrocarbon molecules forms gasoline, which by its chemical state, or configuration, is a great energy source, or potential energy. *Kinetic energy is the capacity to do work which a body has in consequence of its velocity.* Kinetic energy is the measurement of the *work* done by the velocity of a body. Momentum is the measurement of the impulse given the moving body.

Every type of motion and of work done, whether rectilinear, rotational, or *angular, can be computed by the basic concepts of mechanics.* In general, statics considers the effects on bodies from the point of view of the maintenance or disturbance of equilibrium, while kinetics considers the process of so moving. This extends not only from billiard balls to projectiles, but also to planets, satellites, stars, and galaxies. Herein lies the genius of Galileo, Copernicus, Newton, and Kepler. Relativity is a more accurate and more realistic development of the fundamental concepts we have seen above.

Since the accepted concepts of the atom and its particles are based on comparisons to orbital or planetary systems, the principles of mechanics can be applied to the atomic theory. There need be only two further considerations, that of *vibratory motion* and that of *random motion.* Nevertheless since these can be covered by both statics and kinetics, at least by averages, these two can fit into a mechanical explanation of the atom.

The term "mechanical" is applied to the atom, inasmuch as the concepts of mechanics can be extended to the forces at work in the atom. Mechanics is further specified according to the forces that influence equilibrium or motion. If the force is heat, we have thermo*dynamics*. If the force is electricity, we have electro*statics* or electro*dynamics*. These developments of mechanics are also applied to the consideration of the atom and its particles.

We may close this section by noting that although the Greeks, and especially Aristotle, attained most of the concepts in mechanics, especially those of statics, their emphasis was more on *what* these are rather than *how* the respective forces operate. Hence, they did not undertake much measurement. Since the time of Galileo, the emphasis has been on measurement. This has brought a rapid development of theories of measurement, so that physics and mathematics have grown hand in hand by mutual contribution. There is a danger that mathematics might predominate and lead physics into the purely conceptual order of mathematics and away from the real problems that physics should deal with. Relativity is the latest warning against this epistemological danger.

ORIGINS OF ATOMIC THEORY

Although atomic and nuclear theories are vastly complex today, they have their origins in three of the most familiar phenomena we know: the diffusion of gases, the evaporation of liquids, and the expansion of solids when heated. These phenomena had never, as far as we know, entered into earlier atomic theories. Greek atomism simply looked to composition of the whole in terms of minimal parts. The whole was the association of the parts. Generation was the coming together of atoms. Corruption was their separation.

This is also true of the atomism of the Middle Ages. The latter developed largely from Aristotle's emphasis on elements and his opinion that atoms were the smallest parts of bodies, whether compound or simple, and that atoms were also the smallest parts of elements when elements existed by themselves, "in the free state," as we would say today. Medieval thinkers did not pay too much attention to atoms or elements since they were more concerned with *essences* than with structures. Physical structure did occupy the attention of some philosophers, but they were almost indifferent when it came to explaining structure through elements or atoms or elements *and* atoms. The latter was the point of view of Aristotle, and was generally followed by the Arabians, St. Albert, and St. Thomas.

Galileo, and later Priestley and Boyle, who tried to reject such *philosophical* principles as matter and form because of *physical* and *chemical* problems showed that they misunderstood the state of the question. Some decadent Aristotelians had almost made matter and form identical with atoms and elements. This is the type of thinking to which Galileo, Newton, and Boyle were opposed, and rightly so. But Aristotle himself and his genuine followers of the Middle Age kept the problems of physical structures and intrinsic essence distinct. By attempting to explain how atoms unite and separate Priestley, Boyle, and other early modern scientists introduced the concepts of diffusion, evaporation, and expansion as the key to atomic power.

We all know that if a bottle of gas is opened in one corner of a room, the gas will have a tendency to diffuse itself throughout the room. If the gas is heavier than air, it will distribute itself along the floor of the room. If it is lighter than air, it will distribute itself throughout the entire room.

Similarly, we know that the average liquid, when left in an open dish or area, will evaporate. As a matter of fact, one reason why life is fairly acceptable on earth is that there is a cycle of evaporation from seas, oceans, rivers, and lakes, and a redistribution of water through precipitation.

Finally, we know that solids expand when heated. We think of this, generally, in terms of metals. However, we also know that concrete blocks on highways expand when heated and that, consequently, expansion spaces must be left between the blocks lest the entire surface buckle. Warm air rises because the same amount of air, on being heated, expands and has less density than the surrounding air. Being less dense, it is also lighter, and is forced upward by its heavier surroundings. These, in turn, expand and are forced upward, etc.

The easiest way to explain these three phenomena is to suppose that matter of any sort consists of extremely small particles existing in random motion. According to the random character of the motion, particles generally collide with one another. This raises the energy level of the particles involved in the collision. Both the collision and the greater activity consequent to the raised energy state have a tendency to separate the particles. This could take place in one area of the whole, but, as we know, bodies rarely become energetic in only one part. There is a statistical distribution of their energy. Thus, despite the collision of the particles, the statistics of the randomness of their motions indicate that the energy levels of the particles that separate become lower and the activities more restricted in their distribution.

The *diffusion of gases* is, therefore, explained in the following way. A gas is a loosely organized fluid that takes its shape from the container. As the gas is released from the container, the particles have a greater area in which to move. They follow this tendency, and the gas diffuses.

The motion of the gas particles must be *random*. If it were not, it would be directed, and the gas would diffuse in one direction. As a matter of fact, it does not do so, and, hence, the diffusion of the gas is in every direction. The motion of the gas can be directed by ionizing the particles. However, this is a somewhat unusual state, artificially created by passing an electric charge through the gas to give a direction to its particles. The *randomness* of the motion does not mean that it is aimless. It simply means that it is directionless. The amount of the area covered by the random motion of the particles can be estimated. From random motions on the macroscopic level we know that the motion can be averaged as triangular. Hence, the actual area would be as the hypotenuse of a triangle, and is represented as $\sqrt{N}$, where N represents the squared number of changes of direction on the part of a moving particle.

We cannot know the precise position of any individual particle at any time. However, we can know the density of the entire gas as an average of both the number of particles and their activity states at a given temperature. Thus, we explain the outward pressure of a gas on the walls of a container as the average of the motions against the walls by an average number of particles. When the temperature of the contained gas is raised, the pressure on the walls is greater in direct proportion to the temperature, according to the formula: $P = N \times T$, where N represents the number of particles and T represents the temperature. The rise in temperature is a rise in an energy state, and the particles react by a wider scope of more rapid motions. This increases the number and momentum of collisions with the wall as well as with the particles themselves. This is manifested in an increased pressure on the walls of the container.

On the other hand, compression restricts the area of the motions of the particles. This increases the number of collisions and the chances for such a continuation, and the higher energy level brought about by the increased and continued number of collisions is manifested by a higher temperature. The gas gets hotter. Similarly, the release of compression, rarefaction, brings about a cooling of the gas.

The explanation of the *evaporation* of liquids is similar. Again, we have the random motion of particles and chance collisions with other particles. The chance collisions deflect the particles in such a way as to prevent their moving around in the same area. Periodically, a particle near the top of the liquid is deflected directly upward to escape from the common mass of the liquid. It is absorbed in the interstices of the air molecules and is held therein in suspension. Since the particle p has mass m, there is a reduction of the mass of the whole at the ratio of $M - p$. If four particles escape, the reduction is $M - 4p$. In any event, the density always remains the same, and in evaporation can be generalized as $D = M - Np$. Since the density remains, the energy level allowing for evaporation remains the same and evaporation continues until all the particles have evaporated.

The *expansion of solids* is explained in the same way. In this case, however, there is no escape of particles, save in the rare instance of the sublimation of certain gases frozen solid. Rather, as the increased energy level causes more rapid and more widespread areas of activity, since the particles cannot escape or diffuse, the mass of the whole solid increases, and the solid expands.

Historically, it was the question of the heating of solids that opened up this new facet of the interpretation of atoms and their random motions. For centuries, scientists had pondered over the problem of heat. Having rejected the four element theory with the discovery of true elements by Priestly and his successors, they had no element of fire as an explanation of heat. They fell back upon a hypothetical entity called *phlogiston*. This was considered an imponderable and imperceptible entity that flowed into an object causing it to become hot. When it flowed out of the same object, the object cooled off. This is known as the "fluid theory of heat."

The rejection of the fluid theory was the work of Benjamin Thompson, Count Rumford, of Woburn, Massachusetts. Earlier chemists such as Robert Boyle and Daniel Bernouilli had tried to interpret heat in terms of molecular activity. Rumford added empirical verification to their suggestions. He performed his experiments on cannons.

Today cannons are cast as such. In Rumford's day, they were cast as ingots and then the barrels were bored. Since such tedious work created heat, they were sunk into a pit of sand which was kept watered constantly. Nevertheless, the bits broke from the heat. Rumford theorized that the act of boring could so disturb the molecules of both the bit and the ingot that the collisions between particles would become more frequent and would raise the energy state of the whole. This energy would take on the nature of heat and would radiate into the surroundings.

Rumford put this to the test. In a container of water he arranged two spheres in contact, with a device to spin one against the other. He also inserted a thermometer in the water. As the spheres rubbed against one another, the water was soon brought to a boil.

The phlogiston theory had some respectability because it made it possible to measure quantities of heat. It also explained radiation by considering it the flow of phlogiston from the body. There are two kinds of transmission of heat, convection and radiation. Convection is the result of the energizing of the surroundings of the hot body. Radiation is the direct emission of energy particles. Now, since Rumford demonstrated that heat is nothing other than the higher agitation of particles, radiation could also be considered the emission of energy in the form of particles.

Heat, then, for Rumford, was simply an energy state, and thermodynamics is the scientific investigation of the work done by heat interpreted as an energy state. Thermodynamics has introduced a very significant concept, that of *specific heat*. All bodies exist in one of two states: solid or fluid. Fluid states are subdivided into liquid and gaseous. Any body, then, can pass from the solid to the liquid to the gaseous state. However, all do not do so at the same energy levels, or temperatures. We generally consider the normal range of temperatures on this earth as those that range from the solid and gaseous states of water. However, if this is the normal range, the question arises why such elements as iron remain solid at normal temperatures, whereas such metals as mercury remain liquid save in combination, and such elements as hydrogen remain gaseous. The only answer is that there is something about each element whereby it has its own melting point and boiling point. This differs widely from element to element, as was discovered by a Scotch chemist named Black, who found that the heat given off by a gram of lead while cooling one degree was quite different than that given off by iron when cooled the same degree. This means that each element has its own energy level and requires different amounts of heat energy to raise its temperature. *The specific heat of any element is the number of calories required to raise the temperature of one gram of that element one degree Centigrade.* Specific heat is not only a problem in physics but also in molecular chemistry.

A body can be so activated or affected that it can be reduced to a state called *plasma* by the breakdown of its atoms into fundamental ionized particles. Ordinarily, when electrons and ions are produced they soon combine with the opposite charge for an entropic balance. However, above the energy of two electron volts — approximately 20,000 degrees Centigrade — they remain as ions and electrons. In the free state, as, for example, in interstellar gases, they retain some liquid properties. They spread, but do not diffuse. Under pressure, as in stars, they closely resemble dense liquids. The penetration barrier, the strength required by particles or cosmic rays to penetrate plasma without being trapped by it, is 35×10^{15} electron volts. At higher energies than this, matter is generally *radiant*.

THE ELECTROMAGNETIC BACKGROUND OF THE ATOM

The accepted modern considerations of the nuclear atom are an application of the laws of dynamics to the problem of the structure of matter. These include the laws of electrostatics and electrodynamics. Although the considerations of the atom have become highly ornate, the developed concepts have simple beginnings in far-seeing pioneers. Just as the thermodynamical concept can be traced to Count Rumford, so also the electrodynamical concept must be traced back to Benjamin Franklin, Michael Faraday, and James Clerk Maxwell.

The accepted concept of electricity in Franklin's day was the "electric fluid" theory, which considered electricity something of a flow, mysterious in origin. The only attention paid to electricity in the eighteenth century was by way of parlor entertainment and therapeutic experiment.

Franklin's basic principle is what we call the *conservation of charge*. He maintained that matter is electrical by nature and that a passage of electricity is simply the redistribution of a natural force, not the arousing of an exceptional energy. As he envisioned electricity, bodies consist of variations of "common matter," and each body has its quota of "electrical fluid." Rubbing and agitation in electrostatic devices, chemical changes in cells, etc., merely make latent electricity available. It then flows from the excess (+) to the defect (–), whether this transmission be a spark, a shock, or a lightning flash. The amount lost from the source is the same as the amount gained by the receiver.

There were more particular conclusions deduced by Franklin from his experiments. For example, he experimented with Leyden jars to show that the charge is deposited on the glass between the electrodes, and is not proper to either of them. His experiment with the kite was not only to show that lightning is an electrical discharge but also that the direction of lightning can be upward as well as downward. That is, if there is a predominance of charge in the cloud, there is the accumulation of an opposite charge on objects beneath the cloud. If the cloud is negative a positive potential is built up underneath it.

Like everyone else at the time, Franklin considered matter to consist of atoms. His notion of electricity as a fluid that all bodies have is somewhat inconsistent with his simple atomism. However, his position that electricity is *not something over and above* the material structure of bodies is so overwhelming as to submerge the slight inconsistency. The force of his position is this: if matter is naturally electrical, and if matter is atomic-kinetic, then the atoms and their forces must be naturally electrical. About twenty-five years after Franklin's death, a British physicist, Stoney, made the statement explicit and advocated that henceforth all atoms be called "electrons."

This conclusion cleared the way for extremely rapid advances in atomic and nuclear physics. For about one hundred years, physicists considered electricity a problem in chemistry and chemists considered it a problem in physics. When the breakthrough came, however, with the discovery of radioactivity, it was seen that Franklin had paved the way for the consideration that radiation proceeds *from the body as a source.* This saved subsequent physicists the embarrassing problem of trying to eliminate other sources. That is, they did not have to try to prove that it was not from surrounding bodies, etc., but properly from the object under consideration.

Although all devices using electricity or producing electricity are applications of modern theory to practice, they are variations of fundamental discoveries, experiments, devices, and hypotheses advanced by Benjamin Franklin.

Michael Faraday was another scientist who anticipated much modern theory. In his work with dynamos Faraday discovered alternating and direct current. He was fascinated by the surge of electricity when a circuit is first closed, and he noticed that electricity travels in amounts, whether in the wavelike ripples of direct current or in the back-and-forth agitation of alternating current. The notion that electricity travels in packets is basic to modern quantum theory.

The basic principles behind any induction of electricity are that the disturbance of a magnetic field creates a charge and that the transmission of a charge through a conductor creates a field. Faraday became interested in the magnetic field, whether around a magnet or around a conductor. In fact, he was the first to establish that it is a field, and he was the first to experiment on it with iron filings. Long in anticipation of general relativity, he advanced the view that the importance of the attractor and the attracted is not in their mass but in their position in a field. He even suggested that this might be the case in gravitational attraction as well as in the strength of a magnetic field. However, this opinion seemed so opposed to Newton's principles that it was scarcely considered. Nevertheless, when contemporary physicists apply the laws of mechanics to the activities of the atom, they are following Faraday rather than Newton.

The work of Faraday on the direction of currents and on conductors led to investigations into the conductivity of gases. An outstanding investigator in this field was Sir William Crookes, who devised the tube named after him for the tracing of the direction of the current. In a Crookes tube, electrons can be made to flow from the cathode (negative pole) to the anode tube (positive pole). This is the ordinary direction of flow, despite Franklin's convictions to the opposite. Such rays within a vacuum tube are called cathode rays. The opposite flow, from the positive pole to the negative pole, is a canal ray.

In operation, a Crookes tube is a vacuum tube wherein a small amount of gas is allowed to remain as a conductor. When the circuit is closed the current flows through the gas and the gas glows according to the spectroscopic color proper to the gas as an element. Thus, helium glows with a faint pink tinge. Mercury vapor glows with a bluish white tinge, neon with a red tinge.

One of the problems about the conductivity of gases is this. Only a slight amount of current is required to make the gas glow, and glow brilliantly. In fact, its radiation output seems far out of proportion to the small amount of current needed. This, naturally, raises the question of the source of all of this extra energy. Gradually, physicists began to consider that the "flow" or current might be a stream of some kind of particles whose collisions released the extra energy in the form of brighter light. Hence, the current itself was considered to be a stream of "electrons." Since the normal direction of the flow is from the negative to the positive pole, the electrons were considered to be particles having a negative charge.

The above theorizing, rather than the discovery of x rays, gave rise to advances in atomic theory on the part of Sir J. J. Thomson, Sir Ernest Rutherford, and Niels Bohr. It is the theory put into practice in mercury vapor lamps and in television picture tubes.

Nevertheless, x rays gave a startling argument for the corpuscular nature not only of electricity but also of all matter. In 1895, Professor Wilhelm Konrad Roentgen of Munich noticed that photographic plates kept in the vicinity of Crookes tubes became fogged as though they were affected by some type of rays escaping from the equipment. Roentgen decided to experiment. He made a phosphorescent screen of barium platinocynanide. When the Crookes tube was turned on in a dark room, the plate glowed. Roentgen suggested that these escaping rays, which he called x rays (x for unknown), had the properties of particles. He then interpreted the nearby glow in terms of the release of a particle from the phosphorescent screen. He considered that the rays might be particles. When one particle strikes the surface of the screen, it knocks off a particle. The collision itself is a source of energy which manifests itself as a glow.

Spontaneous radioactivity, discovered in 1896 by Henri Becquerel, as well as the isolation of the radioactive element radium by Eve and Pierre Curie, introduced again the notion of the constitution of matter as a structure of particles having electromagnetic properties. Radioactivity would thus be the escape of some of the energy.

SUMMARY

1. Modern atomic and nuclear theory has a remote background in the persistence of atomism. Its modern development is an application of the principles of mechanics to the forces and operations of the atom.
2. Mechanics is the treatment of the motions of masses and the effects of motions and forces. *Kinematics* treats of the effects of the forces on bodies in strain and rigidity. Dynamics treats of the operations of forces.

   Dynamics is subdivided into *statics,* which deals with the disturbance of equilibrium by the effects of forces on masses, and *kinetics,* which deals with the forces on forces.
3. Modern atomic theory can be traced to the problem of the diffusion of gases, the evaporation of liquids, and the expansion of solids. These are explained by the random motions of intrinsically energetic particles.

   This notion was extended into thermodynamics by Count Rumford, into electrodynamics by Benjamin Franklin, Michael Faraday, John Henry, and James Clerk Maxwell.

   It opened up the theory of the x ray, discovered by Roentgen, and spontaneous radioactivity, discovered by Becquerel.

CHAPTER FIFTEEN

MODERN NUCLEAR THEORY

Modern nuclear theory begins properly with the experimentation of Sir Joseph Thomson, Master of Trinity College, Cambridge. It is to Thomson more than anyone else that we owe our modern concept of the atom. He attained the first *model,* that is *concept,* of the atom, and most successive models have been developments of Thomson's model.

THE THOMSON MODEL OF THE ATOM

Thomson envisioned the atom as an electrostatic balance of forces. It consisted, as he thought, of a semiliquid, positively charged nucleus with electrons, or negatively charged particles, embedded in the nucleus. He explained electrodynamic radiation as the flow of the electrons from the nucleus because of some agitation such as heat. The mass of the atom is in the nucleus and its charge balances the number of electrons embedded in it.

His problem was to isolate the electron. To do this he devised a Crookes tube, as in the diagram below, consisting of a cathode whence came the flow of electrons. Instead of the conventional anode plate, he had an anode consisting of two slit devices through which the electrons would pass because of their attained velocity. After passing through the anode, they passed through an electric field created by plates P_1 and P_2. The strength of these plates could be varied so as to deflect the particles upward or downward. Knowing the original charge, and computing both the angle of deflection and the amount of current needed to deflect the particle at the angle, Thomson found it a matter of simple mechanics to discover the mass. He concluded that the mass of the electron is $1/1836$ of the mass of the nucleus.

This is the theory of the television tube, except that the deflecting is both vertical and horizontal. A scanning device is required at the termination of the tube — the "screen" — to wipe away the electrons before they accumulate and spoil the picture.

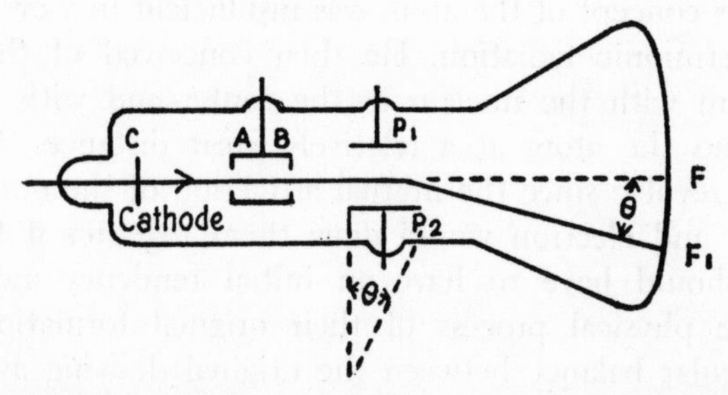

Thomson's Apparatus for Determining the Mass of the Electron
F represents the ordinary path of the electron after being passed through the slit system *AB*
F' is the actual path after its deflection by variation of the force of *Plate 2*

There are many ways of separating electrons from nuclei. The most common way is by thermionic radiation. Heating an object so raises its energy level that sooner or later a stream of electrons begins to flow from the heated object. In ordinary heating, the heated object regains its complement of electrons from its surroundings. In vacuum tubes, where the surroundings are relatively scarce, the electrons flow toward the opposite pole, the anode.

However, there is the phenomenon of ionization, wherein a body becomes positively charged if electrons are stripped from the atom or negatively charged as the atom accumulates electrons. Ionization is fairly common, as for example in a thunderstorm where there is not enough heat for thermionic radiation. Similarly, rubbing certain surfaces ionizes the molecules on the surface by stripping off electrons.

If Thomson's concept of the atom were correct, it would be difficult to strip off electrons since he regarded them as embedded within the whole body of the atom. An electrostatic balance is fairly stable. The comparison might be made of trying to strip plums out of a pudding merely by rubbing the surface of the pudding. In an atom, the electrons are closely united to the nucleus by the mutual attraction of positive and negative electricity rather than by the mere structure of the atom, as in the case of the pudding. We all know how difficult it is to separate magnets when their opposite poles are in contact. It is much more difficult in the case of electrons and nuclei.

THE RUTHERFORD MODEL OF THE ATOM

Sir Ernest Rutherford, the Canadian and British physicist, thought that Thomson's concept of the atom was insufficient in view of ionization other than thermionic radiation. He then conceived of the atom as a planetary system with the nucleus as the center and with the electrons revolving around the atom at a relatively great distance. The electrons would have to revolve since the mutual attraction of the opposite charges of the nucleus and electron would draw them together if they did not. Hence, they should have to have an initial tendency away from the nucleus in the physical process of their original formation, and then achieve an angular balance between the original drawing away from the nucleus and the mutual attraction of their opposite forces.

The simplest presentation of this, then, is that of an atom which is a balance of a positive (+) charges equal to the number of the electrons. Thus a hydrogen atom would have one electron (-) revolving about a nucleus with the charge +e. A helium atom would have two electrons revolving around a nucleus of +2e. The charge is called atomic number, and is the positive charge of the nucleus balancing the number of electrons.

Two further factors enter into this consideration. One is that x rays emit more than electrons. Besides electrons — called *beta* particles — they also emit *gamma* particles, which seem to be intensified photons, or light particles, and *alpha* particles. Alpha particles have the same properties, charge, and penetration as helium ions.

The second factor is that *radon gas*, a product of the spontaneous radioactive decay of radium, frequently suffers atomic explosions. In the process, alpha particles are produced. By the close observation of radon gas, by noticing the radiogenic effects of radium on platinum and platinum on sulphuric acid, and by noticing the effects of x-ray bombardment on lead and various metallic foils, Rutherford was able to come to the conclusion of the existence of the *proton*, or the positive particle within the nucleus.

The proton explains the electrostatic balance of the atom. It does not explain the weight of the atom. For example, the charge of helium is 2. That is, its electrostatic balance is two protons having a charge of +2 balanced by two electrons. This is reconstructed by the isolation of helium ions and by the emission of protons from reactions on such unstable elements as thorium. Nevertheless, even though the atomic charge, or atomic number of helium is 2, its atomic weight is 4; that is, although its charge is twice that of hydrogen, its weight is four times greater. This leads to the question of a particle within the nucleus to explain for the difference in weight. This particle would have to be electrically neutral, otherwise the electrostatic balance of the atom would be other than it is. The name *neutron* was suggested.

MODEL OF THE ATOM ACCORDING TO RUTHERFORD

Hydrogen

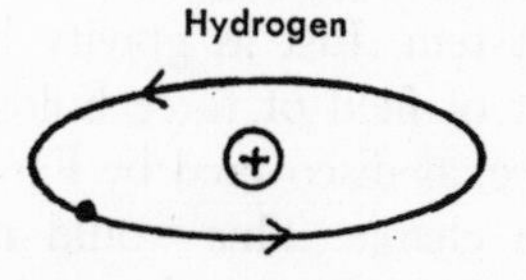

1 proton (+) and 1 electron (—) give hydrogen both a charge of 1 and a weight of 1.

Helium

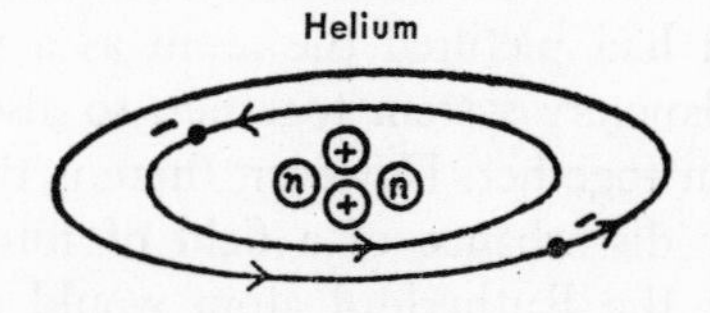

2 protons and 2 electrons give it a charge of 2.
2 protons and 2 neutrons give it a weight of 4.

The existence of the neutron was further hinted by Bohr's concept of the atom. If the atom is a planetary system, it must be not only an electrostatic balance but also a mechanical balance. If the atom is a planetary system, then it follows the laws of angular momentum. Just as a mechanical system consists of the sum of all the motions within the system, so also the total of an angular momentum system is the sum of all the rotations and movements of all of the parts composing the system. This means that any variation in the motion or orbit of any one of the components will be manifest throughout the entire system by: (1) a change of rotation of the other members; (2) a change in their proper orbits — where they are in relation to the focus and each other; and (3) a change in the velocity of their orbits. This is illustrated by the spinning skater who slows down when he extends his arms and who speeds up when he draws his arms close to his body.

In a planetary system, a change in any component of the system has widespread changes. For example, should any one of our planets change in its orbit, there would be resulting changes in the sun and in the orbits and rotations of the other planets. Gradually, however, the original planet would reassume its first orbit and spin. However, should one of the planets be greatly influenced, or explode, or be destroyed, the others would readjust to new orbits, slowing down or speeding up their orbits and rotations as the case might be. This would be normal for the entire system since it would be the tendency toward mechanical stability on the part of a self-contained system. It would involve stresses and strains in the components with consequent readjustment to the new state of physical conditions. It would be normal to the system, although disastrous to the inhabitants of the earth.

THE BOHR MODEL OF THE ATOM

Niels Bohr envisioned a similar set of conditions for the atom. In order to fulfill the conditions of ionization and thermionic radiation, Rutherford had pictured the atom as a planetary system. Just as gravity holds a planetary system together, so also some sort of field of force holds the atom together. However, there is this difference, as discovered by Faraday. Any disturbance of a field of force creates a charge. This would mean that the Rutherford atom would constantly be creating a charge which would manifest itself as instability in the form of radiation. Yet this is not the case. On the other hand, we cannot consider the electrons at rest in relation to the nucleus any more than we can consider a planet at rest in relation to the sun. The electron would be drawn into the nucleus exactly as a planet at rest would be drawn into the sun.

We can draw further on the analogy of a planetary system. One reason why the planets do not fall into the sun is not only that they are constantly rotating about the sun, but also that each is in its proper orbit in relation to the sun and in relation to the other planets. Bohr thus pictured the electrons as having proper orbits. If properly distributed, any slight charge created would be absorbed by the slight shifting of the electrons in their orbits.

The orbits of planets in relation to the sun, with the exception of Uranus, are roughly on the same ecliptic or plane. Similarly, the moons of Mars, Jupiter, and Saturn are on the same ecliptic in relation to their proper planets. Once again, however, one of the moons of Uranus is off its ecliptic. As things are, the planets seem to perform the function of retaining stability in relation to the sun and each other. They also seem to retain the sun's rotation at a proper balance of internal radiant energy and the pressure of gravity in such a way that the sun can keep a balance of the production of helium from hydrogen so that it does not burn up too rapidly.

This same ecliptic is not necessary in an atom. Furthermore, since an electronic field of force is three-dimensional, Bohr envisioned the electrons on many planes in their orbits. In this way, they act as a shield to absorb radiation coming from the outside. These were called "electronic shells." In this theory, when an atom emits an electron, the other electrons distribute themselves outwardly to readjust to the electrostatic balance. When an electron is picked up, the electrons adjust themselves inwardly.

MODEL OF THE ATOM ACCORDING TO BOHR

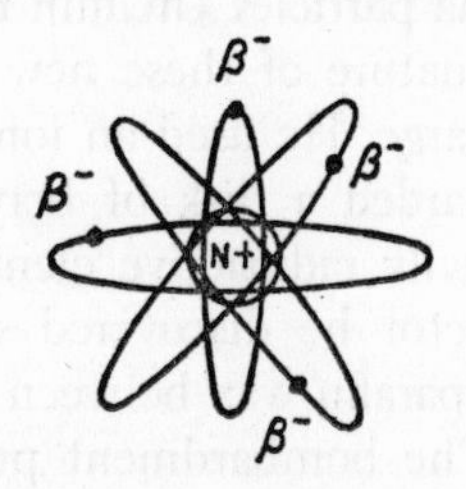

The above concept also fits in with the chemical theory of the manner of the combination of atoms into a chemical molecule. The pioneer in this field was John Dalton, early in the nineteenth century. Elements do not combine with each other indiscriminately. Some elements, such as gold, helium, and the inert gases, resist combination quite efficiently. Even the highly combinable elements such as hydrogen, carbon, and silicon, do not combine with other elements haphazardly. They combine in proper proportion. Dalton was the first to regard the atom as the smallest unit retaining the properties of the element and a molecule as the smallest unit retaining the properties of a chemical compound. He also worked out the proportions of elements in relation to compounds. This was developed further by Jacob Berzelius and Sir Humphrey Davy.

The Russian chemist, Dmitri Mendeleeff, had discovered the table of elements, a list of elements according to their relative weights from hydrogen, the lightest, to uranium, the heaviest. He also noticed periodic similarities among the elements according to proportionate multiples of weights. He thus devised the periodic table of elements, a listing of the elements according to the multiples of their weight and the similarity of their properties. This proportionality of atomic weights as developed by Mendeleeff and later by the British chemist Frederic Soddy gave rise to significant research in isotopes, those elements that remain the same in charge but vary in properties according to their weight. We shall see more of these in a later chapter.

CHADWICK AND THE NEUTRON

The proportionality in weights seemed further confirmation to Bohr and Soddy of the existence of a particle called the neutron, the particle described above. Long periods of observation of the penetration of radioactive particles by Bothe and Becker as well as by Irene Curie-Joliot (daughter of Madame Curie, co-discoverer of radium), led to the discovery of types of penetration by particles other than x rays, beta particles (electrons), and alpha particles (helium nuclei). This led Chadwick to further investigate the nature of these new particles in an attempt to discover their mass and charge. He used an ionization chamber, a Wilson cloud chamber. He bombarded a disk of beryllium with particles from a disk of polonium, a heavily radioactive element. By the use of a gold filter and a sensitive detector he discovered some unforeseen radiation. He then placed a filter of parafin wax between the target (the beryllium) and the cloud chamber. The bombardment produced an increased number of protons. He then inferred that these were knocked out of the paraffin by the particles. Since the penetration of protons had been fairly well measured, he was able to reconstruct from the further penetration of these new protons the size of the particles that knocked them out of the paraffin. He concluded that their mass was slightly larger than that of the proton. He also concluded that they have no known charge. This would explain the depth of their penetration. Since they have no charge, they were neither attracted nor deflected by charged particles. This explains the name given to them, *neutrons*. This also explains why they are used in atom bombs and thermonuclear devices.

Chadwick's experimentation gives us the picture of the atom as a nucleus consisting of protons and neutrons surrounded by electrons. The neutron is responsible for the weight of the atom while the protons and electrons are responsible for the electrostatic balance and any variations of it. This allows for two variations in the normal existence of elements. There may be variations in weight while the same charge is retained. These are called *isotopes*, and the changes in properties therefrom are marked. We have all heard of "heavy hydrogen," or deuterium. Its nucleus contains a neutron not found in ordinary hydrogen, giving it added mass. Deuterium is an isotope of hydrogen. Both deuterium and ordinary hydrogen retain the same charge and the same place in the table of elements. There are also variations in charge while the weight remains the same. These are *isotones*. The consequent changes in properties are generally slight and of short duration.

Chemical combinations are explained by the interlocking of electrons as these new combinations affect the electrostatic balance of the union of the two or several atoms. If the electron combination produces an ideal electrostatic balance, the resulting molecule will be chemically stable. An example of this is the union of sodium and chlorine — both extremely active elements. Their union, sodium chloride (table salt), is quite stable. The same principle is also true for extremely complex combinations; for example, both carbon monoxide and human blood are unstable. The latter has to be unstable to carry on the vital functions of the interchange of oxygen and carbon dioxide, of food and waste. Yet, the union of carbon monoxide and blood is so stable that death occurs rapidly and the poisoned blood remains unchanged for years. We shall see more of this in the next chapter.

We distinguish between slow neutrons and fast neutrons. There is a certain emission of incidental neutrons. However when these collide with a nucleus they produce a "scattered" neutron and a "recoil" nucleus as in the diagram below. The incident neutron is the slow neutron while

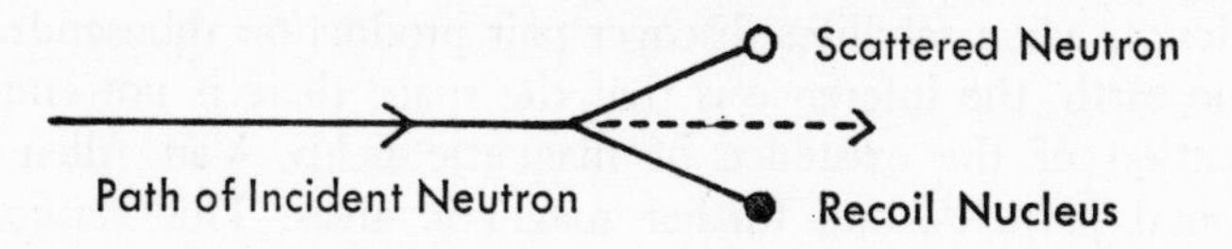

the scattered neutron, because of its further penetration, is called a fast neutron.

In an atomic bomb neutrons are released into the critical mass. Since neutrons are not deflected, some of them hit nuclei thus releasing other fast neutrons, which in turn hit nuclei, etc. In every collision, a great amount of energy is released almost with the speed of light. The result is an intense explosion.

Before Chadwick's isolation of neutrons, it was generally considered that the electrostatic stability of atoms was solely due to the balance of charges between the particles. It was even considered that neutrons were produced by the uniting of protons and electrons. However, this view is no longer held. The more widely accepted viewpoint is that the neutron is the "core" of the nucleus about which charged particles accumulate.

In pursuing the existence and properties of "fundamental particles," Carl Anderson, of the California Institute of Technology, discovered that certain types of bombardment, or "scattering" as it is generally called, produced particles with the mass and properties of the electron except that their charge is positive. These he called "positrons," and he urged that the name "electron" be replaced by "negatron." This substitution was not widely accepted. Instead, the custom has arisen to call the positron either a positive electron, or a *positive beta particle* (β^+), and to call the electron a *negative beta particle* (β^-).

Further work by Anderson and Blackett discovered that frequently the production of a positron also releases a matching electron, as in the diagram below. This production is called the production of "paired particles," or, more briefly, "pair production." Pair production seems to

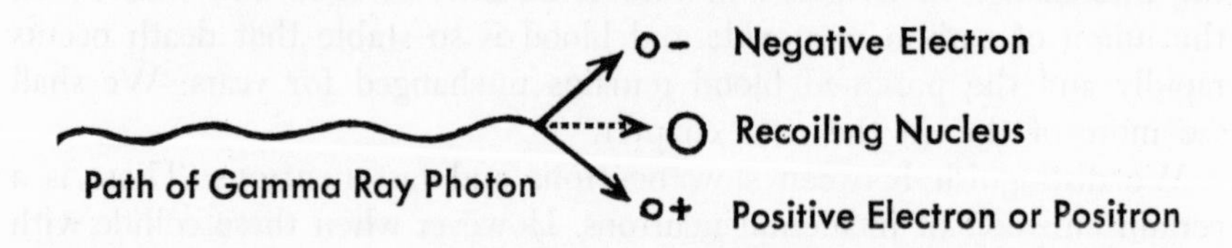

occur only in the presence of a strong field of force, and not in empty space. Hence, when satellites discover pair production thousands of miles above the earth, the inference is that the space there is not empty. This is verification of the existence of magnetic fields, Van Allen belts of fundamental particles, and further magnetic areas. This verifies certain discoveries of radioastronomy concerning conditions in and between distant stars and galaxies.

REVIEW

It is now time to review what we have seen of the nature and structure of the atom. In so doing, we must first look to what we may consider facts and what we must consider hypothesis.

Among the facts we may list the following:

1. We should expect that material bodies are made up of minimal parts in their structure. Matter is divisible into smaller and smaller parts, although the smaller the part the more difficult it becomes to divide it. We should expect that there is a limitation to division. We cannot reduce matter to points because every remnant will have some extension, no matter how minute, and because points are mathematical, not real, entities. Furthermore, since matter is made up of these minimal parts, they should have some extension.

2. We should expect that these minimal parts should have some of the physical properties of the whole, if not all of their chemical properties. A basic supposition is that if we can apply the principles of mechanics to the whole, we can apply them to any of the parts.

3. We have seen that energy can be explained most easily by considering it the degree of the activity of the random motion of fundamental particles.

4. We have also seen that since matter in itself has many electro-

magnetic properties, we can expect certain electromagnetic properties in its fundamental parts.

5. The ordinary behavior of matter when treated as a gas and when subject to the forces of both heat and electricity shows the emission of a particle with a negative charge called an *electron* or a *negative beta* particle. This suggested the existence of a *positive* particle to balance the charge for electromagnetic stability and to explain why all matter is not ionized.

6. The isolation of this particle, called the *proton*, explained the balance of charges but not the differences in weight. Hence, another particle, the *neutron*, was suggested. This, in turn, was isolated, and the experiments involved in its isolation indicated the existence of a positively charged electron, called a *positron*, or a *positive beta* particle.

All of the above particles can be produced and identified quite easily by modern techniques. However, they were produced and identified before modern techniques reached the height of their achievement. Concerning their existence in the atom, the most we can say is that by agitation particles corresponding to the concepts advanced are produced. At least, *something* is produced that corresponds more or less accurately to the concept of its suggested existence. In the history of the progress in nuclear physics, the isolation of one particle has led to hypothetical particles to fill out the needs of the problem. Hence, *the scheme of the atom is primarily the answer to a succession of problems initiated by the discovery of the first problem*. Although we may say that the particles produced have some manner of existence, we cannot say that they exist in perfect correspondence to the model, or the concept, of the atom. Hence, in nuclear physics we deal with nature *as it is thought about* and not *necessarily as it is*.

The introduction of modern techniques introduces *hypothetical and conceptual* elements into the problem. Here we are dealing with results whose origin we cannot draw from existence. We really do not know the origin of many of the results obtained today. Hence, they must be judged not against real problems about the real nature of real matter but against their fulfilling the demands of a series of interrelated concepts within a mental framework.

PROBLEMS OF MODERN TECHNIQUE

These problems originated with the discovery of paired particles. The earlier particles can be produced with simple techniques — spontaneous decay of radioactive elements, x-ray tubes, and radio tubes. Furthermore, the conditions under which they are produced are similar enough to natural events that we do not have to be too much concerned by the interference of the instrument. Similarly, the manners of noticing their effect were: (1) the disturbance of moist air in cloud chamber; (2) the tracking of the paths of particles across the emulsion of a photographic plate; and (3) the penetration of particles through a thin screen of paraffin wax.

Both photo-emulsion and paraffin wax are chemically complex. There is the chance of the production of particles from the target. However, the collision of the primary particles produces such a marked effect — as below — that it is easy to distinguish between the primary particles from the source and the "secondary" particles produced by the collision.

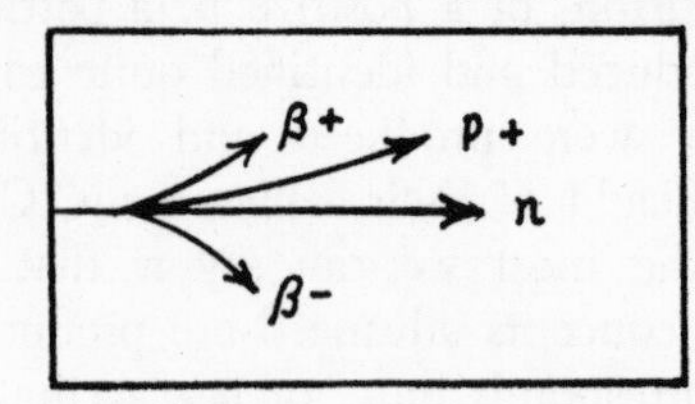

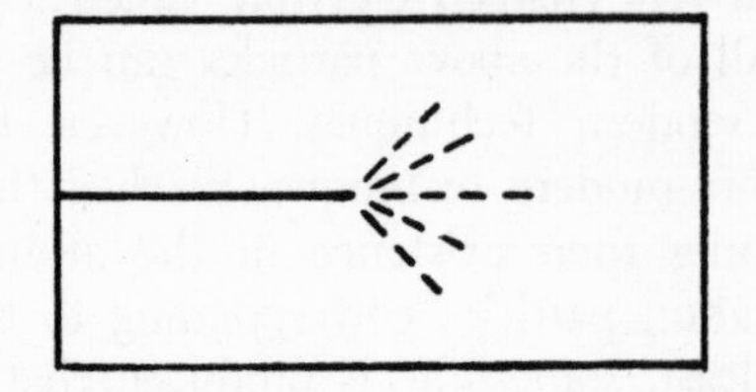

The production of paired particles is different. These are produced only in the presence of an electromagnetic field, and hence are valuable in the study of cosmic rays. However, for the problems at hand — suggested by cosmic radiation — there is the lurking doubt that these may be produced by the collision of the source particle with the components (we do not know what they are!) of the field itself. These problems originated with the use of modern accelerators which make great use of magnetic fields. As a matter of fact, there is an intricate interweaving of theory herein. What we learn from accelerators we can apply to the space between the planets, stars, and galaxies in the case of cosmic rays. What we discover about cosmic rays from observation seems to verify some ideas which we have discovered from accelerators but also seems to suggest further problems. We go to work on these problems in accelerators and seem to find solutions to our difficulties. However, these solutions suggest further investigation applicable to cosmic rays. In order to untangle this interweaving of theory and discovery, we must spend some time on the manner of experiment in nuclear physics and the types of instruments used.

ACCELERATORS AND THEIR RESULTS

The *theory of experiment* is that of a controlled observation in the quest of the uniformity of physical phenomena. We try to see the phenomena unified under one space and time, or space-time, continuity. For this, we must have a theory of measurement and we must apply what we know about measurement to the new direction of experiment. That is why we must know the simple laws of mechanics before we can go into nuclear physics. When we cannot observe the phenomena directly, we must try to reproduce the conditions under which we think they should occur. If they do occur, then we have some verification. If they do not occur, then any number of possibilities open up, and this means that we must pursue these possibilities before ruling out our original position.

We devise an instrument for what we expect we might discover. The reasoning behind this is that from what we know about something we are able to infer how it should act under unusual, or at least different, conditions. Hence, we try to set up those conditions. The epistemological principle behind this is that we pass from the known to the unknown. From the known we are able to infer something of the unknown possibilities, and we try to achieve these. Thus, the theory behind accelerators is that since what we have discovered about the atom indicates not only other possibilities but also problems that demand resolution, we must first formulate in our minds what these other possibilities and problems might be. Since we cannot observe an atom, we must infer from its direct action and from its reactions when it is agitated. Hence we agitate it by bombarding it with particles.

There are special difficulties with attempts at reconstruction after disturbing an atom. Since it is so intrinsically energetic, its debris after a collision consists of flashes of energy that last for several millionths of a second. This could be compared with firing in the dark to attempt to discover what we hit by the sparks produced.

As noted above, the development of devices began with observation. The particle constitution of matter was suggested by collisions of particles, by the spontaneous emission of radium, and by certain radioactive isotopes of uranium. Particle constitution also leads into wave theory, about which we shall see later. Radium is expensive, too expensive for widespread laboratory use. The emission of alpha, gamma, and beta rays, or particles, from x rays led into the consideration of bombardment of targets with consequent scattering. The first device suggested was the Wilson cloud chamber. This consists of a chamber with a quartz window containing a supersaturated solution of water in air. It is compressed, and then suddenly released. The rapid expansion both brings down the temperature and holds the water vapor in the air. Ions are simultaneously beamed into the chamber. Their collisions with the molecules of the water, especially the hydrogen, shows up in vapor trails in the chamber much after the fashion of the contrails of high flying aircraft.

Nevertheless, the voltage is low in such experiments. A way had to be devised to experiment with high voltage. X-ray tubes of extremely high voltage were used, but, again, this gradually proved impractical. One of the most useful devices is the Van de Graaff generator, the theory of which is based upon certain phenomena of static electricity. Static electricity is the separation of charges by the rubbing of unlike substances. An electrostatic generator is a device for rubbing unlike substances together to produce a charge. Sometimes an accumulated charge can be of high potential. We see and experience static electricity in the rubbing of certain types of shoe soles on heavy carpets while walking on them. The trailing edges of airplanes have small rods extended from them to drain off the static electricity which accumulates on the wings by the rubbing of the air over them. Static electricity is produced in clouds by the rubbing of air and water molecules together.

Since static electricity is the separation of charges, and since the negative charge is an electron and the positive charge a proton, if the electrons can be separated from the proton in a controlled manner, the protons might be used to bombard atoms for the purposes of discerning the components of the atoms. This is the theory of the Van de Graaff generator.

THE VAN DE GRAAFF GENERATOR

In design, the Van de Graaff electrostatic generator consists of a large metallic sphere on insulated supports. A belt on a pulley arrangement is fed into the sphere. An electric charge raised to a high potential by a "step-up" transformer is fed into the entrance to the chamber. This ionizes the air or gas of the chamber. A charge is also fed onto the belt and introduced into the chamber. The separation of particles is immediate, the electrons coating the outside of the sphere and the ions being collected at a point called an "ion source." The latter are led through a series of auxiliary electrodes to the target chamber. At every step of the process, the desired ions are accelerated in such way that they pick up voltage. Van de Graaff generators, in general, are able to work up voltages of about one to six million electron volts (1–6 MEV).

The target is an element that releases a type of particle upon bombardment. If neutrons are desired, thorium or beryllium is the target.

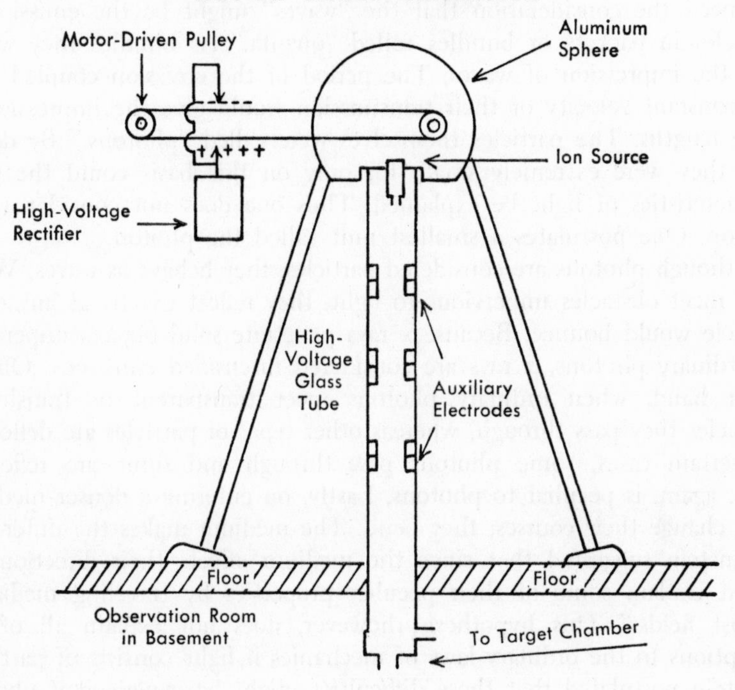

If electrons are desired, some compound rich in hydrogen, such as paraffin, is used.

By today's standards, electrostatic accelerators are of low voltage. The particles emitted and dealt with act according to the laws of mechanics, especially of dynamics. There are but few theoretical difficulties resulting, and it is possible to erect good working models of the atom in its nucleus and electrons.

However, the introduction of wave mechanics suggested higher and higher voltage accelerators; that is to say, the concepts of wave mechanics introduced theoretical suggestions that were not satisfied by the results of low voltage accelerators.

THE THEORY OF HIGHER ENERGY ACCELERATORS

The difficulties are these. In 1886, Michelson and Morley had suggested that the "luminiferous ether," a hypothetical, all-pervading medium postulated for the transmission of light waves, did not exist. Max Planck advanced the consideration that the "waves" might be the emission of particles in packets or bundles called "quanta." As bundles they would give the impression of waves. The period of the emission coupled with the constant velocity of their transmission would give the impression of wave lengths. The particles themselves were called "photons." *By definition* they were extremely small, for only on this basis could the wave characteristics of light be explained. Thus one does not consider a half photon. One postulates a smallest unit called the photon.

Although photons are considered particles, they behave as waves. When they meet obstacles impervious to light, they reflect exactly as any other particle would bounce. Because x rays penetrate solid objects impervious to ordinary photons, x rays are considered *intensified emissions*. On the other hand, when ordinary photons meet transparent or translucent obstacles they pass through, whereas other types of particles are deflected. In certain cases, some photons pass through and some are reflected. This, again, is peculiar to photons. Lastly, on entering a denser medium, they change their courses; they bend. The medium makes the difference.

Einstein suggested that since the medium affects their direction, we might explain some of their peculiar properties by traveling media, or "ghost fields." This hypothesis, however, does not explain all of the exceptions to the ordinary laws of mechanics if light consists of particles. Einstein postulated that these difficulties might be explained if photons were considered to have zero mass at rest. This means two things: (1) *if* light could be slowed down, the particles would be extremely small; (2) since there is no such thing as light at rest, a photon at rest is inconceivable.

In 1922, Louis de Broglie suggested that electrons, being the smallest particles we know, might behave somewhat like light if they could be accelerated to almost the speed of light; that is to say, under normal conditions of ionization, in the state of static electricity, and such, they behave like particles. Nevertheless, because of their small mass, they might behave like waves if they could be accelerated beyond normal conditions. The only experimentation possible at the time was that of reflection and refraction instead of particle deflection. Davisson and Germer experimented with beaming the electrons of x rays on certain crystal surfaces. They discovered that the beta particles, or electrons, act exactly like photons. As the facets of the crystal changed their angle of incidence, the electrons varied in "wavelengths." This did not prove that electrons are of the same nature as photons, but it suggested an in-between condition. It suggested, for example, that the orbit of the electron is characterized by vibrations as well as by position in an orbit and that there is an amplitude to these vibrations called "psi" (ψ) functions. It also suggested that, in determining the position of electrons, statistical averages rather than geometrical laws would indicate their distribution; that is, we would be unable to say that an electron is here rather than there. Rather, since it is a particle with wave properties, its *chances* are better of being here than there.

This is the basic position of wave mechanics. It does not mean that matter consists of waves. It means that if matter is a particle in constitution, it still seems to manifest wave properties. The best way to make sure is to attempt higher and higher accelerations.

HIGH ENERGY ACCELERATORS

The original device of higher acceleration is the cyclotron. The cyclotron consists of a disklike chamber built between the poles of a huge electromagnet. This creates a forceful magnetic field. Particles are beamed

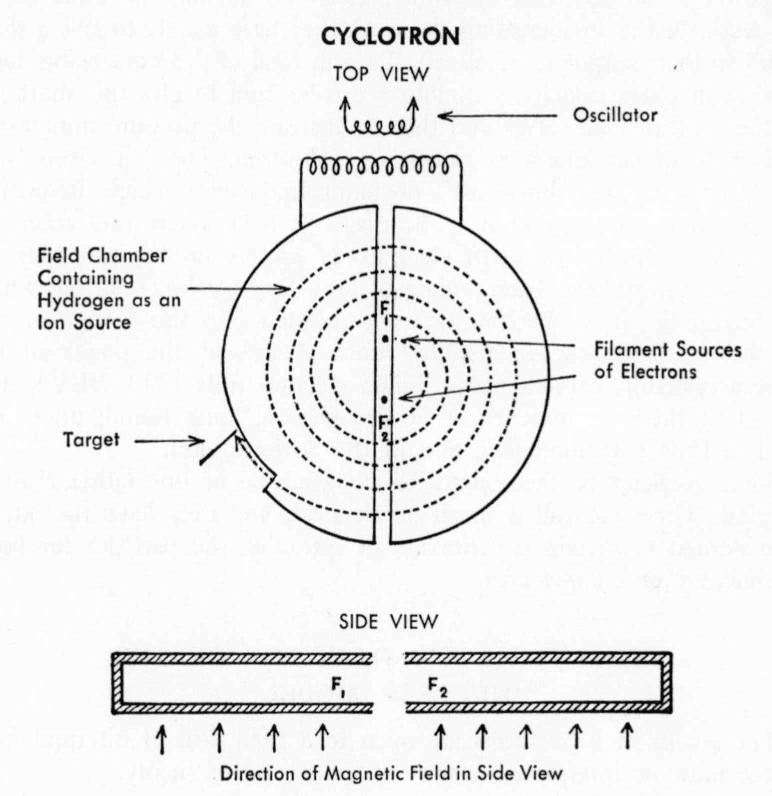

into the field and are accelerated to extremely high velocities and pressures by the field. Furthermore, despite their statistical positions, they are beamed into physical positions. After cycling around within the field, they are directed onto the target at voltages up in the billions. They produce startling results.

If the particles are electrons, they are first produced from cathode-ray emission and then beamed into the cyclotron. If they are protons, they are first produced in an auxiliary Van de Graaff generator and then beamed into the cyclotron.

In keeping with their character as wave functions, after they have achieved a given velocity, they achieve a "phase" velocity; that is to say, their synchronized oscillations help to accelerate each other, just as two pendulums oscillating in phase can help each other. It is as though the waves of the particles pile up on each other and push each other along. Or, it may be like two locomotives pulling a train. After their work has become synchronized, they have merely to ride at a minimum output of power to do the work smoothly, each one helping the other to do the work. Just as in increasing the work they have merely to give a short "jolt" to their output to accelerate the sum total of the work being done, so also, in phase velocity, a cyclotron can be built to give this short jolt to the synchronized waves and thus to increase the pressure immensely. This type of accelerator is called a *synchrotron*. The jolt given by a synchrotron is the "broadcast" of radio frequencies (high frequency, that is, short wavelength) into the magnetic field. These vary according to the wave characteristics of electrons or protons, as the case may be. This instrument has been enlarged into the *synchrocyclotron* which modulates the frequencies as they are injected into the magnetic field. Further accelerations are achieved until at present the power of the huge accelerators exceeds thirty billion electron volts (30+ BEV). The largest of these, at present, are at Brookhaven, Long Island, under the Atomic Energy Commission, and in the Soviet Union.

Some accelerators direct particles along a straight line rather than in a spiral. These are called *linear accelerators*, and they have the advantage desired in certain experiments of spreading the particles for bombardment over a larger area.

CONCEPTUAL CONSTRUCTION OF THE NUCLEAR MODEL

The *results* of accelerators are open to a good deal of interpretation. These must be interpreted against a background of theory.

As we have seen, the simplest model of the atom is that of several charged bodies, the proton and electron, and a neutral particle or neutron. The charged particles explain the electrostatic balance. The neutron explains the mass differences wherein atomic weight is proportionately greater than atomic charge, or number. The presence of the neutron, as well as mechanical problems, suggests a plurality of positively charged particles in the nucleus. The proton, in charge, should balance out the number of electrons. Heavier and radioactive elements are known to have many electrons. There are two ways in which the charge could be balanced, either (1) by a larger and larger proton; or (2) by a plurality of protons proportionate in number to the number of electrons. There are many mechanical difficulties concerning the first alternative. If the electrons are considered to revolve about the nucleus, more electrons revolving in intricate orbits around one proton would cause great strains on the proton, just as many, many planets revolving around a star would cause many strains on that star. Hence, we would expect the proton to break down into chunks. Furthermore, in actual results of low voltage bombardment, the protons emitted from such heavy and highly charged elements as thorium are larger than ordinary alpha particles but not appreciably so. Hence, both from theory and experiment we conclude to a plurality of protons in the nucleus.

What is the binding force of these particles? Like charges, in this case positive particles, repel each other. What holds these positive particles together? It would have to be greater than all of the protons to hold them together. There are two possibilities for this. There could be one force that holds them together. Yet we can only assume that this is a negative charge. Were this the case, what would hold the electrons in relation to the nucleus? It would not be gravity, since gravity is a weak force compared to force between electrons and the nucleus — one million, million times weaker (10^{-12})!

The other possibility was suggested by the Japanese physicist Yukawa. He envisioned a particle midway in mass between the proton and the electron rapidly oscillating between nuclear particles and changing charge as needed. Whereas the former position of the "nuclear glue" might be compared to a net holding a group of sheep together, the latter position, of the oscillating particle, the *meson*, might be compared to a sheep dog which holds the sheep together by dashing about and pulling the sheep into one group.

Yukawa predicted the existence of the meson in 1935. Nature has many huge accelerators in the magnetic fields of stellar and planetary bodies and in the many huge clouds of ionized hydrogen between the stars. Particles radiated from the sun and from other stars and galaxies, called cosmic rays, are accelerated to inconceivable voltages, beginning at about 30 MEV and working up to fantastic voltages. Some of these hit the earth's magnetic belts, Van Allen belts, magnetic field, and atmosphere. They bombard the components of these and produce all known types of particles. In 1933, Kunze noted the traces of an unidentified particle amid the tracks of alpha, beta, and gamma particles on his photographic plates. More convincing pictures of these particles were published in 1938 by Williams and Pickup as well as by Neddermeyer and Anderson. Finally, in 1947 Anderson clearly identified *mu mesons* (μ), sometimes called "muons," while in the same year Lattes, Occhialini, and Powell identified the mesons postulated by Yukawa. These latter are called *pi mesons* (π) and sometimes "pions."

Since modern accelerators are well within the range of cosmic radiation, they produce mesons. In fact, they produce a fantastic array of particles. Actually these particles are flashes of energy that have both wave and mass properties. They are traced either in a Wilson cloud chamber or on the emulsion of photographic plates. They are classified into stable particles, those that can continue to exist in the free state, and particles with a "decay scheme." For example, a proton is stable. It exists as a positive ion. An electron is also stable. On the other hand, a neutron lasts in the free state for a little over eighteen minutes before breaking down into a proton, an electron, and a neutrino. Some particles are extremely short-lived. For example, the negative pi meson, the binding force, exists in the free state for 256 millionths of a second.

Another classification is based on size, running from the smallest particles, using the electron as the standard, to the largest known particles. These are leptons, mesons, nucleons, and hyperons. Thus, if the electron is taken as mass 1, the mass to the negative *xi* (ξ^-) particle is mass 2570. It would seem that the hyperon is larger than the proton, because it seems to be produced by some sort of decay of the components of the bombarded material, and in its rapid acceleration it assumes wave characteristics and spreads, or increases in mass, as its velocity approaches the speed of light.

One may ask the question as to how we are able to measure the mass and duration of extremely tiny particles that last for a few millionths of a second. With the Wilson cloud chamber there was really no way of measuring them. However, with the technique of directing the products of accelerated bombardment across photographic plates, and (1) knowing the direction and displacement of an electron, and (2) knowing its penetration — i.e., how far along the surface of the plate it travels, we are able to reconstruct from the direction and displacement of another particle both its charge and mass, and from its penetration how long it lasts. Since we know that accelerated particles travel at speeds approximating that of light, we know how long it would take a photon, or light particle, to penetrate a given distance at a given time across a photo-emulsion plate. The particle in question is compared to this standard. Even in a few millionths of a second, a photon, traveling at 186,000 miles per second, is going to cover a measurable distance of inches in milliseconds.

If a particle exists in the free state in nature without changing into something else, it is called a stable particle. The only ones we know are: (1) photons — light particles; (2) neutrinos; (3) electrons; (4) positrons; and (5) protons. All the other particles are judged on the basis of their (1) mass; (2) charge; (3) lifetime; and (4) decay scheme. The way of determining these properties consists in measuring: (1) the amount of emulsion displaced — the size of the groove they make; (2) the direction of their paths; (3) the distance they cover; (4) the further products that emerge from them, by their directions, penetrations, etc. For example, a *neutron* produces a proton, an electron and an anti-neutrino. Schematically, this would be represented as $n \rightarrow p^+ + \beta^- + \bar{\nu}$ On a plate it would look like:

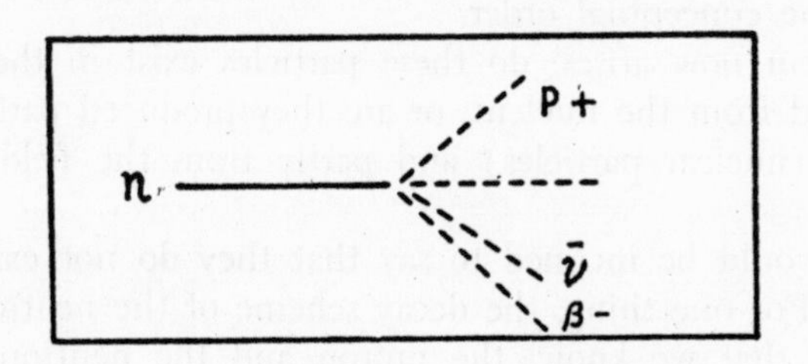

Incidentally, the question that triggered the emphasis on huge accelerators, whether or not particles might behave like waves and thus be better represented by wave mechanics rather than the classical mechanics of simple bodies, was answered in the affirmative. Particles have wave characteristics, and the higher the velocities the more wavelike they are. So much so is this the case that although the term "fundamental particles" is used, we have no way of knowing whether the objects are particles and whether they are fundamental. The term "fundamental particles" is simply a convenient expression.

At this point, we had better have another review. We can summarize what we have seen in the following points:

1. Spontaneous radioactivity and the emissions from x-ray tubes seem to indicate that the atom consists of particles positively charged surrounded by particles negatively charged.

2. This seems to be verified by the results of low-voltage Van de Graaff electrostatic generators. In fact, when it comes to a model of the atom, the use of Van de Graaff generators is now preferred for certain experiments. It does not destroy the material beyond recognition.

3. The suspicion that these particles might have wave properties, suggested by Einstein and further developed by De Broglie, initiated interest in the possibilities of the high acceleration of particles.

4. The resulting instruments, the cyclotron, synchrotron, synchrocyclotron, and cosmotron, accelerated particles with such pressures that they both assumed wave characteristics and gave indication of the increase of mass predicted by Einstein.

5. These instruments also gave rise to many particles, which, in turn, broke down into other particles, most of which have extremely short lifetimes in the free state.

6. Nevertheless, when we say that matter "consists" of particles or waves, we mean that under certain conditions and with a view to certain problems, *it is more convenient to consider them as particles*. Under other conditions *it is more convenient to consider them as waves*. We are still in the *conceptual* order.

The problem now arises: do these particles exist *in* the nucleus; are they produced *from* the nucleus; or are they produced partly by a decay of nucleons (nuclear particles) and partly from the field that accelerates them?

First, we would be inclined to say that they do not exist *as such* in the nucleus. For one thing, the decay scheme of the neutron shows that the nucleons that we know, the proton and the neutron, seem to be changeable, possibly interchangeable.

Furthermore, when we bombard protons with protons, we get protons, neutrons, positive pions, and neutral pions. The schematic representation is:

$$p + p \rightarrow p + n + \pi^+$$
$$p + p \rightarrow p + p + \pi^0$$

When we bombard neutrons with protons we get protons, neutrons, negative, positive, and neutral pions. The scheme is:

$$p + n \rightarrow p + p + \pi^-$$
$$p + n \rightarrow n + n + \pi^+$$
$$p + n \rightarrow p + n + \pi^0$$

When we bombard neutrons with neutrons we get neutrons, protons, and negative and neutral pions. The scheme is:

$$n + n \rightarrow n + p + \pi^-$$
$$n + n \rightarrow n + n + \pi^0$$

We further get the proper decay schemes of the pions involved. Thus, the full expression of one change would be:

$$p + n \rightarrow p + n + (\pi^0 \rightarrow \gamma + \beta^- + \beta^+)$$

Second, certain breakdowns of nuclei indicate the elimination of an electron from the nucleus. Now there are overwhelming theoretical difficulties about the continued existence of an electron in the nucleus. The only conclusion to be drawn from this production is that the fundamental nucleons, the proton and neutron, can come from something more fundamental and can become something else and of a different charge.

In general, the statement of Heisenberg that the nucleus is relatively simple and that it gives rise to other products seems the more accurate assumption, at least more accurate than the opinion that all of the known and produced particles have existed in the nucleus and have been released by excitation.

Third, there is the suggestion that some of these particles might derive in part from the field through which they are accelerated. This hypothesis comes to us from the production of paired particles. Paired particles were produced before accelerators became so powerful. Their production depends not so much upon the velocity of acceleration as upon the strength of the field. Although they are produced only in the presence of a strong field, this does not mean that they are produced from the field, but it does open up the possibility that the field contributes something. The contribution of something of the field might explain some of the wave characteristics of excited particles. It is interesting to notice that Einstein's "ghost field" concepts gave rise to the gradual acceptance to his universal field theory. Geometrically this means that position is more important than mass. Physically it means that space is never empty and that there is always something of a field of force maintaining some electromagnetic properties as well as gravitational properties.

Since we are not by any means sure of any answers to the above questions, it is now necessary to construct a model of the atom. There is no ultimate reconciliation of the particle or wave nature of fundamental particles. Hence, we find it convenient to consider matter at rest (relatively), "discontinuous matter," to consist of particles, and radiant matter, "continuous matter," to consist of waves. This does not mean that we believe that particles change into waves. We simply consider their wave functions more pronounced in a radiant state. They are still assumed to have some wave functions in the unexcited atom.

Since the particles are assumed to have some wave functions in the unexcited state, we cannot consider any atomic particle as having a given position. Nor can we consider the shell of any electron as a definite orbit. We must take a statistical point of view of this and consider the orbits of electrons as being oscillations, the possible movings of nucleons as also being oscillations.

Consequently, in any considerations of action on or by an atom, we must consider the atom as a multibody problem. Nevertheless, in representing these "bodies," we would do better to regard them as forces along the line of activity. This is what is called the *barrier model* of the atom. It is not much different from considering the strains imposed on the sun by the masses and motions of the planets as simple forces, regardless of the individual variations of individual planets.

RECONSTRUCTED MODEL OF THE NUCLEUS

There are two forms of the barrier model, the shell model and the random distribution model.

Before examining these models, however, we must look to the origin of the *concept of a barrier*. Any model of the atom that implies a notion of discreet particles in relation to each other must face the problem of the forces involved in these relations. These problems involve the masses and charges of the particles as well as the field of force and the binding energy. At the end of the eighteenth century, the French physicist, Coulomb, had determined that the attraction of particles in a magnetic field was that of the charges over the inverse square of the distance. Refinement of this concept was advanced by Michael Faraday and John Henry. Maxwell noted the similarity of the ratio to that of gravitational attraction, and he worked out more systematic formulae of the strength of a field and the forces of attraction and repulsion involved in the field. This is the basis of Einstein's field theories.

If the atom is an electrostatic balance, then the Coulomb-Maxwell formulae can be applied to it. In practice, then, these formulae are expressions of (1) the forces of attraction between the nucleons — one hundred million, million times that of gravity (10^{14}); (2) the forces between the nucleus and the electrons — one million, million times that of gravity (10^{12}); and (3) the proportionate amount of energy required to release a nucleon or an electron from the electrostatic balance of a stable atom. The force resisting such a release can be considered a barrier to the energies attempting to bring about such a separation. It is thus called the "Coulomb barrier."

The Coulomb barrier simplifies problems in atomics and nucleonics to the extent that it allows us to regard them in terms of forces rather than in terms of positions. Seen in the perspective of this basic position, the shell nuclei model and the random nuclei model differ in elegance.

The shell concept arises out of the emphasis on the mechanical problems of body upon body in a common field of force. Its basis is the transformation of the concepts of pure mechanics to electromechanics. It thus reflects the continuation of the developments of the outstanding work of James Clerk Maxwell. It also fits in with refined observations of nuclear particles after high acceleration scattering.

The mechanical basis is this. One body moving around another body exerts a number of strains on that body. For example, the moon exerts all kinds of strains on the earth over and above ocean tides. The planets exert far greater strains on the sun. There must be some compensation for this. In the sun it is fairly easy. Since the outer parts of the sun are gaseous, helium and hydrogen, the compensation is like that of a fluid. In other words, the compensation takes the form of tides. The core of the sun is compressed radiance called plasma. Again, this reacts like a fluid. In a rigid body it is not so easy to explain compensation. We would expect a gradual wearing down, cracks appearing on the surface, gradual splits in the structure, etc. One way to avoid this expectation would be to consider the body in question as made up of smaller bodies free in their movements. The compensation, then, could be by the moving of the smaller bodies. For example, a bag of marbles resists strains more easily than a similar mass of clay crockery.

Now let us apply this to the atom. Although the electrons apply strains to the nucleus, the compensation could be by way of adjustment of the nucleons with relation to one another and to the electrons if the nucleus consists of nucleons rather than a semiliquid state of positive energy. This would involve rotations on axes ("spins") and changes of position ("orbits"). It would also involve moments of force, points where the forces could be considered to be applied, called "magnetic moments" and "electric moments," according to the principles of angular momentum.

All of these concepts seem to be verified in the traces left on plates. Besides the proper angular directions as the results of direction, collision, and charge, the particles show other manifestations that would indicate some such proper movements as spins. We could compare it to the added motion given to a billiard ball beyond directional velocity because of the "english" (or spin).

Reconstructing from this theory and data, then, we can envision the model of the atom as electrons oscillating about the nucleus, itself composed of particles rotating and orbiting. By the same principles of angular momentum that envision electrons orbiting around the nucleus, we can consider the nucleons as having their regular — but oscillating — orbits and spins. As a matter of fact, the spectroscopic analysis of certain heavy atoms does show the presence of certain "spectral" lines in the regular spectroscopic picture that would indicate some kind of steady oscillating on the part of the component particles. The oscillation also accounts for the wave effects.

On the other hand, equally sound and valid arguments can be marshaled for the *random distribution* of nucleons. All of the effects of scattering can be equally explained in terms of releases of energy that have mass effects according to the formula: $m = \frac{E}{c^2}$. The spectral lines in the spectroanalysis could be explained by harmonic random distribution of the particles and harmonic motions on their part. It is no more unusual than saying that in a given group in a series of popular lectures, the number of listeners and the space that they occupy will average out the same regardless of the fact that they change places from week to week.

The difference between the two models of the atom are that the former would consider the atom as a fairly average distribution of nucleons in oscillating orbits surrounded by electrons in similarly oscillating orbits. The latter would have the atom a random distribution of electromagnetic forces in oscillation.

EVALUATION

The frequent use of the term "model," of the verb "to suppose," and of the verbal expression "to find convenient," should indicate to us the proper nature of physical theory, especially as it pertains to the atom and to any theoretical deductions therefrom.

We have no direct experience of the atom. Every form of atomism in ancient times and atomic theory in modern times is a conceptual reconstruction of the most convenient way to explain familiar problems. We must *envision* a structure of indivisible particles with certain energetic and electromagnetic properties. In view of what we know more directly of nature, we must fit this envisioning into a properly comprehensive concept — or model. This model must be sufficiently adequate to take care of all of the phenomena of matter. Among these are purely mechanical phenomena — the relations of mass and energy in the activities of forces at work. For this purpose, a particle-like atom is the most convenient model. On the other hand, we must also account for wave phenomena, and we must enlarge our model to include these. Hence, we must envision a particle constitution of more than merely mechanical or electromagnetic properties to account for wave theory. We do not really know whether that is the way nature *is,* but in view of the way nature acts we find it the best way *to think about it.* Hence, we are properly in the conceptual order.

In an attempt to discover whether or not our concepts are true, we try to put them to the test by exciting nature in such way as to make it indicate a wave constitution, particle consitution, a particle constitution allowing for wave properties, or an energetic and wave constitution allowing for particle properties. If our conceptual models are insufficient for this enlargement, we attempt to include therein some influence of a hypothetical environment postulated for this particular experiment or observation — the field.

In our experiments, we sometimes perceive a spark of energy. We sometimes perceive a track in a cloud chamber. We most frequently observe a disturbance of the pointer reading of a dial. We also perceive strange tracks across a photographic plate. Knowing the strength of the electromagnetic field (although we do not know what the field is, and hence must interpret it in terms of the theory we are trying to establish) we can suppose what amount and charge of electromagnetic energy disturbed it by traveling through it at a given velocity. Knowing something of the permeability of the photographic emulsion, we can interpret the tracks on it in terms of waves or particles of a given mass traveling at a given velocity.

The norm we are using in this development of theory is the *fittingness of concept to concept*. When we state that one of the basic truths of nuclear physics is the decay of nuclear particles, we are not using the term "truth" as a relation of the agreement of a concept to an extramental entity, situation, or event. We are using it in the sense of the agreement of one concept with another concept. The norm of truth in this type of theorizing is the adequacy of one concept within a general conceptual system.

This is perfectly valid within physical theory. However, we must be careful in philosophizing therefrom. We must not attach too much *real* value to what is primarily a *conceptual development*. This warning comes to us from such philosophers as the almost (unfortunately) unknown Charles Sanders Peirce, William James, Ernst Mach, Karl Pearson, Lord Russell, Alfred North Whitehead. Like warnings come to us from such physical theorists as P. A. M. Dirac, Albert Einstein, and Werner Heisenberg.

When we put too much emphasis on the conceptual system, nature frequently upsets our calculations. Several years ago the physical world was upset by the "overthrow" of the Law of Parity. The upset was a bit premature since parity was not that important. What happened was that the basic assumption for certain decay schemes of mesons was oversimplified. There was an assumption that two objects indistinguishable from each other would be indistinguishable in their operations if acted upon by the same forces. If acted upon by the same type of forces but in opposite directions, they would offer "mirror images." Variations in the decay scheme were dismissed as temporary interferences on the part of environment, the accelerating device, etc.

As physical theory stands, what actually happens is that the conceptual expectation anticipates the actuality corresponding to it. This gives the impression that the idea is the principle of the entity. For this reason, we can see how it is that philosophers that put heavy and even undue metaphysical emphasis on ideas, such as Plato and Kant, are popular with the physical theorists. Yet, insofar as Aristotle developed Plato in a realistic way, we could expect that more and more attention be paid him by those physical theorists interested in the problem of reality as it is. We find this to be the case with Werner Heisenberg.

NUCLEAR THEORY AND HYLOMORPHISM

Even though physical theory is heavily conceptual, and even though its norm of truth is more logical than realistic through its emphasis on the interrelation of concepts, we must say that something corresponds to a certain extent with the concepts. *Something* is making tracks on plates and manifesting wave properties. At any event, we can say that matter is granular rather than smooth, that it seems to be composed of particles in its normal state, and that it seems to manifest wave properties in its radiant state.

This we should expect. Regardless of what matter consists of, it is divisible into minimal parts that to a certain extent maintain the properties of the whole. This was widely maintained by philosophers of both the Platonic and Aristotelian tradition. It is not anything that began with Joseph Priestley, Robert Boyle, or John Dalton. Among the properties of matter is intrinsic energy. If energy comes *from* a body, it must somehow be *in* that body, in its structure if not in its essence. Even the consideration that there is a natural limitation to the retention of the properties of elements in the component atoms is implicit in the Aristotelian-scholastic tradition. Aristotle looked upon elements as simple bodies composed of atoms. A change in the element either to something else or in combination with something else must be effected throughout the whole, hence in the atoms.

Consequently, the problem of hylomorphism is not that of structural composition of energetic atoms. It is more the problem of the relationship of parts to the whole.

Even if matter consists, structurally, of all the particles with their particle and wave properties, decay schemes, charges, and all the rest postulated by contemporary nuclear theory, we must then see how this is to be interpreted from the point of view of fundamental particles. For this purpose, we must review, briefly, our concept of substance and of the integrity of parts in the whole.

Substance is potential autonomy, that is, it is that type of being that can exist in itself. A substance need not be structurally homogeneous. As long as it is capable of independent existence, it is a substance. There must be a unity of parts toward this end, otherwise it would be the accidental union of several substances. A machine is a type of the latter. An animal illustrates the former.

What was a substance can later become a part of a new substance. In becoming a part, it loses its former substantiality. On the other hand, what is a part of a substance can be separated from the substance and become a substance on its own. It gains substantiality. For example, a limb of a tree is a part of the tree. It exists in virtue of the tree. It can be cut off from the tree, and it is now either one substance or a union of several substances in itself. It has its own independence. It can be grafted onto another tree, and it reverts to becoming a part.

If we suppose that the atom is exactly what is pictured by the model, it consists of a nucleus and its parts surrounded by electrons. In the natural order, an atom is the smallest part of an element. If it exists in isolated fashion, it is a substance having its own parts. Furthermore, when it is broken down into its component parts, they assume substantiality, whether they are protons, electrons, neutrons, and neutrinos. When reunited into an integral whole, they once again become parts. In other words, as long as a component particle is a part of an atom, it partakes of the substantiality of the atom. As long as an atom is a part of an element, it partakes of the substantiality of the element. When a part is able to exist on its own, it assumes its own substantiality.

Hence, the problem is to see how the parts are united to the whole. If they are so united as to draw their existence and their outstanding properties from the whole, they are parts of a substance. If they retain their identities and their properties with no subordination to the whole, then the whole is an accidental organization of substances. As a matter of fact, there is subordination of the parts of the atom to the whole atom. The identity of the atom seems to be in the nucleus, and there is cooperation of the parts to that end. Furthermore, the electrons, as long as they are associated with the nucleus, subordinate their properties to the electrostatic balance of the whole. They are parts subordinating their independence and properties to the whole. Similarly, when the atoms are allied with other atoms in the element, there is subordination to the substantiality of the element.

There is a similar subordination of elements to the compound in chemical compounds. Here subordination is clearly suggested by the fact that proper proportion is demanded and that frequently there are marked changes in properties — more marked, let us say, than in the isotopes of elements.

The problem, then, is not that there are parts. It is rather *how* these parts are subordinated to the whole. If the subordination is such that in this or that case the parts exist in virtue of the whole, then there is substantial unity. On the other hand, if there is simply union without subordination, then the result is an accidental union.

The one fundamental factor involved in all of this is that if these atoms are *actually* the same as they are in the conceptual model, then their combinations, changes, developments are in virtue of their *capacity* to undergo these combinations, changes, and developments. The whole theory of the atom depends upon the changeability of the component particles. It depends upon their potency, or *primary matter*. Hence, nuclear theory, if properly representative of the objective, is an argument in favor of primary matter, but with a deeper understanding of it than is frequently presented. As we shall see in the last chapter, if all of the elements in the universe, and from them all of the galaxies, stars, planets, non-living and living entities are developments out of one source — perhaps hydrogen and a few particles, perhaps only the particles, this process develops not only out of the *actuality* of the source as being *what* it is, but also out of the *potentiality* within that source to become every other being in the universe.

The difference between an accidental union and a substantial composite can perhaps best be seen in the manner of fulfillment. If the fulfillment goes beyond the individual fulfillments of the sum of the components, we have a good argument for a substantial union. If it does not do so, then we can infer that it is an accidental union. There will still be difficulties in identifying the types of union and change, but the question of the manner of fulfillment, added to the consideration of a marked change in properties, gives us a good basis for determining whether the union in question is accidental or substantial. Nevertheless, it must always be traced back to the potentiality for change in the actual component, that is, to matter and form.

HYLOSYSTEMISM

Contemporary scholastic cosmology will always be in debt to Albrecht Mitterer, who was one of the first to face the problem of atomic structure in his theory of *hylosystemism*. When Mitterer first published his views in 1935, cosmology was still the stepchild of scholastic philosophy.

In the history of cosmology, largely as a result of Cartesianism, there crept in the assumption that substantial unity meant homogeneity of structure. When it was pointed out that man in his structure is anything but homogeneous, and that, in fact, he has many disparate and discrete organs, the answer was advanced that man's substantiality is based on the unifying influence of the one human soul. When a similar difficulty was pointed out about lower animals, the answer was given either in terms of "animal souls," or in terms of the differences between life and non-life. In order to justify the latter position, biological vitalism was elevated beyond its scientific merits. Spontaneous generation and evolution — both of which had been accepted inchoatively by St. Gregory of Nyssa, St. Augustine, St. Albert, and St. Thomas — were considered almost heresy.

Further difficulties occurred in the relation of substance to accidents. Most accidents are qualities. Thus, they have a formal nature. They are different from their subject substances and from each other. Without a fundamental appreciation of hylomorphism, the existence of substance began to be doubted. The nineteenth century pointed out that many qualities, such as color, are in the senses as much as in the object, and that frequently objective qualities can be considered aspects of mass-energy relationships.

Third, the decadent hylomorphism of the nineteenth century did not face the problem of substantial change. Substantial change is brought about by sufficient accidental changes. This means that any substantial change is brought about by modifications of bodily structure. Yet, when hylomorphism concentrated on the order to life, and for all practical purposes limited itself to the relation of soul and body in man, it was unprepared to face scientific and philosophical mechanism which explained all phenomena in terms of structural organization and forces.

Mitterer's theory is based on the composition of matter out of fundamental particles. He based himself on a literal acceptance of the Bohr atom, the planetary atom of proper orbits. He looked upon the atom as a cooperative system rather than as a unit, and he considered the structure of matter to be that of discrete particles. He used three important Greek terms: *hyle* (ὕλη), matter; *systema* (συστῆμα), system; and *meros* (μέρος), particle. Mitterer's theory may be called *hylomeric* because it is a theory of particles of matter. It is called *hylosystemism* because it deals essentially with the organization of these matter-particles.

He attributed a proper matter and form to each particle. Thus, involved in his theory is a plurality of forms. He claimed that the organization of particles not only explains diversity in structure in the one entity or substance, it *is* the substance. The substance is an organization of different essences unified by an overall form of organization.

This organization in various degrees not only explains the many differences in a substance and its operations but also gives a realistic answer to the problem of substance and accidents. Furthermore, just as a substantial change involves change in structure and is brought about by such, hylosystemism gives a philosophical basis for the process of such changes.

Hylosystemism brought about gradual reactions among hylomorphists. For one thing, it stirred them to action. Only a few scholastics, such as Cardinal Mercier, Nys, Fulton Sheen, Edward A. Pace, and James A. McWilliams, had taken an interest in the sciences. Interest in the physical sciences became necessary for scholastic cosmologists. It was only by such interest that they were able to philosophize about the *conceptual atom* and the particle constitution of matter, as explained above.

A further consequence of hylosystemism among cosmologists was the consideration of the principle of the hylomerons in relationship to the organization. The hylomorphists discovered that Mitterer was, in the main, restating the almost forgotten Aristotelian, Albertian, Thomistic, and Scotistic doctrine of the existence of minimal parts in relation to elements, and elements actually existing in a substance. They discovered that in the Aristotelian explanation there is no need either to postulate homogeneity of structure or to limit hylomorphism to living beings. On the contrary, Aristotle begins with inorganic matter and works up, by gradually higher organization, to hylomorphism in living entities. In the Christian consideration as developed by St. Augustine, St. Albert, St. Thomas, and Scotus, hylomorphism in man is based on hylomorphism in all below man.

Thus, by viewing the matter in the light of genuine Aristotelian hylomorphism, if Mitterer's particles enter into organization, they do so only because they *can* enter into such organization. The *potency*, the capacity for organization and organized existence is the old Aristotelian, Albertian, Thomistic, and Scotistic *primary matter*. Although the forms of the elements, or atoms, may be present in their essences, their existence is due to the *determination* of the whole organization in the order of existence. This determination is the *form*. This is the essential difference between hylosystemism and hylomorphism. In hylosystemism, the essence of a body is the *organization* of elements by an over-all form. In hylomorphism it is the *fulfillment* of the organized atoms.

We do not hear very much about hylosystemism today since we have discovered that Mitterer was restating a classical resolution of elements in relationship to parts and to the whole. Nevertheless, scholastic cosmology owes a great debt to Albrecht Mitterer. He took up the challenge of realistic problems in philosophy and the sciences. In so doing, he directed cosmologists back to neglected sources.

SUMMARY

1. The basic models — that is, concepts — of the atom are: Thomson's electrostatic model; Rutherford's planetary model; Bohr's model of electronic shells.
2. The atom is considered to be a positively charged nucleus having a positive charge surrounded by negative electrons.

   The nucleus is considered to consist of positively charged particles, *protons*, and particles with no charge, *neutrons*.

   Atomic number is the positive charge of the protons balancing the number of electrons. The standard is hydrogen, having number one, since it consists of one electron and one proton.

   Atomic weight is the weight of an element compared to hydrogen, the lightest of the elements.

   Protons are responsible for the charge. Protons and neutrons are responsible for the weight.
3. Isotopes are variations in the weight of an element that retains the same charge. Isotones are variations in the charge of an element retaining the same weight.
4. Results of spontaneous radioactivity, cosmic rays, and accelerating devices have shown up the evidence of other nuclear particles. Whether these exist

in the nucleus or, as suggested by the formation of the positron, may be produced from the nucleus is not determined.

5. Experiment has also shown that matter has many wave properties in high energy transmission.
6. We do not know what the fundamental structure of matter really is, since nuclear and atomic theory deals directly with *models*, that is to say, *concepts*. Theory does not tell us what matter is but how best to think about it.
7. If there is a problem about hylomorphism arising from nuclear physics, it must be resolved in terms of the parts in the whole of a material substance, and this in terms of potency and act, matter and form.
8. Hylosystemism looks upon bodily essence as an organization of components under a form. Hylomorphism explains the essence as the fulfillment of the potencies of the organized components.

CHAPTER SIXTEEN

EXTENSIONS of PHYSICAL THEORY

One of man's oldest intellectual goals is to give a unified physical theory for the universe. We have already shown the growth of physical theory, both philosophical and scientific; with respect to the intrinsic nature and structure of mobile, changing being. It is now appropriate to examine the extension of these views into areas of chemistry, astronomy, and biology.

THE DEVELOPMENT OF CHEMISTRY

For centuries, chemistry was the science of elements and their combinations. Many chemical problems of this nature were investigated by alchemists, who were particularly interested in the transformation of any one of the "four elements" into any other. Their interest in the transformation of base metals into gold was a logical consequence of the four element theory. They considered both gold and any other heavy metal such as lead as different forms of the element earth. Hence, by some addition of weight to lead they might be able to transform it into gold; that is, they attempted to change one form of earth into another form of earth.

These alchemical investigations led the Arabian physicians to new theories of the elements, to grasp the shortcomings of the four element explanation, and to the supposition that there might be more than four elements. Hence, when in the seventeenth century Robert Boyle wrote *The Skeptical Chemist*, the stage was set for the gradual development of what we ordinarily consider chemistry.

The isolation of gaseous elements, such as Priestley's isolation of oxygen, led to the consideration of other elements in the free state and in combinations. Outstanding work in the listing of elements in a table was done by Lavoisier, the unfortunate victim of the French Revolution, and his disciple Berthollet.

All of this was behind the work of John Dalton. Dalton advanced three significant points in chemistry:

1. Elements exist either as compounds or in the free state.
2. The smallest particles of compounds, what today we call molecules, can be broken down into atoms, that is, the smallest particles of elements that retain the properties of the entire element.
3. There are definite proportions in the combinations of elements in compounds.

The consideration of proportions is not particularly new. However, the fact that certain elements will not combine with other elements, and that, on the other hand, elements such as carbon and silicon combine most readily and most widely, gave rise to a theory of types. Williamson found certain types of combinations, and Gerhardt advanced the theory that certain types of elements combine only with other types of elements. However he did not attempt to explain why certain types of elements would combine only with certain others.

The type theory was based on the element as a whole. The hypothesis that the key to combinations might be in the shape of the component atoms is called the theory of *valence*, or *valency*. It can be traced back to Frankland, in 1852. By experimentation, it was discovered that some elements tend to enter into combinations whereas others do not, and valency was considered the tendency of elements to form combinations. Elements were said to have either Valency I (readily combinable), Valency II (active, but less combinable), or Valency III (even less combinable). Some elements have two valences. Iron, for example, has a valence of 2 and 3. The modern theory of valence is due to two theoretical advances, the discovery of the periodic table of elements and the Bohr model of the atom.

Lavoisier had listed a table of elements. Some of the members of his table were not properly elements. For example, light is listed as an element. Again, he did not know of fluorine and boron. Hence, he speaks of the radical or root of hydrofluoric acid, and the root of boric acid.

A Louvain chemist, Jean Servais Stas, discovered that the easiest way to list the elements was by their atomic weights; for example, the lightest of the elements is hydrogen. It is number one on the table. The second lightest is helium, number two; then lithium, number three; beryllium, number four; and so on down to uranium, number ninety-two, the heaviest of the elements found in nature. He also noted that periodically elements have similar properties. For example, there are inert gases, helium, neon, argon, krypton, and xenon. There are also very active elements, carbon, silicon, titanium. He noticed that these appear periodically in the table of elements. He fell back upon Avogadro's distinction between the physical atom, in which weight does not mean too much — save in neutron theory — and the chemical atom, in which weight is the key to activity. This is still a significant point in chemistry. The whole theory of isotopes is based upon different weights of the same element.

The British chemist, Mosely, investigated the periodic character of elements from the point of view of atomic number, or charge, providing the basis of modern theories of valence. The latter owe much to the Bohr model of the atom.

As we saw in the past chapter, the Bohr model attributes proper orbits, called "electron shells," to the electrons about the nucleus. Each electron is matched by a proton in the nucleus. This explains the electrically neutral character of the atom. Thus, the *atomic number* is the number of electrons, or the matching charge of the protons. The *atomic weight* is the combined weight of the protons and neutrons. The orbits of the electrons are somewhat complicated, but their arrangement in shells makes a convenient model for both chemical and physical problems. The electron shells are considered outwardly from the nucleus and labeled *k, l, m, n, o, p* respectively. The maximum number of electrons in each shell are as follows: in the k shell, up to 2; in the l shell, up to 8; in the m shell, up to 18; in the n shell, up to 32. In the outermost shell, no more than eight electrons are posited. If more electrons are added, then a new shell begins. The acquisition of electrons is always in the outermost shell.

Combinations of elements are considered to take place when the electrons of the outermost shells of elements interlink. This is explained by the fact that there are types of elements such as sodium, potassium, calcium, magnesium, and aluminum, that have an electron, two electrons, or three electrons, to spare. On the other hand, there are elements such as nitrogen, oxygen, sulphur, fluorine, and chlorine, that lack three, two, or one electron on their outer shell. The linking of atoms by the transfer of an electron from an atom with plus valency (with electrons to spare) to an atom with minus valency (lacking electrons), is called *electrovalence*. In this scheme, valence is numbered one, two, three, etc., according as the atom of the element can spare or needs one, two, three, etc., electrons. The most active elements are those with the lowest valence, either having one electron to spare, such as sodium (Na), or lacking one electron, such as chlorine (Cl). The most stable compounds are those of elements having +1 valence and –1 valence, such as sodium chloride (NaCl), common table salt. Valency is the key to the activity of the element.

Valency number matches the place in the periodic table. Thus, the elements in Tables I, II, and III have positive valence of one, two, and three electrons respectively. On the other hand, the elements in Tables V, VI, and VII have a negative valence of three, two, and one, respectively.

We would expect that an element like carbon, which is in Table IV, and is called *tetravalent*, would be inert. As a matter of fact, carbon forms more combinations than all the other elements combined. The only convenient way to explain this is to suppose that there is a linking, a bond, an interpenetration of electron shells. This is called *covalence*, and is represented as:

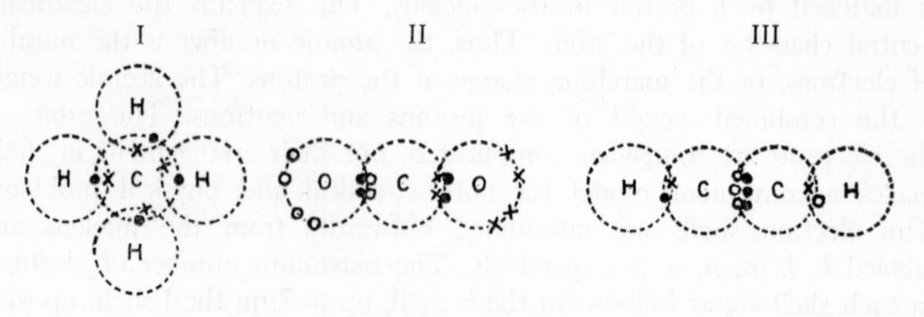

These are the atoms of methane (CH_4), carbon dioxide (CO_2), and acetylene (C_2H_2) respectively. Compounds of carbon are, accordingly, always represented by way of *bonds*, and this requires frequent change in chemical notation. It is not enough to abbreviate formic acid to H_2CO_2 and formaldehyde to H_2CO. They are, respectively, HCOOH and HCOH. This latter type of nomenclature becomes extremely significant in organic chemistry, which considers the many carbon combinations.

All of the above is what we might call electrochemistry. The great breakthrough, however, came with nuclear chemistry. This links both the commonness of elements throughout the universe with the common understanding of forces required to bring about both the physical and chemical effects that are postulated in any single plan for the universe.

We must note here that there is no single mechanical model for the universe. Any application of either physical or chemical models to other problems — and there are many such in any scheme about the entire universe — involve such a stretching of principles that one begins to wonder at the validity of the transformation. We have seen some of this in the past chapter, especially in extending the concepts of wave mechanics with respect to the wave and particle properties of light to the assumption that the same might be said for accelerated electrons. The statement that matter at rest is discontinuous, or constituted by particles, and that radiant matter is continuous, or constituted by waves, does not answer the problem. It simply gives us a convenient set of concepts as a starting point for further investigation. Nevertheless, it indicates a possible direction.

Similarly, the drawing together of what were once considered disparate principles of chemistry, physics, astronomy, and geology into an attempted unified scheme may not present us with one mechanical model, but it does indicate a possible avenue of exploration.

In general, any such drawing together depends upon three assumptions: (1) the validity of the spectroscope; (2) the nature of cosmic rays; and (3) the chemical investigation into atomic nuclei in the experiments carried out in "hot-atom" chemistry.

THE SPECTROSCOPE

The spectroscope was devised about 1860 by Bunsen, who had noticed that certain elements burn with a characteristic color. This was no new fact. The manufacturers of fireworks had based their entire industry on that fact. For example, sodium burns with a yellow flame, iodine with a violet flame, neon with a reddish-pink flame, argon with a blue flame, and so on. However, Bunsen noticed that a prism helped break down the colors of the components of a compound, and the narrower the flame, the more distinct did the colors appear. Hence, he invented a slit device wherein the flame appeared extremely narrow. The delineation of the colors then became quite sharp. The theory of the spectroscope is that the energy emitted by the element or compound has a periodic release of energy corresponding to wavelengths. Each element has, so to speak, its own wavelength or its own periodic emission. In compounds, the wavelengths of the component elements appear.

THE SPECTROSCOPE

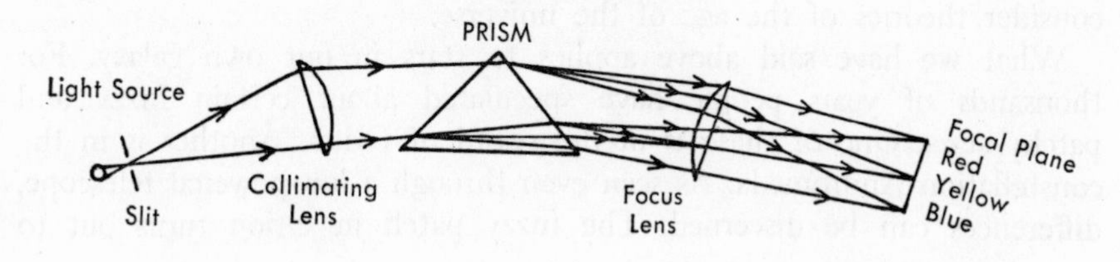

If light or any other wave force passes through some medium having harmonic vibrations similar to those of the radiant source, the waves of the radiant source are absorbed in the vibrations of the medium, and black lines appear in the part of the spectrum proper to the emitting element. Hence, since we suppose that the energy of the surface of the sun is in harmonic vibration with the elements composing the sun, when dark lines appear in the hydrogen and helium bands, we suppose that the sun is composed of hydrogen and helium. This is extremely significant, since it allows us to use the sun as a standard and to obtain, if we can, spectroscopic analyses of stars to discover what elements they contain within them. This can be done in any of the stars that we can isolate as individuals. This means all the stars in our galaxy. For example, the familiar North Star, Polaris, is really four stars appearing as one to the naked eye. A high-powered telescope with good resolution sees them as four.

Let us see what we can do with our facts about the North Star. Since the four stars constitute one highly involved mechanical system, we are led to infer that they originated out of the same source. The chances of their coming together and being trapped in the same system are extremely remote. If they originated at the same time, we must explain the differences in their colors and masses. Their relative masses and densities we can infer from their actions on one another. Their colors are analyzed spectroscopically, and we discover that the redder they are the more helium they contain. This gives us an indication of their relative ages; that is, we do not know how long it has been since they were formed, but since the sequence of a hypothetical development of elements would be from hydrogen to helium, and not the other way around, we suppose that those stars with the more helium should be the older stars. A difference of color results from this, and hence we can use the different colors of stars as a rough estimate of relative ages. In general we can infer that red stars are older than yellow stars. This means that, if they originated at the same time, some of them must be burning at a faster rate than others. Hence, we have two suggested principles: (1) the more helium a star has the older it is; or (2) the more helium it has, the faster it is burning. We will come back to this point later when we consider theories of the age of the universe.

What we have said above applies to stars in our own galaxy. For thousands of years people have speculated about certain fuzzy and patchy stars. One of these is in the sword of Orion. Another is in the constellation Andromeda. As seen even through a low-powered telescope, differences can be discerned. The fuzzy patch in Orion turns out to look like an incandescent cloud. The one in Andromeda resembles a fiery pinwheel. In the eighteenth century, Immanuel Kant suggested that the latter is a collection of stars similar to the distribution of stars in what we call the Milky Way, which resembles a cloud to the naked eye but which can be seen to be an immense distribution of stars when seen even through field glasses. In 1931, Edwin P. Hubble, at the time astronomer of the Mount Wilson Observatory in California, was able to distinguish individual types of stars in the Andromeda galaxy, thus proving it to be a collection of stars and not a cloud of incandescent gas as in the nebula in Orion. Furthermore, he was able to obtain spectroscopic analyses of stars in the same galaxy. He discovered, as have other astronomers later, that these stars — in fact, all of the matter in the universe — seem to be composed of the same elements and in about the same proportions as matter with which we are familiar.

Knowing that the matter throughout the universe seems to consist of the same elements is a big start toward further understanding of the components and operations of the universe as a whole. Nevertheless, there is much about the universe that we have found difficult to understand, in particular, exactly what goes on in the interiors of stars. We cannot properly face the problem of the origin or age of the universe until we know the processes going on in the majority of the physical inhabitants of the universe, the stars.

COSMIC RAYS

A new mystery was added with the discovery of *cosmic rays*. Cosmic radiation first came to the attention of physicists in 1900, when it was discovered that glass-enclosed gases used in experiments on electrical conductivity became ionized even when not in use. This was thought to be the result of terrestrial radiation, but two facts militated against this supposition. These were: (1) gases over the sea showed the same ionization even though sea water has practically no radioactive elements; and (2) gases raised to the same height over both land and sea (in one case, the top of the Eiffel Tower — 300 meters; in another, in a balloon 300 meters above the sea) showed the same results. In 1912 and 1913, Hess raised his instruments in several balloon flights up to 5000 meters above sea level, and found that the ionization increased suddenly and sharply with the increase in elevation. This seemed to show that the ionizing energy was extra terrestrial in source.

Since there are practical limits to the heights of balloon ascensions, Millikan, Cameron, and Anderson took on the problem from the point of view of penetration. They noted the standard of ionization at sea level, and then lowered their instruments below water and below the surface of the earth. They noticed an immediate decrease. However, they lowered them deeper, into lakes and in mines under water, and they noted that after an initial decrease of penetration, the penetration continued to an almost fantastic depth. Since this penetration is far more than the penetration which normally proceeds from sun energy, it was inferred that its origin was from a source or sources other than the sun, that its origin was interstellar and perhaps even intergalactic. This extreme penetration also showed that there must be tremendous amounts of energy within and outside our galaxy.

The advances made by aerologists in the technique of balloon ascensions during World War II, as well as the new technique of photo-emulsion plates to record cosmic radiation at extremely high altitudes, brought about rather startling results. The former view was that cosmic rays were alpha, beta, and gamma rays. For this reason, cosmic rays were frequently called "ultra-gamma" rays. However, photo-emulsion plates exposed at extremely high altitudes, as well as those exposed at sea level, showed quite different results. They show tracks of all of the particles that we know. In other words, they seem to be the records of nuclear and atomic disintegration under conditions of extreme acceleration.

The records of cosmic radiation show us that the energies required in the universe to accelerate particles to such an extreme penetration are far higher than had been anticipated. Some of the particles bombard the earth with energy higher than thirty billion electron volts. Since the present theory of cosmic radiation, largely dependent on the discovery of the Van Allen belts and the magnetic belts surrounding the earth, supposes that the cosmic rays that we receive are the results of collisions of ions and electrons emitted from the sun and from stars with the magnetic belts, the Van Allen belts, and the atmosphere, there must be some extreme acceleration in outer space.

Some cosmic rays come from the sun. The majority do not. We know that the direction from which they come is equal in all directions, although they are directed by the Van Allen belts toward the poles. The intensity of radiation from the sun or any other star is not regarded as exceeding the speed of light. Nevertheless, since the energy of cosmic rays is so tremendous, and since we rarely experience cosmic rays directly but rather the results of their collisions, cosmic rays must be pressurized by magnetic fields and by clouds of ionized hydrogen between the stars and galaxies. We know that the clouds exist. We can perceive them with a good telescope. We know that energy comes to us not only from the stars within our own galaxy but also from galaxies as far as six billion light years away. This energy is both light energy and radio energy. Hence, we infer that the primary radiation from such distant objects can reach us. After all, there is nothing to slow it down significantly. Because its penetration is so deep, an acceleration or intensification is implied that, as far as we know, can come about only by huge magnetic fields and clouds of ionized hydrogen.

All of the above can be reproduced at lower scales by accelerators. It was mentioned above that cosmic rays have been detected at about thirty billion electron volts. Ordinarily, they come to us at lower acceleration, well within the range of present accelerators (30+ MEV). The top range supposed for cosmic radiation is one hundred million billion electron volts (1×10^{17} EV). This has been detected. In fact, radiation of the intensity of ten billion, billion electron volts (1×10^{19}) has been detected. With magnetic storms on the sun there are sharp rises in the peak of detectable cosmic radiation, most particularly of x rays. There are also other sharp peaks observed, whereby we infer similar storms on other stars or major disturbances in interstellar matter. Extrapolating the trend of the observed peak, we arrive at the figure above. Nevertheless, within the common field of observed cosmic rays and accelerator scattering of particles, we have learned more about fundamental particles. At lower energies (below 10 MEV) we get sharp delineation of nucleons. Above 10 MEV disintegration processes become more complex. Mesons begin to appear. At much higher energies we enter into the field of "fundamental particles." We find this common to artificial accelerators and cosmic rays.

The observation of accelerators and cosmic rays shows a commonness throughout the universe. Hence, from the spectroscope we have learned of the commonness of elements throughout the universe. With cosmic-ray observation we attain to a commonness both of electromagnetic forces and of nuclear structure throughout the universe. The one remaining problem is the transferral from physical to chemical principles.

NUCLEAR CHEMISTRY

As noted earlier, modern chemistry was based on electron theory. Slight attention was paid either to nuclear theory or to energy within the nucleus. Part of the difficulty was that even the lowest acceleration by electrostatic generators so disturbed the target material that its chemical properties were lost. Yet this need not necessarily be so. After all, we live on a hard radiation planet. We are being bombarded at all times by extremely hard radiation in the form of x rays, infra-red and ultra-violet light, as well as all of the cosmic-ray energy mentioned above. Yet there are no significant chemical changes in natural bodies. This means that they have become accustomed to such energy. A way had to be devised for a chemical investigation of the nucleus of the atom without the smashing up produced by accelerators. This is the field of hot atom chemistry.

Hot atom chemistry is only part of the new chemistry. Actually, it deals with chemical combinations that occur when one or all of the component elements have been exposed to some type of radioactive emanation. Such elements are called "hot" elements. As they enter into combination, the neutrons they have picked up influence not only their own nuclei but also the nuclei of those elements with which they combine. The results are startling insofar as different properties appear for a time. At the same time, this is in harmony with ordinary chemical concepts in that the properties are the result of the mass, not the charge, of the nucleus; that they are to be traced to the neutrons, not to the protons. This is what occurs in the combinations of hot elements.

However, there is more to it than that. The nucleus or nuclei involved become unstable and give off gamma radiation. This, in turn, affects surrounding atoms and the process can easily be traced by the surroundings. For this reason, they are called "tracer" elements. It is as though we were to trace the course of a mad dog by the paths of the spectators trying to get out of his way.

What is significant in the above experiments — first begun by the British chemists Szilard and Chalmers — is that the first step is a chemical development accepted from physical means and that the second is a change in chemical concepts. The traditional chemical concept was to tie up stability or instability to the electron shells. We now see another source of instability in the physical state of the nucleus, not only for the free element but also for the combinations of elements.

The significance of all this is an interchange of physical and chemical concepts. Apart from the wide practical results from "hot" and tracer elements in medicine, botany, and industry, the theoretical contribution of hot atom chemistry — for that matter, of the entire new chemistry — is that of the proper interaction of concepts in physical and chemical theory. In other words, chemical problems can be considered with physical concepts, and chemical concepts can contribute to physical problems. For example, hot atom chemistry has opened up new fields of investigation in the processes of the elements of the outer atmosphere when they are bombarded by alpha, beta, gamma particles, by photons, by infra-red and ultra-violet light, and by cosmic rays.

Insofar as there can be the interchange of concepts in experimentation, the way has been opened up for rapid developments in element transformation. In the old chemistry, based as it was on electron transference or exchange, transformation of elements was considered the dream of the alchemists. Now that chemistry has entered the problems of the nucleus, transformation is taken for granted. Chemists, as well as physicists, have been active in the development of new elements, whether they be elements missing from the periodic table or whether they be the new artificial elements beyond uranium 238.

Nuclear chemistry has opened up a new investigation into the rare earths, those metallic ores that are so remarkably alike that they are difficult to separate from their oxides and from each other. Lastly, and this is the most important from the needs of scientific cosmology, it has given us a unified system of analyzing the activities of elements in the centers of stars. Under the old electron chemistry, scientists were at a loss to account for the intense energies whereby the stars burned for billions of years without losing much of their mass. Physics attacked the problem from the point of view of nuclear activities. Chemistry has allied itself to this consideration with the concept of nuclear transformations.

As we now face the main problems of scientific cosmology, we have three points as a basis for investigation. These are: (1) a commonness of elements throughout the universe; (2) a commonness of forces; (3) a commonness of concepts whereby we can transform our understandings of elements, particles, waves, molecules, transformations of elements, all in their normal states or all in highly energetic states.

THE DIRECTION OF THE PROCESSES OF THE UNIVERSE

Although scientific cosmology is a modern development insofar as we now have the means to extend what we know of the elements and energies with which we are familiar to elements and energies elsewhere in the universe, scientific cosmology may be said to have begun with thermodynamics.

Classical thermodynamics hinges about three points: (1) There is a conservation of energy. (2) Any transfer of energy is unidirectional, from the higher energetic state to the lower. (3) Energy is thus becoming unavailable. The first point can neither be proven nor disproven, but it is a basic and extremely useful concept in physics. The second point cannot be properly explained. We do not know why energy flows in one direction save on the hypothesis of entropy, that it is a fulfillment of energy, or that a low energy state is more normal. However, we cannot establish this latter point, either.

The last point needs to be expanded a bit in view of the second point. Energy is becoming unavailable because: (1) it never passes from the lower to the higher, never reverses its direction, and consequently the flow is unidirectional; (2) when the source and receiver become equal in energy possession, the flow stops and the process stops. Thus, cold objects are heated by warm objects, but the reverse process does not occur. Moreover, in the case of two objects of the same temperature, neither heats the other. Even if all the energy were utilized, that is, even if no energy were lost in the transfer, the energy would eventually become unavailable and the process would be unidirectional because of the entropy that would be attained.

Undoubtedly energy escapes. Most of the fuel in a steam engine is used not only in raising steam but also in compensating for the heat lost. However, the heat loss of a closed system might be utilized for other purposes than the system. For example, a small steam engine could be used not only to do its proper work, but also to heat the shed in which it is. The heat thus lost from the point of view of the machine's work is not a total loss. Hence, we must be careful in thinking of energy becoming unavailable simply because from a given point of view it is not used. We think of most of the sun's energy as lost (1) because the total area of all planetary surfaces is small compared to the sun's energy output; and (2) since the planets, which are, with the exception of Uranus, all generally on the same ecliptic, receive little of the sun's energy. Most of the sun's radiance is thus unavailable from our point of view. However, it may very well be doing work of another sort elsewhere, for example, heating, compressing, and ionizing clouds of interstellar hydrogen for the formation of new stars.

In other words, we must be careful in applying the laws of thermodynamics to processes in the universe to determine whether or not the universe is running down. For one thing, the Sadi Carnot interpretation is based on such closed systems as steam engines in their exemplification of the principle of the conservation of energy. However, we cannot rule out the possibility that the universe is not a closed system, and then the basis of the laws of thermodynamics, the conservation of energy, becomes in fact no wider than our observations and their applications.

The calculus of probabilities. One attempt to face the difficulties of the possible renovation of energy was to make a statistical investigation of the probability of the recurrence of events. This was advanced by Rudolf Clausius in his calculus of probabilities.

The calculus of probabilities expresses the chances of the occurrences, reversals, repetitions, and renewal of events. The fact is that there are many possible variations in any event and geometrically higher variations in the continued repetition of an event. For example, since the motions of the molecules of air are random motions, there is no reason why all the air in a given assembly hall should not all flow to one corner, leaving the members of the assembly to suffocate. This is not impossible, but it is extremely improbable. We might see this reasoning in the following example. If all amateur tennis players were exactly equal in talent, there should be no national champion. If we follow one player up through the various competitions we can see how chance can be calculated.

Let us say that a player starts off with a city championship involving four seeding matches. He then passes on to a state championship, a district championship, and finally a national championship. In the first seeding match, let us suppose that he faces eight players. His chances of winning this match are one in eight. If he wins, he passes on to the city championship. Again, let us suppose that his chances are one in eight, insofar as he must play eight winners. Already, his chances now are one in sixteen. In the state championship, his chances may be one in twenty, that is, a total now of one in thirty-six. Again, chances are against him in the regional match and in the national championship. The odds might be one in one hundred or more against his winning the championship even before he starts. The fact that he does win indicates that all players are not equal and that he has skills and talents that can overcome his opponents, one by one, and that can be predicted if sufficiently known.

Our example of the tennis player is quite restricted. On the cosmic order, there is a much wider chance for different eventualities. The fact that such do not occur shows that all things are not equal, that there are forces and tendencies operating in one direction rather than operating in random fashion. These forces and tendencies are called "anti-chance," and they are a mathematical expression of the order in the universe. They do not prove that there is order in the universe, or that disorder may not break out on a much wider scale than it now exists. They simply state that it is improbable, and that we are quite safe in expecting a continuation of order that we know. Since this order involves the non-repetition of events, we can expect that events are not going to repeat themselves, that once something is done it is done once and for all.

Since there are many non-repetitious events in the universe, we may expect that the totality of these events over repetitious events is such that the universe is going in a definite direction. If we can say further that these events involve more absorption of energy than output of energy, than the order of the universe is a running down, a process whereby the ultimate order is not going to be work done but work finished.

Notice that we have not proven anything. We have simply stated that, as far as we know, the chances are that the universe is moving toward a maximum of entropy. Whether the universe is actually doing so or not is a problem in astrophysics involving the possible beginning — or "creation" — of the universe and a possible ending to it. The reasoning is that if the universe is running down, there must have been a time when it was started, and we may be able to discover this. Oddly enough, could we discover this, we would not thereby prove that it is running down. We would only prove that it is operating as the result of a beginning.

THE AGE OR ETERNITY OF THE UNIVERSE

The problem of assigning a time value to the universe began in 1828 with *Olbers' Paradox*. Before the astronomer Olbers raised the question of star energy, the universe was thought to be a careful balance of bodies and forces all operating according to Newton's laws. In this scheme, the question of the finiteness or infinity of the universe did not arise, because if we followed Euclidean geometry, space could extend infinitely and there was no reason why there should not be stars and planets in this infinity of space. In the twentieth century Albert Einstein was to point out the physical difficulties of this position. If the universe were one, and if it were infinite, the binding force would be gravity. Gravity would be infinite. However, the closest we can come to any infinite force is radiant energy. Hence, the universe would have to be radiant energy.

This was not foreseen by Olbers. Yet he did raise contemporary difficulties by asking the superficially simple question: Why is the sky dark at night? It seems obvious that the sky is dark because the sun has set, until we realize that, sun or no sun, the sky should be much brighter than it is if we take into account the tremendous amounts of starlight and other forms of radiant energy that reach the earth.

The stars, of course, are much farther away than the sun, and their brightness as we see them varies according to the inverse square of their distance. The light from a star twice as far away as another will be four times as weak if they have the same magnitude or absolute surface brightness. On the other hand, no matter how weak the light may be when it reaches us, no matter how variably distant the stars may be, their light still reaches us. In fact, the light from colliding galaxies six billion light years away reaches us. When we realize the amount of light emitted by these billions and billions of sources, no matter how large or small the universe may be, no matter how distant the stars may be, the total amount of light reaching the earth should make the night sky far brighter than daylight.

Such should be true no matter how large or small the universe may be. Granted an average or quasi-average distribution of stars in the universe, with magnitude *M*, then the light reaching us will be the total of the magnitude of stars as divided by the square of the distances of the individual stars. Taking *L* for light as it reaches us and *N* for the number of stars, it will be $L = N(M/r^2)$. A smaller universe will mean a lesser number of stars, but also smaller distances over which the radiant light would be diffused. A larger universe will mean more stars, but there will always be the increased distances cutting down on the power of the light received. No matter how large or small the universe may be, the light received will always be $L = N(M/r^2)$. Notice that the power of light, or magnitude, is always proportionately cut down by the inverse square of the distance. Consequently, taking any sized universe, there is always going to be an average amount of light striking the earth, and taking the totality of stars and galaxies that we know, any size of the universe will add up to an extremely bright sky, day or night.

Why is the sky dark at night? There is no reason why light should weaken. If it is a wave, it spreads a bit, but it also travels too fast to spread much. We know now that the cause of darkness must mean that the light is being weakened by some factor other than distance. We cannot say that something is blocking off the light, since such interstellar matter is shown up by being energized, or at least outlined after the manner of a silhouette, as in the case of the Horse Head Nebula. The conclusion seems to be that light must be weakened because the source is going away from us.

The Doppler effect. Light never really dies out, and that raises the question as to the manner of its weakening. If we consider that light is a wave, then we need not take into account whether the emitting source is coming toward us, going away from us, or standing still. The wave will travel as a constant velocity. This phenomenon is seen in sound waves. These travel at a constant velocity whether or not the source is moving toward us or away from us. However, when the object is traveling toward us, the sound is at a higher pitch because the pressure of the motion of the emitting object crowds the wavelengths together and does not allow them to spread too much. On the other hand, when the source is moving away, the lack of forward pressure allows the wavelengths to be farther apart and the waves themselves to spread further. In the former case, the pitch of the sound is higher. In the latter case it is lower. In both cases the speed of the sound is constant. The difference is in the wavelengths and the wave spread. This is the Doppler effect, and it can be demonstrated for shock waves, wakes of ships, as well as for sound waves.

This has been applied to light. It is based on the supposition that light travels at a constant velocity, after the manner of sound, and that light is a wave. Actually, light behaves like a wave, and quantum theory is based on the supposition that even if light were particles, for which there is evidence, it would still behave like a wave if photons travel in quanta, just as a blast of buckshot will spread like a wave and give off wave phenomena. As applied to light, the supposition is that light from a source moving toward us will have its wavelength crowded together and will give off the characteristic spectrum of short-wave light, violet light. Light from a receding body will have longer wavelengths and waves more spread out, and will be characteristically red. In the former case, the analogy of the high pitch will be violet light. In the latter case, the low pitch, the light will be red, and the farther away the source is, the more rapid its recession, the redder will be its light.

Tests for the red shift. This theory has two factors in its favor. The first is that every experiment on the constancy of light has shown that the light travels at a constant velocity whether the source is advancing or receding. There are tests for this carried out on terrestrial objects, but binary stars, rotating about a common center, give more natural evidence. In such cases, one star is traveling toward us during somewhat less than the period of its orbital rotation while the other is traveling away during the same period. In all observed cases, the velocity of light, timed when one eclipses the other, is the same for both stars.

The second factor, the difference in color, is also confirmed by binary stars, but this time by spectroscopic analysis. The light from the receding star is characteristically and progressively reddened, while the light from the advancing star becomes characteristically and progressively more violet; that is to say, there is a period when the stars are equally distant from the earth, and during this their spectra — apart from the differences in their chemical composition — show the same proportion of red and violet in their wavelengths. However, as they continue in their orbits, one appears to begin to advance and to pick up speed toward us, while the other correspondingly appears to begin to recede and to pick up speed away from us. The light of the first begins to show more violet in the spectrum. Similarly, as the receding star recedes farther and faster, its spectrum becomes more and more red. This phenomenon, the "red shift," was first investigated in 1889 by E. C. Pickering in the case of the double star Zeta Ursa Major.

There are many reasons for the reddening of light, for example, passage through such media as interstellar and intergalactic dust clouds, but there are no known media which would make light become more violet apart from the advance of the source. Hence, we can infer that light from a receding star is characteristically red, and that the faster it is receding, its light becomes proportionately more red.

Inferences from the red shift. The above reasoning awaits application to the distribution of observable stars and galaxies. In making this application, we must consider the means we have of determining the distances of stars. Our basic tool is *luminosity*, that is, the brightness of the star as it appears to us. If we could triangulate the distance and luminosity of one star, we could use that as a standard and compare other stars to it. We could use this exactly as a photographer can judge distances by his light meter. The difficulty with this, however, is that stars are not all of the same color. They are classified as Population I stars, those that become blue giants, and Population II stars, those that become red giants and red supergiants. In general, Population I stars are found in the arms of spiral galaxies, whereas Population II stars are found in the centers of galaxies. There are types of galaxies called "globular clusters," generally surrounding the spiral galaxies, that seem to be populated exclusively by Population II, that is, red, stars.

Nevertheless, we must start somewhere. We must find a star whose *magnitude* we know, that is to say, whose intrinsic brightness we know, to realize that its luminosity, its brightness as we see it, is the product of its magnitude over the inverse square of the distance, and then use it as the standard of other stars. The standard was found with Cepheid variables. There is a star in the constellation *Cepheus* called *Delta Cephei* that is a pulsating star. It flares to brightness, then dims, and flares to brightness again in a period of 5.366 days. There are many such Cepheids, and after a long period of observing many of them in the Southern Hemisphere, Henrietta S. Leavitt observed that there is a regularity about their luminosity and the period of their flares and diminutions. Harlow Shapley concluded that if we take an *average* of their brightness and dimness, we have their absolute magnitude, their intrinsic brightness. These, then, can be the standards of light against which we can compare the other stars. All that is needed is to triangulate one.

The triangulation of a star is exceedingly difficult. Even if we use the orbit of the earth in position six months apart, a distance of 186,000,600 miles, it is quite difficult to notice a significant displacement in one star, simply because the stars are so far away. Yet, in 1832 such a measurement was made on this star by Henderson at the Cape of Good Hope. Accurate measurements were similarly made by Bessel and Struve in 1838. Shapley made triangulations of about 2000 stars.

Among these 2000 were several variables of extremely rapid period called RR Lyra stars. Shapley used them as a basis of magnitude, considering their magnitude as 0.00, and then made comparisons to certain Cepheids in the Magellenic clouds, globular clusters surrounding our galaxy. In this way he measured the extent of our galaxy. After Hubble was able to distinguish a Cepheid in the Andromeda galaxy, its distance was concluded from this variable as a standard and comparing its luminosity with the other variables. In this way, Hubble was able to use the Andromeda galaxy as a standard for the distances of other spiral-type galaxies, and he was the first to advance a statement of the extent of the universe visible to the 100-inch telescope at Mt. Wilson.

In the early 1950's, Walter Baade of Palomar Mountain tried to discover RR Lyra stars in the Andromeda galaxy, and he failed completely. Since they are within the visible power of the 200-inch telescope — they are 100 times brighter than the sun — he concluded that the Andromeda galaxy is much farther away than Hubble had estimated. After much thought he concluded that RR Lyra stars are variables proper to Population II stars. The variables used by Hubble were among Population I stars in the arms of the Andromeda galaxy. Implicit in this conclusion is the warning that a mistake had been made in using one as a standard for the other. Actually, the Andromeda galaxy is most likely twice as far away as we thought.

Using the above standards, we really have no idea how big the universe is, except that its vastness is indescribable. It consists of galaxy after galaxy extending indefinitely outward. Here we find an interesting point. The farther away the stars are known to be, the redder is their light. Now, as seen earlier, redness indicates recession and progressively recessive velocity. Apart from a few exceptions, the light from stars and galaxies received by us from all directions shows the red shift. In other words, all the stars and galaxies seem to be receding at an increasingly rapid rate. The answer to Olbers' question about the darkness of the sky seems to be that the universe is expanding.

THE EXPANSION OF THE UNIVERSE

This expansion of the universe has a time value, since we can infer the rate of its expansion in terms of miles or kilometers per second, and we measure its distance in terms of parsecs, which we break down into light years. We are able to calibrate this with other known temporal processes carried on throughout the universe, and we are able to consider the age of the process of the expansion. We are thus able to consider whether or not the universe had a beginning, and, if so, when that beginning was. This is the field of two theories of the processes of the universe: the expanding universe theory and the steady state theory.

The expanding universe theory is based on the assumption that, if the universe is expanding, at one time its components were all closer together. From the rate of expansion we can infer when the process began. From what we know about matter, we can infer something of material conditions before the expansion. From what we know about nuclear processes in the stars, both from physics and chemistry, we can infer something about the energy processes that caused the expansion. This, at least, is the argumentation of the exponents of the expanding universe theory. On the other hand, these factors, with certain modifications, are used to support *the steady state theory* in denying the character of the beginning postulated by the expanding universe theory, if there was a beginning. Thus, the two theories differ not according to what the universe *is*, but according to what it *was*.

THE EXPANDING UNIVERSE THEORY

The expanding universe theory was first advanced by Edwin P. Hubble. He interpreted the red shift as an argument in favor of the supposition of the expansion of all celestial bodies from a common center. Abbé Georges Eduard Lemaitre, the Belgian scientist, saw a possible correlation between this and the postulates of Einstein's general relativity theory as corrected by A. Friedmann. The implications of this theory with nuclear theory had been developed by E. A. Milne and are now developed by Hans Bethe. Correlations of this theory with radio stars and galaxies in radio astronomy have drawn Martin Ryle into supporting the theory.

In brief, this theory maintains that if the universe is now expanding, in times past it must have been much denser. Density, of course, implies a higher energy level. In the beginning there must have been a gathering of primordial matter, because of gravitational attraction, into one superdense mass, perhaps hydrogen, or perhaps fundamental particles. Because of the intense pressures built up in this superdense mass, in the breaking down and building up of particles and atoms, and perhaps in the building up of elements, the mass exploded after the manner of a thermonuclear device. This explosion, on a cosmic scale, sent matter scattering in all directions throughout empty space. As matter scattered at tremendous velocities, it fell apart of its own weight and localized into huge gaseous nebulae, which in turn broke down into smaller clouds (each tremendously vast, each millions of light years across), which, in turn, broke down into smaller clouds building up into stars.

Within the galaxies we find different-colored stars, incandescent gases, and dust. It has been debated whether the dust becomes stars or the stars produce the dust. However, since the stars are moving through the dust, the older the stars are the more dust they will have gathered into themselves and hence the less dust will be around them. The older they are, the more they will have moved, and the less dust they will have about them. As a matter of fact, the red giants have little dust about them, whereas the blue stars and main sequence stars have a good deal of dust about them, and are considered to be in the process of building up. (Red stars are considered older, not only because of more helium in their composition, but also because their redness seems due to lower temperatures. They have cooled off.) Since red stars are usually in the centers of galaxies and blue and yellow stars in the arms of galaxies, the arms are considered to be still in the process of building up. This fits in with the principles of mechanics, since it would be supposed that the main amounts of gas would be gathered in the center and would go to work in building up stars earlier. Similarly, in the globular clusters, the stars are mainly red, that is, older, and the globular clusters are almost dust free.

Will the universe continue to expand indefinitely into "infinite space"? Or will it double back on itself? Are its intrinsic forces sufficient to draw it back on itself to begin the process of re-formation, re-explosion, re-expansion after the manner of a cepheid variable? This supposition is known as the "pulsating universe." Or will it reach escape velocity and continue out infinitely after the manner of the Crab nebula? All of these are questions which must be correlated into a whole with a maximum of evidence and a minimum of supposition before this can be accepted as an established theory.

The direction of expansion depends upon the distribution of matter, the direction of space. Following the statements of the general relativity theory, it is taken for granted that interstellar and intergalactic space is curved. The basis for this is seen in the bending of light in a gravitational field. This was first observed in a solar eclipse and is since confirmed quite freely by use of the coronascope. The supposition is that light, in following the line of least resistance — the old Aristotelian concept of natural motion — follows the distribution of matter. However, if this distribution, following the fields of force, is curved, then both matter and the field must be curved.

The direction in which it is curved, back on itself ("positive curvature") or away from itself ("negative curvature"), is determined by geometry. We apply various geometries to find which one best fits according to the least amount of correction needed to explain the positions of celestial bodies with the least amount of displacement. Einstein, before the observation of light curvature, worked out the statistics into a geometrical pattern and concluded with positive curvature according to the geometry of Riemann. In this he was followed by De Sitter and Weyl. The universe was thus pictured as closed, in a rough cylindrical (Einstein) or spherical (Weyl) shape. This would mean that the expanding universe was already in the process of closing back on itself. However, Friedmann, in reviewing Einstein's work, noticed a mistaken value carried out in the subsequent inferences and deductions. In correcting this, the geometry was found to fit the postulates of the negatively curved system of Lobartchesvski. As applied to the universe, this would mean that the direction of the expansion was not doubling back, but according to the pattern of a negative sphere, the shape of a baseball cover or a saddle, expanding infinitely into space.

There is no doubt about sufficient physical force in the initial explosion to carry this out. As a matter of fact, the velocities of receding objects are far beyond the escape velocities required to get out of the influence of any gravitational field. The evidence of this last statement is seen in random sampling of celestial objects according to distance and velocity. The distance, once again, is inferred from the amount of red in the spectrum. For example, we may see the superescape velocity in the following cases:

Object in:	Distance (in millions of light years)	Velocity (in miles per second)
Virgo	22	750
Ursa Major I	255	9,300
Corona Borealis	390	13,400
Bootes	685	24,500
Ursa Major II	700	26,000
Hydra	1,100	38,000
Bootes II	6,000	90,000

There seems to be no intrinsic limit to this. If gravity is the binding force of the universe, it is insufficient to hold the universe together. Consequently, the universe seems to be expanding into infinite space—which in this case means the absence of matter and the projection of geometrical concepts.

Is there any extrinsic force to limit the expansion? We do not know, and it is difficult to consider how we might discover such. Einstein postulated a repulsion force, but only to save his Riemannian geometry. After Friedmann pointed out the error in his calculations, he abandoned the repulsion field, which should show up, supposing that we could ever have sufficiently powerful instruments to detect the edges of the universe, in some sort of energy manifestation.

The theory of anti-matter has been tentatively advanced as some such stabilizing force. Anti-matter is a theoretical possibility. It would be matter with a negative nucleus and positive electrons. It gained some credence with the production of the positron, and later with the production of negative nuclear particles. The intrinsic spin independent of force fields that brought serious doubt about the law of parity further suggested a balance of matter of opposite charges throughout the universe. Some tracks of unusual energy releases on photo-emulsion plates exposed at high altitudes lead to the conclusion of energy releases of the force $2(mc^2)$, which would indicate anti-matter. Again, the unusually high energy output of certain radio stars leads to the suggestion of their being affected by anti-matter.

However, the assumption of the universe being a balance of positive-negative matter, or bounded by anti-matter, is rather gratuitous. There is always the question of how the two could be produced together and exist side by side. There should be mutual annihilation, complete reduction of mass into energy according to the proportion $2(mc^2)$. This would be like trying to keep an animal alive in formaldehyde. Again, could we reach the edges of the universe, the anti-matter boundary should show up somehow according to the tremendous energy output brought about by the meeting of the two forms of energy. That does not mean that anti-matter does not exist. Nevertheless, it will be difficult to detect and even more difficult to prove until we know more about terrestrial matter.

Consequently, as far as we know, there is nothing to prevent the continued expansion of the universe. If this is the case, that means that the universe had the beginning of an expansion, and that is the point denied by the steady state theory of the universe.

THE STEADY STATE THEORY OF THE UNIVERSE

In physics, a steady state is a difficult physical condition. It is a physical system wherein there is an input of energy matched by an output of energy without any major disturbance of the whole system. An example of it would be the steady dripping of drops of water into a bucket matched by a steady dribbling of water over the edge of the bucket without any significant disturbance of the general mass of water in the bucket.

The steady state or "continued creation" theory was first advanced about 1950 by Herman Bondi and Thomas Gold. They based themselves on the assumption that matter is distributed throughout the universe homogeneously, that is, with a geometrically average distribution. They further considered that if the universe is homogeneous as regards space, it is also homogeneous as regards time. It is more convenient to regard the different ages of stars in the galaxies by supposing that matter is being constantly created in a constant present. Consequently, any look at the universe, past, present, or future, would show the universe to be just about the same as it is now. Hence, any expansion is not an evolution. It is rather a process of making room for more and newly created matter. This theory was formulated mathematically by Fred Hoyle in such way as to be consistent with the general relativity formulae.

In the physical order, Hoyle argues that there is no need to postulate a past superdense state culminating in an initial explosion. Instead, since the average distribution of matter throughout the universe seems to give no evidence of a past superdense state, we may substitute a "creation field" analogous to a field of force that "creates" an electron. Needless to say, this is not creation but transmutation of energy. The creation field is as gratuitous an assumption as the superdense state and the initial explosion. Hoyle also falls back on the supposition of the continued building up of elements in the present stars, or at least in supernovae, rather than the initial building up of elements in the superdense state. There is evidence, as we shall see, that the elements in the solar system seem no older than 4.5 billion years, which at first sight seems to lend support to the supposition of the steady state theory but on second sight can be used for or against any theory.

The exponents of the expanding universe theory claim to show the astronomical evidence of a superdense state. The furthest we can penetrate astronomically (at the present state) is about six billion light years. From about two billion light years outwardly we find an unusual factor.

We find many galaxies, all closer together. We also find several radio stars which are colliding galaxies; that is to say, two at least prove to be colliding galaxies, strictly speaking. They interpenetrate (one in Cygnus A; one, NGC 1275 in Perseus). About ten are close enough together to have their gases greatly disturbed by the proximity which is characteristic of all galaxies at this extreme distance.

It does not take much inference to conclude that if this is the case far out in space, then far out in space matter is closer together. Furthermore, the further we penetrate toward the limit of apprehension, the closer we find galaxies bunched. Since distance in space is also a view into the past, the inference is that in the past, our past as well as the past of any section of the universe, matter was a lot closer together, and this inference is used to argue to a past superdense state.

In February, 1961, Professor Martin Ryle, radioastronomer of Cambridge University, announced the significant findings of four years' patient observation.

In 1957 he had announced the existence of a number of "radio stars," and had interpreted these as colliding galaxies, especially when a closer one was verified visually at Palomar Mountain, out beyond six billion light years. This was interpreted as an argument in favor of the past superdense state. However, observations by a number of radioastronomers, both in the United States and in Australia, raised serious doubts about the precision of Ryle's observations. These doubts seemed to weaken his conclusions about the expanding universe theory, and the steady state theory gained more adherents.

Professor Ryle is a first-class and patient scientist. He did his work all over again. This time he redesigned his original radio receiver into an interferometer in such a way as to achieve greater accuracy in perception, an accuracy far more precise than that of any dish antenna.

Astronomical radio receivers are generally dish antennas. These have the advantage of mobility. They also suffer the disadvantage of having to become bigger and bigger for accurate perception of more distant objects.

Radio perception is done as follows. When an object is perceived, generally on a wavelength of 3.57 meters, the receiver is slowly rotated like a radio directional finder. The amount and angle of rotation required between the first signal, the centered and strong signal, and the last signal, can be extrapolated as base angle for delineation, again after the fashion of a direction finder. Obviously, the wider the antenna, the better is the base for precision. This is especially necessary since many radio stars are too distant to be detected visually. We can perceive them since radio signals are stronger than light. The largest dish antenna is at Jodrell Bank, England. It is a huge, saucer-shaped receiver having a diameter of two hundred and fifty feet. The United States is building one having a diameter of six hundred feet at Green Bank, West Virginia.

The Cambridge observatory, with which the author is somewhat familiar, is different, as is the radio observatory in Australia. The Cambridge observatory consists of antennas strung north and south, east and west. Each is 1437 feet long.

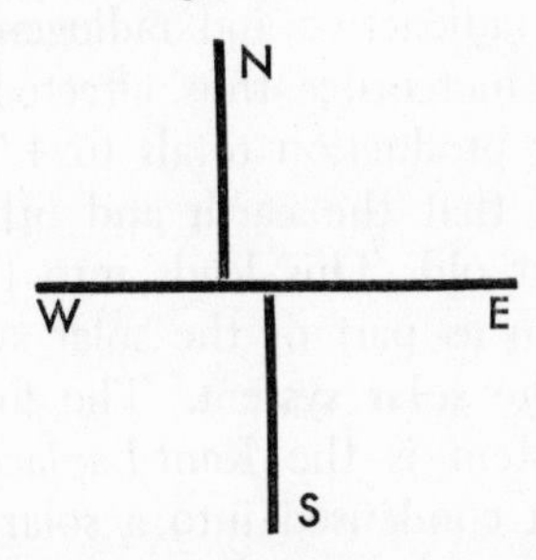

The rotation of the earth takes care of the north-south variations, while the east-west antenna is adjustable north and south for an angle of about forty degrees. This gives an altazimuth system of locating objects that can be calibrated with the equatorial positions of visual astronomy.

In order to delineate radio stars more precisely, in fact, more precisely than any dish antenna, Ryle mounted a movable dish antenna on a set of tracks parallel to the east-west antenna. In this way he could have a variable and yet large base for interferometer measurements.

Ryle detected over one thousand radio stars from eight to twelve billion light years away. Since there now seems little chance of questioning the accuracy of his observations, and since these seem to be colliding galaxies, there would appear to be a strong argument of a past superdense state and the expanding universe theory.

We have thus the picture of the two theories. The steady state theory maintains that the present universe cannot be proved to have had a beginning. It is a steady state of continued creation of new material. The expanding universe theory maintains that there was a beginning in an initial explosion which started off the expansion.

DETERMINATION OF THE AGE OF THE UNIVERSE

If there was a beginning, when was it? To answer this we must correlate considerable data from several fields. Although there is general agreement, there are still sufficient differences to make any correlation at best an average. The fields of correlation are: (1) the age of the earth, which involves (2) a theory of the age of the sun and the stars; (3) the selection of a theory of the origin of the elements.

The age of the earth. The first accounting is based on the half life of the spontaneous radioactivity of radium into lead, of rubidium into a strontium isotope, of a radioactive isotope of uranium into helium, and of a naturally radioactive isotope of potassium into argon. Taking the known distribution of radioactive and radiogenic materials thus affected both on earth and in meteorites thus affected and produced, the best statistical time of their production totals to 4.5 billion years, and would lead to the conclusion that the earth and other members of the solar system are at least that old. This leads into the theory of the manner of the earth's formation as part of the solar system.

The formation of the solar system. The first modern theory of the origin of the solar system is the *Kant-Laplace theory*. This maintains that a spherical nebula condensed into a solar nebula, that is, into the sun and a lens-shaped envelope of incandescent gases. As this increased in its rotation, it brought about a condensation of masses of gas into the planets which gradually condensed into solid bodies. In the condensing bodies, the heavy elements began to be formed, and their gravitational tendency toward the center, as opposed to the tendency of the latent gases to expand, brought about the rotations of the planets. This perhaps formed their satellites by ejecting molten masses of the parent planets because of centrifugal force.

Were this theory correct, it would make the sun not much older than the earth. It would also explain the interior heat of the earth and other planets. It would further explain why all the planets have their orbits in the same direction as the sun's rotation, and why all are generally on the same ecliptic. It was accepted by Lord Kelvin, who saw in it an explanation of the volcanoes because of the still molten interior of the earth.

However, there are difficulties in this theory. For one thing, the formation of the elements in a nebula involves insuperable difficulties. The tendency of elements to concentrate in the center is not enough to explain rotation. It would more likely set up a shearing effect, rather than a rotational motion, as pointed out by Maxwell. It is true that Laplace had considered the formation of orbital rings which coalesced into protoplanets. However, the force would still be shearing, preventing coalescence into one mass. There would more likely be many planetoids after the manner of the rings of Saturn.

A much more serious difficulty is suggested by the mechanics of angular momentum. The angular momentum of any system is the totality of the sums of all the masses, rotations, orbits, and distances of all the components of the system. Even should the components change in distance, density, etc., the sum of the angular momentum would remain the same. In the solar system, if the Kant-Laplace theory is correct, things are quite wrong. When we take into account the mass, velocity, and distance ratios of the components and of the whole, we discover that Jupiter has well over one third the angular momentum of the entire system. Yet, were the Kant-Laplace theory correct, it is difficult to see how this can be the case. Second, in view of the condensation theory of the dense planets in the nebula, it is difficult to see how the sun and planets rotate with a speed any different than the rotation of the whole, that is, proportionate to the orbit of Pluto, or perhaps Neptune. Finally, the rotation of any and all the individual planets according to the possession of elements in their composition is quite wrong according to the moment of force in a rotating body. The small, heavy, dense, inner planets should be speeding up in their rotation while the outer, larger, and less dense planets should be slowing down proportionately. Yet, of the inner planets, Mercury and Venus rotate slowly, the same as their orbits. The earth is slowing down. Jupiter and Saturn, on the other hand, rotate at an extremely rapid rate for their masses.

In brief, even though the Kant-Laplace theory has some attractive features that can be pictured readily and that, as a whole, could make the problem of the age of the sun easy to solve at first sight, it is so fraught with objections as to make it difficult to accept.

For these reasons, Sir James Jeans advanced his *"tidal" theory*. Since so many of the stars we know are multiple stars, Jeans assumes that the sun was once part of a double-star system. Out of space came some sort of object that dragged the sun's partner after it. This raised huge tides on the sun, which, on being detached and dragged away by the interloper, became the planets.

However, this does not necessarily clear up the difficulties. It does not, for example, explain why there is a concentration of the heavier elements in the inner planets all out of proportion to the rest of the solar system. We could say that they come from the twin sun, basing ourselves on the assumption that the latter was extremely dense, having a concentration of heavy elements. However, although there are pairs of stars in which one is large and the other comparatively small and dense, after the manner of Sirius Alpha and Sirius Beta, nevertheless, in this supposition, the twin star to our sun would have to be about the size of

Jupiter, about one thousandth of the sun's mass, and have the density of a white dwarf star to balance the sun's mass. How anything could be torn from such a dense mass is difficult to see.

All in all, even though the tidal theory is more satisfactory than the Kant-Laplace theory, still there are many difficulties involved. A paramount objection notes the odds against one star coming sufficiently close to raise the tides and separations postulated. These chances are rare and remote. Jeans suggested that the stars were a lot closer together than now if the expanding universe theory is true, and that the chances of near collision were greater.

However, if the expanding universe theory is true, the closeness is seen in galaxies rather than in stars. Moreover, on the supposition that the expanding universe theory is true, there is no need to fall back upon a double star or a traveling star.

Later speculations. The difficulty about any theory of the solar system is not to explain why the planets exist but why certain planets are where they are. In the solar system, the concentration of the heavy elements in the inner planets poses a problem that is not explained by any theory of the formation of the elements. This difficulty is tentatively answered by supposing that the heavier elements come from meteorites.

The age of the sun and the stars. There are several factors in favor of this supposition. We know that meteorites are stony and metallic. We know that the earth has been bombarded by heavy meteors more frequently in the past than in recorded times. The problem, then, is to establish the origin of the meteorites. They might have been formed in the orbital rings of spiral nebulae and because of their greater density, veered in toward the sun and collided with the inner planets. These planets, through combinations of elements already in existence, were condensed water, ammonia, and methane. Because of the gravitational fields of the other planets, they have retained most of these substances, which exist chiefly as frozen atmospheres. The inner planets lost most of their hydrogen and were bombarded by meteorites and chondrites from the planetoids. Thus, the planets are about as old as the sun, and the sun's age can be fairly well determined. In general, it is considered, from the amount of helium built up in the sun, to be about six billion years. The age of the earth, both from the dating of terrestrial elements and from the dating of meteorites, seems to be about 4.5 billion years.

The sun is a *main sequence star of G2 spectral type;* that is, the sun is an average star that is considered to go through a predictable process from what we can infer from nuclear physics. The process is: (1) condensation of interstellar gas and dust from a combination of the pressure of starlight and gravitational forces; (2) a controlled thermonuclear process of the building up of helium from hydrogen; (3) a series of readjustments in the star as the helium built up collapses, because of its greater weight, to the center of the star; (4) a gradual dying down of the star as the helium uses up the hydrogen until its only intrinsic energy is the energy of gravitational pressure.

This process should be estimated in terms of about twelve billion years. Furthermore, there are other elements in small proportion in the stars, and perhaps there is the building up of elements in stars, which fits in the time element. Thus, from spectroscopy we can discover the proportion of helium to hydrogen and the other elements to learn the average ages and processes of the stars. According to theory, the ages of the main sequence stars should terminate in about twelve billion years before the final collapse. The stars then shine by their gravitational pressures. There are some stars in the Magellenic clouds that have been claimed to give evidence of being about twenty-four billion years old. However, we cannot prove that these might not have sped up in their processes.

There seem to be exceptions to the main sequence. Main sequence stars would normally progress from reddish, low-temperature stars, along through yellow and hotter stars, whitish and still hotter stages, and terminate in blue giants. Besides their intrinsic energy development, they seem also to pick up heat by tunneling through dust, by an infall of dust. These are called *Population I stars.** *Population II stars* are the different stars. They are such as red supergiants. Somewhere in the scheme are also the white dwarfs. There are also stars which, because of different proportions of elements, perhaps because of a planetary system to slow down their rotation, hasten or delay along the main sequence. Nevertheless, they appear to be stars which seem to have started along the main sequence but which, because of different proportions of elements to initial masses, and again, perhaps planetary systems or their lack, seem to have swung off the main sequence. However, their ages can be calibrated with the main sequence and the amounts of dust around them. This leads to the conclusion that Population I stars (yellow, white, and blue)

* A new interpretation of the main sequence has been advanced from observations made by Professor Holton Arp of the Mount Wilson and Palomar observatories. The accepted interpretation is that as stars carry on their processes they become blue or red supergiants. Professor Arp's theory would have stars start as blue supergiants, become smaller yellowish-white stars, and end their evolution as red supergiants before a final collapse into red or white dwarfs. If the reader is familiar with the constellations, he can see in Orion the beginning and end of this process in a brilliant blue star (Riga) and a sullen red star (Betalgeuse) of the same constellation.

are comparatively young, whereas Population II stars (especially red supergiants) are old stars.

Population I stars are surrounded by dust envelopes and are in the arms of spiral galaxies. Population II stars are not surrounded by dust and are in the centers of galaxies. This leads us to infer that the stars are made of dust and gases, and not the other way around, and that the centers of galaxies are the older sections. It also suggests that cluster galaxies, characterized by being dust free and by being populated with red stars, are old spiral galaxies, or at least spiral galaxies that have sped through their processes.

On the grounds above, and with the exception of the disturbing facts of certain aspects of some of the stars in globular clusters, theory leads us to a universal age of about six or eight billion years. Nevertheless, since the oldest objects we know by distance are the colliding galaxies in Bootes, six billion light years, we must state that the universe is older than that figure. Granting about six billion years for the stars of these galaxies to have reached the state of their developments, we reach an age of about twelve billion years. Most of the difficulty with trying to attain the age of the universe from astronomical data is that almost every discovery makes us push the time table of the universe back a few billion years.

There is one more factor to be considered in the age problem, and that is the origin of the elements.

The origin of the elements. We are spoiled on earth. We have a relative abundance of the ninety-two natural elements. The same is not true throughout the universe. This raises the question as to the distribution and the origin of the elements. By distribution through the universe, the average is:

Hydrogen:	$\pm 92\%$ by volume,	$\pm 73\%$ by weight
Helium:	$\pm 6\%$ by volume,	$\pm 20\%$ by weight
Others:	$\pm 2\%$ by volume,	$\pm 7\%$ by weight

There are two theories to explain this: the carbon-nitrogen cycle and the proton-proton cycle.

The carbon-nitrogen cycle, advocated by Bethe, supposes that hydrogen in the presence of carbon 12 can go through a process of exchange of energies building up nitrogen isotopes and helium with the release of energy and the restoration of carbon 12 in such way as to continue the process. The process is:

$$
\begin{aligned}
C^{12} + H^{1} + p^{+}\downarrow &\rightarrow N^{13} + \gamma\uparrow \\
N^{13} &\rightarrow C^{13} + \beta\uparrow \\
C^{13} + H^{1} + p^{+}\downarrow &\rightarrow N^{14} + \gamma\uparrow \\
N^{14} + H^{1} + p^{+}\downarrow &\rightarrow O^{15} + \gamma\uparrow \\
O^{15} &\rightarrow N^{15} + \beta\uparrow \\
N^{15} + H^{1} + p^{+}\downarrow &\rightarrow C^{12} + He^{4} \\
&\quad\downarrow \\
&\quad C^{12} + H^{1} + p^{+} \rightarrow N^{13} + \gamma\uparrow, \text{ etc.}
\end{aligned}
$$

If this process is going on, it would necessitate the previous existence of carbon and nitrogen, and suppose that the initial process would have to have been from fundamental particles rather than from hydrogen. However, hydrogen, having these particles under sufficient energies, could produce them. This would seem to require a highly energetic state, which could be explained in a superdense state.

The other process, the proton-proton cycle, supposes that hydrogen can build up by the assimilation of a proton to deuterium, tritium, a rare helium isotope, normal helium, and hydrogen to continue the cycle. This is a complicated procedure, as exemplified in the long years of theoretical and practical work put into the first thermonuclear device. In an extremely simplified scheme, the process would be:

$$
\begin{aligned}
H^{1} + p^{+}\downarrow &\rightarrow H^{2} \\
H^{2} + p^{+}\downarrow &\rightarrow H^{3} \\
2H^{3} &\longrightarrow He + H^{1} + p^{+}\downarrow \\
&\qquad\qquad\downarrow \\
&\qquad\qquad H^{1} + p^{+}\downarrow \rightarrow H^{2}, \text{ etc.}
\end{aligned}
$$

Parts of this process have been carried out in the laboratory, and apparently this is the process of the nuclear bomb. As remarked by Sir James Jeans, what can be carried out in the laboratories can take place in the sun and the stars.

Before anyone were to commit himself to either or both of these theories, he should realize that they not only *release* great amounts of energies, but also *require* a lot of energy. That is one reason why the expanding universe theory postulates the superdense state and why the steady state theory postulates the intense energy conditions found only (as far as we know) in the centers of stars. For some advocates of the former theory, all the elements were formed in a few moments after the initial radiance of the explosion became mass energy. These energies are thus available for the carbon-nitrogen cycle, and there does not have to be the continued absorption of huge amounts of energy required in either cycle to explain the further build-up of heavier elements. They are already built up. Furthermore, there is the difficulty involved in the absence of atomic number 5 of atomic mass 8. The instability of this prevents any permanent existence of such. It *might* be explained by a fractionally temporal existence of a helium isotope ($He^4 + n \rightarrow He^5$), but this is extremely unstable and momentary. Gamow claims to answer this by postulating a rapid, twenty-minute process of building up all the elements. It is rather risky. On the other hand, Hoyle and Fowler postulate the interior of the stars to be sufficiently energetic to carry on the process according to the proton-proton cycle. If carbon and nitrogen are needed, they might have been obtained from supernovae, exploding stars. Since very little of these elements would be needed, there are enough supernovae in any galaxy to supply these elements.

How old is the universe? We simply do not know. Modern theory is an extremely ingenious and noteworthy associating of data and hypothesis. It leans heavily on conclusions drawn from the assumption of either random or average distribution of matter throughout the universe. New techniques of investigation could easily modify accepted theories on this point and accepted inferences therefrom. Another key tenet subject to further investigation and possible variation is the interpretation of Cepheid variable and RR Lyra stars as indicative of the relation between magnitude and period for distance. Different interpretations of the magnitude and color of these stars can vary the interpretation of distances, and since in the expanding universe theories distance indicates age, greater distances would mean an older universe.

Modern theories are divided as to its beginning or eternity, and no one theory answers the question. Theories do not speak of creation. They speak of an origin from previous sources. In the case of the expanding universe, the origin of the present process, which is not the origin of *being*, and hence not creation philosophically and theologically understood, supposes some previous material — particles and hydrogen, that is, material causes. In the case of the steady state theory, there is no beginning. There is the steady and eternal production of matter from a "creation field." Consequently, throughout all of this fascinating investigation by the astronomers and astrophysicists, the term "creation" is used in an adapted sense. The proper term is "process."

It is interesting to note that all of this theory seems to be among the implications of St. Thomas Aquinas' stand that it is impossible to prove creation in time from reasoning. Any investigation in this problem raises further problems that both weaken the timetable and seem to do away with it. One can understand why some scientists hold that the clearest statement of creation is from revelation and not from science: "In the beginning God created heaven and earth."

SUMMARY

1. Modern scientific cosmology attempts to unify its concepts of the entire universe, and has received great assistance from the conceptual scheme of modern nuclear chemistry.
2. Chemistry deals with elements and their combinations. The rate of their combinations is called "valence." Valence is explained by an exchange of electrons (electrovalence) or by a linking of electrons (covalence).
3. Isotopes are variations in the properties of an element according to weight. However, chemistry now accepts variations according to nuclear properties, thus inaugurating nuclear chemistry.
4. Nuclear chemistry validates spectroscopic and chemical analysis of stars and galaxies elsewhere in the universe. This opens up the problem of theories of the age and evolution of the universe.
5. Much of physical and chemical theory is verified by cosmic rays, types of radiation coming to us from the sun, other stars, and other galaxies. The particles detected are of the same nature as terrestrial matter. Hence, from chemistry and from cosmic rays we can infer that the entire universe consists of the same material and goes through the same processes.
6. There are two theories of the direction of the processes of the universe: the expanding universe theory and the steady state theory. The former maintains that the universe began as a superdense state of element-forming matter that exploded throughout all of space. The latter maintains that new matter is constantly being created and that elements are formed in stars and supernovae.
7. Speculation about the age of the universe is drawn from: (1) geological and physical data about the age of the earth — about 4.5 billion years; (2) the formation of the solar system and the age of the sun — about 6 billion years; (3) the distribution of elements and types of stars.

   From the above we infer that the universe is 12–24 billion years old, if the expanding universe theory is correct. We really do not know.

CHAPTER SEVENTEEN

The NATURE and PHILOSOPHY of LIFE

Aristotle opens the second book of his *Physics* with the following words:

> Of things that exist, some exist by nature, some from other causes. "By nature" the animals and their parts exist, and the plants and the simple bodies (earth, fire, air, water) — for we say that these and the like exist "by nature" (*Physics*, II, 1, 192b9–12).

Undoubtedly life is a natural phenomenon and has spread itself all over the earth. Nevertheless, familiar as life may be to us, there are many things we do not know about it. We do not know exactly what life is, nor do we know when or how it originated on earth. Hence, in any treatment of life, we must reconstruct from what we do know about it.

THE NATURE OF LIFE

We describe life through four outstanding properties. These are: mobility, growth from within, self-development of parts, and self-repair of parts. The feature common to these properties is that they proceed *from within* the living thing. Things other than living beings have some of these properties, but they are put into the object by an extrinsic principle: for example, every machine and every motor has mobility. Types of machines can govern their own operations, correct their own mistakes, and repair their own parts. Nevertheless, these operations do not develop from an intrinsic principle. They are not natural developments. They are put into or designed into the machine by the ingenuity of human intelligence. Perhaps the best definition of life is by St. Thomas Aquinas when he calls it the "existence of a living nature."

What we do know about life is drawn from the chemistry of life. We know many chemical facts about life without knowing why they are so.

Life centers about the most versatile of the elements, carbon. Carbon, as we saw, is a tetravalent element whose atom combines by covalence rather than by electrovalence. That is to say, it forms links by the interchange of electrons rather than by the supplying or absorbing of an electron in an electrostatic balance. In practice, this means that the combinations formed by carbon may be chemically stable but are more changeable than ordinary electrovalent compounds. This implies that such energy states as heat and cold have more immediate effect on organic compounds than on other compounds. This is why, for example, butter turns rancid and meat spoils.

The other elements associated with carbon in organisms are oxygen, hydrogen, and nitrogen. All forms of life that we know involve combinations of carbon, hydrogen, and oxygen. In some forms, in fats, we also find nitrogen. We do not really know why this is the case, although we can speculate about it and advance some reasons.

The first of these is that life in any form, low or high, demands the expenditure of relatively great amounts of energy. Hence, life requires ready sources of energy. These postulated elements are all highly energetic. The energy is available in them.

The second reason is that the continuation of life itself through its vital functions demands that these elements not only be the sources of energy but that they also carry off the waste products of vital functions; for example, an animal body needs energy in a readily assimilable form. For this, simple sugar is most excellent. Insofar as all energy is not used at once — otherwise the animal would always have to be eating and would not be free to move around for the pursuit of food and the escape from enemies — this sugar must be stored up. However, sugar has a tendency to ferment into alcohols. Hence, the carbohydrate that we call sugar must be extracted from starches and stored as fats. The simple exchange of oxygen for nitrogen transforms the sugar into adipose fat which is stored in layers on the animal body. This also serves as a protection from cold. Since nitrogen is also a factor in decay, it is united to the byproducts of living matter to become waste in various forms. Other wastes are attached to carbon and exhaled as carbon dioxide.

These functions become amazingly complex in the chemical order; they take place because carbon is a versatile element and because of the valency of the elements that readily associate with and dissociate from carbon. Carbon is the key to all of this because of its covalent character.

The actual elements that enter into the only life that we know, life on earth, are carbon, hydrogen, oxygen, and nitrogen. Yet are they the *only* elements that do enter into life? We know of no others on earth that do so, although we cannot claim to know that much about life on earth. We can only look to other tetravalent elements. These are silicon, germanium, tin, and lead. The last three are metals. Because of this they tend toward weights that would hamper the mobility required of life. That leaves us silicon. This also offers difficulties as a possible constituent of living bodies, among them the fact that combinations of silicon normally take on stony or glassy properties; for example, a silicon-based life would have silicon dioxide as one of its waste products. This, however, is quartz. The general stoniness of silicon compounds, if combined with fluorine and various methane and chlorine compounds, might suit plants, but would present a serious difficulty for animals and other more mobile forms of life. Furthermore, atom for atom, silicon is over twice as heavy as carbon. Thus silicon would add physical difficulties to the problem of living. It might be suitable for life on a planet of different gravitational attraction, but the gravitational forces required would make difficult the retention or availability of the gaseous elements that would be required for silicon-based life.

Hence, we may conclude as probable that life as we know it seems to be based on a long molecule consisting of carbon, hydrogen, oxygen, and nitrogen. These elements are most suitable because of their energy in combination and because of the ease with which they combine.

Because of this physical basis for life, we can also conclude that two sets of circumstances would limit life or render it impossible. These are: (1) elements that would destroy life — toxic elements; and (2) physical conditions that prevent the formation of compounds necessary for life or destroy them once they have been formed — temperature conditions.

Toxic elements or compounds stabilize the chemical states of an organism in such a way that they prevent the necessary exchange of elements and compounds. For example, methane (CH_4), ammonia (NH_3), and chlorine (Cl) are toxic because they prevent the interchange of oxygen for carbon dioxide on the part of plants and carbon dioxide for oxygen on the parts of animals. Similarly, formaldehyde (HCOH) takes one oxygen molecule out of animal tissue and becomes formic acid (HCOOH), thus stabilizing the oxidation and glycolosis of the cell. The individual cells cease to breathe and to assimilate food.

Toxic agents and poisons vary depending upon the form of life. For carbon-based life certain elements and compounds interfere with vital processes in such a way that we call them toxic. If there were other forms of life, elements and compounds beneficial for our form might be toxic.

The second limitation to life is the energy range. This is closely associated with temperature. If the environment is too cold, vital energy is drained off and the sources necessary for the continuation of life become unavailable. Crystallization sets in liquid cells, and although some forms of life go into a suspension, the entire ecology, the balance of life, suffers serious interference. On the other hand, if the temperature is too high, complex organisms are broken down into their components. Thus, since life is organization, life ceases when the organization ceases. We cannot lay down any hard and fast rules about the temperature range necessary for life, but we can state it roughly as between –100 degrees F. and +150 degrees F.

This opens up two problems to us. One is that of the formation and evolution of life on earth. The other is the possibility of life elsewhere in the universe.

THE ORIGIN OF LIFE

We do not know when or how life was formed on earth. The best we can do is to reconstruct ideal conditions and try to find when such conditions appeared on earth. In this we must be prepared to accept spontaneous generation as a working concept. It does not mean that spontaneous generation is proven. On the other hand, it has never been disproven. We must simply use it as a convenient possibility, a fitting concept.

Evolution based upon spontaneous generation had been accepted for centuries. Aristotle accepted it, pointing out the obvious fact that we do not know where non-life leaves off and where life begins, and that we do not know the boundaries between one form of life and another (*On the History of Animals*, VIII, 1, 588b4). Aristotle's reasoning was followed, with modifications, by St. Augustine, who considered that God created simple and fundamental types of realities out of which evolved higher types of beings (cf. *De Genesi ad Litteram*, VI, 10). St. Albert and St. Thomas also acknowledged this. The Christian philosophers made exception for man's soul, knowing that a spiritual soul can in no way emerge from the potencies of matter. Apart from that, their position was simple. If a higher entity emerges from a lower source, then the higher product was within the potency of the source. All that was required was sufficient energy (efficient cause) to educe the act from the potency, and in Aristotelian science, the universe was considered to be full of available energy.

Spontaneous generation was denied when more discoveries were made about the cell nature of life. It was gradually assumed that the living cell was too intricate and too highly organized to have emerged from non-living elements. Sooner or later, this unfortunately became a religious issue insofar as it gave certain superficial verification of a literal and fundamentalist interpretation of the first chapters of *Genesis*.

Louis Pasteur, a commercial chemist, seemed to have established that there are no known cases of spontaneous generation. As a matter of fact, that is true. Even now, if we should discover some apparently spontaneous forms of life, we could not eliminate the possibility that these were caused by unknown living cells already in existence. Nevertheless, although we know of no cases of spontaneous generation under contemporary physical conditions, we cannot eliminate the possibility of spontaneous generation in the past. Nor can we overlook the possibility of the production of life in the laboratory. In fact, we are very close to such in truly significant work done on amino acids, generally considered the sources of proteins.

It is true that there is a theory, or at least an hypothesis, that life did not originate on earth spontaneously, that it was carried here by cosmic dust particles from some other world where life already existed. There is a popular expression to the effect that life is here from "cosmic garbage." However, in such theorizing, we would do better to base ourselves on what we know than on what we do not know.

Some advance the theory that after the geological formation of the earth, when the earth's crust began to appear and the oceans were formed, enough vital elements were produced that a catalyst such as formic acid (HCOOH) and an energy source such as lightning — itself a producer of ozone (O_3) — would be able to produce simple hydrocarbons and carbohydrates. From these — again through the agency of lightning working on hydrogen — methane, ammonia, and the amino acids could have been built up for the production of proteins, and life would have appeared in the warm oceans. This theory is grounded on an intrinsic possibility that seems close to realization in the laboratory.

We do not know when this might have occurred. If we consider the earth to be about 4.5 billion years old, it is conceivable that it could have reached its life-producing possibilities several billion years ago. Man is generally considered to have appeared about a million or a million and a half years ago, although we have no accurate timetable for this. The evidence is deduced from human traces in geological formations which we can date approximately.

We must keep in mind, of course, that all of this is supposition. Nevertheless, we can produce amino acids in the laboratory by treating free methane, free hydrogen, and free ammonia with an electric spark. Furthermore, if chemistry means anything, we are led to suppose the existence of more of these elements and compounds in the early cooling-off period in the earth's history. Hence, the supposition has a fairly good basis in what we know. If life proceeds from spontaneous generation, then conditions were fitting for it. Since life is present, then we must give more than idle consideration to our supposition.

EVOLUTION

The process of evolution is a more difficult one to determine, although we have far more evidence for it than for the spontaneous generation of life. Evolution is based upon our knowledge of already formed and highly developed fossils. The trilobite may be the earliest form of animal life that we know, but simple as it is, it is still highly complicated.

Philosophical theories of evolution as applied to life have always been accepted. Besides the pagan philosophers Plato and Aristotle, St. Gregory of Nyssa (cf. *Hexaemeron,* I) and St. Augustine maintained that the account of creation in the Bible had to be interpreted metaphorically and had to be rounded out by realistic theories of evolution. They were followed by St. Albert and St. Thomas.

The present direction of *scientific evolution* can be traced largely to Charles Darwin and Alfred Wallace, both of whom released their theories in 1859. Very little is held of their theories any more, especially the supposed descent of man from the ape, except for Darwin's principle of the struggle for existence, concretized in Spencer's ready phrase, "survival of the fittest." Survival is an accepted basis in all organic evolutionary theories.

Darwin noticed that even if we take the short biblical age of the earth literally there should be many more plants and animals than there are. He noticed that all plants and animals reproduce more than once and most frequently produce several offspring at one time. Simply put, this means that if one set of parents produced two offspring, and if these mated and each new family produced two offspring, and so on, there would be the progression of 2, 4, 8, 16, etc., in a comparatively short time. As a matter of fact, there is a lot of reproduction going on in both the vegetative and animal kingdoms, but the rate is not so fast as it should be in its simplest mathematical expression. Hence, something is preventing it.

One preventative would be warfare between different types of entities, for example, between carnivorous and herbiverous animals. This, however, is not a complete explanation. If we take all the lions and all the cattle in Africa, there never have been enough lions to catch up with the reproduction rate of the cattle.

Hence, the vital competition must be *within* species, not between them. Most of the members of a given species simply are not able to cope with their environment. They must struggle with their environment, and most fail in the struggle. Only the fittest survive in the struggle for existence.

The ablest weapon in this struggle for existence is adaptation. The lizard that can achieve protective coloration is the one that escapes the hawk. Only the heron which blends against its background escapes the wolf. Only the dog that can domesticate escapes death in the dog pound.

Darwin saw this adaptation against a spatial and temporal background. After making a voyage in the *Beagle* (1831–1833), he had a chance to observe the flora and fauna in such isolated places as Australia, the Barrier Reef, and Tasmania. Here he noted forms of life that were generally similar to others, for example marsupials, but having local developments quite different from others of the same biological family. For example, both kangaroos and opossums are marsupials, but the development of the kangaroo is quite different from that of the opossum. In some cases, these can be explained by "land bridges," that is, possible connections between one land mass and another land mass. In cases, however, where a land bridge cannot be established, we must look to the past as an explanation. We must find some way in which life became what it is in terms of a long, long evolution.

For centuries men had been puzzled by fossils, bones of animals, reptiles, and impressions of sea life often found on mountain tops. In the nineteenth century many people such as Buffon, Cuvier, and Lyell looked upon them as stages in the development of present forms of life. Many theories were advanced about their disappearance. Darwin added the note of struggle for existence. They did not survive because they were not able to struggle successfully against their environment. For example, the huge brontosauri of the late Jurassic period and the Cretaceous period were so heavy that they had to live in swamps not only to eat but also to have their weight supported by water. When the swamps dried up because of various geological changes, they were unable to survive.

Necessary to the process of survival was adaptation. Hence, in the process of evolution animals found means to compromise with their environment and passed this means on to subsequent generations. This is the great disputed point in Darwin's evolution: transmission of acquired characteristics. Such transmission was widely doubted for many years. Some sort of substitution had to be made. Lamarck had supposed that there were "sudden leaps" from one type to the next. People began to talk in hushed tones about transmutations, but this was never held too seriously. However, with the actual evidence of mutations in fruit flies that have been exposed to radiation, the question of mutations has come to the fore.

The points mentioned above, with the possible exceptions of mutations, are those that are accepted in almost all evolutionary theories. Although we do not know when or how life began, the fact that fossils show a progression from the more simple to the more complex, gives us reason to believe that life began in its simplest forms billions of years ago.

Billions of years must be postulated simply because of the problem of chance and probabilities. When we analyze the intricate complexities involved in one protein molecule, the chances of its being developed spontaneously according to any physical or chemical principles that we know are overwhelmingly in the negative. It is time that is on the side of life; that is, granted enough time, the chances against the spontaneous appearance of life are reduced. Nevertheless, because of the time element, it must have been a long time ago.

MECHANISM AND VITALISM

We must interrupt these speculations about the origin and evolution of life to introduce some of the hesitations — and sometimes open opposition — of *vitalism*. Vitalism opposes the above positions, which are those of *mechanism*.

Mechanism maintains that life can be produced, given the proper sources and adequate energies. There is no need to fall back upon a vital principle or anything of that sort. Mechanism can be represented as:

$$\text{elements} + \text{organization} + \text{energy} \rightarrow \text{life}.$$

Vitalism maintains that this is not enough. There are two really distinct vitalistic trends.

Older vitalism maintained that in every type of life there must be a vital principle, a "soul," over and above organization. This was, among pagan philosophers, the Platonic type or form. Among Christians it was an extension downward of the properties of the human soul. The human soul transcends matter, and yet is the form of man. Comparisons were made in the case of animals and plants, and there was quite a bit of talk about "animal souls" and "plant souls." Its expression would be:

$$\text{elements} + \text{organization} + \text{energy} + \text{vital principle} \rightarrow \text{life}.$$

This is not in the Aristotelian-scholastic tradition. Since we find the same elements in living beings as in non-living beings, Aristotle held we must look upon living beings as higher organizations of sources according to the actualizations of the potencies of the elements (*On the Parts of Animals,* I, 1, 640b1 ff.).

Modern vitalism is a mathematical rather than a biological position. It maintains that the statistical chances of a spontaneous origin of life and of the mutations required in many evolutionary theories are forbidding. In fact, as the vitalists argue, if chances are weighed and applied, life must be older than the oldest known date of the universe. The chances that "somehow a fortuitous event occurred," and that "somehow a fish learned to live on the land," are overwhelmingly forbidding. The conclusion of the vitalists is that some other explanation must be adopted. They do not tell us what explanation. They simply advance criticisms of some of the principles of spontaneous generation and evolution.

THE AGE OF LIFE

The earliest geological age is the Pre-Cambrian period of over 500 million years ago. The name "Cambrian" is a variation on "cumbrian," which, in turn, is a development of the ancient name of the Welsh people, the *cymbri.* The Cambrian period is so named because first evidences of it were discovered in diggings in Wales and Cumberland. Even though the Cambrian period is dated at 500 million years ago, before this time, called the Pre-Cambrian period, we have the fossil imprint of a trilobite. Trilobites are highly organized types of life. Hence, life must have been formed long periods before the Cambrian period. That is why we have to think in terms of several billions of years. We find no evidences of earlier forms of life, most likely because their structure was soft and did not leave any fossil imprints.

We may list the geological periods and their types of life as follows:

Period	Time	Life Forms
	PALEOZOIC	
Pre-Cambrian	Before 600 million years	Simple cells, jellyfish, trilobites
Cambrian	500 million years	Fish, sea plants
Ordovician	425 million	Fish, sea plants
Silurian	350 million	Land reptiles and land plants
Devonian	225 million	Conifers, ferns, dessiduous trees, simple reptiles
	MEZOZOIC	
Triassic	205–165 million	Early great reptiles
Jurassic	165 million	Development of reptiles in size
Cretaceous	135 million	Great dinosaurs
	CENOZOIC — *The Age of Mammals*	
Paleocene	75 million	Small camels
Eocene	60 million	Prototype of modern camel
Oligocene	40 million	Early rhinocerous
Miocene	30 million	Prototype of deer
Pliocene	10 million	Prototype of elephant
Pleistocene	1 million	Woolly mammal, giant camel, saber-toothed tiger, etc.

We do not know when man appeared in the Cenozoic Era, except that the type of stone he used in his tools, as found in graves, and the carbon dating of human bones seem to push his appearance back to about one million years. There are human fossils, and there are such prehistoric men as the Neanderthal man, the Java man, the Peking man, and the Cro-Magnon man. These are named after the places where they are found, and they show ascending resemblances to modern man. Even though they resemble apes in various reproductions found in museums, they are clearly men. They had a much more highly organized brain than apes, central nervous system, and they were toolmakers. As a matter of fact, even in biology, we must be somewhat careful of reproductions. There has always been a school of anthropologists who maintain that these types still exist today but that, dressed in the clothing of modern man, they pass unnoticed.

If, however, these types no longer exist, how do we go about dating their time on earth? There are three methods: (1) their geological position; (2) chemical changes in the bones; and (3) carbon 14 dating.

There is a rough rule in geology that the deeper we go in the earth the earlier we go. Hence, we would think that we could date human remains according to the depth at which we find them. However, one characteristic of man is that he almost always buries his dead. In the very act of interment, the burial party may be going down thousands of years. Furthermore, if man did not always bury his dead, it is hard to see how bodies would remain where they fell. Human bodies do not simply lie around after death. They are devoured by scavengers. This would greatly reduce the chances of any human fossils being discovered. The third possibility is that the men so discovered might have been the victims of some such natural disaster as an earthquake or a flood. This, too, poses difficulties for the investigator. Dating seems possible because of tools and implements buried with the body. However, there are difficulties here, too. Arrowheads, for example, were either of bone or of stone or metal. If they were of bone, they had small chance of lasting long underground because they are organic. If they are of stone or metal, we are faced with the difficulty that many contemporary cultures are Stone Age cultures.

The second manner of dating human fossils is by the chemical changes undergone by bone. Bone consists of the other elements found in human tissue as well as calcium and phosphorus. While the softer sections of bone, such as marrow, tend to decay, calcium tends to harden and phosphorus tends to enter into compounds with the surrounding soil. The rate of these changes can be computed with fair accuracy. Hence both calcification and the amounts of phosphates found in or with the fossil give a fair indication of its age.

Atomic physics indicated a third and more accurate method of dating fossils. This is the carbon 14 method. Carbon 14 is an isotope of carbon 12 produced by radiation. Calcium is a great storehouse both of radiation and of radiation products.* We know the half life of carbon 14, and hence a measurement of carbon 14 in human fossils gives a date accurate to about fifty years of the existence of the remains.

Taking all of the three means above, it seems that we must push the existence of man back to about one million years.**

* This is the reason for the concern over radioactive fallout. Radiation products can be stored in the calcium of bone tissue. However, bones are also the sources of red blood corpuscles, which are manufactured in bone marrow. Radiation effects in bone calcium also break down the manufacture of corpuscles, and this is the essence of radiation sickness.

** Since this writing, a newer and much more accurate method of dating organic remains has come into use. It is based on the decay scheme of radiogenic potassium into an isotope of argon and various particles and energies. It is accurate to a few years in an area of several million years, and as used in connection with new human fossils discovered in Africa, it seems to push man's presence on earth to well over a million years.

This consideration of billions and millions of years of the earth's age and the appearance of life seems a far cry from the simple, geocentric earth of somewhat over 6000 biblical years, if Genesis is taken literally. For this reason, evolution has always been a fair target for some religious thinkers. It has never been much of a problem for philosophers, most of whom were anticipated by ancient and medieval philosophers. Theologians have come to accept evolution as a fact and to follow the advice of SS. Gregory of Nyssa and Augustine that there are sections in the Bible that must be interpreted metaphorically.

Nevertheless, we must look to the value of the evolutionary theories. We shall see them, briefly, from the scientific point of view, the philosophical point of view, with some attention to their theological implications.

SCIENTIFIC EVALUATION OF EVOLUTION

Scientifically, evolution is most peculiar insofar as it is characterized by an overwhelming amount of data and a paucity of theoretical interpretation. No other science has as much evidence, by way of actual remnants, fossils, and ancient artifacts as evolution. On the other hand, few other sciences have as little theoretical unity. As a fact, evolution is overwhelming. As a theory it often lacks conviction. This is a result of the conceptual nature of scientific thinking, and its value in correlating discoveries and phenomena. The representations of discoveries and phenomena are themselves concepts, and hence they must be assimilated into a larger conceptual system. Thus, the proper note of a science is to be able to justify one concept by another concept. If the concepts are properly representative of reality, then their association gives us a more valuable appreciation of reality. If the concepts are hypothetical, then the science suffers, although it always has the force of its logic. Evolution breaks down on the conceptual level. Its concepts are drawn from widely diverse fields: from biology, from geology, from chemistry, from anatomy, from physics, and all more from the development of resemblances than from the proper and intrinsic relationship of concepts. Nevertheless, evolution has sufficient cumulative force, despite some theoretical weaknesses, to be a commanding fact. We must be prepared to accept evolution, especially insofar as arguments marshaled against it are either far weaker than the weakest points of evolution or are simply questionings of some point or other in connection with the whole.

PHILOSOPHICAL EVALUATION

Philosophically, evolution is nothing new. Every great philosopher from Plato on has either accepted some evolutionary system or been prepared to accept it. For Plato it was simply the further unfolding of the superplenitude of the Forms in the material world. For Aristotle it was the actualization of the potentialities of the sources whence higher entities emerged; that is, since the higher comes from the lower, it was in potency in the lower and was educed from the lower by sufficient causes.

Aristotle deserves a closer look. He gets quite metaphysical about evolution. Aristotle maintained that the same elements that make up non-living beings also make up living beings. Furthermore, we do not know where non-life leaves off and life begins. Nor do we know where one form of life leaves off and another form begins. Hence, all we can say is that degrees of material being are different and higher degrees of organization of the elements. The higher forms are, thus, the higher proportions of the elements, the fulfillment, through higher forms, of the potentialities for existence.

Since the new entities come from sources, and since these sources, or material causes, are also temporal antecedents of the products, time enters into universal processes. Even if a change were to reverse itself, it would still take time. Thus, the change from *A* to *B* would take one time, and the reversal from *B* to *A* would take a later time. Since Aristotle could not envision a time when this process began, he considered the process of the universe to be eternal. In the *Metaphysics*, he gives a strongly metaphysical treatment of this. He considers that this process is meaningless unless we see it tending toward participation in the life of the Prime Mover or Mind of the Universe. It can never reach this goal, and hence the process can never end, since the energies of the universe contribute to the constant emerging of newer and higher beings from older and lower sources.

St. Augustine deserves special consideration in any philosophy of evolution. Once he had become convinced of the necessity to interpret some portions of the Bible metaphorically, he felt free to philosophize about questions not dealt with in revelation. Among these was the manner of the creation of the universe. He believed that God created certain fundamental types, called *rationes seminales*, that potentially contained future and more specific types within themselves. As listed by St. Augustine, the *rationes* are:

1. The creative plan in God's creative knowledge — the exemplars of beings to be created;
2. The elements of the world as universal causes — that is, sources and energies in the world whence come subsequent products;
3. Particular causes — that is, the convergence of forces on particular events;
4. What both St. Augustine and St. Thomas call "seeds" — that is, more particular types as potential further developments.

Taking the processes of nature as we understand them, it is difficult to see how one could get a more comprehensive philosophical view of the evolutionary character of nature and its processes.

In the Middle Ages, St. Albert generally followed Aristotle, especially in the question of degrees of being as higher and higher organizations from common sources or elements. St. Thomas owed much to both Aristotle and St. Albert. Moreover he was influenced by St. Augustine's doctrine of the *rationes seminales*, adapting and modifying Augustine's teaching to his own metaphysics. The philosophers of the Platonic-Aristotelian tradition explained evolution as exemplifications of the doctrine of potency and act. The actually newer product was the actualization of a potency from its sources.

Modern philosophy has been largely influenced by scientific evolution. Here we must distinguish between philosophers and popular writers. For example, among the popular writers was H. G. Wells, a literary critic and essayist. He used popular notions of evolution in his history of the human race, and he shaped his novels by envisioning a future evolution of the human race. When he was optimistic, his future humans were supermen, as in *Men Like Gods*. When he was somewhat pessimistic, his future humans were degraded into effetes or brutes, as in *The Time Machine*.

As mentioned above, most modern philosophers have been influenced by evolution. Hence, we must single out those philosophers who have either done the most with evolution or who have had the most philosophical influence.

The philosopher of *mechanistic evolution* was Herbert Spencer (1820–1903). Spencer's philosophy of evolution is based on the application of the principle of the conservation of energy to the unfolding of new entities. Spencer's "agnosticism" enters indirectly into his evolution theory. By agnosticism, Spencer did not mean that we are unable to know whether God exists. On the contrary, we must affirm that some absolute being does exist since everything in the universe is related to everything else. Since all of these are relative, and the relative has no meaning without the absolute, the very existence of this relative implies the existence of some absolute. However, and here agnosticism comes in, neither theology nor the physical sciences have the proper concepts to investigate and to explain the nature of this absolute. We cannot even know if it is the God in whom Jews and Christians believe.

Since Spencer has ruled God out of the picture, so to speak, he must undertake to explain the universe in terms of a limited amount of energy proceeding from and operating on a universal interrelation of material entities. Spencer does so in terms of the direction of the expenditure of this energy. This direction is inward and outward. In simple beings, little inward energy is required, so that their activities are predominantly outward. In highly complex entities, the energy is predominantly inward, to maintain their complex structures, and there is little outward activity. Furthermore, there must be some opposition to the energy before it will do anything significant. If there is no opposition, it simply dissipates. It is like gunpowder burning in the open air. On the other hand, when the gunpowder is in a restrictive case, it explodes. When the energy of bodies meets outward restriction, it does work.

The upward development of energy falters on two levels. The first occurs when there is no opposition to the energy. It continues to dissipate and does no work. The entity simply remains on the same level of being until it runs out of energy. This is the case, for example, in the stars and in other forms of almost pure energy. (Spencer's view was proposed before we knew about the evolution of the stars.) The other level of stagnation occurs when the entity is so concerned with the maintenance of its own organized state that it does no outward work at all. It is unable to resist its encroaching environment.

Those entities that evolve do so by overcoming their environment. The fittest survive. In the biological field, it is the simple cell that can become tissue, develop organs to move around for protection. It is the fish that can move onto the land to become a reptile. This goes all the way up, and in man achieves a peculiar trend. Man's instrument of survival is the development of moral values through his conscience. We can summarize this type of evolution in the expression *challenge and response*. If the developing entity does not respond to the challenge, it stagnates and gradually fails to survive.

This theory has many scientific weaknesses. We could accept it on the basis of potency and act, except that we must grant the human soul spiritual value and we cannot expect any evolving of the soul from matter. On the other hand, we can grant the evolution of man's nervous system, upon which the soul depends so heavily that it would be almost helpless without it.

Spencer's philosophy of evolution was built up on the principle of the conservation of energy. Hence, it suffers any weaknesses in variations of either biological or physical theory. For example, if vitalism could be proved, then Spencer's philosophy would suffer. Another and more modern philosophy of evolution is the *emergent evolution* of Samuel Alexander (1859–1938).

Emergent evolution is more conceptual than Spencer's. Alexander's philosophy is described as "stratified." It is an evolution into distinct stages, each dependent upon the lower and earlier. The foundation of all is space-time, a matrix whose only property is motion. This motion sets up "spots," or localizations, some of which become permanent and are the basic substances. Those spots which are not permanent are set up as relationships. All these are the first stratum. The substantial spots set up qualities which are geometrically describable. They acquire material properties and become material substances with secondary qualities. This is the second stratum. The third stratum arises when organized matter becomes organic, vital. Substances become living bodies. They acquire, in succession, trophisms, senses, consciousness and awareness of each other and of themselves.

The Real is the challenge of the next step. It has been called "God in the making." In other words, then, it is the ultimate reason for evolution, the tending toward God. The tendency is never fully realized, and hence the evolution continues. We can, then, never say that any stage or stratum in evolution is the last. We can only say that it is the latest, with more to come.

The above, especially the consideration of space-time as the matrix, contains some elements of Platonic philosophy. Moreover, since it views evolution as a process toward a never achieved final cause, it has a close resemblance to Aristotle's theory.

A sharply divergent system of metaphysical evolution was advanced by the French philosopher, *Henri Bergson* (1859–1941). Bergson did not have much patience with emergent universes striving for a never attainable God. If God is anything, He is the force and drive of the evolving universe. Bergson's philosophy hinges about two points: the nature of useful ideas and the nature of intuition.

Bergson was influenced by the phenomenologists Husserl and Meinong. Perhaps he was also influenced by Kierkegaard's emphasis on suprarational consciousness. At any event, he maintains that experience is the real and that the real is experience. Experience is not transitory. It piles up in one's consciousness. This accumulation of experience is what he calls memory. Memory and experience are the basis of useful ideas — and among useful ideas he includes what we call scientific, philosophical, and theological concepts. These give us only a measured, limited, and fragmentary glimpse of reality. To attain reality, we must experience it intuitively, not rationally. After we clear our experience from conceptual thinking we arrive at what we experience through intuition, and this is duration. However, by duration Bergson does not mean the *realization* that things persist. This is simply a static acceptance of something. It is the *feeling* that things are going somewhere, that this duration is a living drive. The expression he uses is *élan vital*.

Since stagnancy is abhorrent to this vital force, the universe is peeling away any static remnants. The force behind this dynamic drive is God, who is both at the center of the movement and also in the movement itself. This drive extends upward from simplicity in the physical order to the complexity of human culture which also has a future of vital perfection to be achieved, even though this will not be the ultimate state. In fact, there is no ultimate state — simply a future of striving toward a further future. To stop anywhere is the stagnation that brought about the downfall of the dinosaur as well as of the Roman empire or the Napoleonic empire.

It is a common fallacy today to confuse *dialectical materialism* with communism. As a matter of fact, dialectical materialism is a philosophy of nature of which communism is a part. Moreover, it is an evolutionary philosophy that assimilated wholeheartedly the principles of Darwin and of Spencer.

Dialectical materialism is a development of the *dialectical idealism* of Hegel (1770–1831). Oftentimes, we cannot obtain a universal concept. Hence, our notion is a general notion with the possibility of its contradictory concept being acceptable. This means that its contradictory concept is not truly contradictory, but rather contrary. In dialectical thinking, we accept our first concept as a tentative thesis, and then investigate its denial (antithesis). Often we arrive at a more consistent idea developed out of both the thesis and the antithesis. This idea is a *synthesis* of the acceptable notes of both the *thesis* and *antithesis*. The above process, as mentioned before, is what Aristotle called a *dialectic*.

The dialectic is a process of ideas. Hegel, who admired Greek thought, was profoundly influenced by Kant. Part of Kant's difficulty was to discover where mental operations left off and physical operations began. Hegel advanced the opinion that there was no breaking-off point. Physical and mental operations are but two aspects of the operations of nature, which itself follows the dialectic characteristic of so much thinking. As applied to the problem of evolution, the dialectic might be:

Homogeneous mass Differentiation	Simple bodies Environment	Higher entities Greater differentiation	Living bodies

As developed by Hegel, dialectical evolution means that just as the knowledge of man is a history of ideas, so also the evolution of the world is a history of processes. In fact, nature is not so much the interactions of types of things as a history of the development of entities. Nature is history.

Marx turned Hegel's dialectical idealism "upside down," making it a dialectic of matter and looking upon ideas merely as operations of the central nervous system. He then pushed the dialectic into social problems. The following might be an example:

Downtrodden workers Concentrated wealth	Class warfare Dictatorship of the proletariate	Communistic society

Here we are not concerned with the problem of communism, but we do want to show that communism is a special application of a philosophy of nature wherein nature is considered history and is an evolution. This explains the conviction of the communist. He believes that all of history, that is to say, nature, is on his side. He accepts the evolutionary phrase "survival of the fittest," but he maintains that Marx's dialectical materialism indicates that he is among the fittest to survive.

Undoubtedly, one of the greatest philosophers of modern times is Alfred North Whitehead (1861–1947). His philosophy is *metaphysical*, and he was influenced by *evolution*, although we cannot call his philosophy a metaphysics of evolution or anything of that sort. He was by training a mathematician, one of the greatest. In mathematics, his field was logistics, that is, the mathematical treatment of the logical relations between mathematical concepts and values. Hence, logistics is characterized with problems about rules.

One would think that with this background, Whitehead's philosophy would be extremely conceptual. As a matter of fact, the opposite is true. He realized that his theory of mathematics and of physics was static. It dealt with ideas rather than with reality. He also noted that in reality, beings are constantly perfecting themselves by their very survival—

their past contributes to their present — and by their relationships with other beings.

Maintaining that nothing is static, that all things change, and that everything that exists is not only the total of all that has happened to it but also reflects the entire past of the universe, Whitehead is interested in explaining why there is order in the universe rather than the chaos that such emphasis on change might indicate. His aim is to find the general in the particular, the eternal in the changing temporal.

He falls back upon Platonic Forms, which he calls "eternal objects." These are the essences of each real being. He calls these real beings "actual events." The term "actual" indicates that it is a reality, not a concept. The term "event" means that, even though it maintains its essence, its "eternal object," it is still changing in many ways, and is subject to change into another actual event. Although Whitehead is opposed to the concept of substance, he is really opposed to Locke's notion of substance which is about the same as the logical concept of subject of a proposition. His actual event is a twentieth-century analogue of Aristotle's substance or *ousia*.

Changes are brought about by the "lure for feelings" and "prehensions." These are similar to the Aristotelian appetites and privations.

A word must be said about the expression "actual event." This is in contrast to the mathematical term "point event." In analytic geometry, a position is a point on a set of coordinates. So also, real events are frequently plotted on a set of coordinates, except that instead of the *x* axis and *y* axis, there is a *space* axis and a *time* axis. We can represent an historical event in this manner. However, for Whitehead, this is to conceptualize the event to such an extent that it loses its real value, Hence, in his break with the conceptualism of mathematics and physical theory, he emphasizes the reality of the event and calls it an *actual* — not point — event.

Whitehead disagreed with the Platonic and Aristotelian notions of the divine. He considered that both Plato and Aristotle kept their highest entity out of touch with reality. Plato's Idea of the Good has some, but not enough, contact with reality. Aristotle's self-thinking thought has none at all. Hence, he considers process, evolution, not God, to be the ultimate. God is the self-perfecting and universe-perfecting intrinsic reason of the universe. He is, as it were, the world soul, and His aim is to make things work out correctly and for the best of each individual in the whole. Whitehead's God is also somewhat like Spinoza's. Whitehead was concerned with God as love, and for Whitehead, He must be part of the process, ". . . with tender patience leading it by his vision of truth, beauty, and goodness." It is unfortunate that Whitehead, who did a remarkable piece of work in reconstructing the philosophies of Plato and Aristotle almost unaided, was not more familiar with St. Thomas' unifying of the metaphysical greatness of Plato and Aristotle with the warmth of the Judeo-Christian tradition. He would have realized that both Plato and Aristotle were, in their philosophical greatness, trying also to say that God is Love.

It is rare that a thinker achieves recognized philosophical status in one work. Yet this has been done in a truly *metaphysical evolution* by Pierre Teilhard de Chardin in his work *The Phenomenon of Man*. Teilhard was a Jesuit priest, an anthropologist. He achieved fame first by his discovery of the Peking man.

Teilhard looks upon the universe as a preparation for its latest production, man. Hence, he looks upon man as a *phenomenon*, a fact to be explained. He also looks upon man as the final product of evolution, not to become a more developed organism but to advance himself as social man. There is no concern about supermen or superior men. There is concern about better society.

The universe consists of the evolution of a number of stages, each the potential and source of the higher development. These stages are characterized by two properties: an outward, radiating movement, and an inward, perfecting movement. The outward movement diffuses matter throughout space, sets up relations and conditions. The inward movement is that of interior organization. In the original expansion of the universe, the outward movement consisted in the diffusion of matter throughout space, setting up space-time conditions. The inward movement was the coalescence of matter into galaxies and stars.

This outward and inward motion takes place in successive stages, each a potential for the next and higher stage. At each stage, the motion is radiation through space and time to set up the organization of the components. The movement is diffusion for organization. Thus, matter was diffused throughout all of space to set up the creation of the elements. The elements were diffused to set up life. Life was diffused to work around in various stages of which man is the ultimate.

The stages are physical, chemical, biotic, and noetic — the "noösphere," or the sphere of the mind. Teilhard apparently means that there is a stage in higher organization when matter seems to reflect. This is not intellectual reflection, nor does Teilhard mean that the universe below man thinks. Apparently he means that there is a stage in evolution when there is some improvisation on the part of the organized entities. This is reactive, trophic, and sensile. Furthermore, even on the animal level, this reflection is to a certain extent intelligent. Instinct takes the form of a certain amount of reaction and particular choice. On this level, it is similar to what St. Albert and St. Thomas call the *vis aestimativa*, the improvising power of animals.

Man is the culmination of all. Even though Teilhard maintains, as do all evolutionists, that man's *body* and its central nervous system may have evolved from lower matter, he does *not* maintain that man's soul has done so. It is man's soul that makes him unique. It is man's soul that indicates that he is the termination of evolution. Any further development of man must be in the use of his spiritual powers to perfect himself both as an individual and as a member of society. Since man is naturally social, it stands to reason that when God founded a Church for man's supernatural perfection He would make it a society. The challenge for man, then, is not a superhuman state, a society of supermen according to the tradition of H. G. Wells, Aldous Huxley, and Julian Huxley. It is the perfecting of his social nature and the supernatural perfecting of himself in grace through the Church.

Philosophically, there is little to be said about evolution. Its validity will always rest on the actualization of potency. We must explain reality in terms of potency and act simply because an entity can change or develop only according to its capacities. The organization of new beings, higher beings, must similarly be explained. The tendency of potency, primary matter, to exist through organization into a new formal essence is the Aristotelian tradition accepted and developed by St. Albert and St. Thomas. Insofar as any evolutionary system must think in terms of the new as the fulfillment of the old, it exemplifies to that extent these basic philosophical principles. It is on the same ground that we must draw the line at the supposition of the evolution of the complete man. We can accept the evolution of man's body. However, we cannot accept the evolution of his soul. The soul is an immaterial, spiritual principle, and in no way can it be educed from the potencies of matter.

Any evolutionary theory must be judged more by its scientific contents than by its philosophical implications. Although there is an impressive sweep of evidence in favor of evolutionary theory, there is often a lack of detail. There is, for example, the embarrassing gap between the highest of the anthropoids and man — the "missing link." Nevertheless, these are details that may be filled in.

EVOLUTION AND THEOLOGY

There are few, but only few, *theological* problems posed by evolution.

These hinge about the biblical account of creation. The book of Genesis speaks of creation in six "days." Long before modern evolution was devised, Scripture scholars, among them such Fathers of the Church as St. Gregory of Nyssa and St. Augustine, maintained that this was one of the many places in the Old Testament where a metaphorical interpretation would be better than a literal interpretation. St. Thomas Aquinas considers the account in Genesis as a statement of two facts: (1) God is the creator of the universe, and (2) there is an order in His work. St. Gregory of Nyssa maintained that the account was Messianic, that is, that it is an account of creation *and* original sin with a view to redemption by Christ. The emphasis is upon the fact that *one* God and only God — not some satanic principle — created the universe and that His work is good.

There was a time, not so long ago, when "reconciliations" of Genesis with science were advanced. These tried to line up the work of the days with accepted geological accounts of the formation and evolution of the earth as a planet. Such attempts were bound to suffer from inaccuracies, and perhaps the best position to take is that the biblical account portrays God's creative act in the imagery of the people to whom the revelation was given. Certainly, God adapts His revelation to the limitations of the human intellect and imagination, and there is no reason to think that this would be an exception.

The second point is that of the age of the human race. If we count up the events and generations as given in the Old Testament, in the Gospels of St. Matthew and St. Luke, we find an account of human existence totaling about six thousand years. Obviously, man has been on earth longer than six thousand years. Here we should note that the genealogies in the Bible are *liturgical* rather than literal; that is, they record family descendants for purposes of worship and Hebrew privileges of the temple. Hence, there are undoubtedly huge gaps between a significant ancestor and a significant descendant, for example, Christ called Himself "the Son of David" — and He was truly a lineal descendant from David — and yet there are about eight hundred years between Christ and David. Consequently, we must be careful in trying to pin down the age of the human race from the Bible. It really gives us no indication. Nor need it. Its purpose is religious instruction, not scientific knowledge.

LIFE ELSEWHERE IN THE UNIVERSE

The last problem to be considered is that of possible life elsewhere in the universe. Two questions have been debated: (1) Is life possible elsewhere in the universe? (2) If so, is such life rational? Both questions have been favorite themes with writers for centuries and are of serious concern to contemporary science. In fact, the National Space Administration has recently completed what it calls *Project Ozma,* the emission of a code of signals into space from Green Bank, West Virginia, in the attempt to see if, years and perhaps centuries afterward, there might be replies.

Any serious investigation into the possibility of life elsewhere in the universe is based on the commonness of physical conditions and chemical elements throughout the universe. We think that we have a good notion of physical conditions throughout the universe from what we know of the observable universe. As far as anyone can tell from analysis of radiations within the known universe, the elements found on earth are also present in just about the same proportions throughout the universe. This means that we can extrapolate our knowledge of the actual into the realm of the possible

At first sight it seems rather arrogant to suppose that we are the only form of rational life in the universe. The universe is vast and we are small. The suspicion creeps in that surely, somewhere, there are conditions akin to ours and that there should be cultures like ours, perhaps superior, perhaps inferior. Since we do not know, then we must ask the question about the chances of such.

Here we meet difficulties. Chances involve statistics, and we find several statistical tables involved, depending upon the science on which they are based. There are astronomical and biological statistics. There are statistics based upon physical conditions and upon meteorology.

The astronomer notes that we live on a dense, inner planet in an orbital system surrounding a G2 spectral type of star which seems to be midway in its internal development. Hence, his first task is to find out whether there are other such stars. He finds that such stars are fairly common among Population I stars in our galaxy and in other galaxies.

The next task is to see whether planetary systems are common to such types of stars. He cannot see planets for stars. Hence, he must approach the problem from what we know about the sun. The sun is a controlled thermonuclear production of helium from hydrogen. It is controlled by a balance of radiation with gravitational pressure. Many other stars are similar. In fact, if stellar theory is correct, all stars should be. Yet, there are stars that seem to go wild, that seem to hasten their processes, and some even explode. Hence, he introduces the rate of rotation, adding centrifugal force as an influence toward stability to prevent the collapse of the star by the increasing weight of the produced helium. Rotation in a system is estimated according to the principles of angular momentum. These are influenced by any components of the system. The planets influence the sun's rotation, and if the balance of the sun's processes is influenced by its rotation, then the existence of planets enters in as a factor toward stability in a star.

Can we say, then, that planets are the normal accompaniment of a certain type of spectral-type star to keep it stable much as a system of anchors is used to hold a great ship steadily in place? Many astronomers seem to think so, and this would give us an average of 1 star in 100,000 with supposed planetary systems. This means that from the astronomer's point of view, the chances of a vital environment are about 1 in 100,000. Furthermore, because of some spectral perturbations in the star Sirius, some astronomers are inclined to extend the possibility of planetary systems to F and K type stars. This raises the chances of a vital environment a good deal.

However, we must face chemical conditions. As we have seen earlier, the most economical form of life from the point of view of energy and interchange of elements is a life form based upon carbon. Once we admit this, then we must admit that hydrogen, oxygen, and nitrogen are also necessary. The availability of these elements depends upon physical conditions. We have seen some of these, and briefly they are the gravitational field and the temperature of the planet.

If the gravitational field is too light, hydrogen and oxygen will never combine into water and will drift off into space. If the gravity is too strong, hydrogen will never escape and will form methane (CH_4) and ammonia (NH_3), both of which are toxic to a carbon-based life. Moreover, life could have been formed only at a sensitive point in the evolution of the planet. If contemporary theory is correct, then there must be sufficient methane and ammonia to help form amino acids, yet not enough to form large quantities of these toxic gases. This imposes a delicate balance that, statistically, would be difficult to reproduce.

The temperature must not be so hot that the elements cannot combine, as is the case on the planet Mercury. Nor should it be so cold as to drain off vital energy, as in the case of the outer planets.

There is a further delicate balance on earth that makes it unique among our planets. Its gravitational field is such that there is a balance between the hydrogen that drifts off into space (or is trapped in the magnetic and Van Allen belts surrounding the earth) and is replaced by hydrogen from rocks. Not only that, there is the vital part played by the ionosphere. In general, the atmosphere protects life from harmful radiation — especially x rays and other forms of hard radiation — proceeding from the sun. Most particularly, some of this same radiation is trapped in the ionosphere, that part of the atmosphere consisting of charged particles, where oxygen is changed into ozone. Ozone is heavier than ordinary oxygen, and its weight keeps atmospheric oxygen from escaping the earth. Not only that, some of the ozone produced is sufficiently struck by radiation to become ordinary oxygen again.

As far as anyone can tell, such conditions are not present on the other planets of our solar system. Mercury is too hot, and its gravity is too weak to hold an atmosphere. No one has ever seen the surface of Venus, but its atmosphere seems to be carbon dioxide, which is heavier than oxygen and thus seems to preclude an oxygen atmosphere, let alone water, on the planet. Furthermore, it is too hot. There is a remote chance of low forms of plant life, but almost no chance of even the lowest forms of animal life.

Mars, which deserves special mention, may once have had some form of animal life, but the chances of such are difficult now. Its atmosphere is very, very thin, and traces of ammonia and methane have been detected in it. We do not know whether its polar caps, which vary with the seasons as do ours, may be a very slight amount of thin water vapor or frozen carbon dioxide. At one time the presence of "canals" on Mars was taken to indicate an intelligent attempt to draw water from the ice caps to the vast deserts that seem to constitute most of the Martian landscape. However, these "canals" are now regarded as some low, lichenlike form of vegetation undergoing seasonal changes. Furthermore, the Mars atmosphere is so thin that it is subject to lethal radiation from the sun and from the stars and galaxies. The Martian day is about the same length as ours, but because of the rarity of its atmosphere, its present temperature range is over one hundred degrees Fahrenheit in one day. Finally, its gravitational field is only .38 that of the earth, and this implies that the vital elements of hydrogen and oxygen have drifted off into space.

The outer planets must be ruled out as possible sites for living organisms. Jupiter is too cold and its gravity too immense. Saturn, Uranus, Neptune, Pluto, and their satellites are too cold. Jupiter and Saturn are probably mostly frozen atmospheres with a smaller solid center. Uranus and Neptune are probably still in a gaseous state, their gas molecules never having come together sufficiently to coalesce into one frozen mass. Pluto is dense and frozen.

In addition, the statistics against earthlike conditions on planets that may surround other stars are formidable. Hence, the chances are that, if there are other planetary systems, the component planets are probably not like the earth. The chances are several million to one against another earth.

Let us consider one more difficulty. Granting the likelihood of some form of life elsewhere in the universe, the chances of its evolving into a rational form of life are formidable. Evolution of life into a rational-type body involves such a delicate balance of physical, geological, and weather conditions, that the chances of its occurring are overwhelmingly negative. Thus, the chances of rational life elsewhere in the universe are billions to one. Nevertheless, there are billions of stars in each galaxy, and we estimate that there are over 200 billion galaxies. Thus there is a slight theoretical possibility that there is, somewhere in the universe, another earth with rational creatures inhabiting it. We cannot be too optimistic about this possibility, but we cannot rule it out.

If there is rational life elsewhere, what would it be like? Most likely it would be like us. The human body is so economical for its activity that a form of life radically different would be too uneconomical. Despite the popularity of strange types that we read about in science fiction — rational lizards, rational insects, rational monsters — evidence available would indicate that rational beings, if existent elsewhere in the universe, would be much like us.

Any form of rational life must be as self-contained as possible. This rules out reptiles and fish. They are cold-blooded, and hence they are completely dependent upon their environment for vital heat. When we place a warm-water fish in cold water, it dies.

Moreover, rational life is social. Hence, it must communicate for cultural development and build for family purposes. The very building process means that it must stand erect in order to free its forelimbs for building. Extra limbs would demand a different skeletal arrangement, different muscles, tissues, and, in general, an increase in mass that gets uneconomical. Yet, the very economy required in planning and building cuts down on protective efficiency. Hence, man must plan for his own protection. He must rely upon planning rather than cunning, speed, or strength. His brain power must be extremely complicated. His senses must be sharper, and hence they should be centered about his head — two eyes for depth perception, two ears for direction finding, nostrils and mouth for a protected and yet short distance to his lungs and stomach. He needs bone and muscle structure, rather than tentacles. Tentacles can only pull. Bone and muscle structure can both pull and push. Taking one thing with another, the human body is about the most efficient type of structure for any rational purposes. There would be no point, for example, in having a rational soul in a dog. A dog could neither speak nor write. He might devise a code of barks, but since he does not have an opposable thumb, he could not build telegraphic equipment; and since his brain is so limited, he probably could not even envision one. Hence, taking all things into consideration, any other rational life form is most likely like man. Does it exist? We simply do not know. But if it does exist, we would probably find in it a sympathetic brother rather than a hostile rival.

Philosophically, there is no difficulty about possible life elsewhere. The fact of rational life on earth is automatically a statement of its possibility elsewhere. We simply must await further evidence while we speculate.

Theologically, we know there would be no difference concerning the nature of God. He is still the Trinity, still the Creator, still the providential and loving Protector. Those doctrines peculiar to *this* human race — original sin, Redemption, the foundation of the Church, the Immaculate Conception of the Blessed Virgin and her Assumption — would not apply to rational life elsewhere. Their providence and salvation would be peculiar to them if God wished to raise them to the supernatural order. If they were in the supernatural order and remained in their innocence, they would need no redemption. Had they sinned, then if God willed a redemption, it would be peculiar to them, and might be different from our redemption. Whether God's concern for us would militate against a reduplication elsewhere, we cannot say.

We can conclude this work by noting that cosmology begins with matter and terminates in man. This is most fitting, for not only is man the highest in the material order, but he is also the substantial link to the spiritual order, and through this to the supernatural order. He is, indeed, the microcosm, the little universe, the only material creature we know who not only can understand the universe but also God and himself.

SUMMARY

1. We do not know what life is, although we know that it occurs naturally and that its properties are mobility, growth from within, self-development of parts, and self-repair of parts, all from within.
2. Chemically, life seems to require combinations of oxygen, hydrogen, and nitrogen, all about carbon. These combinations are essential for the energy and chemical changeability required for living processes. Other elements, even silicon, are deficient in one or both of these properties.
3. Life may have been formed spontaneously and may have evolved into its present forms — with the exception of the soul of man — over the course of billions of years. The production of amino acids, the sources of pro-

teins, in the laboratory seems to verify the possibility of spontaneous generation. Mutations seem to argue the possibility of evolution. The purely scientific consideration of this is called *mechanism*. It is denied on statistical grounds by *vitalism*.

4. Evolution is philosophically acceptable on the grounds of potency, again allowing direct creation for man's spiritual soul.

   Philosophies of evolution are: Spencer's survival of the fittest, Alexander's emergent evolution, Bergson's metaphysical evolution, dialectical materialism, Whitehead's philosophy of organism.

5. If we grant that the Bible is literal in doctrine but frequently metaphorical in historical expression, then evolution poses no difficulty to either the biblical narration of creation or to the age of the human race.

GENERAL BIBLIOGRAPHY

PHILOSOPHICAL SOURCES

Albert the Great, St., *Omnia Opera*, Vivès, Paris, 1890–1899.
Aquinas, St. Thomas, *Omnia Opera*, Vivès, Paris, 1871–1880.
——— *Omnia Opera* (incomplete), Leonine Edition, Typographia Polyglotta, S. C. de Propaganda Fidei, Rome, 1882.
Aristotle, *Works*, Oxford, at the Clarendon Press, 1952; Harvard University Press, Cambridge, 1935.
Plato, *Works*, Oxford, at the Clarendon Press.
Scotus, *Omnia Opera*, Vivès, Paris, 1891–1895.

PHILOSOPHICAL WORKS*

Alexander, S., *Space, Time, and Deity*, Macmillan, London, 1927
Bridgman, Percy, *The Logic of Modern Physics*, Macmillan, New York, 1927.
Burnet, John, *Early Greek Philosophy*, Adam and Charles Black, London, 1958.
——— *Greek Philosophy from Thales to Plato*, Macmillan, London, 1958.
Burtt, E. A., *The Metaphysical Foundations of Modern Science*, Doubleday, Garden City, 1954.
Collingwood, R. G., *The Idea of Nature*, Oxford, at the Clarendon Press, 1949.
Conant, James B., *On Understanding Science*, Yale University Press, New Haven, 1947.
Engels, F., *The Dialectics of Nature*, Foreign Languages Publishing House, Moscow, 1954.
Haldane, John Scott, *The Sciences and Philosophy*, Doubleday, New York, 1929.
Haldane, Richard B., *The Philosophy of Humanism*, J. Murray, London, 1922.
Jaeger, Werner, *Paideia: The Ideals of Greek Culture*, Oxford University Press, New York, 1945.
Joad, C. E. M., *Philosophical Aspects of Modern Science*, Allen and Unwin, London, 1932.
Lucretius, *On the Nature of Things*, E. P. Dutton & Co., Inc., New York, 1957.
McWilliams, James A., *Cosmology*, Macmillan, New York, 1933.
Maritain, Jacques, *The Philosophy of Nature*, Philosophical Library, New York, 1954.
Maziarz, Edward A., *The Philosophy of Mathematics*, Philosophical Library, New York, 1950.
Mitterer, Albert, *Das Ringen der alten Stoff-Form-Metaphysik mit der heutigen Stoff-Physik*, Tyrolia, Innsbruck, 1935.

* Many of these works are now available in paperback.

——— *Wesensartwandel und Artensystem der Physikalischen Körperwelt*, Weger, Bressanone, 1936.

Nahm, Milton, *Selections from Early Greek Philosophy*, F. S. Crofts, New York, 1940.

Nys, D., *Cosmology*, tr. S. Raemers, The Bruce Publishing Co., Milwaukee, 1942.

Price, Lucien, *The Dialogues of Alfred North Whitehead*, New American Library, New York, 1956.

Randall, John Herman, Jr., *Aristotle*, Columbia University Press, New York, 1960.

Reichenbach, Hans, *The Rise of Scientific Philosophy*, University of California Press, Berkeley, 1951.

Russell, Bertrand, *A B C of Relativity*, Harper and Bros., New York, 1925.

——— *Analysis of Matter*, Harcourt, Brace, New York, 1927.

——— *Our Knowledge of the External World*, Norton, New York, 1929.

——— *The Scientific Outlook*, Norton, New York, 1931.

Sampson, R. A., *Science and Reality*, Benn, London, 1928.

Sheen, Fulton J., *The Philosophy of Science*, The Bruce Publishing Co., Milwaukee, 1934.

Smith, Vincent E., *The General Science of Nature*, The Bruce Publishing Co., Milwaukee, 1958.

——— *Philosophical Physics*, Harper and Bros., New York, 1950.

Teilhard de Chardin, Pierre, *The Phenomenon of Man*, Harper, New York, 1959.

Van Melsen, Andrew G., *The Philosophy of Nature*, Duquesne University, Pittsburgh, 2nd ed., 1954.

Whitehead, A. N., *Adventures of Ideas*, Macmillan, New York, 1933.

——— *The Concept of Nature*, Cambridge, at the University Press, 1920.

——— *Process and Reality*, Macmillan, New York, 1929.

——— *Science and the Modern World*, Macmillan, New York, 1925.

SCIENTIFIC WORKS

Annual Report of the Smithsonian Institution, U. S. Government Printing Office, Washington, D. C., 1948–1960.

Atomic Physics, The Physics Staff of the University of Pittsburgh, John Wiley & Sons, New York, 1946.

Blatt, John M., and Weisskopf, Victor H., *Theoretical Nuclear Physics*, John Wiley & Sons, New York, 1954.

Bohr, Niels H., *Atomic Theory and the Description of Nature*, Cambridge, at the University Press, 1934.

Bonala, Roberto, *Non-Euclidean Geometry*, Dover, New York, 1955.

Boole, George, *The Mathematical Analysis of Logic*, George Bell, London, 1847.

Born, Max, *The Constitution of Matter*, Dutton, New York, 1923.

——— *The Restless Universe*, Dover, New York, 1951.

Brinkley, Stuart Robert, *Introduction to General Chemistry*, Macmillan, New York, 1938.

Colerus, Egmont, *From Simple Numbers to the Calculus*, Wm. Heineman, Ltd., London, 1955.
Condon, Edward Uhler, and Morse, Philip M., *Quantum Mechanics*, McGraw-Hill, New York, 1929.
Crombie, A. C., *Medieval and Early Modern Science*, Doubleday, Garden City, 1959.
Crowther, James Arnold, *Ions, Electrons, and Ionizing Radiations*, Longmans, Green, New York, 1934.
d'Abro, *The Evolution of Scientific Thought*, Dover Publications, Inc., New York, 1950.
——— *The Rise of the New Physics*, Dover, New York, 1951.
Dampier, William Cecil, *A History of Science and Its Relations with Philosophy and Religion*, Cambridge, at the University Press, 1948.
Dantzig, Tobias, *Number, the Language of Science*, Doubleday, Garden City, 1956.
Darrow, Karl K., *The Renaissance of Physics*, Macmillan, New York, 1936.
Darwin, Charles G., *The New Conceptions of Matter*, Macmillan, New York, 1931.
Darwin, Charles Robert, *The Descent of Man*, Collier & Son, New York, 1901.
——— *The Origin of the Species by Means of Natural Selection*, D. Appleton & Co., New York, 1896.
DeBroglie, Louis, *Corpuscular Waves*, Annual Report of the Smithsonian Institution, Washington, D. C., 1930.
Dirac, P. A. M., *Quantum Mechanics*, Oxford, at the Clarendon Press, 1956.
Dreyer, J. L. E., *A History of Astronomy from Thales to Kepler*, Dover, New York, 1953.
Eddington, Arthur, *The Expanding Universe*, Macmillan, New York, 1933.
——— *The Mathematical Theory of Relativity*, Cambridge, at the University Press, 1923.
——— *The Nature of the Physical World*, Macmillan, New York, 1933.
——— *New Pathways in Science*, Macmillan, New York, 1935.
——— *The Philosophy of Physical Science*, Macmillan, New York, 1939.
——— *Science and the Unseen World*, Macmillan, New York, 1929.
——— *Space, Time, and Gravitation*, Cambridge, at the University Press, 1929.
Einstein, Albert, *Relativity, the Special and General Theory*, Henry Holt, New York, 1929.
Frank, Philipp, *Philosophy of Science*, Prentice-Hall, Englewood, N. J., 1957.
Galileo Galilei, *Dialogue Concerning Two New Sciences*, Dover, New York, 1914.
——— *Dialogue on the Great World Systems*, Chicago, New York, 1953.
Gamow, G., *The Creation of the Universe*, Viking, New York, 1952.
Gamow, G., and Critchfield, C. L., *Theory of Atomic Nucleus and Nuclear Energy Sources*, Oxford, at the Clarendon Press, 1950.
Heath, T. L., *The Works of Archimedes*, Dover, New York, 1912.
Heisenberg, Werner, *The Physical Principles of the Quantum Theory*, Dover, New York, 1930.
Hopkins, B., *General Chemistry for Colleges*, Heath, New York, 1937.

Houston, Wm. V., *Principles of Mathematical Physics*, McGraw-Hill, New York, 1948.
Hoyle, Fred, *Frontiers of Astronomy*, Heineman, London, 1955.
Jánossy, L., *Cosmic Rays*, Oxford, at the Clarendon Press, 1950.
Jeans, James, *Astronomy and Cosmogony*, Cambridge, at the University Press, New York, 1928.
——— *The Mysterious Universe*, Macmillan, New York, 1932.
——— *The New Background of Science*, Macmillan, New York, 1934.
Jones, G. O., Rotblat, J., Whitrow, G. J., *Atoms and the Universe*, Scribner's, New York, 1956.
Jones, H. Spenser, *Life on Other Worlds*, Macmillan, New York, 1954.
Koyré, Alexander, *From the Closed World to the Infinite Universe*, Harper, New York, 1958.
Lewis, Gilbert Newman, *Valence and the Structure of Atoms and Molecules*, The Chemical Catalogue Co., New York, 1923.
Lindsay, Robert Bruce, and Margenau, Henry, *Foundations of Physics*, Dover, New York, 1957.
Lodge, Sir Oliver, *Ether and Reality*, Hodder and Stoughton, London, 1925.
Lorentz, Einstein, Minkowski, Weyl, *The Principle of Relativity*, Dodd, Mead, New York, 1923.
Manning, Henry Parker, *The Geometry of Four Dimensions*, Dover, New York, 1956.
May, Kenneth, *Elementary Analysis*, Wiley, New York, 1952.
Menzel, Donald H., *Stars and Planets*, University Society, New York, 1938.
Millikan, Robert, *Cosmic Rays*, Chicago University Press, Chicago, 1939.
——— *Electrons, Protons, Photons, Neutrons, and Cosmic Rays*, Chicago University Press, Chicago, 1935.
——— *Science and the New Civilization*, Scribner's, New York, 1930.
——— *Time, Matter, and Values*, University of North Carolina Press, Chapel Hill, 1932.
New Astronomy, The, Scientific American Company, Simon and Schuster, New York, 1957.
New Chemistry, The, Scientific American . . . 1957.
Newton, Isaac, *Opticks*, Dover, New York, 1952.
——— *The Principles of Mathematical Physics*, University of California Press, Berkeley, 1934.
——— *Papers and Letters on Natural Philosophy*, Harvard University Press, Cambridge, 1958.
Physics Review, The, Scientific American Company . . . 1947–1960.
Planck, Max, *The Philosophy of Physics*, Norton, New York, 1936.
——— *Survey of Physics*, Methuen, London, 1925.
——— *The University in the Light of Modern Physics*, Norton, New York, 1931.
——— *Where is Science Going?* Norton, New York, 1932.
Poincaré, Henri, *Science and Hypothesis*, Dover, New York, 1952.
——— *Science and Method*, Dover, New York, 1952.
Ruark, A., and Urey, H. C., *Atoms, Molecules, and Quanta*, McGraw-Hill, New York, 1930,

Sarton, Georges, *A Guide to the History of Science*, Chronica Botanica Co., Waltham, 1952.

——— *The History of Science*, Harvard University Press, Cambridge, 1952.

——— *Six Wings: Men of Science in the Renaissance*, Indiana University Press, Bloomington, 1957.

Shilling, Hugh, *Fundamentals of Electric Waves*, Wiley, New York, 1957.

Simon, Pierre, Marquis de La Place, *A Philosophical Essay on Probabilities*, Dover, New York, 1951.

Soddy, Frederick, *The Interpretation of the Atom*, Putnam's, New York, 1932.

Sommerfeld, Arnold, *Atomic Structure and Spectral Lines*, Dutton, New York, 1929.

Thomson, J. J., *Beyond the Electron*, Cambridge, at the University Press, 1928.

Tutton, A. E. H., *Crystalline Form and Chemical Constitution*, Macmillan, New York, 1926.

Universe, The, Scientific American, Schuster, New York, 1957.

Vinci, Leonardo Da, *Notebooks*, Reprint Society, London, 1954.

Whitehead, A. N., *An Introduction to Mathematics*, Oxford University Press, London, 1948.

Whittaker, Edmund, *Space and Spirit*, Regnery, Hindsdale, Ill., 1948.

Wold, Peter, *Kimball's College Physics*, Henry Holt, New York, 1939.

PERIODIC TABLE OF ELEMENTS

TRANSITION ELEMENTS

GROUP I	GROUP II												GROUP III	GROUP IV	GROUP V	GROUP VI	GROUP VII	INERT ELEMENTS
1 H 1.0081																		2 He 4.003
3 Li 6.940	4 Be 9.02												5 B 10.82	6 C 12.010	7 N 14.008	8 O 16.000	9 F 19.00	10 Ne 20.183
11 Na 22.997	12 Mg 24.32												13 Al 26.97	14 Si 28.06	15 P 30.98	16 S 32.06	17 Cl 35.457	18 A 39.944
19 K 39.096	20 Ca 40.08	21 Sc 45.10		22 Ti 47.90	23 V 50.95	24 Cr 52.01	25 Mn 54.93	26 Fe 55.85	27 Co 58.94	28 Ni 58.69	29 Cu 63.57	30 Zn 65.38	31 Ga 69.72	32 Ge 72.60	33 As 74.91	34 Se 78.96	35 Br 79.916	36 Kr 83.70
37 Rb 85.48	38 Sr 87.63	39 Y 88.92		40 Zr 91.22	41 Nb 92.91	42 Mo 95.95	43 Tc [99]	44 Ru 101.7	45 Rh 102.91	46 Pd 106.7	47 Ag 107.880	48 Cd 112.41	49 In 114.76	50 Sn 118.70	51 Sb 121.76	52 Te 127.61	53 I 126.92	54 Xe 131.3
55 Cs 132.91	56 Ba 137.36	57 La 138.92	58 To 71	72 Hf 178.6	73 Ta 180.88	74 W 183.92	75 Re 186.31	76 Os 190.2	77 Ir 193.1	78 Pt 195.23	79 Au 197.2	80 Hg 200.61	81 Tl 204.39	82 Pb 207.21	83 Bi 209.00	84 Po [210]	85 At [210]	86 Rn [222]
87 Fr [223]	88 Ra 226.05	89 Ac [227]	90 to 103															

LANTHANIDE SERIES	57 La 138.92	58 Ce 140.13	59 Pr 140.92	60 Nd 144.27	61 Pm [145]	62 Sm 150.43	63 Eu 152.00	64 Gd 156.9	65 Tb 159.2	66 Dy 162.46	67 Ho 163.5	68 Er 167.2	69 Tm 169.4	70 Yb 173.04	71 Lu 174.99
ACTINIDE SERIES	89 Ac [227]	90 Th 232.12	91 Pa 231	92 U 238.07	93 Np 237	94 Pu [242]	95 Am [243]	96 Cm [243]	97 Bk [245]	98 Cf [246]	99 Es [254]	100 Fm [255]	101 Md [256]	102 No [253]	103

RARE EARTH ELEMENTS

TABLE OF ELEMENTS AND THEIR ISOTOPES

At. No.	Element	Symbol	Atomic Weight	Isotopes
1	Hydrogen	H	1.0081	1, 2
2	Helium	He	4.003	4
3	Lithium	Li	6.940	6, 7
4	Beryllium	Be	9.02	9
5	Boron	B	10.82	10, 11
6	Carbon	C	12.010	13, 14
7	Nitrogen	N	14.008	13, 15
8	Oxygen	O	16.000	17, 18
9	Fluorine	F	19.000	
10	Neon	Ne	20.183	21, 22
11	Sodium	Na	22.997	23
12	Magnesium	Mg	24.32	24, 25, 26
13	Aluminum	Al	26.97	
14	Silicon	Si	28.06	29, 30
15	Phosphorus	P	30.98	31
16	Sulphur	S	32.06	32, 33, 34
17	Chlorine	Cl	35.457	37
18	Argon	A	39.944	36, 40
19	Potassium	K	39.096	41
20	Calcium	Ca	40.08	44
21	Scandium	Sc	45.10	
22	Titanium	Ti	47.90	
23	Vanadium	V	50.95	
24	Chromium	Cr	52.01	52, 53, 54
25	Manganese	Mn	54.93	
26	Iron	Fe	55.85	56
27	Cobalt	Co	58.94	59
28	Nickel	Ni	58.69	58, 60
29	Copper	Cu	63.57	65
30	Zinc	Zn	65.38	64, 66, 67, 68, 70
31	Gallium	Ga	69.72	69, 71
32	Germanium	Ge	72.60	70, 72, 73, 74, 76
33	Arsenic	As	74.91	
34	Selenium	Se	78.96	74, 76, 77, 78, 80, 82
35	Bromine	Br	79.916	79, 81
36	Krypton	Kr	83.70	78, 80, 82
37	Rubidium	Rb	85.48	87
38	Strontium	Sr	87.63	86, 87, 88, 90
39	Yttrium	Y	88.92	
40	Zirconium	Zr	91.22	90, 92, 94
41	Niobium	Nb	92.91	
42	Molybdenum	Mo	95.95	92, 94, 95, 96, 97, 98, 100
43	Technetium	Tc	99	
44	Ruthenium	Ru	101.7	96, 98, 99, 100, 101, 102, 104
45	Rhodium	Rh	102.91	
46	Palladium	Pd	106.7	
47	Silver	Ag	107.880	107, 109
48	Cadmium	Cd	112.41	110, 111, 112, 113, 114, 116
49	Indium	In	114.76	
50	Tin	Sn	118.70	112, 114, 115, 116, 117, 118, 119, 120, 121, 122, 124
51	Antinomy	Sb	121.76	121, 123, 124
52	Tellurium	Te	127.61	125, 126, 128, 130
53	Iodine	I	126.92	
54	Xenon	Xe	131.3	124, 126, 128, 129, 130, 131, 132, 134, 136
55	Caesium	Cs	132.91	

TABLE OF ELEMENTS AND THEIR ISOTOPES (continued)

At. No.	Element	Symbol	Atomic Weight	Isotopes
56	Barium	Ba	137.36	135, 136, 137
57	Lanthanum	La	138.92	
58	Cerium	Ce	140.13	142
59	Praseodymium	Pr	140.92	
60	Neodymium	Nd	144.27	
61	Promethium	Pm	145	
62	Samarium	Sm	150.43	
63	Europium	Eu	152.00	
64	Gadolinium	Gd	156.9	
65	Terbium	Tb	159.2	
66	Dysprosium	Dy	162.46	
67	Holmium	Ho	163.5	
68	Erbium	Er	167.2	
69	Thulium	Tm	169.4	
70	Ytterbium	Yb	173.04	
71	Lutetium	Lu	174.99	
72	Hafnium	Hf	178.6	
73	Tantalum	Ta	180.88	
74	Tungsten	W	183.92	182, 183, 184, 186
75	Rhenium	Re	186.31	185, 187
76	Osmium	Os	190.2	186, 187, 188, 189, 190, 192
77	Iridium	Ir	193.1	
78	Platinum	Pt	195.23	
79	Gold	Au	197.2	
80	Mercury	Hg	200.61	196, 197, 198, 199, 200, 201, 202, 203, 204
81	Thallium	Tl	204.39	203, 205
82	Lead	Pb	207.21	203, 204, 205, 206, 207, 208, 209, 210
83	Bismuth	Bi	209.00	
84	Polonium	Po	210.00	
85	Astatine	At	210.00	
86	Radon	Rn	222.00	
87	Francium	Fr	223.00	
88	Radium	Ra	226.05	
89	Actinium	Ac	227.00	
90	Thorium	Th	232.12	
91	Protoactinium	Pa	231.00	
92	Uranium	U	238.07	235, 237
93	Neptunium	Np	237	
94	Plutonium	Pu	242	
95	Americium	Am	243	
96	Curium	Cm	243	
97	Berkelium	Bk	245	
98	Californium	Cf	246	
99	Einsteinium	Es	254	
100	Fermium	Fm	255	
101	Mendelevium	Md	256	
102	Nobelium	No	253	

INDEX